SMALL BUSINESS FOR DUMMIES®

by Eric Tyson and Jim Schell

IDG
BOOKS
WORLDWIDE

IDG Books Worldwide, Inc.
An International Data Group Company

Foster City, CA ♦ Chicago, IL ♦ Indianapolis, IN ♦ New York, NY

Small Business For Dummies®

Published by
IDG Books Worldwide, Inc.
An International Data Group Company
919 E. Hillsdale Blvd.
Suite 400
Foster City, CA 94404
www.idgbooks.com (IDG Books Worldwide Web site)
www.dummies.com (Dummies Press Web site)

Library of Congress Catalog Card No.: 98-86177

ISBN: 0-7645-5094-2

Printed in the United States of America

10 9 8 7 6 5 4 3 2 1

1E/QT/QY/ZY/IN

Distributed in the United States by IDG Books Worldwide, Inc.

Distributed by Macmillan Canada for Canada; by Transworld Publishers Limited in the United Kingdom; by IDG Norge Books for Norway; by IDG Sweden Books for Sweden; by Woodslane Pty. Ltd. for Australia; by Woodslane (NZ) Ltd. for New Zealand; by Addison Wesley Longman Singapore Pte Ltd. for Singapore, Malaysia, Thailand, Indonesia and Korea; by Norma Comunicaciones S.A. for Colombia; by Intersoft for South Africa; by International Thomson Publishing for Germany, Austria and Switzerland; by Toppan Company Ltd. for Japan; by Distribuidora Cuspide for Argentina; by Livraria Cultura for Brazil; by Ediciencia S.A. for Ecuador; by Ediciones ZETA S.C.R. Ltda. for Peru; by WS Computer Publishing Corporation, Inc., for the Philippines; by Unalis Corporation for Taiwan; by Contemporanea de Ediciones for Venezuela; by Computer Book & Magazine Store for Puerto Rico; by Express Computer Distributors for the Caribbean and West Indies. Authorized Sales Agent: Anthony Rudkin Associates for the Middle East and North Africa.

For general information on IDG Books Worldwide's books in the U.S., please call our Consumer Customer Service department at 800-762-2974. For reseller information, including discounts and premium sales, please call our Reseller Customer Service department at 800-434-3422.

For information on where to purchase IDG Books Worldwide's books outside the U.S., please contact our International Sales department at 650-655-3200 or fax 650-655-3297.

For information on foreign language translations, please contact our Foreign & Subsidiary Rights department at 650-655-3021 or fax 650-655-3281.

For sales inquiries and special prices for bulk quantities, please contact our Sales department at 650-655-3200 or write to the address above.

For information on using IDG Books Worldwide's books in the classroom or for ordering examination copies, please contact our Educational Sales department at 800-434-2086 or fax 317-596-5499.

For press review copies, author interviews, or other publicity information, please contact our Public Relations department at 650-655-3000 or fax 650-655-3299.

For authorization to photocopy items for corporate, personal, or educational use, please contact Copyright Clearance Center, 222 Rosewood Drive, Danvers, MA 01923, or fax 978-750-4470.

is a trademark under exclusive license to IDG Books Worldwide, Inc., from International Data Group, Inc.

About the Authors

Eric Tyson, MBA, is a personal financial writer, lecturer, and counselor. For most of the past two-plus decades, he has been his own boss. He works with and teaches people from a myriad of income levels and backgrounds, so he knows the small business ownership concerns and questions of real folks just like you.

After toiling away for too many years as a management consultant to behemoth financial-service firms, Eric decided to take his knowledge of the industry and commit himself to making personal financial management accessible to all of us. Despite being handicapped by a joint B.S. in Economics and Biology from Yale and an MBA from Stanford, Eric remains a master at "keeping it simple."

An accomplished freelance personal finance writer, Eric is the author or co-author of numerous other ...*For Dummies* national bestsellers on personal finance, taxes, investing, and home buying, and is a syndicated columnist. His work has been critically acclaimed in hundreds of publications and programs including *Newsweek,* The *Los Angeles Times, Chicago Tribune, Kiplinger's Personal Finance Magazine, The Wall Street Journal,* and on NBC's Today Show, ABC, CNBC, PBS's Nightly Business Report, CNN, FOX-TV, CBS national radio, Bloomberg Business Radio, and Business Radio Network.

Jim Schell, contrary to what some people may think, has not always been a grizzled veteran of the small business wars. Raised in Des Moines, Iowa, and earning a B.A. in Economics (1958), Jim served in the U.S. Air Force in Klammath Falls, Oregon, followed by six unhappy years underperforming for a variety of businesses in Moline, Illinois, and Minneapolis, Minnesota. Finally, Jim's entre-preneurial genes were allowed to surface. In 1968, when Jim was 34, he and three Minneapolis friends started The Kings Court, at the time the nation's first racquetball club. Two years later, Jim bought General Sports Inc.; after another two years, he started National Screenprint, and, finally, in 1974, he partnered with an ex-employee in Fitness and Weight Training Corp. Each of the start-ups was bootstrapped, and each was privately held. For several years, Jim involved himself in the management of all four businesses at the same time. His third business, National Screenprint, ultimately grew to $25 million in sales and 200 employees. He sold his final business in 1990.

Relocating to San Diego, Jim began a long-simmering writing career, authoring four books *(The Brass Tacks Entrepreneur, Small Business Management Guide, The Small Business Answer Book,* and *Winning Together)* and numerous columns for business and trade magazines.

Citing culture shock, Jim and his wife Mary, a sales trainer and long-time business partner, relocated to Bend, Oregon, in 1994 where he continued his writing career. He also kicked off his fifth start-up, The Advisory Board (TAB), a business that uses volunteers to organize, administrate, and facilitate the formation of small business owners into teams that will serve as a member's board of directors. Jim has three grown sons, Jim, Todd, and Mike, and five grandchildren. He and Mary have been spotted frequently in the summer strolling any one of a number of Central Oregon's fine golf courses.

ABOUT IDG BOOKS WORLDWIDE

Welcome to the world of IDG Books Worldwide.

IDG Books Worldwide, Inc., is a subsidiary of International Data Group, the world's largest publisher of computer-related information and the leading global provider of information services on information technology. IDG was founded more than 25 years ago and now employs more than 8,500 people worldwide. IDG publishes more than 275 computer publications in over 75 countries (see listing below). More than 90 million people read one or more IDG publications each month.

Launched in 1990, IDG Books Worldwide is today the #1 publisher of best-selling computer books in the United States. We are proud to have received eight awards from the Computer Press Association in recognition of editorial excellence and three from *Computer Currents'* First Annual Readers' Choice Awards. Our best-selling *...For Dummies®* series has more than 50 million copies in print with translations in 38 languages. IDG Books Worldwide, through a joint venture with IDG's Hi-Tech Beijing, became the first U.S. publisher to publish a computer book in the People's Republic of China. In record time, IDG Books Worldwide has become the first choice for millions of readers around the world who want to learn how to better manage their businesses.

Our mission is simple: Every one of our books is designed to bring extra value and skill-building instructions to the reader. Our books are written by experts who understand and care about our readers. The knowledge base of our editorial staff comes from years of experience in publishing, education, and journalism — experience we use to produce books for the '90s. In short, we care about books, so we attract the best people. We devote special attention to details such as audience, interior design, use of icons, and illustrations. And because we use an efficient process of authoring, editing, and desktop publishing our books electronically, we can spend more time ensuring superior content and spend less time on the technicalities of making books.

You can count on our commitment to deliver high-quality books at competitive prices on topics you want to read about. At IDG Books Worldwide, we continue in the IDG tradition of delivering quality for more than 25 years. You'll find no better book on a subject than one from IDG Books Worldwide.

**IDG
BOOKS
WORLDWIDE**

John Kilcullen
CEO
IDG Books Worldwide, Inc.

Steven Berkowitz
President and Publisher
IDG Books Worldwide, Inc.

*Eighth Annual
Computer Press
Awards ≥1992*

WINNER

*Ninth Annual
Computer Press
Awards ≥1993*

WINNER

*Tenth Annual
Computer Press
Awards ≥1994*

WINNER

*Eleventh Annual
Computer Press
Awards ≥1995*

Dedications

To my wife, Judy; my family, especially my parents Charles and Paulina; my friends; and to my counseling clients and students of my courses for teaching me how to teach them about managing their finances.
Eric Tyson

This book is dedicated to The Rocky Road, and to all those friends, employees, and customers who have traversed it with me. Most of all, it is dedicated to my wife, Mary, without whom The Rocky Road would have been The Dead End.
Jim Schell

Authors' Acknowledgments

Many people contribute to the birth of a book, and this book is no exception. First, Eric would like to express his deep debt of gratitude to James Collins, who inspired him when he was a young and impressionable business school student. Jim encouraged Eric to try to improve some small part of the business world by being an entrepreneur and focusing solely on what customers needed rather than on what made the quickest buck.

The technical reviewers for this book, Bill Friedman and Chris Santas, helped improve each and every chapter, and we are thankful for that.

Thanks to all the good people in the media and other fields who have taken the time to critique and praise my previous writing so that others may know that it exists and is worth reading. And to those who may not open the book because of its bright yellow color and low-brow title, "You can't judge a book by its cover!" Now that we've got your attention, flip through the pages and find out why readers everywhere know and trust books ...*For Dummies.*

And a final and heartfelt thanks to all the people on the front lines and behind the scenes at IDG Books who helped to make this book and Eric's others a success. A big round of applause, please, for Kathy Cox as project editor and Gwenette Gaddis as copy editor. Special thanks to Kathy Welton, publisher, for her many timely and thoughtful ideas, and to John Kilcullen for cajoling me into writing these books in the first place. Thanks also to the Production, Graphics, Proofreading, and Indexing staffs for their great efforts in producing this book.

P.S. Thanks to you, dear reader, for buying this book.

Publisher's Acknowledgments

We're proud of this book; please register your comments through our IDG Books Worldwide Online Registration Form located at http://my2cents.dummies.com.

Some of the people who helped bring this book to market include the following:

Acquisitions, Editorial, and Media Development

Project Editor: Kathleen M. Cox

Acquisitions Editor: Mark Butler

Copy Editor: Gwenette Gaddis

Technical Editors: William Friedman, owner, Cascade Bookkeeping, and Chris Santas, accountant

Editorial Manager: Colleen Rainsberger

Media Development Manager: Heather Heath Dismore

Editorial Assistant: Paul Kuzmic

Production

Project Coordinator: Valery Bourke

Layout and Graphics: Lou Boudreau, Linda M. Boyer, J. Tyler Connor, Angela F. Hunckler, Brent Savage

Proofreaders: Christine Berman, Melissa D. Buddendeck, Nancy Price, Rebecca Senninger

Indexer: Mary Mortensen

Special Help: Ted Cains, Tamara Castleman, Wendy Hatch, Stephanie Koutek, Diane Smith

---

General and Administrative

IDG Books Worldwide, Inc.: John Kilcullen, CEO; Steven Berkowitz, President and Publisher

IDG Books Technology Publishing: Brenda McLaughlin, Senior Vice President and Group Publisher

Dummies Technology Press and Dummies Editorial: Diane Graves Steele, Vice President and Associate Publisher; Mary Bednarek, Director of Acquisitions and Product Development; Kristin A. Cocks, Editorial Director

Dummies Trade Press: Kathleen A. Welton, Vice President and Publisher; Kevin Thornton, Acquisitions Manager

IDG Books Production for Dummies Press: Michael R. Britton, Vice President of Production and Creative Services; Beth Jenkins Roberts, Production Director; Cindy L. Phipps, Manager of Project Coordination, Production Proofreading, and Indexing; Kathie S. Schutte, Supervisor of Page Layout; Shelley Lea, Supervisor of Graphics and Design; Debbie J. Gates, Production Systems Specialist; Robert Springer, Supervisor of Proofreading; Debbie Stailey, Special Projects Coordinator; Tony Augsburger, Supervisor of Reprints and Bluelines

Dummies Packaging and Book Design: Robin Seaman, Creative Director; Jocelyn Kelaita, Product Packaging Coordinator; Kavish + Kavish, Cover Design

◆

The publisher would like to give special thanks to Patrick J. McGovern, without whom this book would not have been possible.

◆

Contents at a Glance

Introduction 1

Part I: Becoming an Entrepreneur 9
Chapter 1: Is Small Business for You? 11
Chapter 2: Laying Your Personal Financial Foundation 35
Chapter 3: Finding Your Niche 51
Chapter 4: Turning Your Ideas into Plans 65
Chapter 5: Financing, Ownership, and Organizational Options 85

Part II: Buying an Existing Business 113
Chapter 6: Identifying the Right Business to Buy 115
Chapter 7: Making a Successful Offer to Buy 133

Part III: The Keys to Running a Successful Small Business 159
Chapter 8: The Owner as Jack or Jill of All Trades 161
Chapter 9: Defining a Marketing Strategy: Product Development,
Promotion, Sales, Distribution, and Pricing 187
Chapter 10: Keeping Your Customers Happy 219
Chapter 11: Minding the Financials: Cash Flow, Costs, and Profitability 233
Chapter 12: Escaping the #1 Cause of Failure on the Road to Success 257

Part IV: Keeping Your Business in Business 267
Chapter 13: Finding and Keeping Superstar Employees 269
Chapter 14: Providing Employee Benefits 297
Chapter 15: The Long Arm of the Law: Regulatory and Legal Issues 315
Chapter 16: Taming Your Small Business's Taxes 329
Chapter 17: Issues for Growing Businesses 343

Part V: The Part of Tens 363
Chapter 18: Ten Tips for Home-Based Businesses 365
Chapter 19: Ten Ways Computers Can Help Your Small Business 377
Chapter 20: Ten Tips for Managing Your Growing Business 383

Index 391

Book Registration Information .... Back of Book

Cartoons at a Glance

By Rich Tennant

page 363

"Well, there's another caravan that didn't stop. Now will you let me add salted dates to the menu?!"

page 159

"I don't know, Art. I think you're just ahead of your time."

page 9

page 267

"What made you think you were the one to own and operate a china shop, I'll never know."

page 113

Fax: 978-546-7747 • E-mail: the5wave@tiac.net

Table of Contents

Introduction *1*

Why This Small-Business Book? 1
What We Assume about You 2
How to Use This Book 3
   . . . for making big decisions 3
   . . . as a road map 4
   . . . as a problem solver and a frame of reference 4
   . . . as a mentor 5
Icons Used in This Book 6
The One Common Denominator 7

Part I: Becoming an Entrepreneur *9*

Chapter 1: Is Small Business for You? **11**

What Is a Business? 12
   Small (and large) business basics 12
   Small business as a role model for big business 16
   Different people, different businesses, similar issues 16
   Our definition of an entrepreneur 17
Small Business or Monkey Business? 18
   Pyramid schemes and the like 18
   Work-from-home opportunities 19
The Small-Business Owner's Aptitude Test:
   Do You Have the Right Stuff? 20
   Preparation 20
   The test questions 21
   Scoring the test 24
   Does passing this test guarantee a successful
      entrepreneurial career? 25
Making the Decision to Own a Small Business 26
   The reasons to own 27
   The reasons not to own 28
Options to Starting Your Own Business 29
   Becoming a better employee 29
   Entrepreneuring inside a larger company 30
   Moving from a large company to a small company 31
   Buying an existing business 31
   Investing in someone else's business 33

Chapter 2: Laying Your Personal Financial Foundation 35

The Value of Personal Financial Order 36
 Greater ease of cutting the umbilical cord 36
 Increased probability of business survival 37
 Harmony on the home front 37
Your Personal Financial To-Do List 38
 Assess your financial position and goals 39
  Measuring net worth 39
  Telling good debt from bad 40
  Reducing debt 40
  Buying insurance 41
  Planning for the long term 41
 Shrinking your spending 42
 Building up your cash reserves 44
 Keeping your income stable through part-time work 44
Assessing and Replacing Benefits 45
 Retirement savings plans and pensions 45
 Health insurance 46
 Disability insurance 46
 Life insurance 47
 Dental, vision, and other insurance 48
 Social Security taxes 49
 Time off 49
Managing Your Personal Finances Post-Launch 49

Chapter 3: Finding Your Niche 51

Why You Don't Need a New Niche or a Great Idea 51
How to Choose Your Business 53
 Consider your category 54
 Take advantage of "accidental opportunities" 56
 Inventory your skills, interests, and job history 56
 Narrow your choices 59
 Take advantage of government resources 62
Recognizing Your Number One Asset — You 64

Chapter 4: Turning Your Ideas into Plans 65

Your Mission — As You Choose to Define It 65
 Writing your mission statement 67
 Keeping your mission in people's minds 67
Your Business Plan: Don't Start Up without It 68
 The business plan as a road map 68
 The business plan as a tool for financing 69
Writing Your Business Plan 70
 Part 1: Description of the Business 71
  A. Mission statement 71
  B. Summary of the business 71

C. Legal description 71
D. Competitive edge 72
Part 2: Management 73
Part 3: Marketing plan 73
A. The industry at large 74
B. Identify potential customers 75
C. Geography 75
D. Distribution 75
E. Advertising 75
F. Public relations 75
G. Pricing 76
H. Sales terms and credit policies 76
Part 4: Management plan 77
A. Employees 77
B. Compensation 77
C. Vendors and outside resources 78
D. Accounting and/or bookkeeping 78
Part 5: Risks 78
Part 6: Financial management plan 80
A. Pro forma profit-and-loss statement 80
B. Balance sheet 81
C. Cash-flow projections 81
Keeping Your Plan Current 83

Chapter 5: Financing, Ownership, and Organizational Options 85

Determining Your Initial Cash Needs 85
Bootstrapping: Using Your Own Resources 88
Profiles of bootstrappers 89
Bootstrapping sources for financing 90
Outsourcing for Your Capital Needs 92
Banks 92
Asset-based financing 93
Line of credit 93
Letter of credit 94
Floor planning 94
Nonbanks 95
The Small Business Administration (SBA) 95
Small Business Investment Companies (SBICs) 96
Certified Development Companies (CDCs) 96
Angels: Investors with heart 96
Venture capital 97
Minority funding resources 99
Ownership Options: Going It Alone versus Partners and Shareholders ... 99
You as the one and only owner 101
Sharing ownership with partners or minority shareholders 102
Going public: Cashing in 103

The Entity Decision: Should You Incorporate? 105
Unincorporated options 105
Sole proprietorship 106
Partnerships 107
Incorporated business entities 108
C Corporations: The norm 109
Subchapter S Corporation: Liability protection 110
Limited Liability Corporations: A hybrid invention 111

Part II: Buying an Existing Business *113*

Chapter 6: Identifying the Right Business to Buy 115

Why Buy? 116
You want to reduce start-up hassles and headaches 116
You want to lessen risk 117
You can increase profits by adding value 117
You want an established cash flow 117
You don't have a good business idea 118
You want to open locked doors 118
You're not a great salesperson 118
Why NOT Buy? 119
You dislike inherited baggage 119
You're going to skimp on inspections 119
You lack capital 120
You can't handle lower potential returns 121
You don't get the satisfaction of creating a business 121
What Should You Have Before You Buy? 121
Business experience and training 121
Down payment money 122
How Do You Find Good Businesses? 124
Name your preferences 124
Generate leads 125
Peruse publications 125
Network with advisors 126
Knock on some doors 126
Consider enlisting business brokers 127
Should You Consider a Franchise? 129
Franchise advantages 129
Franchise disadvantages 130
What About Multilevel Marketing Companies? 131
Beware of the pyramid 131
Finding the better MLMs 132

Chapter 7: Making a Successful Offer to Buy **133**

Evaluating a Small Business for Sale 134
What is the background of owners and key employees? 135
Why is the owner selling? 136
What kind of company culture are you buying into? 138
What do the financial statements reveal? 140
The income statement (P&L) 140
The balance sheet 142
What are the terms of the company's lease contracts? 144
Special issues when evaluating a franchise 145
Thoroughly review regulatory filings 145
Evaluate the motives of the franchisers 146
Interview lots of franchisees 146
Understand what you're buying and examine comparables 146
Check with federal and state regulators 147
Investigate the company's credit history 147
Analyze and negotiate the franchise contract 147
Making an Offer to Purchase a Business 148
Assembling an all-star advisory team 148
Negotiating a good deal 149
Resources for valuing (determining the worth of) 149
Multiple of earnings and book value 150
Business appraisers 151
Businesses you've explored that have sold 151
Advisors who work with comparable companies 151
Research firms and publications 152
Trade publications 152
Business brokers 153
Purchase offer contingencies 153
Allocation of the purchase price 154
Due diligence 155
Income statement issues 156
Legal and tax issues 156
Moving into Your Newly Bought Business 157

**Part III: The Keys to Running a
Successful Small Business** **159**

Chapter 8: The Owner as Jack or Jill of All Trades **161**

The Nitty-Gritty Details of the Start-Up 161
Buying insurance 162
Workers' Compensation Insurance 163
Paying federal, state, and local taxes 163
Negotiating leases 164

Maintaining employee records 164
Getting licenses and permits — city, state, and federal 164
Check signing 165
Deciding What Tasks to Outsource 165
Typical small business jobs which are outsourced 165
Questions to determine what to outsource 166
Why You Need a Good Accounting System 167
Which accounting system should you use? 168
Manual bookkeeping systems 168
Computer-based systems 170
Category #1: Quick and easy 170
Category #2: Plus payroll and inventory 172
Category #3: Marching the audit trail 172
Category #4: Modular power 172
Determining the system that's right for you 173
Controlling Your Expenses 174
Fixed versus variable expenses 175
Zero-based budgeting 176
Managing Vendor Relationships 177
Dealing with Bankers, Lawyers, and Other
Folks Outside Your Business 179
Bankers 179
Recognizing risk 180
Working with your existing banker 180
Lawyers 181
Tax advisors 183
Consultants 184
Governments 185

**Chapter 9: Defining a Marketing Strategy: Product Development,
Promotion, Sales, Distribution, and Pricing 187**

Marketing Illustrated; Marketing Defined 188
Product and Service Development 188
Promotion: Getting Out the Word 190
Networking 191
Word-of-mouth: The power of referrals 192
Media advertising 193
Yellow Pages 195
Newspapers 195
Radio 196
Television 196
Magazines (local and national) 197
Online advertising 198
Other advertising vehicles 198
Publicity 199
The news release 199
The hook 200

Distribution: Moving Products into Channels 201
Product distribution versus service distribution 201
Direct distribution of products 202
Retail 202
Direct mail 202
Mail order catalogs 203
Internet sales 204
Indirect distribution 204
Retailers 204
Wholesalers/distributors 205
Repackaging 206
Deciding on distribution 206
Pricing: A Matter of Cost Plus Value 207
The six factors to consider when developing
your pricing strategy 207
Your marketing objectives 208
Cost to produce the product (or service) 209
Customer demand 210
Comparative value to customer 210
Competition 210
Substitute products 211
Deciding on price 211
Pricing new products or services 211
Updating prices of existing products and services 212
Sales: Where the Rubber Hits the Road 214
Going in-house, or not in-house; that is the question 214
Using an in-house sales force 215
Using manufacturers' representatives 215
Becoming a sales-driven company 217

Chapter 10: Keeping Your Customers Happy 219

The Keys to Retaining Good Customers 220
Get it right the first time 221
Keep offering more value 222
Company policy is meant to be bent 222
Learn from customer defections 224
The value of customer loyalty 224
Tracking customer defections 225
Customer service is part of what your customers buy 226
Customer service before the sale 228
Customer service during the sale 228
Customer service after the sale 229
Dealing With Unhappy (and Difficult) Customers 230
Listen, listen, listen 230
Develop a solution 231

Chapter 11: Minding the Financials: Cash Flow, Costs, and Profitability 233

Cash Flow — the Fuel That Drives Your Business 234
Getting to Know Your Financial Statements 237
    The Profit & Loss Statement 237
    The Balance Sheet 240
Turning the Numbers into Action 242
    Your business's key ratios and percentages 244
        Return on sales (R.O.S.) 245
        Return on equity (R.O.E.) 245
        Gross margin 245
        Quick ratio 246
        Debt-to-equity ratio 246
        Inventory turn 246
        Number of days in receivables 247
Managing Your Inventory 247
Collecting Your Accounts Receivables 249
    Finding customers likely to pay 250
    Managing your accounts receivables 251
The Three Ways to Improve Profitability 251
    Decreasing (or controlling) expenses 252
        Zero-based budgeting 253
        Tips for controlling the fat 254
    Increasing margins 255
    Increasing sales 256

Chapter 12: Escaping the #1 Cause of Failure on the Road to Success 257

Overcoming Isolation 258
    Soak up information like a sponge 258
    Find a mentor 258
    Network with peers 260
    Form a Board of Advisors 261
    Get a partner 263
    Join a trade association 265
    Stay informed 266

Part IV: Keeping Your Business in Business 267

Chapter 13: Finding and Keeping Superstar Employees 269

Why You Need Superstars 269
Assembling a Team of Superstar Employees 270
    Hints for hiring 271
    The interview process 273

Training Your Team: It's an Investment 274
Motivating Your Team: Issues of Pay and Performance 276
    Designing a compensation plan 277
        Types of compensation 278
        Ways to create a plan that works 279
    Get SMART! Goal-setting that works for everyone 281
    Writing performance expectations 282
    Reviewing your employees' performance 283
    Parting company — firing an employee 286
Working Relationships: Designing a Flexible Organization Chart 289
Why You Need an Employee Manual 290
What Makes a Successful Employer? 292
    Flexibility: Some rules are meant to be bent 292
    Accountability: Performers and non-performers
       are accordingly noted 293
    Follow-up: The more you do it, the less you need it 294
The Option of Leasing Employees 295

Chapter 14: Providing Employee Benefits **297**
Small-Business Retirement Plans: The Underappreciated Benefit 298
Getting the Most Value from Your Small-Business Retirement Plan 299
    SEP-IRAs 300
    Keoghs 300
    401(k) plans 302
    403(b) plans 302
    SIMPLE plans 303
    Convincing employees that retirement plans matter 303
To Share or Not Share the Equity 305
    Stock and stock options 306
    Employee stock ownership plans (ESOPs) 307
    Buy-sell agreements 307
Insurance and Other Benefits 308
    Health insurance 308
        Issues to consider when establishing health insurance 308
        Select higher deductibles and co-payments 309
        Be sure to shop around 310
    Disability insurance 310
    Life insurance 311
    Dependent care plans 312
    Flexible benefit plans 312
    Vacation 314

**Chapter 15: The Long Arm of the Law: Regulatory
and Legal Issues** **315**
A Whole Lotta Laws for Small Business 315
Regulatory Concerns of the Start-Up 317
    Licensing, registrations, and permits 317
        The realities of compliance 318
        Local regulations: Taxes, zoning, and health 320

State regulations: More taxes, licensing, insurance,
and the environment 322
Federal regulations: Still more taxes, licenses,
and requirements 323
Selection of a business entity 324
Protecting ideas and plans: Trademarks, patents,
NDAs, and copyrights 324
Nondisclosure agreements (NDAs) 325
Patents, trademarks, and copyrights 326
Contracts with customers and suppliers 327
Hiring and Labor Laws 328

Chapter 16: Taming Your Small Business's Taxes 329

Get Smarter About Taxes 330
Reading income tax guides 330
Using income tax-preparation software 331
Hiring help 331
Keep Good Financial Records 334
Know Your Income Tax Bracket 335
Stay on Top of Employment Tax Issues 336
Know your benefits options 336
Keep current on those taxes 336
Be careful with "independent contractor" hirings 337
Hire your kids! 338
Spend Your Money Tax-Wisely 339
Take equipment write-offs sensibly 339
Don't waste extra money on a business car 340
Minimize entertainment and travel expenditures 340
Taxes and Selecting the Right Corporate Entity 341

Chapter 17: Issues for Growing Businesses 343

Recognizing the Three Stages of a Business 344
The start-up years 344
The growth years 345
The transition period 345
Feeling the Impact of Human Resources Issues 346
Human resources concerns 346
The three stages of human resources development 347
Stage 1: Dealing with human resources issues yourself 347
Stage 2: Delegating human resources
responsibilities to others 348
Stage 3: Hiring a human resources director 348
Addressing Time-Management Issues 348
Time wasters 349
Time savers 349

Choosing the Best Management System for Your Small Business 350
    Management by objective (MBO) 352
    Participatory management 352
    Employee ownership 352
    Quality circles 353
    Total Quality Management (TQM) 353
    Reengineering 353
    Open-book management 355
Troubleshooting Your Business 355
    Troubleshooting checklist 355
    Taking the five-minute appearance test 357
Finding Your Role in an Evolving Business 358
    Dealing with growing pains 359
    Making the transition to manager 360
    Making big changes 361
        Downsizing your business 361
        Taking a personal inventory.. 361
        Hiring a replacement 362
        Selling the business 362

Part V: The Part of Tens 363

Chapter 18: Ten Tips for Home-Based Businesses 365

Run your business like a business 366
Keep things legal.. 366
Do things right the first time around! 367
Put on a professional face 367
Choose the right technology.. 369
Develop a marketing strategy 371
Manage your time effectively 372
Motivate yourself (if you don't, who will?) 373
Include your spouse or significant other 373
Stay in the loop 374
Recognize that working from home isn't a free lunch 375

Chapter 19: Ten Ways Computers Can Help Your Small Business ... 377

Brainstorming and researching business ideas 378
Finding a mentor 379
Buying a business or franchise 379
Searching for financing 379
Marketing your business 380
Maintaining and analyzing your financials 380
Filing your taxes.. 381
Avoiding attorneys 381
Saving time and money 382
Keeping track of technology 382

Chapter 20: Ten Tips for Managing Your Growing Business 383

Keep focus on what you can do and what you do best 383
Bend the rules when necessary 384
Hold your employees accountable 385
Consider the 80-20 rule 385
Think ahead: What happens today was yesterday's fault 386
Sleep on it 387
Resolve conflicts (the meek may inherit the Earth,
   but their employees may revolt) 388
Walk your talk: The message you send is vital 388
Remember and review your mission 389
Follow the Rule of Many Reasons 390

Index *391*

Book Registration Information .... *Back of Book*

Introduction

• •

*I*f you visit the small-business section of a larger bookstore, you'll soon find that there's no shortage of books on the topic of small business. The problem we see, however, is that most of them aren't worthy of your time or dollars. *Forbes* magazine once said of the marketplace for small-business books, "Warning: Most how-to books on entrepreneurship aren't worth a dime." We agree with that statement, except for the "dime" part. We think it's more like a nickel.

Why This Small-Business Book?

Here are the backgrounds and philosophies we have that serve as a guide to the advice we are about to offer, advice from the field that we believe makes our book different from other small-business books:

First, we're small-business experienced and we share the benefits of that experience with you. Between us, we have four decades of experience in starting and running seven successful small businesses. In addition, we work with small-business owners on a daily basis. Jim leads numerous small-business peer networking groups and provides volunteer counseling services to small-business owners under the Small Business Administration umbrella. Eric provides financial counseling to small-business owners, teaches financial management courses, and is a former management consultant.

Throughout this book, we share the experience we've gained, in the hopes that you'll use our advice to purge some of the trial-and-error from your inventory of management tools. We also share an ample collection of straight-from-the-horse's-mouth anecdotes in the following pages, each one based on a true story.

Second, we take an objective view of small-business ownership. Although we firmly believe in the creative power of small business, we're not here to be its pitchmen.

Sadly, too many small-business books are written by folks with an agenda: a franchise to sell, a multilevel marketing scheme to promote, a high-priced seminar to foist on the reader. As a result, small business often looks rosier than it really is, sort of like having children appears to wannabe parents. But you won't see us pretending that your baby won't require a fair amount of midnight diaper changes and early morning feedings. We're here to pass on the bad news as well as the good. If you're the type of person who wants to get into this competitive career field, we'd like you to enter the race informed as well as inspired.

We take a holistic approach. Because small business can at times be both demanding and intoxicating, running your own shop can threaten to consume your life. Although everyone knows that life is more than just business, striking a balance and staying in control can represent a stifling challenge. With that in mind, we take particular care to present the realities of running a small business within the larger (and more important) framework of maintaining a happy personal and financial life.

What We Assume about You

Many small-business books make a host of dangerous assumptions. For one, too many of those books assume that their readers are ready to make the leap into small business. We don't make that assumption here and neither should you. That's why we include sections designed to help you decide whether or not small business is really for you. We spell out the terms of starting your own business, break down the tasks, and point out the danger signals. We don't think that you're incapable of making the decision yourself; we just know that time is your most precious resource, and we think we can help you save it. Too many years of your life will be lost if you make the wrong choice.

Small business is many things to those of us who have participated in it or have dreamed about participating in it. Owning a small business is "The American Dream," "The Road to Great Riches," and "The Incubator of Capitalism," all rolled into one. Without a doubt, this concept of "being your own boss" is an alluring one.

Not everyone can be a boss, however. For those of you who currently are not bosses, fantasizing about owning a business of your own is perfectly natural on those days when you're fed up with your current boss or job. Your fantasy is made even more attractive by the rags-to-riches stories we hear about those entrepreneurs who have turned their visions into millions and or even billions of dollars.

But in the midst of your dreams, know that small business ownership has some not-so-appealing aspects as well. Most often, many years of hard work and tons of tough choices are required before the risks we take are turned into rewards. And, most difficult of all, the entrepreneurial career can be lonely at the top.

We're not talking about the kind of loneliness that solitude breeds either, although if you happen to be the boss as well as the only employee, that too may be a part of your job description. What we are talking about is the kind of loneliness that is common to many new small-business owners, whether you're a coffee shop owner, a plumber, or running a small printing shop: We're talking about the loneliness of responsibility — the loneliness that happens when the buck stops only with you.

Of course, the thrill of being the ultimate decision-maker may be exactly what attracts you to small business in the first place, but you should realize that this attraction has its downsides as well, the most prominent of which is that it breeds trial-and-error, and trial-and-error begets mistakes, and mistakes are the most expensive (and most dangerous) way for the small-business owner to learn.

But wait, before you plod back to your day job, we've got some good news for you. The mistakes that you're likely to make have been already made by those who have gone before you — including us. If you can somehow avoid the trial-and-error that leads to them (which is what we're here to help you do), your chances for success will multiply many times over.

How to Use This Book

We've organized this book to satisfy different reading and personal styles. Some of you may read it from cover to cover, while others will refer to it to answer a specific question or address an immediate concern. For this reason, each chapter of the book is designed to stand on its own.

Much like every small-business owner, this book must wear a number of hats. Here are the ways in which it can serve as your resource.

. . . for making big decisions

Your very first small-business decision may be to admit that you're not ready for this career — at least not yet. Chapter 1 is intended to help those of you who are straddling the fence to dismount onto one side or the other. We help you make the right choice by presenting you with a test designed to assist in determining whether or not this career works for you.

Make no mistake about it, no matter how creatively you and your lawyer may attempt to structure your deal, this business of small business involves risk. Therefore, before exposing yourself to such risk, we suggest that you get your personal finances in order. Enter Chapter 2, which covers personal finances.

. . . as a road map

The road in the early stages of a small business has so many detours and Y's that you're bound to lose sight of the road itself. Chapters 3, 4 and 5 provide you with the map you need to reach your destination. All the stones of a typical start-up are overturned in these two chapters, from writing a gangbuster business plan to creating the right legal framework to locating the financing that suits your needs.

Wait. You say you're considering buying an existing business as opposed to starting one from scratch? That's fine too, but you should ask some questions prior to making that decision. What are the advantages of buying an existing business over starting a new one? What kind of business should I buy? How should I determine the price I can pay? What are the tax implications? What are the first things I should do after the sale is completed? You find the answers to these questions (and many more) in Chapters 6 and 7.

. . . as a problem solver and a frame of reference

You'll soon discover that small-business ownership is really one never-ending exercise in problem solving. Chapters 8 through 17 are designed to help solve small business's most compelling problems. A partial list of those problems includes the following:

- ✔ **Sales creation:** No sales, no income. Period.

- ✔ **Marketing:** Although such small-business functions as sales, accounting, and operations are primarily black-and-white issues, not so with marketing. Marketing is gray, fuzzy, and hard to define (try defining the word *marketing* right now in one easy sentence), one of those aspects of doing business that doesn't come naturally to most of us.

- ✔ **Employees:** Deciding when and whom to hire is a vital but difficult decision. Then, even when you have hired the right employees for the right jobs, you're faced with the never-ending task of motivating and retaining them — and sometimes replacing them.

- ✔ **Operational issues:** Operations is that long list of day-to-day responsibilities, beginning with how you spend your day from the time you walk in the office or store in the morning until the time you go home at night. These issues include everything from collecting accounts receivable to understanding financial statements to taking good care of your customers. And don't forget the foremost operational issue of them all: managing cash.

✔ **Long-range planning:** Small-business owners recognize that long-range planning is important, but unfortunately they're too busy unloading the UPS truck to get around to it. They say they'll do planning tomorrow, but alas, tomorrow never comes.

✔ **Accounting and bookkeeping issues:** Double-entry accounting systems? Cash flow projections? Current ratios and quick ratios and inventory turns? You're probably saying, "Give me a break. What does all this have to do with the chocolate chip cookie business?" You'll see!

✔ **Technology issues:** It seems like only yesterday the fax machine was invented. Today, new telecommunications and information-gathering tools are appearing faster than politicians promising to cut taxes and improve government services. Keeping up is sometimes challenging, but you can do it.

✔ **Locating new financing or revising existing financing:** Money is the food that feeds every small business. If you lack money, you may not be able to get your business headed in the desired direction. No money equals no energy to make your business go.

✔ **Everything else:** This category includes, but is not limited to, such issues as product development, pricing, budgeting, business expansion, government regulations, customer service, ownership issues, and lifestyle issues.

. . . *as a mentor*

It oughta be a rule: Every small-business owner should have his or her own mentor. Sadly, too few of us do. Meanwhile, our Fortune 500 cousins long ago learned the mentorship lesson, resulting in the fact that every new management employee today has a mentor lurking in the wings nearby. Those mentors are typically grizzled old business veterans, people who have learned business's lessons the hard way.

Chapters 18 through 20 act as the mentor you need to assist you in building your business. These chapters share a collection of suggestions, advice, and tips on subjects designed to make the difference between maintaining a stagnant or mediocre business and growing a healthy one. Included in these chapters are tips on such topics as how to effectively utilize computers, how to improve your personal management skills, and where to find the best learning tools with which to grow your business.

Mentors guide and teach, and that is what these chapters are intended to do.

Icons Used in This Book

To help you find the information you need to help you on your entrepreneurial path, we've placed signposts called icons throughout the text to highlight important points.

This symbol indicates on-target tips to make your journey into small business safer and easier.

We present tales from our own experience to save you some trial-and-error. Enjoy the company of your fellow entrepreneurs and benefit from the lessons they've learned.

Straight from the heart of experience, we'll clue you in on what works for us as we navigate the oft-troubled waters of small-business life.

We stay away from lawyers as much as we can, and we recommend that you do, too. But sometimes, asking a lawyer is the safest and most efficient way to solve your business problem. This icon denotes those times.

The path of small-business ownership can be fraught with peril. This icon points out the dangers and helps steer you clear.

This icon points out stuff too good to forget.

The heart of our message; you'll find only one of these in a chapter. When you see this sign, sit up and take notice — this advice will help you get to the top.

Watch out for the shark in sheep's clothing. Some deals may be too good to be true, and some people may have their own interests at heart, not yours.

This icon warns you to do some thinking and checking before you take the plunge. You have a lot of important choices here, so don't rush in.

For those of you who like to sweat the dull stuff, this icon points out the inner workings of the business world that you are likely to ignore as you get down to the real work.

The One Common Denominator

Michael Gerber, author of *The E-Myth Revisited* (published by HarperBusiness), makes the point that "the one common denominator in every successful entrepreneur is an insatiable appetite to learn." If Michael is right, and we believe that he is, then you've passed the first test of the successful entrepreneur. By purchasing this book, you've displayed a desire to learn. Keep it up — you're on the right track.

Small business is not rocket science. You don't need an off-the-charts IQ to start and run a successful small business. What you do need is help. And that's exactly why we wrote this book.

We're pleased that you chose us as your guides into the stimulating world of small business.

Part I

Becoming an Entrepreneur

The 5th Wave   By Rich Tennant

Art's AUTO PARTS

GIFT BASKETS

Gasket Greetings | Valentine Tune up | Spark plug Sampler

SALE
~~1/3 OFF~~
1/2 OFF

"I don't know, Art. I think you're just ahead of your time."

In this part . . .

Your very first small-business decision may be to admit that you're not ready for this career — at least not yet. This part is intended to help those of you who are straddling the fence to dismount onto one side or the other. You can test your entrepreneurial aptitude, insure that your personal finances can withstand the strain, and then start making your dream a reality with a well-designed business plan and a survey of financial and ownership options.

Chapter 1

Is Small Business for You?

In This Chapter

▶ The role of small business and the people who participate in it

▶ Small-business "opportunities" to avoid

▶ A test to help you determine whether you should consider owning a small business

▶ The skills required of a small-business owner

▶ Reasons to own (and not to own) a small business

▶ Options to starting your own business

*E*veryone has his or her own definitions of small business. One of the more descriptive of those definitions, although possibly not the most accurate, came from an old friend of ours who has been a small-business owner for more years than many of us have been alive. What's more, he has not only been an active small-business participant, he has also been a small-business writer, consultant, and trainer, all rolled into one. He definitely has earned his small-business stripes in many ways.

"Small business is a place where you can take your dog to the office whenever you choose," he says in answer to our question about what a small business is. You can almost hear his German shepherd panting in the background, can't you?

Not a bad definition, when you think about it. That's because most small-business veterans will cite freedom of choice as the number one reason that they selected their vocation. What better expression of freedom than to have Old Shep snoozing happily at your side while you work?

However, deciding to start or buy a small business is a lot more complex than considering whether you'd like the ability to take your favorite pet (or family member) to work! And, the reality of small business isn't as simple as assuming that you'll have all the freedom in the world, nor are you correct in assuming that the converse (being an employee) offers you little freedom. In fact, we know an employee (a lawyer, no less) who took his full-grown Doberman to the small law firm where he (the lawyer, not the dog) worked! However, because some small businesses have lots of clients/customers coming in the door, having a pet in the office may not always be feasible.

Of course, most people won't make the decision about whether to go into the small-business world based upon their desire to spend more time with their pets! Lots of important issues, from your financial situation, to your desire to create a needed product or provide a needed service, to your ability to be a jack-of-all-trades, will influence your decision to become an entrepreneur. This chapter helps you understand the realities of running your own business and how it may or may not work for you.

What Is a Business?

The lingo of the business world — cash flow, profit & loss statements, accounts receivable, debt-to-equity ratio, and so on — makes the world of small-business ownership appear far more complicated than it really is. Don't be fooled. You're probably more acquainted with the basic concepts of doing business than you think. If you've ever participated in a bake sale, been paid for a musical performance, or operated a baby-sitting, painting, or gardening service, you've been involved in a small business.

Being a small-business owner doesn't mean that you must work 70 hours a week, make a six-figure income, or have a breakthrough product or service that lands you on the cover of a national business magazine. We know many successful small-business owners who work at their craft 40 hours a week or less and some who work part time at their business while on someone else's payroll. The vast majority of small-business owners who we know provide products or services quite similar to what's already in the marketplace and make reasonable but not extraordinary sums of money — and are perfectly happy doing so!

Small (and large) business basics

It's a hot summer afternoon, and you and your friend Jenny, who lives down the street, are sweating it out under the shade of an elm tree in your front yard.

"Boy, it's hot," sighs Jenny. "I could sure go for a glass of lemonade. But I don't feel like walking eight blocks to get to Timmy's lemonade stand."

And that's when you seize upon your business idea. With no lemonade stand for eight blocks, you and Jenny figure that you have found an untapped market of thirsty customers.

You start by asking some of your neighbors if they would buy lemonade from you, and you quickly learn that the quality, service, and location of your proposed business may attract a fair number of customers. You've just conducted your first *market research.*

You and Jenny also need to determine the location of your business. Although you could set up in front of her house or your house, you both agree that your respective streets don't get enough traffic. To maximize sales, you decide to set up your stand on the corner down the road. Luckily, Mrs. Ormsby gives you permission to set up in front of her house, provided that she gets a free glass of lemonade. You've just negotiated your first *lease,* and you've just had your first experience at *bartering.*

With a flip of the coin (Jenny wins), the name — Jenny's Lemonade Stand — is determined. Several transactions with parents and the grocery store later, and you have your lemonade stand (the *store*), your cash box, table, and pitcher (your *furniture* and *fixtures*), and the lemonade (your *inventory*). Jenny's Lemonade Stand is now ready for business!

Jenny didn't know it at the time, but she faced the same business challenges and issues that all small-business owners face. As a matter of fact, the business challenges and issues Jenny's Lemonade Stand faced are the same that General Motors and every other Fortune 500 company faced. And still face today.

Here is a comparison of the basics of doing business for General Motors, as well as for Jenny's Lemonade Stand:

- ✔ **Sales:** General Motors sells automobiles; Jenny sells lemonade. A sale is a sale no matter what the product or service or how large or small the ticket price.

- ✔ **Cost of goods:** General Motors buys steel and tires for its vehicles from its vendors and suppliers; Jenny buys lemons and sugar and paper cups for her lemonade from her parents and the grocery store.

- ✔ **Expenses:** General Motors has employee wages and pension plans (or employee benefits); Jenny has sign-making costs and bubble gum expenditures to keep her employees happy (also employee benefits).

- ✔ **Profit:** Profit is what's left over after General Motors and Jenny subtract the cost of the goods and the expenses from their sales. This simple equation works for General Motors and Jenny, and it will work for you.

And there you have it: the formula for Business 101.

To take this Business 101 concept one step further, not only is the preceding formula the same for any and every business, many of the formula's subsidiary financial basics are the same, too. Here's what we mean:

- ✔ **Accounts payable:** General Motors owes money to the vendors who provide it with steel and tires; Jenny owes money to her parents who provide her with lemons.

✔ **Accounts receivable:** General Motors has money due from its dealers who stock the company's cars on their lots; Jenny has money due her from Mrs. Cratchett, who wandered by thirsty and without her purse.

✔ **Cash flow:** General Motors has cash flows (sometimes positively, sometimes negatively), and so does Jenny. (For much, much more on this concept, see Chapter 11.)

✔ **Assets:** General Motors has its plants and equipment; Jenny has her lemonade stand and cash box.

✔ **Liabilities:** General Motors owes people money (vendors); so does Jenny (her parents).

✔ **Net worth:** Net worth is what's left over after General Motors subtracts what it owes (its liabilities) from what it owns (its assets). Ditto with Jenny's small enterprise.

This comparison between Jenny's Lemonade Stand and General Motors could go much deeper and longer. Suffice it to say here that the basics of the two businesses are the same; the differences are primarily due to size. Size is a synonym for complexity in business.

So, you must be thinking, if business is so simple, why isn't everyone doing it — and succeeding at it?

The reason is that while the basics of business are simple, the details are not. Consider the various ways in which you grant your customers credit, collect the resulting accounts receivable, and unfortunately sometimes write them off when you're not paid. Consider the simple concept of sales: How do you pay the people who do make those sales, where and how do you deploy them, and how do you organize and supervise and motivate them? And how do you compile and make sense of your financial figures? How much should you pay your vendors for their products? And when you need money, should you consider taking in shareholders or should you borrow from the bank? And how should you deal with the IRS and OSHA and your state's workers' compensation department? These are but a few of the complex details that take the basics of business and muddy the waters.

In this chapter, we help you to assess whether you've got what it takes to make it in the small-business world. And, in the rest of the book, we cover the important concepts that you and Jenny and General Motors must know in order to succeed.

Small business by the numbers

Contrast our dog-owner-friend's definition of small business at the start of this chapter to that of the Small Business Administration (SBA). The SBA defines small business as any business with fewer than 500 employees. If that's small, then the U.S. Government pays bottom dollar for its military purchases!

Jim's fourth small business had 200 employees, and in our minds anyway, that wasn't small. With 200 employees, you have, say 400 dependents, maybe 1,000 customers, and 100 or so of the business's vendors all depending on you, trusting in you, waiting for the mail to deliver their next check. That certainly isn't small by our standards — not if you measure size in terms of responsibility anyway.

For those to whom numbers are important, however, our own reluctant definition of small business is any business with 100 employees or less, a category that includes the majority of the nation's entrepreneurial endeavors.

The Internal Revenue Service (using the SBA definition) tells us that more than 22 million nonfarm businesses exist in the United States, of which 99 percent meet our definition of "small." These 22 million include corporations, partnerships, and sole proprietorships. Almost two-thirds of the 22 million businesses operate full time; the rest operate part time.

No matter how you slice it, more than 22 million small businesses in a nation of about 270 million people translates into one heck of a lot of economic activity. As a matter of fact, if the small businesses in the U.S. were their own country, that country would be the third largest in the world in terms of gross national product, trailing only the United States and Japan.

The number of people owning or employed in small businesses is on the rise. Over the past five years, Cognetics (a firm that conducts surveys and tracks employment patterns in businesses of all sizes) found that total employment rose by more than 11 percent in firms with fewer than 19 employees, grew less than 2 percent at companies with between 100 and 4,999 employees, and shrank more than 1 percent at companies with more than 5,000 employees.

Small business's continued success is not without its counterpoint, however. Futurist John Naisbitt points out that the 500 largest American businesses now account for only 10 percent of the American economy, down from 20 percent in 1970. As judged by the continuing popularity of "downsizing" by the Fortune 500 companies, this trend is expected to continue.

An even more startling figure is that 50 percent of U.S. exports are created by companies that have 19 or fewer employees. Meanwhile, only 7 percent of U.S. exports are created by companies with 500 or more employees. The lesson? No matter how small your business is, you, too, may have a chance to get in on the global boom.

What all this says is that small business is not really *small* — it is large, and growing. Not only is it not small when speaking in terms of the sheer numbers of small businesses and their employees, it's also not small when talking about the tenacity and knowledge required to start and run a small business, which is where the remainder of this book comes in. You will provide the tenacity part of the equation; we will provide the knowledge.

Small business as a role model for big business

Jack Welch, CEO of General Electric, stated in his company's corporate message for the '90s: "Think small. What General Electric is trying relentlessly to do is to get that small-company soul . . . and small-company speed . . . inside our big-company body."

Think small? What's happening here? Why would the CEO of a gigantic company like GE want his employees to be thinking *small?*

Small can be beautiful because success and survival in the business arena favors the agile over the cumbersome, the small over the big. Encouraging this trend is the fact that, thanks to the increasing pace of technology, you no longer have to *be* big to appear big; thus, everyone can compete in most of today's marketplaces.

Different people, different businesses, similar issues

Okay, so we've defined the term "small business" and identified the people who create and run one, but what about *your particular* small business? After all, in your eyes anyway, the business you have in mind or are already running is different than anyone else's. Different products, different services, different legal entity, and the list goes on. We'd bet that you have some specific concerns about whether this book will address your needs.

Yes, this book will address your needs if your endeavor (actual or proposed) intends to create revenue by offering a product or a service to a customer, thereby generating a profit in the process. If that's what your business is presently doing or if that's what you intend your business to do, then this book is for you. We've got you covered.

The term "small business" covers a wide range of product and service offerings. A ten-person law practice is a small business. A doctor's office is a small business. Architects, surveyors, and dentists are also in the business of owning and operating small businesses.

How about a Dairy Queen franchisee? You guessed it. Small business. Ditto with freelance writers (hence, we, your humble authors, are both small-business owners), consultants, and the dry cleaner on the corner of Elm and Main Street. Each one is a small business.

A business is also a small business regardless of its entity. You say that you're a partner in a limited partnership? Then you're involved in a small business. Sole proprietorships, C Corporations, and Limited Liability Corporations — all are small businesses, as long as they have fewer than 100 employees.

Think about it. All of these businesses have several common denominators. They all need "marketing" (to make their products or services known), they all need sales (to get their products or services in the hands of the customer), and they all need varying degrees of administration and financial accounting (to satisfy a number of internal informational needs, as well as the IRS). From that point forward, each business is significantly different from another: Some need employees, some don't; some require vast investments in real estate, equipment, and elaborate information systems; some can get by with a desk, computer, modem, and phone; some may need to borrow money to get the business up and running; many others get by with what's in the owner's savings account.

As far as this book is concerned, however, the size, shape, or form of your business matters not. As long as you're creating revenues and striving to generate profits, that's enough. We've got you covered.

Our definition of an entrepreneur

A small-business owner (or entrepreneur), by our definition anyway, is anyone who owns a business that has 100 or fewer employees. Period. Everyone who hangs out a shingle qualifies for the title no matter whether the business is private, public, barely surviving, or soaring off the charts.

You're a small-business owner if you've been in the saddle one day, one week, or one decade. You're a small-business owner if you're male or female, don't have a college degree, or have an MBA. You're a small-business owner if you work out of your home or on a fishing boat somewhere off the coast of Alaska.

Everyone has his or her own definition of the small-business owner. We find these three of particular interest; pick one or pick them all:

- ✔ **Webster's Dictionary:** A person who organizes and manages a business undertaking, assuming the risk for sake of profit.
- ✔ **Peter Drucker:** Someone who gets something new done. (Peter Drucker is the "father of modern management." His books have virtually defined contemporary U.S. management theory. Drucker primarily writes for large companies.)
- ✔ **Us:** A person who is motivated by independence, creativity, and growth, rather than by the security of an employer's paycheck.

All people have their own collection of unique characteristics that determine who they are, what makes them happy, and where they belong in this world. On those not-as-frequent-as-they-should-be occasions when our characteristics align with the kind of work we are doing, we know how Cinderella felt when her foot slipped snugly into the slipper offered by the Prince.

In all fairness, we must warn those of you who are considering our vocation that owning your own business can be addictive. We hate it occasionally, love it usually, and need it always, and we wouldn't trade professions with anybody, except for maybe Michael Jordan.

Small Business or Monkey Business?

As you navigate through the landscape of small-business opportunities, you're bound to encounter some land mines planted by those who don't have your best interests at heart. This section discusses some common land mines to watch out for when deciding to buy a small business, invest in one, or start up your own.

Pyramid schemes and the like

Unfortunately, plenty of businesses derive their incomes purely from the "signing-up" process. They "sign up" their investors/customers/suckers to sell their products or services or to buy their franchises, and then poof! After the money has changed hands, the relationship is kaput. No discernible products or services are offered, and all the investor has to show for the deal is a worthless agreement and a canceled check.

Some multilevel marketing (MLM) companies (which we cover in more detail in Chapter 6) have a reputation for falling into this category. Also known as network marketing or direct selling companies, MLMs have been known to offer the pitch that you can make tens of thousands of dollars monthly while sitting on your duff and letting someone else do the work. All you have to do is sign up a few friends and relatives to sell the company's widgets: Before you can shout the words "easy money," the big bucks come rolling in. We know many people who have been taken for hundreds of dollars in multilevel marketing schemes, only to discover that all they've stumbled upon is a quick way to lose a buck.

Anyone considering becoming an MLM investor should keep in mind that any network marketing arrangement is really just another form of a job. No company, MLM or otherwise, can offer to pay you money while you're busy watching the soaps. As with any other worthwhile venture, time — three to five years in most cases — and lots of hard work are required to create a business that will provide you with a decent living. If the MLM business were as simple as some in the business would lead us to believe, everyone would dive in.

For sure, some legitimate and successful companies are MLMs — Mary Kay and Tupperware, for example. However, they are the exception rather than the rule, particularly among the types of MLMs that you are likely to have aggressively pitched to you by others.

If you do decide to buy into an MLM that seems reputable, think twice before signing up relatives, friends, and coworkers in your MLM venture — at least until you are satisfied that the concept is a viable one. The particular danger in doing business with people you care for, and who care for you, is that in addition to your reputation and integrity, your friendships and family relations are also on the line.

Quality multilevel marketing companies make sense for people who really believe in, and want to sell, a particular product or service but don't want to, or can't afford to, tie up a lot of money in the process. Be sure to remember to check the references of the MLM company that you're considering (do the same homework we recommend in Chapter 6 for buying a franchise). Also, remember that you won't get rich in a hurry, or probably ever. And finally, remember that those people who do get "rich" in the MLM business pay the same price — lots of hard, smart work over a number of years — that the rest of us pay for success.

Work-from-home opportunities

Ads promoting ways to make piles of cash while working out of your home are easy to find these days, especially in the magazines that cater to small-business owners and wannabes. In many cases, these ads are another form of overhyped multilevel marketing scam and should be avoided.

> "Earn $10,000 monthly! We'll even help you hire agents to do the work for you. . . . FREE! Thirty days is all that it takes!"

> "Work out of your home. Company needs help. Earn $500–$900 per week. Anyone can do this — will train. Full time or part time. Only for the serious — please!"

> "Earn $4,000 per month on the new instant information superhighway."

And so the refrain goes. In these and other similar ads, no legitimate company may exist, but rather, you'll find a person or two with a post office box somewhere who wants to sell you a package of "confidential information" explaining the business opportunity du jour. This package of confidential information may cost several hundred dollars or more. More often than not, this information ends up being worthless marketing propaganda and is rarely useful.

Our advice? Read this book and tap the other helpful resources we list in it to understand more about legitimate small-business opportunities. You'll find more and better information, and the price will be far lower.

And remember one more thing on such money making "opportunities." Never buy into one that is pitched over the telephone or that requires a non-refundable cash outlay — unless, that is, you want to lighten your pocketbook and feel like a doofus, both at the same time.

The Small-Business Owner's Aptitude Test: Do You Have the Right Stuff?

Tests don't always have to a pain in the posterior, and they especially don't have to be a pain when you don't have to study for them, there are no right or wrong answers, and you're the only one who needs to know the outcome. So be prepared to take a painless but potentially telling test: **The Small-Business Owner's Aptitude Test.**

Some words of caution here: This test is not scientific in its basis. However, we think it's potentially useful because it's based on our many combined years of experience working as entrepreneurs, as well as alongside them. This test is meant to provide a guideline and not to cast in concrete your choice to start or buy a business. Although the results will be meaningful when it comes time to make your decision (especially if you are in the highest- or the lowest-scoring groups), for those of you who fall somewhere in the middle, we recommend some serious soul searching, consultation with friends and other small-business owners, and a large grain of salt. Your decision about starting a business should ultimately depend on your tenacity to achieve and your passion to own a business. And no test can accurately measure either of those.

Preparation

Score each of the following 20 questions with a number from 1 (the entrepreneurially unfriendly response) to 5 (the entrepreneurially friendly response). You determine your appropriate numerical score by assessing the relative difference between the two options and by how fervently you feel about the answer.

For example, one question asks, "Do you daydream about business opportunities while commuting to work, flying on an airplane, or waiting in the doctor's office?" Give yourself a 5 if you find yourself doing this a lot, a 1 if you never do this, and a 2, 3, or 4, depending upon the degree of work-related daydreaming you do. (The meaning of this one? Business, especially one that you own yourself, can be downright fun and all-consuming. For most successful entrepreneurs, their minds are rarely far away from their businesses, often thinking of new products, new marketing plans, and new ways to find customers.)

To make the test even more meaningful, have someone who doesn't have a vested interest in or strong opinions about your decision — such as a good friend or coworker — also independently take the test, with you as the subject. We seldom have unbiased opinions of ourselves, and having an unrelated third party score the test gives a more accurate view. Then compare the two scores — the score you arrived at when you took the test compared to the score your friend or peer compiled for you. Our guess is that your true entrepreneurial aptitude, at least according to our experience, will lie somewhere between the two scores.

The test questions

#1: In the games that you play, do you play harder when you fall behind, or do you have a tendency to fold your cards and cut your losses? (5 if you play harder, 1 if you wilt under pressure)

5	4	3	2	1

SCORE _____

#2: When you go to a sports event or concert, do you try to figure out the promoter's or the owner's gross revenues? (5 if you often do, 1 if you never do)

5	4	3	2	1

SCORE _____

#3: When things take a serious turn for the worse, is your first impulse to look for someone to blame, or is it to look for alternatives and solutions? (5 if you look for alternatives and solutions, 1 if you complain)

5	4	3	2	1

SCORE _____

#4: Using your friends and/or coworkers as a barometer, how would you rate your energy level? (5 if it is high, 1 if it is low)

5   4   3   2   1

SCORE _____

#5: Do you daydream about business opportunities while commuting to work, flying on an airplane, waiting in the doctor's office, or other quiet times? (5 if you often do, 1 if you never do)

5   4   3   2   1

SCORE _____

#6: Look back on the significant changes you've made in your life — schools, jobs, relocations, relationships. Have you fretted and worried about those changes and not acted, or have you looked forward to them with excitement and been able to make those tough decisions after doing some research? (5 if you looked forward to the decisions and tackled them after doing your homework, 1 if you've been overwhelmed with worry about them and paralyzed from action for too long)

5   4   3   2   1

SCORE _____

#7: Is your first consideration of any opportunity always the upside or is it always the downside? (5 if you always see the upside and recognize the risks, 1 if you dwell on the downside to the exclusion of considering the benefits)

5   4   3   2   1

SCORE _____

#8: Are you happiest when you are busy or when you have nothing to do? (5 if you are *always* happiest when busy, 1 if you are *always* happiest when you have nothing to do)

5   4   3   2   1

SCORE _____

#9: As an older child, did you often have a job or a scheme or an idea to make money? (5 if always, 1 if never)

| 5 | 4 | 3 | 2 | 1 |

SCORE _____

#10: Did you work part-time or summer jobs as a youth, or did you do nothing over the summer? (5 if you often worked, 1 if you never did)

| 5 | 4 | 3 | 2 | 1 |

SCORE _____

#11: Did your parents own a small business? (5 if they worked many years owning small businesses, 1 if they never did)

| 5 | 4 | 3 | 2 | 1 |

SCORE _____

#12: Have you worked for a small business for more than one year? (5 if you have, 1 if you haven't)

| 5 | 4 | 3 | 2 | 1 |

SCORE _____

#13: Do you like being in charge, in control, and at the center of attention? (5 if you really crave those things, 1 if you detest those things)

| 5 | 4 | 3 | 2 | 1 |

SCORE _____

#14: How comfortable are you with borrowing money to finance an investment, such as buying a home? (5 if owing money is not a problem, 1 if it's a huge problem)

| 5 | 4 | 3 | 2 | 1 |

SCORE _____

#15: How creative are you? (5 if extremely creative, 1 if not creative at all)

5	4	3	2	1

SCORE _____

#16: Do you have to balance your checkbook to the penny or is "close" good enough? (5 if "close" is good enough, 1 if to the penny)

5	4	3	2	1

SCORE _____

#17: When you fail at a project or task, does it scar you forever or does it inspire you to do it better the next time? (5 if it inspires you for the next time, 1 if it scars you forever)

5	4	3	2	1

SCORE _____

#18: When you truly believe in something, whether it's an idea, a product, or a service, are you able to sell it? (5 if almost always, 1 if never)

5	4	3	2	1

SCORE _____

#19: In your current social and business environment, are you most often a follower or a leader? (5 if almost always a leader, 1 if always a follower)

5	4	3	2	1

SCORE _____

#20: How good are you at achieving/keeping your New Year's resolutions? (5 if you almost always achieve/keep them, 1 if you never do)

5	4	3	2	1

SCORE _____

Scoring the test

Now total your score. Here's how to assess your totals:

80 to 100: Go for it. If you read this book and continue to show a willingness to be a sponge, you should succeed!

60 to 79: You probably have what it takes to successfully run your own business, but take some time to look back over the questions you scored the lowest on and see if you can discern any trends.

40 to 59: Too close to call. Review the questions on which you scored poorly and don't scrimp on learning more to tilt the scales in your favor.

0 to 39: We could be wrong, but you're probably better off working as an employee or pursuing one of the other alternatives to starting your own business.

Good luck in your new career. Or in your old one.

Does passing this test guarantee a successful entrepreneurial career?

The truth about a good test is that it can serve as a helpful indicator, but it isn't always right. Too many other factors go into the passing, or failing, of tests. And so it is with The Small-Business Owner's Aptitude Test. It can be a helpful indicator, but it won't be the definitive answer. We issue this disclaimer because The Small-Business Owner's Aptitude Test is, in effect, a measure of the way you have acted in the past.

Unfortunately, your future as a small-business owner will hold many surprises. (By the time you finish this book, we'll have prepared you for many of them.) The skills and traits that you need to cope with those surprises will ultimately determine whether your choice to start or buy a small business is the right one.

Just exactly what are those skills?

- ✔ **Numbers skills:** These skills include those related to borrowing money, accounting for it, and reporting on the financial performance of your company. (See Chapters 5, 8, and 11 for more information.)
- ✔ **Sales skills:** The small-business owner is always selling someone — be it his customers, employees, or vendors. (See Chapter 9 for more information.)
- ✔ **Marketing skills:** Everyone has to market her product or service — no one is exempt. (See Chapter 9 for details on marketing.)
- ✔ **Leadership skills:** The small-business owner is the grand poobah of his venture. Grand poobahs are only as good as the manner in which the business's employees are led. (See Chapter 13 for more information.)

Does this mean that if you don't have these skills, you should remain on the receiving end of a paycheck? Thankfully, it does not.

Many successful entrepreneurs who have come before you made it without being able to personally perform all the skills necessary to run a business. But what we *are* saying is that over the course of your career, you'll have to either develop these skills or involve someone in the business who already has them (a partner, a key employee, or a hired adviser or consultant).

And what about those traits?

- **The ability to coexist with risk and possibly debt:** Capitalism offers its participants no guarantees; thus the small business and consequently its owner are often at risk and sometimes in debt. And yet, its owner still has to sleep at night.

- **Intuition:** Call it intuition or call it gut instinct, the small-business owner has to call things right more often than wrong, or he will be calling it quits.

- **Optimism:** Rarely pessimistic, successful small-business owners see good fortune, not misfortune; upsides, not downsides; and opportunities, not problems. The small-business owner can always hire a devil's advocate (that's what lawyers and accountants are for), but the enthusiasm and optimism necessary to drive the vision must come from the entrepreneur.

- **Driven:** Successful small-business owners are driven to create a product, to service a customer, to build a successful business. Like the craving for chocolate, this drive doesn't go away.

Does this mean that if you don't have these four traits, you should remain on the receiving end of a paycheck?

Well, let us answer by saying that we also recognize that being a good employee today also requires some of the above traits. However, if you don't have most of the above traits in healthy supply, you're probably going to be better off as an employee instead of a small-business owner.

Making the Decision to Own a Small Business

Assuming that you've determined that you *do* have what it takes to own a small business, allow us to help you take the next step. Allow us to help you make the decision to dive in.

Even if you passed the test and qualify as a prospective small-business owner, this is not a slam-dunk decision you are about to make. After all, there are as many compelling reasons why you should not own a business as there are why you should. Here's what we mean.

The reasons to own

The following are some reasons why people choose to own a business:

- **The satisfaction of creation:** Have you ever experienced the pride of building a chair, preparing a gourmet meal, or repairing a vacuum cleaner? Or, how about providing a needed counseling service that helps people solve their vexing financial problems? The small-business owner is treated to the thrill of creation on a daily basis, not to mention the thrill of solving a customer's problem.

- **Establishment of their own culture:** No more standing around the water cooler complaining about "the way things are around here." After you've started your own business, the way things are around here is a direct function of the way you intend them to be.

- **Financial upside:** Consider Oprah Winfrey, Ted Turner, Steven Jobs, and Debbi Fields. It's no surprise that these one-time small-business owners are among the nation's wealthiest individuals.

- **Self-sufficiency:** For many of us, working for someone else has proven to be a less-than-gratifying experience. As a result of such unfulfilling experiences, some people have learned that if they wish to provide for themselves and their families, they'd better create the opportunity themselves. It's either that, or be willing to occasionally spend a long wait in the unemployment line.

- **Flexibility:** Perhaps you prefer to work in the evenings because that's when your spouse works, or perhaps you want to spend more time with the kids during the day. Or you may prefer taking frequent three-day-weekend jaunts rather than a few full-week vacations. As a small-business owner, despite the long hours you work, you should have more control over keeping a schedule that works best for you. After all, you're the boss, and you can usually tailor your schedule to meet your personal needs, as well as those of your customers.

- **Special perks:** As you see later in the book (see Chapter 15), small-business owners have several advantages over many employees. For example, small-business owners can sock away up to $30,000 per year free of federal and state income taxes into their retirement accounts. And yes, similar to those corporate execs who wine and dine their clients and then write off the expenses, small-business owners also have the option to write off such costs as long as they adhere to IRS rules. We explain later (see Chapter 16) what makes these rules tick and how they can work for you.

The reasons not to own

In light of the resounding potential benefits, why would any reasonable soul elect to continue receiving a paycheck? Why wouldn't everyone want to own a business? Let us count the nays:

- ✔ **Responsibility:** As a small-business owner, not only does your family depend on your business success, so do your partners, your employees and their families, your customers, and sometimes your vendors. As much as we love our small businesses, every now and then even the most enthusiastic of us wax nostalgic for the good old days when we would punch our time card and leisurely walk out the door — really, truly, done for the day. If you're the type of person who sometimes or often takes on more responsibility than you can handle and work too many hours, beware that another drawback of running your own business is that you may be prone to becoming a workaholic.

- ✔ **Competition:** When push comes to shove, the lure of competition helps prompt us to open the doors of our small businesses, but that same competition comes back to haunt us by threatening our security. We soon find out that a host of hungry competitors is pursuing our customers and threatening our livelihood, whether by cutting their prices or offering a more complete package of unique services. Sure, competition is what makes capitalism go 'round, but you should remember that in order to have a competition, someone's got to win and someone's got to lose.

- ✔ **Change:** Products and services come, and products and services go. Nothing is sacred in the business of doing business, and the pace of change today is significantly faster than it was a generation ago — and it shows no signs of slowing down. If you don't like change and the commotion it causes, then perhaps the stability that a larger, more bureaucratic organization provides is best for you.

- ✔ **Chance:** Interest rates, the economy, theft, fire, natural disasters, sickness, pestilence — the list goes on. Any of these can send your business reeling.

- ✔ **Red tape:** Taxes, health care reform, bureaucracy, tariffs, duties, treaties, OSHA, FDA, NAFTA, glurg, glurg, glurg.

- ✔ **Business failure:** And finally, as if this list of a small-business's enemies isn't enough, the owner faces the specter of the ultimate downside: business failure in the form of bankruptcy. This is the stage where the owner stands back and watches the creditors walk off with everything he or she owns, from the president's desk to the fax machine to the potted plants in the office. Now contrast the small-business owner's failure to the Fortune 500 employee who fails, collecting a tidy severance check as he packs up his calculator and waves good-bye on his way to register for unemployment compensation. No life's savings lost for this person, no second mortgages hanging over his or her home, no asterisks on the credit report. In our opinion, no other failure in the business world is as painful as that facing the small-business owner. More than any other reason, this cost of failure is the primary reason that owning a small business isn't for everyone.

These two lists, incidentally, are in no particular order. Everyone is different. The reasons Bill Gates may have decided to start Microsoft may be vastly different than the reason John Dough decided to buy his own pizza business. You won't find right or wrong reasons to start or buy a business; you'll only find right or wrong criteria that go into forming those reasons.

Options to Starting Your Own Business

More than a few small-business owners and entrepreneurial cheerleaders would have you believe that every employee would be happy and financially better off running his own small business. The reality is, of course, that the grass is not always greener on the other side of the fence. Small business isn't the only game in town; in some cases, it isn't even the best option available.

If, after taking The Small-Business Owner's Aptitude Test, you feel that you don't fit the profile of the typical entrepreneur, don't despair. Some folks are happier working *for* a company, be it either for-profit or nonprofit. This section provides several options for you to consider, in lieu of becoming an entrepreneur.

Becoming a better employee

If you are one of the many people who are mostly satisfied being an employee, you'll be happy to know, if you don't already, that companies of all sizes need good employees. Furthermore, good companies are willing to go to a lot of trouble and expense to hire, retain, and pay them. (If you're not presently working for one of those good companies, there are plenty to choose from. Get your resume updated!)

A variety of approaches work when it comes to improving your employee skills, but here are our favorites:

> ✔ **Keep improving your work ethic.** Your willingness to put in the extra hours when needed and your accompanying willingness to accept more responsibility will bring a smile to the faces of employers. Those employees who take the extra initiative and subsequently deliver will

rise to the top, especially in those organizations (both in the private and nonprofit sectors) where too many salaried employees have the 9-to-5 mentality.

Be careful, however, not to commit to more than you are capable of delivering in a high-quality and timely fashion. The downside of non-deliverance: Your supervisors will rightfully feel that they can't count on you if you consistently fall short of meeting your commitments. Another downside to overcommitting: Your personal life probably will be in a shambles, too.

✔ **Keep learning.** You don't need a Ph.D., a master's degree, or even an undergraduate college degree to succeed in business because of the amount of knowledge that's available for you to pick up on your own. These options to a full-degree program include mentors, experience, and plenty of reading, as well as higher education.

If you haven't completed your college or graduate degree and the industry you're in places particular value in those who have, investing the time and money it takes to finish your degree can pay big dividends. (More than a few of today's enlightened businesses will finance all or at least a part of that education for you. Just ask.) Talk to others who have taken a similar midcareer educational path, and see what they have to say.

Entrepreneuring inside a larger company

You can sometimes enjoy some of the best aspects of owning a small business at the same time that you are avoiding most of its downsides. How? By leading an entrepreneurial venture at your present company or for some other employer.

If you can find or create an entrepreneurial enterprise inside of (or alongside of) a larger company, in addition to significant managerial and operational responsibility, in many cases you can also negotiate sharing in the financial success that you help to create. Many enlightened companies' senior managers want you to have the incentive that comes from sharing in the financial success of your endeavors. The granting of bonuses, stock options, and in some cases outright ownership may be tied to the performance of your division.

Entrepreneurial opportunities can come from within businesses of all sizes, shapes, and forms. One large company — 3M, a Fortune 500 company — has long taken pride in a corporate culture that allows its employees to take an idea and build it into a separate company within 3M. Post-it Notes, those sticky notes that can be found everywhere in the offices of the world, is an example of a business started within a business by 3M employees.

Similar examples can be found at smaller companies with even better results for the entrepreneurial employee. Jim owned a sporting goods retail and wholesale business at the time one of his employees suggested that the company start a separate fitness and weight training division. The company did just that. The employee and Jim became the only two shareholders of the spin-off business, and the employee assumed its presidency. Four years of profitability later, Jim sold his stock to the ex-employee-now-sole-owner, who went on to build the company into a greatly successful small business. That business (now known as Pro Source Fitness), we're happy to report, is still alive and healthy today.

Developing a business within a business is a win-win situation for everyone — the employees involved are compensated for the results of their new-found business, companies like 3M add another terrific and profitable product to their empire, and a new business venture may be spun off to make more products and hire more employees, keeping the local economy humming.

Moving from a large company to a small company

Although we're not aware of any statistics measuring the movement of employees from large businesses to small businesses (or vice versa), we would guess the scale tilts significantly in favor of employees moving from large businesses to small businesses for several reasons:

- ✔ Employees get well-rounded experience working with small companies. The business equation is closer to home.
- ✔ Small-business employees have opportunities for more responsibility.
- ✔ Employee decisions and actions have much more impact on a small business, and that impact is more visible than in a large business.
- ✔ The small-business experience provides a logical stepping stone for those who eventually aspire to owning their own businesses.

Buying an existing business

In the likely event that you don't have a specific idea for a business you want to start, but you have exhibited business-management skills and you possess the ability to improve existing businesses, buying an established business may be right for you. Although buying someone else's business can, in some cases, be riskier than starting your own, at least you know exactly what you're getting into right from the start. You don't have to go through the risky start-up period when you take this acquiring route.

Minimizing the risk of start-up: Developing a part-time business

Some people believe that starting your own business is the riskiest of all small-business options. However, if you're starting a business that specifically uses your skills and expertise, the risk may not be nearly as great as you think. Besides, risk is relative: Those who are employed by someone else are taking a risk, too — a risk that their employer will continue to offer them the opportunity to work.

One way to minimize the risk of starting a full-time business is to work into a part-time one. Suppose for a moment that you're a computer troubleshooter at a large company and making $40,000 per year. You're considering establishing your own computer consulting service and would be happy making a comparable amount of money. If you find through your research that others performing the services you intend to provide are charging $40 per hour, you'll need to actually spend about 20 hours a week consulting (assuming that you work 50 weeks per year). Because you can run your consulting business from your home (which can generate small tax breaks) and you can do it without purchasing costly new equipment, your expenses should be minimal. (*Note:* We've ignored your employer's benefits here, which, of course, have value, too.)

Rather than leaving your day job and diving cold turkey into your new business without the safety of a regular paycheck, you have the option to start moonlighting as a consultant. Over the course of a year or two, if you can average 10 hours a week of consulting, you're halfway to your goal. Then, after you leave your job and can focus all your energies on your business, getting to 20 hours per week of billable work won't be such a stretch.

Many businesses, by virtue of leveraging their owner's existing skills and expertise, can be started with low start-up costs. You can begin building the framework of your company using "sweat equity" (the time and energy you invest in your business, as opposed to the capital) in the early, part-time years. As long as you know your competition and can offer your customers a valued service at a reasonable cost, the principal risk with your part-time business is that you won't do a good job marketing what you have to offer. When you can learn how to market your skills, that's the time to make the break.

You will probably need more capital to buy an ongoing enterprise than to start a new one. Buying an existing business can also mean that you'll have to shell out more money at the outset, in the form of a down payment to buy the business. Thus, if you don't have the ability to run the business and it does poorly, you have a lot more to lose financially. Another risk that start-ups don't face is that businesses for sale are generally for sale for a reason: The business may not be profitable or may be in a state of continual decline, or in an industry that doesn't exactly have a glowing future. Don't expect the seller to volunteer such negatives.

The good businesses, those with a track record of performance, don't come inexpensively. If the business has been a success under its current owner-ship, the owner has removed the risk from the business, so the price of the business will be at a premium. Be prepared to reach deep into your wallet for a business like this.

One particular idiosyncrasy of buying an existing business is that you will be required to deal with sticky personnel and management issues. The culture of the business that you are buying will predate your ownership of the business, so you will probably have to deal with several long-term loyal employees who preferred the old ownership and who don't want to work for you. If you don't like making tough decisions, firing people who don't fit into your management scheme, and coercing employees into changing the way they have "always done things around here," buying an existing business may not be right for you.

If you do have the capital to buy an established business and you do have the management skills to run it, you should always consider this route in lieu of a start-up business. See Chapters 6 and 7 for the inside scoop on how to buy a good business.

Investing in someone else's business

If you find that managing the day-to-day headaches of a small business is not for you, perhaps a viable alternative would be to consider investing in someone else's small business — assuming that you have the ability to identify potentially successful businesses.

You may want to consider investing in someone else's business if you meet the following criteria:

- ✔ You have enough assets so that the amount you invest in small, pri-vately held companies is a small portion (20 percent or less) of your total financial assets.

- ✔ You can afford to lose 100 percent of the amount that you're investing. Investing in a small business is a risky pastime; even sophisticated venture capitalists, who make their living investing in small businesses, lose on specific investments a significant amount of the time.

- ✔ You're proficient at evaluating corporate financial statements and capable of recognizing good business strategy. Investing in a small, privately held company has much in common with investing in a publicly traded firm. The difference is that private firms aren't gov-erned by SEC (Securities and Exchange Commission) guidelines and aren't required to produce comprehensive, audited financial statements that adhere to the same generally accepted accounting principles that public companies are.

✔ You can live with a lack of liquidity. Getting a return on your investment from a small business, especially in the early, formative years, is almost impossible. In most cases, it takes many years for a small business to build up the reserves (and track record to sell the business) necessary to cash out its equity investors.

In our experience, however, few people have the knowledge to be investors in other people's businesses. (For more information on this subject, see the discussion on "Angels" in Chapter 5.)

Chapter 2

Laying Your Personal Financial Foundation

In This Chapter

▶ Getting your personal finances in order before launch

▶ Examining short-term and long-range tasks

▶ Valuing and replacing your job benefits

▶ Managing your money after you're in business

*W*hether you dream about owning your own business or whether you're currently living the reality of the good and the bad that comes from being your own boss, you know that money is important. Just as your car won't run without gasoline, you can't sustain a roof over your head and provide food, clothing, and the rest of life's necessities if you can't pay for them.

Likewise, you can't continue buying what you want and need for your business without money. Of course, today's easy access to consumer credit — witness the never-ending stream of credit card solicitations cramming your mailbox and some retailers' E-Z layaway terms — can allow you to live beyond your means for quite a while.

But if you continue spending more money than you take in and adding to your debt pile, you can easily and quickly end up with more debt and interest on that debt than you can handle. Your next stop will be bankruptcy, a fate this chapter would like to help you avoid.

Consider the case of Sara, who grew up in a family where she and the other children got fabulous presents at the holidays even though her family was poor. "I picked up my parents' habit of living in the moment and spending money as soon as you earn it," she says. Sara is a self-employed consultant with an educational background that includes a master's degree from an Ivy League university.

"Sara" prefers that her real name not be used because she is ashamed of her financial habits and is worried about how work colleagues will view her.

Sara, like many people in her situation, doesn't know how common her spending and debt problems are. More than half of all American households carry high-interest consumer debt, such as credit card debt, on a month-to-month basis. Over the past year, more than 1 million people filed personal bankruptcy.

In her sixth year of marriage, Sara left her job at a large corporation to start her own company. She used the increased flexibility in her work schedule to join a dance troupe. Sara was doing what she loved; everything seemed to be going right for her.

In the early months of her business, as is typical with start-ups, Sara earned little income. Meanwhile, Sara's husband was growing increasingly upset with her spending. He was a saver and disliked her carrying credit card balances at double-digit interest rates. Sara used the credit cards to finance her business purchases. Her outstanding balances grew as she developed her business and continued spending money just as if she was working at a generous salary with benefits from an employer.

Rather than scaling back on her purchases to compensate for her reduced income, Sara's wallet full of plastic tempted her like a stocked liquor cabinet tempts an alcoholic. She became addicted to her multiple lines of credit, which gave her the temporary ability to live a lifestyle beyond her means. But much like alcoholism, Sara relates today, her addiction was ultimately uncontrollable and contributed heavily to the failure of her marriage.

Stressed, exhausted, and unable to come up with her quarterly tax payments, Sara ultimately filed personal bankruptcy. Following on the heels of the failure of her marriage, Sara was "bankrupt" now financially as well as emotionally.

The Value of Personal Financial Order

Having your personal finances in order is one of the most underrated keys to achieving success in your small business. If your finances are in reasonably good shape, a story like Sara's in the introduction to this chapter may not seem relevant to you. However, even one oversight or mistake can derail your entrepreneurial dreams or venture. Here are several good reasons why your chances for success as a small-business owner are higher if your personal finances are in top shape.

Greater ease of cutting the umbilical cord

One of the primary reasons that many aspiring entrepreneurs remain employees is the financial and accompanying psychological obstacles they face in leaving the security of a regular paycheck. The pressure of living paycheck to paycheck to meet monthly obligations serves as a huge wet blanket for most budding entrepreneurs' enthusiasm and resolve to leave the comfort of their paychecks and benefits.

Unless you prepare yourself fiscally and emotionally to leave your job, you may never discover that you have untapped potential to run your own business (and perhaps never discover that you had a good idea to boot). Money and mind issues cause many aspiring entrepreneurs to remain indentured servants of their employers, and cause those who do break their bondage to soon return to being employees.

If you decide to start your own business, you will quickly learn what every successful entrepreneur before you has learned: You have a finite amount of time every day and a finite amount of energy. If your mind is preoccupied with personal financial problems and resolving those problems requires too much of your time and energy, something is going to give. That something is likely to be either your family or your business — and perhaps both.

In the early years of your business, you will almost surely experience a reduction in your take-home income. You must accept this as fact, plan accordingly, stick with those plans, and make them work.

Increased probability of business survival

If you are successful in leaving your job and getting your business venture off the ground, you'll need to manage your money well if you don't want to greatly increase your chances of failure. Money is a precious resource that once squandered is gone forever.

Of course, if you're wealthy to begin with, you can go on squandering and screwing up for quite some time before you're forced to give up your venture. But most of us who start small businesses aren't Rockefellers or Gettys to begin with — after all, one of the attractions of achieving small-business success is to build your own nest egg. Getting your financial house in order before you start your business can buy you critical time to make a success of your start-up.

Harmony on the home front

The financial and emotional stress that small business puts on many entre-preneurs not only affects them directly but also impacts family members — especially spouses and children — even more. Young children can pick up on the stress and feel the hurt of neglect from parents who forget their role as parents in their quest to be successful (workaholic) business owners. Spouses can grow resentful of all the money and time their workaholic partners put into the business.

After years of hard work in the business and neglect of their partners and friends, successful and unsuccessful small-business owners alike can end up with a set of divorce papers and few friends. (Of course, workaholic employees and company executives can end up in the same lonely boat, too.) Business success, if it comes as the result of ignoring one's personal life, can be a lonely and unfulfilling reward.

Before you commit to launching your small business, consider this short but highly important list of things to accomplish on the home front:

- ✔ **Set aside time to talk concerns.** Schedule time with your spouse and other family members to discuss their concerns and needs as those concerns and needs relate to your starting a small business. How do they feel about the financial burden? What do they think about leaving the corporate security? What concerns do they have about your working late hours? How about working from home — do they see that as a good thing or a bad thing? What role, if any, would they like to play in the business? Especially important is to come to an understanding as to what personal assets you all agree can be used in the business. If you haven't discussed and assessed your personal financial situation, now's the time to do so.

  Let your family members speak their minds and get their concerns out on the table. Although this is easy to say and much harder to do, it's important that you don't get defensive or make them feel that they can't be heard. Your first job is to listen and really hear what they have to say.

- ✔ **Seek outside assistance for impasses**. Running your own business is demanding and stressful. You don't want the added pressure of problems on the home front. If your initial discussions with family members reveal problems that aren't easily resolved, now's the time to get help. After your spouse has filed for divorce or your kids are messed up on drugs, the damage too often is done. Marriage/family counseling with an experienced counselor can be an invaluable investment. Finding a mentor or another entrepreneur who has built a business of his or her own can give you the additional insight of experience. You may also try reading some of the better self-help family relationship books.

Your Personal Financial To-Do List

We hope you agree that getting your personal finances in order before you set up shop makes a lot of sense. But you have so much to do and so little time! Where to begin and what to do?

This section provides a short list of the important financial tasks you'll need to undertake.

Assess your financial position and goals

Where do you stand in terms of retirement planning?

How much do you want to have saved to pay for your children's educational costs?

What kind of a home do you want to buy?

These and other important questions can help shape your personal financial plans. Sound financial planning isn't accomplished by faithfully balancing your checkbook or investing in stocks based upon a friend's tip. Rather, smart financial management is about taking a hard look at where you are, figuring out where you want to go, and making sure that you're prepared for occasional adverse conditions on the road (a process, incidentally, that is not unlike what you'll be doing when you run your own business).

Measuring net worth

First, give yourself a financial physical. The math is simple, the process shouldn't take you long, and you won't have to give even a drop of blood — unless you're applying for certain insurance coverages.

Begin by totaling up your financial assets (all your various bank accounts, stocks, mutual funds, and so on) and subtracting from that the sum total of all your liabilities (credit card debt, auto loans, student loans, and so on).

Now, don't jump to conclusions based on the size of the resulting number, commonly referred to as *net worth*. If you're young and still breaking into your working years, your net worth is bound to be relatively low — perhaps even negative. Relax. Sure, you've got some work to do, but you've got plenty of time ahead of you.

Ideally, as you approach the age of 40, your net worth should be greater than a year's worth of gross income; if your net worth equals more than a few years of income, you're well on the road toward meeting larger financial goals, such as retirement.

Of course, the key to increasing your net worth is making sure that more money is coming in than is going out. To achieve typical goals such as retirement, you should probably be saving about 10 percent of your gross (pretax) income. If you've got big dreams or are behind in the game, you may need to save 15 percent or more.

If you know that you're saving enough, or if you know it won't be that hard to start saving enough, then don't bother tracking your spending. On the other hand, if you have no idea how you'll start saving that much, you're going to need to detail where you are spending your money.

Telling good debt from bad

Next, categorize your liabilities as either "good debt" or "bad debt."

- *Good debt* refers to money borrowed for a long-term investment that appreciates over time, such as a home, an education, or a small business.
- *Bad debt* is money borrowed for a consumer purchase, such as a car, an Italian silk suit, or a vacation to Cancun.

Why is bad debt bad? Because it's costly to carry, and if you carry too much, it's like a financial cancer. If the outstanding balances of all your credit cards and auto loans divided by your annual gross income is pushing beyond 25 percent of your income, you've entered a danger zone, where interest payments can start to snowball out of control.

Don't even consider starting a small business until you've got all of your consumer debt paid off.

Not only are the interest rates on consumer debt high, but also the things you buy with consumer debt lose their value over time. The financially healthy amount of bad debt — like the healthy amount of cigarette smoking — is none.

Reducing debt

If you have outstanding consumer debt, get it paid off sooner rather than later. If you must tap into savings to pay down your consumer debts, then do it. Many people resist doing this, feeling like they're losing hard-earned money. Remember that the growth of your money is determined by your net worth — the difference between your assets and liabilities. Paying off a 14 percent outstanding credit card balance is like finding an investment with a guaranteed return of 14 percent — *tax free.*

If you don't have any available savings with which to pay off your high-interest-rate debts, you'll have to climb out of debt one month at a time. Anyway, the fact that you're in hock and without savings is a sign that you've been living beyond your means. Devote 10 to 15 percent of your income toward paying down your consumer loans. If you have no idea where you'll get this money, detail your spending by expense category such as rent, eating out, clothing, and so on, as we discussed in the preceding section. You'll probably find that your spending does not reflect what's important to you, and you'll see fat to trim.

While paying down your debt, you should always look for ways to lower your interest rate. Apply for low-interest-rate cards to which you can transfer balances from your highest-interest-rate cards. It sometimes works to haggle with your current credit card company for a lower interest rate.

Also, think about borrowing against the equity in your home, against your employer-sponsored retirement account, or from family — all options which should lower your interest rate significantly.

If you're having a hard time kicking the credit card habit, then get out your scissors and cut up your cards. The convenience of purchasing with plastic can still be had with a VISA or MasterCard *debit card,* which is linked directly to your checking account so you can't spend beyond your means. Merchants who take VISA or MasterCard credit cards also accept these companies' debit cards.

Buying insurance

Another action you should take before you address your longer-term financial goals — even before paying down your consumer debts — is to make sure that you're properly covered by insurance. Without proper insurance coverage, an illness or an accident could quickly turn into a devastating financial storm.

Buy long-term disability insurance if you lack it. This most overlooked form of insurance protects your greatest income-generating asset: your ability to earn money. If anyone depends on your income, buy term life insurance. Make sure that your health insurance policy is a comprehensive one. Ideally, your lifetime benefits should be unlimited; if the policy has a maximum, it should be at least a few million dollars. (We provide more details on these important coverages later in this chapter.)

Also check the liability coverage of your auto and home policies: You should have enough to cover twice your assets.

And for all your insurance policies, take the highest deductible you can afford. Of course, if you have a claim, you'll have to pay more of the initial expense out of your own pocket, but you'll save significantly on premiums. Buy insurance to cover the potentially catastrophic losses, not the small stuff.

Planning for the long term

In Eric's experience as a financial counselor, he has seen many examples to prove that earning a high income does not guarantee a high rate of savings. Rather, the best savers he knows tend to be goal oriented — earmarking savings for specific purposes.

If you know that you're an undisciplined saver, you may consider adopting the technique of designating certain savings or investment accounts toward specific goals. After all, if you're feeling tempted to buy a luxury car, it's a lot harder to take money out of an account earmarked for Timmy's college education than from a general account called "savings."

Perhaps because it's the longest of our long-term goals, retirement is the most difficult to get in focus. Retirement is also much tougher to plan for than most goals because of all the difficult-to-make assumptions — inflation, life expectancy, Social Security benefits, taxes, rate of return, and so on — that go into the calculations.

Use a good retirement planning workbook (check out T. Rowe Price's and Fidelity's), Web site (www.Vanguard.com), or software program (Quicken Financial Planner). These retirement planners help to transform a fuzzy dream into a concrete action plan, forcing you to get specific about retirement issues you may not have thought about and opening your eyes to the power of compounding interest and the importance of saving now.

Goal-specific saving is challenging for most people given competing goals. Even a respectable 10 to 15 percent of your income may not be not enough to accomplish such goals as to save for retirement, accumulate a down payment for a home, save for children's college expenses, and tuck away some money for starting a small business.

So you must make some tough choices and prioritize your goals. Only you know what's important to you, which means that you're the best qualified person to make these decisions. But we want to stress the importance of contributing to retirement accounts, whether you use a 401(k), SEP-IRA, Keogh, or an IRA. Not only do retirement accounts shelter your investment earnings from taxation, but your contributions to these accounts are often tax deductible.

With the money you are socking away, be sure you invest wisely. Doing so is not as difficult as most financial advisors and investment publications make it out to be. (Of course, they want to make it sound complicated in order to gain your confidence and your business.)

What's your reward for whipping your finances into shape and staying the course? Although it's true that money can't buy happiness, managing your personal finances efficiently can open up your future life options, such as switching into a lower-paying but more fulfilling career, starting your own business, or perhaps working part time at a home-based business when you have kids so you can be an involved parent. Work at achieving financial success, and then be sure to make the most of it.

Shrinking your spending

Do all you can to reduce your expenses and lifestyle to a level that fits with the entrepreneurial life that you want to lead. Now is the time to make your budget lean, mean, and entrepreneurially friendly.

Determine what you spend each month on rent, mortgage, groceries, eating out, telephone calls, insurance, and so on. Your checkbook register, credit card statement, and your memory of cash purchases should help you piece together what you spend on various things in a typical month.

Beyond the bare essentials of food, shelter, health care, and clothing, most of what you spend money on is discretionary. In other words, luxuries. Even the dollars you spend on the so-called necessities, such as food and shelter, are usually only part necessity, with the balance being luxury.

If you refuse to question your current spending, if you view all of your current spending as a necessity, then you'll probably have no option but to continue your career as an employee. You'll never be able to pursue your dream! Overspending won't make you happy; you'll be miserable over the years if your excess spending makes you feel chained to a job you don't like. Life is too short to spend most of it working at a full-time job that doesn't make you happy.

Eric's tips for investing your money

Your choice of investment vehicle should depend largely upon your goal and time horizon for the money. If, for example, you're saving money to buy a home in a few years, short-term bond funds are probably your best bet.

When saving for retirement a decade or more away, you can invest more aggressively in growth investments such as stocks (such as through stock mutual funds). Although sometimes volatile, the stock market historically generates higher returns, which most people need to turn retirement dreams into reality.

Here's a general rule for allocating retirement assets: Subtract your age from 110 and treat that number as the percentage you should invest in stocks. Put the remainder of your portfolio in bonds. For example, a 35-year-old would put about 75 percent of his retirement money in stocks with the balance in bonds.

Want to be more aggressive? Subtract your age from 120 — which would have the 35-year-old investing 85 percent in stocks.

No matter how you allocate your assets, consider using mutual funds; Eric advises *against* picking individual stocks, which are not only risky but also time consuming to research and monitor. An efficiently managed mutual fund, by contrast, offers diversification and professional management at a reasonable cost. Pick funds with low operating expenses, with long track records of success, and from well-respected fund companies. Vanguard, T. Rowe Price, and Fidelity are a few of Eric's favorites.

After you've picked your funds, do yourself a favor and put your saving on autopilot. Most fund companies allow for automatic deductions from your paycheck or checking account.

Building up your cash reserves

Shrinking your spending is a means to an end, that end being the ability to save what you don't spend for a rainy day. In the embryonic years of your business, you're going to see lots of rainy days; you may even experience years predominated by rain.

Your wherewithal to stick with an entrepreneurial endeavor will depend in part on your war chest of cash. At a minimum, you should have three to six months of living expenses invested in an accessible account such as a money market fund with low operating expenses. If you have consumer debt, after you finish paying off your debt, your top financial priority should be building this fund. The bigger the war chest the better — if you can build up at least a year's worth of living expenses, great.

Keeping your income stable through part-time work

One way to pursue your entrepreneurial dreams, and not starve while doing so, is to continue working part time in a regular job at the same time you are working part time in your own business. If you have a job that allows you to work part time, seize the opportunity. Some employers will even allow you to maintain your benefits.

This tool is used by many entrepreneurs. When Eric was planning to start his financial counseling business, he was able to cut back his full-time job to half-time for four months, using his time away from his regular job to start his financial counseling business. In the first year of Jim's initial entrepreneurial venture, he also continued his full time job for a wood products business.

In addition to the security of the money from a regular job, splitting your time allows you to adjust gradually to a completely new way of making a living. Some people have a difficult time adjusting if they quit their job cold turkey and start working full time as an entrepreneur.

Another option is to completely leave your current job but line up a portfolio of work that will provide a decent income for at least some of your weekly work hours. Consulting for your former employer is a time-tested first "entrepreneurial" option with low risk.

Another option to going part time is to depend on your spouse's income while you work on beefing up your own. Obviously, this involves great sacrifice from the love of your life, so be sure to talk things through with your partner to minimize misunderstandings and resentments. Maybe someday you can return the favor — that's what Eric was able to do. His wife, Judy, was working in education when Eric started an entrepreneurial venture after business school. They lived a spartan lifestyle on her income. Several years later, when Eric's business was on solid footing, Judy left her job to start her own business.

Assessing and Replacing Benefits

For some aspiring entrepreneurs, the thought of losing their employee benefits is even scarier than cutting off their paychecks. Insurance coverages in particular — especially health insurance — seem daunting to replicate outside of the friendly confines of a corporation.

Some people are so intimidated at giving up their benefits that they give up on their dreams of becoming small-business owners. One father said to Eric, "I can't go into business for myself because health insurance is too costly." That's unfortunate: Neither health insurance nor any other benefit should stand in the way of your small-business dreams.

You may be surprised at how quickly and inexpensively you can replicate your employer's benefits in your own business. And, as you will see in this section and in even more detail in Chapter 14, as a small-business owner, you may have access to some quite valuable benefits that your employer doesn't or can't offer you. So if you're dreaming of starting your own business, don't view your employer's benefits package as a ball and chain to your current job.

Retirement savings plans and pensions

If your employer offers retirement savings programs, such as a 401(k) plan or a pension plan, don't despair about not having these in the future should you start your own business. (Of course, what you've already earned and accumulated as an employee is yours if you're vested.)

One of the best benefits of self-employment are the available retirement savings plans — SEP-IRAs (Simplified Employee Pension Individual Retirement Accounts) and Keoghs. SEP-IRAs and Keoghs allow sheltering of far more money than most corporate retirement plans do. With a Keogh plan, for example, you can plow away up to 20 percent of your net income on a tax-deductible basis.

Retirement plans are a terrific way for you, as a business owner, and your employees to tax-shelter a healthy portion of earnings. Especially if you don't have employees, regular contributions to one of these plans is usually a no-brainer. If you do have employees, the decision is a bit more complicated but still often a great idea. Small businesses with a number of employees should also consider 401(k) plans. We explain how all these plans work in Chapter 14.

Health insurance

Although we don't want to minimize the importance of quality health insurance coverage, getting such insurance as an individual is not difficult, especially if you're in good health. Even if you've had health problems, health insurance regulations have been changed in recent years to allow individuals more ease in securing coverage and minimizing the chances of being denied coverage for pre-existing conditions.

Thanks to the Health Insurance Portability and Accountability Act, you may be able to secure an individual health insurance policy even if you have existing health problems. How? Employers with 20 or more employees are required by law to provide (at your expense) health insurance for 18 months (under government regulations called "COBRA") after you terminate employment. If you've previously had group health insurance coverage for at least 18 consecutive months, you've used up your "COBRA" coverage from your last employer and you apply within two months of the ending of that coverage, you are guaranteed to have access to an individual health insurance policy regardless of your medical condition.

If you're in good health and you've decided to start your own business, by all means start investigating what will happen to your coverage when you leave your job. The first option to explore is whether your existing coverage through your employer's group plan can be converted into individual coverage. If it can, great; just don't act on this option until you've explored other health plans on your own, which may offer similar benefits at lower cost. Also get proposals for individual coverage from Blue Cross and Blue Shield, Kaiser Permanente, and other major health plans in your area. Be sure to take a high deductible, if available, to keep costs down.

Disability insurance

Well in advance of leaving your job, be sure that you secure long-term disability insurance. Long-term disability insurance protects your income in the event of a disability. If you're like most people, your greatest financial asset is your ability to earn employment income. Should you suffer a disability and be unable to work, how would you and your family manage financially? Most people, of course, couldn't manage their current lifestyle if their employment income disappeared.

Don't wait until you leave your job to shop for disability coverage. After you quit your job and no longer have steady employment income, you won't be able to qualify for a long-term disability policy. Most insurers will then want to see at least six months of self-employment income before they're willing to write a policy for you. The risk then is, if you were to become disabled during this time, you would be without insurance.

Here are several proven sources for securing long-term disability insurance:

- ✔ **Professional associations:** Thanks to purchasing power of the group, associations that you may be a member of — or could become a member of — often offer less-costly disability coverage than what you could buy on your own.

- ✔ **USAA:** USAA is one of the nation's leading and best providers of insurance. Call 800-531-8000.

- ✔ **Insurance agents:** Also consider shopping for an individual disability policy through agents who specialize in such coverage.

Life insurance

If you have life insurance coverage through your employer, odds are you can replicate it on your own. If you have dependents (children, spouse, and so on) who rely on your income, you need life insurance.

The amount of life insurance you carry should be determined by how much annual income you're trying to protect and over how many years. For example, to replace your income over the next decade, multiply your annual after-tax income by 8.5.

Thus, if you're annually making $30,000 after taxes, you should buy about $250,000 of life insurance. You only need to replace your after-tax income because the death benefits on a life insurance policy are free of income tax.

Term life insurance, which is pure life insurance protection, offers the best way to buy needed coverage at the lowest cost.

Other policies, such as universal, whole, and variable life, which are collectively referred to as cash value policies, combine life insurance coverage with an investment account. For an equivalent amount of coverage, a cash value policy typically costs about eight times more than a term policy. Furthermore, in the early years of a cash value policy, the bulk of that cost difference builds little in the way of cash value and instead goes mostly to pay insurance agent commissions and administrative costs.

In the long run, you would do best to separate your life insurance from your investments. Buy term insurance and invest your savings through your employer's retirement savings plan. Contributions to 401(k) plans and the like typically offer an up-front tax deduction at the federal and state levels. Money put into a cash value life insurance plan offers no such deduction.

If your current employer does not offer a retirement savings plan or if you are already maximizing your contributions to it, also consider investing in mutual funds inside an individual retirement account (IRA).

The good news is that if you need life insurance, you can probably purchase an individual life insurance policy at a lower cost than you could purchase such coverage through your employer.

Here are some great places to get proposals:

- ✔ **USAA:** A top-notch insurer that sells low-cost term insurance direct to the public (800-531-8000).

- ✔ **Wholesale Insurance Network:** This organization is paid a marketing fee, which is basically a commission, from the companies whose insurance it sells and is another good source for low-cost term insurance (800-808-5810).

- ✔ **Insurance agency quotation services:** These firms send you a handful of relatively user-friendly proposals from the highest-rated, lowest-cost companies available. Like other agencies, the services receive a commission if you buy a policy from them, which you're under no obligation to do. Unlike local insurance agents, they generally won't hound you. Don't give them your phone number if you want to be sure they won't call you. They'll ask you for your date of birth, whether you smoke, and how much coverage you'd like. The best quotation services in terms of customer service, pricing, and presentation of information are SelectQuote (800-343-1985) and Jack White Insurance Services (800-622-3699).

Dental, vision, and other insurance

For those of you who work for a large employer, you may very well have other insurance programs besides the traditional health, life, and disability. Some employers offer insurance plans for dental and vision care, and occasionally some other unusual benefits, such as prepaid legal plans.

As an aspiring or new entrepreneur, you can't afford to waste money. Insurance programs that cover small potential out-of-pocket losses aren't worth purchasing. Don't waste your money buying such policies. Remember that insurance companies are in the business to make money. On average, insurers pay out no more than about 60 cents in claims per dollar paid to them in policyholder premiums. The other 40+ percent goes to administration and profits.

Social Security taxes

Another "benefit" of working for an employer is that the employer pays for half (7.65 percent of your income) of your Social Security and Medicare taxes. Before you despair of the extra cost of having to pay both halves of this tax when operating your own business, know that while you do have to pay the entire tax (15.3 percent of your income) when you're self-employed, the IRS allows you to take half of this amount as a tax deduction on your Form 1040. The value of your deduction depends on your marginal tax rate; if you are in, say, the 28 percent tax bracket, then the actual cost of your self-employment tax is 5.51 percent [7.65-(7.65*28%)]. Thus, the tax is not as painful as you think.

When pricing your products or services, you can build the cost of this tax, as well as other benefits you'll pay for out of your own pocket, into your calculations. (After all, this is what your current employer does.) We explain pricing strategies in Chapter 9.

Time off

All work and no play make Mary and John dull entrepreneurs. When you work for a company, we trust that it provides you with certain holidays and at least a couple of weeks of vacation each year. You may never have considered that your paycheck covers the cost of these normal workdays when you're allowed time off.

Again, when you price your products and services, you should factor in that between holidays and two to three weeks of annual vacation, you'll probably not be working about 5 weeks out of the 52 weeks in a year. While it's true that some new entrepreneurs don't take much vacation or many holidays off, we certainly don't want you to plan for that — you'll burn yourself out and not be much fun to be around!

Managing Your Personal Finances Post-Launch

It continues to amaze us: We see so many savvy small-business owners who are successful when it comes to managing their companies. However, when you glance at their personal finances, they look like total financial misfits —

underinsured, overextended on credit, undiversified in investments, behind on retirement planning, and so forth.

We tend to dismiss this trait as a mere foible, in much the same way that we chuckle at a genius with a messy desk. Such sloppiness with personal financial management is an unfortunate tendency, however, because it downplays the seriousness of the problem: Poorly managed personal finances can destroy a business, no matter how successful and well run it is. Also, it has been our observation that poor personal financial management often leads to more of the same on a business level. Old habits are not easily changed.

This chapter has focused on getting your finances in order before you start your business. However, keeping your personal finances on track (living within your means, planning how much you need to save for various goals, selecting sound investments, and maintaining catastrophic and cost-effective insurance coverage) post-launch is vital to your financial future as well as to the viability of your business. If you don't know how to do these things well, we've got a recommendation for you — Eric's book, *Personal Finance For Dummies,* 2nd Edition (published by IDG Books Worldwide, Inc.).

As a small-business owner, you also need to be especially careful to stay on top of your required tax payments for both yourself and your employees (we cover small-business tax issues in Chapter 16). You also need to protect your personal finances from lawsuits — an important topic we cover in Chapters 5 and 15.

Chapter 3

Finding Your Niche

● ●

In This Chapter

▶ Finding a niche

▶ Understanding your business categories

● ●

*B*efore we go any further, you need to get something straight: Although your business niche and the idea behind your business are important, neither the niche nor the idea make the primary difference when it comes to the survival of your business. The niche and the idea are only a small part of the puzzle. In this chapter, we give you more puzzle pieces to play with, and we explain why you need to put them together for business success.

Why You Don't Need a New Niche or a Great Idea

Most small-business owners dive into their niches because they love the product or they love the service they have elected to provide. Check it out: The annals of small business are filled with the tales of founders who cared so deeply about some product or service that they subsequently decided to make it their life's work so they could enjoy getting up in the morning again.

Examples abound of businesses that have grown and prospered as a result of an entrepreneur's passion for an activity:

✔ Jim Gentes was a passionate biker who had ideas about bike helmets that led him to found Giro.

✔ L.L. Bean developed a line of outdoor gear that he couldn't find elsewhere.

✔ John Bogle founded the Vanguard Group of mutual funds in order to deliver low-cost funds that serve investors' best interests rather than those of brokers and money managers.

Of course, many (the vast majority in fact) small-business owners do not break new ground. Lots of tax preparers, dry cleaners, and restaurant owners happily make themselves a living doing what many others before them have already done. Ben & Jerry's is a perfect example of a company founded by two men (Ben Cohen and Jerry Greenfield) who love an everyday product (ice cream) that competes in a tough and well-populated niche — a tough, well-populated niche that had been dominated by a number of large, heavily capitalized, veteran businesses. The rest, as they say, is history; Ben & Jerry's not only went on to survive in its niche, but it also prospered.

These highly successful entrepreneurs are the exception rather than the rule, however. Most small-business owners go on to make a comfortable living doing something we want to do in a field we enjoy without making major waves or accumulating major wealth.

Unfortunately, having a groundbreaking idea or extensive product knowledge and enthusiasm has little real influence on your long-term business success. Even if you make the best chocolate chip cookies this side of Mrs. Fields, your business could still very well crash and burn. Maybe you don't sell enough cookies, or you have a hard time accounting for the ones you do sell, or you sell ocean tankers filled with cookies but your customers don't pay for them.

Having a good product and knowing the product well are only the beginning of building a successful business; you must also perform a long list of sometimes arduous day-to-day chores in order to be a successful small-business owner:

- Find good customers and convince them to buy.
- Deal with difficult, hard-to-please customers.
- Provide cost-effective customer service that retains customer loyalty.
- Understand financial statements, including balance sheets, profit and loss statements, and cash flow statements.
- Grant credit and know how, and to whom, to grant it.
- Collect receivables (the money you're owed).
- Juggle and prioritize the payment of payables (the money you owe to others).
- Understand the mystifying concept of cash flow and then manage it.
- Compute inventory turn, days-in-receivables, current ratios, and return on sales (we cover those in Chapter 11).

✔ Use such management tools as organization charts, job descriptions, and performance reviews.

✔ Purchase the right computer and software and then learn how to use it.

✔ Collect and disburse sales tax, income tax, and FICA, and perform all those other services the government requires of small business (we explain those in Chapter 15).

✔ Protect yourself from lawsuits — both from your employees and your customers — including sexual harassment suits and product liability suits.

✔ Avoid (and deal with when you can't) such headaches as OSHA (Occupational Safety and Health Administration), workmen's compensation, and unemployment problems.

✔ Deal with drug-and-alcohol related problems, pacify smokers and non-smokers, and recognize and deal with the malingerers, the embezzlers, and the shoplifters.

✔ Know how, and when, to use small claims court.

✔ Know how to hire, fire, and train, and motivate, and hold employees accountable, and control expenses, and manage crises, and balance cultures, and deal with bankers, and budget, and forecast, and. . . .

Of course, not all businesses have to deal with all the items in the above list. If your business doesn't have inventory, for instance, you won't have to deal with the myriad of issues relating to that.

Our point here is that the niche or idea won't ultimately make or break your business; the day-to-day running of the business itself is what ultimately determines success — or failure.

Stated another way, you show us a crackerjack business person, and we'll show you someone who can get rich in the cookie business whether or not he or she has the foggiest idea about how to bake the darn things.

How to Choose Your Business

Before we begin helping you decide the business that would be best for you, you need to understand a bit about the four major categories: retailing, service, manufacturing, and wholesaling.

"How hard can it be to run a card shop?"

Our hero (we'll call him Aaron) decides that it's time to make a lifestyle change. He and his family relocate to Bend, Oregon, where, he figures, the world rotates at half the speed it does in the San Francisco Bay Area.

Aaron, a marketing consultant for a high-powered firm, decides to become a Hallmark franchisee, whereupon he and his wife purchase an existing store in a Bend mall. Because Aaron had been consulting with Hallmark for several years on how to resolve its marketing issues, he figures he knows the industry inside out.

"Hey," he told his friends in a statement he would regret for years, "how hard can it be to run a card shop?"

Aaron found out *exactly* how hard it can be to run a card shop. Suddenly, instead of having to know everything there is to know about Fortune 500-style marketing, he has to know a smattering of everything there is to know about accounting and bookkeeping procedures, and hiring, and training, and motivating, and firing, and payroll, and government regulations, and cash flow, and budgeting, and inventory, and dealing with bankers, lawyers, and accountants, and . . . Well, you get the point.

"When I was consulting and would work with Hallmark management in problems relating to its franchisees," he says today, "my marketing firm's management and I would go nuts. We'd say things like 'those little guys just don't get it,' and we'd want to tear out our hair in frustration.

"Well, I'm one of those 'little guys' today, and it's me who's tearing out what's left of my hair in frustration. We small-business owners see the world through a different set of sunglasses than the corporate consultants.

Would Aaron do it all over again?

"Well, y-y-y-ess. The change in scenery has been worth it. But I can tell you this much," he says, returning an out-of-place Charlie Brown birthday card to it's rightful slot. "There are two kinds of businesses in this world. The first is where you have to be a jack-of-only-one-trade. The second is where you have to be a jack-of-all-trades and *you* are the person who is responsible for ensuring that everything else is taken care of.

"I went from the first to the second and now I know. The two aren't even in the same universe."

Consider your category

As you look across the vast business landscape, you see four major industry groups: retailing, service, manufacturing, and wholesaling. Here are some important characteristics of these groups that you need to know:

> ✔ **Retailing:** Retailing is the general category that most of us are familiar with, since the typical American deals with at least one retailer every day. Because we're familiar with the retail business, the learning curve

is usually much easier in retailing than in the other three categories (although this is true as well for your retailing competitors). Also, because most retail businesses deal primarily with cash or near-cash equivalents (credit cards), funding requirements for accounts receivable are low, which means in turn that the capital requirements for entry are correspondingly low. (See the section in Chapter 5 on determining your initial cash needs.)

✔ **Service:** Service is the fastest growing of the four categories, in part due to the low cost of entry (that is, you need no significant inventory outlays and minimal equipment). Additionally, if you're among the increasing number of service providers who choose to work out of their homes, occupancy expenses are low, and tax advantages a valuable perk.

✔ **Manufacturing:** Save up your hard-earned cash if you're thinking of becoming a manufacturer; this category is a veritable cash-guzzling machine. Inventory, accounts receivable, equipment, physical plant, employees — you name the cash-draining asset and most manufacturers have gotta have it.

Although manufacturing is typically the most expensive of the four categories in terms of capital requirements, it offers great potential for rewards. Look at the high-tech industry for examples of wealth being created (not just for the founders but for key employees as well) in short periods of time; companies such as Microsoft, Intel, and Compaq were start-up manufacturers not too long ago.

✔ **Wholesaling:** The middleman in capitalism's distribution channel, wholesalers act as intermediaries between manufacturers and the retailers or the consumers. The wholesaler's role is to buy large quantities of products at discounted prices from manufacturers, break them down into smaller quantities, and sell them at a mark-up over the wholesale price to retailers or consumers. Like manufacturers, wholesalers require significant cash outlays for inventory, receivables, physical plant, and employees; thus, the start-up capital requirements for wholesalers are correspondingly high.

Okay, you believe that you have what it takes to be a successful small-business owner. (Don't you? If you're still in doubt, see Chapter 1 for a helpful quiz.) You know the complexities of running a small business, you appreciate the role that the owner plays in the process, and you understand the four major categories available. The next logical step is to decide (if you haven't already) what business you want to be in. We'll help you do this by giving you an overview of the options available and then providing guidelines designed to help you narrow your choices to the business that will work best for you.

Ready? Then get started!

Take advantage of "accidental opportunities"

Many small-business owners are "accidental" entrepreneurs; that is, they simply stumble on a business to start or to buy. Maybe a favorite retail store suddenly comes up for sale, or maybe a friend informs them of a can't-miss opportunity, or maybe a customer of the business that person is working for now invites him or her to do some freelance consulting — an invitation that turns into a business opportunity. In these cases, the lucky entrepreneur doesn't set out to own a business, rather he or she stumbles on the right opportunity. As with so many other directions we take in life, the time and the place just happened to be right.

For those of you accidental entrepreneurs who have stumbled on the right business to start or buy, the following sections may be for information only. For those of you who are still looking however, listen up. We'll help you make your decision.

Inventory your skills, interests, and job history

Most people are not lucky or fortunate enough to stumble upon the right business. For them, career opportunities must be discovered. And the kind of people who discover them are those who are willing to go to a lot of trouble to find the right opportunities.

In this section, we want to help those of you who are actively seeking the right business to buy or start. We want to assist you in matching your skills, your interests, and your job history with the right situation. We want to help you select the niche that works best for you, given who you are, what you like to do, and what you are capable of doing.

To properly make this selection, you need to do some introspection. We help in this process by asking you a series of questions.

The following questions are designed to help you take a look at your business acumen. After you answer these questions, you'll have the inventory you need to help select possible businesses for you. Please take your time in completing this exercise. When in doubt as to the answer, ask a friend or a spouse for advice. Oftentimes, they know you better than you know yourself.

Question #1: What top three business skills have you displayed over your business career? (Examples include such categories as sales, accounting, marketing, administration, writing, communications, quantitative analysis, hiring, training, employee motivation, product development, customer service, focus, delegation, accountability, attention to detail, and so on.)

1.

2.

3.

Question #2: Using the same list of examples as included as part of Question #1, in which of the categories are you the weakest?

1.

2.

3.

Question #3: Over your working history (include part-time and full-time jobs), what three jobs have you enjoyed the most? (After listing the three, consider and then list the reasons why you liked those particular jobs.)

Job   *Why liked*

1.

2.

3.

Question #4: Over your working history, what three jobs have you enjoyed the least? (Similar to Question #3, consider and then list the reasons why you disliked those particular jobs.)

Job   *Why disliked*

1.

2.

3.

Question #5: What are your top three overall personal skills? (Leadership, communication, intelligence, creativity, vision, cheerleading, invention and/or innovation, listening, problem solving, counseling and so on.)

1.

2.

3.

Question #6: If this were a perfect world and you could select the industry in which you'd like to spend the rest of your life, what would be your top three choices? (Sports, music, movies, art, finance, education, telecommunications, electronics, computers, medicine, architecture, agriculture, transportation, insurance, real estate, financial services, food and beverage service, apparel design and manufacture, furniture and home products, outdoor products, printing, photography, chemistry, plastics, and so on.)

1.

2.

3.

Question #7: Many people develop a hobby or special interest (such as photography, golf, coin collecting) into a business. What three favorite hobbies or special interests of yours might be conducive to creating a business?

1.

2.

3.

Question #8: Given what you know about the retailing, service, manufacturing, and wholesale career choices, rank the four in order of desirability.

1.

2.

3.

4.

Don't expect to complete this exercise and determine that — Eureeka! — you should immediately open a retail clothing store. Or start a financial consulting business. Or import rare ostrich eggs. This exercise is not designed to provide you with an exact business to start.

Rather, as the sub-chapter heading indicates, this quiz is an attempt to help you take an "inventory of your skills, interests and job history." Then, as a result of that inventory, we hope to stimulate the thought processes that will assist you in developing a list of businesses that might work for you.

If, for example, your strengths (and interests) are in sales, you might want to consider a business where sales is the primary function of the business. If you indicate that you have weaknesses in such areas as attention to detail, delegation, and administration, you might want to consider operating a business solo as opposed to one requiring employees. If you determine that over your job history, you didn't like those jobs where you dealt directly with customers, the retail business would probably not work for you. And so goes the thought process we're trying to instill in you.

This exercise, then, is intended to help you take an introspective look at yourself and lead you to where you would logically fit in the broad spectrum of business opportunities available. That's why we say you'll find no quick answers here, but rather an opportunity to jump start the narrowing-down process.

We can't of course, list every business and the prerequisite inventory of skills and interests that goes along with it, although we can help you narrow your choices. Read on.

Narrow your choices

Drumroll please! We now continue the process of assisting you in selecting the right business for you (if, that is, you haven't already selected it). If you've already chosen your business opportunity, you need to ask yourself the following questions in order to assure yourself that the business you've chosen is the right one for you. These questions, it should be noted, are in no particular order of importance.

Question #1: Is this a business that suits your personality?

✔ Consider a retail business if you like dealing with people, don't mind keeping regular hours and can handle being tied to one spot for long periods of time. (The converse of course, also applies. That is, if you don't like dealing with people, keeping regular hours, or being tied to one spot for long periods of time, don't consider the retail business.)

> ✔ Consider the service business if you like dealing with people, solving problems, and working in spurts and flurries. (The converse also applies.)
>
> ✔ Consider a wholesaling business if you are a detail-oriented person, if you enjoy supervising employees and don't mind risking the significant amount of capital that carrying inventory requires. (The converse also applies.)
>
> ✔ Consider the manufacturing business if you're a quality-conscious and detail-oriented person who enjoys searching for solutions to such engineering-oriented issues as process and flow and quality control. You should also enjoy supervising employees.

Within each of the four major categories, you can get more specific and narrow your choices down to specific industries. For example:

> ✔ If you like working with numbers, consider the financial services or accounting or tax preparation business
>
> ✔ If you don't mind working unusual hours, consider the restaurant or entertainment business
>
> ✔ If you don't mind spending long periods of time sitting at a desk, consider a banking or telephone sales or consulting business

and . . . You get the idea.

Question #2: Is this a business or product in which you have experience? Experience is the world's best teacher. If you don't have it, your competitors who do have it are bound to have a sizable competitive edge over you. According to a recent study, 60 percent of successful business owners have gravitated to products or services in industries with which they were previously familiar.

Question #3: Is this a business you can afford? The service business will usually be the least expensive of the four options, followed by retailing, wholesaling, and finally, manufacturing. For more information on how to compute the cash requirements of your business, see Chapter 5. (Yes, you can take into consideration the amount of money you can borrow or find investors for when considering this question.)

Question #4: Can you live with the risk inherent in this business? Generally, the bigger the capital requirement, the larger the risk. Are you sure you're prepared to live with the risk of starting a manufacturing company? If not, consider becoming a service provider instead; it's more suited to the average pocketbook. (If you have an idea for a new widget but don't have the resources to manufacture it, you could have someone else do the manufacturing, then you can still sell it, service it and maintain it.)

TIP

In search of fast growth

Every year *Inc.* magazine publishes its list of "The 500 Fastest Growing Companies in America."

This list includes tomorrow's potential goliaths of the business world. Such companies as Microsoft, Oracle, and Gateway 2000 have graced and then graduated from the list since its inception.

We've gone through the most recent list and categorized these fast-growing companies by industry. So, if you're looking for the fast track, this list of fastest growing small business niches in the United States may prove helpful to you:

Industry	Percentage of the total
Computers (All aspects: software to service)	36%
Business Services (All aspects: Tax prep to consultants)	22%

Consumer Goods & Services	9%
Telecommunications	8%
Health Care	5%
Construction	5%
Industrial Equipment	5%
Financial Services	4%
Media	2%
Environmental Goods & Services	2%
Transportation	1%

We need to mention here that a number of past *Inc.* 500 fastest-growing companies are no longer in business. Risk and growth are common bedfellows, and one entrepreneur's riches may lead to another entrepreneur's rags. Thankfully for most of us, other, less glamorous industries offer plenty of room for success.

Question #5: *Do you believe in the industry you plan to do business in?* Industries such as the tobacco industry or the firearms industry or the debt-collection industry are not for everyone. Be sure to select an industry that will allow you to sleep at night and feel good about what you're doing.

Question #6: *Is this an industry that is not overcrowded or dominated by a few well-marketed companies?* You say you're thinking about a coffee house or a bagel shop? Good luck. You'd better know something or be prepared to offer a different product or service than Starbucks, or Bruegger's or Noah's Bagels. Every industry has a saturation point; you want to make sure your chosen industry isn't one of them. (You can usually determine the saturation point by observing how successful the existing businesses are. Such success can usually be measured by observation — the condition of the business's premises, the quality and professionalism of the employees and by the prices charged; for example, is there room in the prices to make a profit?)

Question #7: Is this a business in which you have a competitive advantage? Can you make your product better, service it better, or sell it better? If not, you need to ask yourself what will motivate your customers to work with you? (If your answer is price, you're in trouble already unless you've figured out a clear and quality way to create and deliver a product or service cheaper and better than the industry leaders.)

Question #8: Is this a business in which you can become a specialist? There's power in being a specialist; there's danger in being a generalist. Today's movers and shakers have learned from past experience: Do those things you can do better than anyone else and stay away from those things you can't. (Consider all those takeovers of a few years ago, with steel companies buying insurance companies and film-makers buying bookstores. Many of those odd-companions are companions no more. Many were spun off to other businesses more knowledgeable about that industry and better able to provide a quality product at a competitive price.)

Take advantage of government resources

Everyone likes to poke fun at our government (hey, what are governments for anyway?). But now and then, when we least expect it, our governments will surprise us and do something right. The small business arena is one of those areas where, in the last ten years anyway, the government has made giant strides when it comes to doing something right. We cite the following examples:

- ✔ **The Small Business Administration (SBA):** The SBA offers a wide variety of educational materials and seminars for both current and aspiring small-business owners. They also provide financial assistance through loans and loan guarantee programs. In recent years, these programs have become significantly more user-friendly, and today the SBA is an excellent resource for the capital-seeking small-business owner who has trouble finding funding through the conventional private-sector sources. For more information on SBA loans, see Chapter 5; for more information on how the SBA can be of assistance locally, call your nearest field office.

- ✔ **The Small Business Answer Desk:** A complementary service of the SBA, you can call 800-827-5722 to speak with a living, breathing SBA employee who will provide you with a thorough list of governmental resources and referrals, along with a smattering of advice. Questions can be specific or general, ultimately you will be referred to a web site, a SCORE or SBDC chapter, or an SBA publication.

✔ **Service Corps of Retired Executives (SCORE):** Federally funded, SCORE consists of more than 12,000 volunteers in hundreds of cities across the U.S. who provide free counseling and advice to prospective or existing small businesses.

SCORE, an excellent concept to be sure, can be a tad on the hit-or-miss side, however, due to the fact that the majority of SCORE's volunteers are ex-Fortune 500 employees. Thus, not all of them have known what it's like to have "been there" as their own small business takes off. If you happen to be assigned to the right volunteer, however, SCORE can be the best deal in town — occasionally even providing you with a much-needed mentor. SCORE is definitely a service worth trying, especially given its cost to you, which is FREE. Call up their World Wide Web site at 222.score.org to pose online questions to counselors or to contact the office nearest you. Not wired yet? Then call 800-827-5722 (ext. 0) for the SCORE office nearest you.

✔ **Small Business Development Centers (SBDCs):** There are 700 SBDCs in the U.S., most of which are located on college and university campuses. The SBDC program is sponsored by the SBA in partnership with state and local governments, the educational community, and the private sector. Its mission is to provide business counseling, training, and various other educational resources to help both start-ups and existing small businesses.

Unlike SCORE, SBDC services are provided on a fee basis, and SBDC employees (they are not volunteers) are usually educators. Most have not owned a small business of their own. As a result, similar to SCORE, the services they offer can be hit-or-miss. Call 402-595-2387 for the SBDC center nearest you.

✔ **Business Assistance Service-Office of Business Liaison:** Associated with the Department of Commerce, this agency helps guide small businesses through the federal "maze" (their word, not mine). This agency's role is to help the small business owner locate the federal agency best able to serve his or her particular needs. Call 202-483-3176.

✔ **State Department of Commerce:** Most state Departments of Commerce have small business assistance centers. These centers contain information on licensing and permit regulations and provide information packets on starting and running a business. Check your state government pages or call information for your state's Department of Commerce. (Some states include commerce under the Secretary of State.)

Recognizing Your Number One Asset — You

Turn back the clock to the middle of the 20th century. Imagine you're a small-town banker somewhere in the state of Arkansas. In the course of a day's business, you look up from your desk to see a 30-something-year-old man stride into your office and plop down a proposal. It seems this fellow intends to buy a soft ice cream machine to put on the sidewalk outside of his Ben Franklin dime store, and he wants you to help him finance it.

"Oh, brother," you think to yourself, "this guy must be one pickle short of a barrel. If he can't scrape up $1,800 from the profits on his little dime store, what makes him think I should finance this new venture — $1,800 is a lot of ice cream cones."

Then you pause in the midst of your thoughts and take a deeper look into the man's eyes as he passionately describes his vision for peddling ice cream cones on the sidewalk. And lo and behold, you see a fire burning inside as he explains his ideas for selling ice cream and attracting customers to shop in his store while they enjoy his new product. And the more the man talks, the more you come to understand that this fellow is driven by a dream, a dream that goes far beyond peddling ice cream. After listening for longer than you had intended, you make an uncharacteristic decision to cough up the dough — not because of the uniqueness of the entrepreneur's idea but because of the uniqueness of the entrepreneur himself. Despite the humdrum notion of selling ice cream on the sidewalk, you fork over the check. Then you sit back and watch as two years later he pays off the five-year note and goes on to eventually create Wal-Mart, the mightiest retailer in the land.

Yes, you made your decision based on Sam Walton and not an ice cream machine. It was only natural that the success of his business would follow.

And so it will be with the rest of us who follow in Sam Walton's footsteps — we alone will either make our company, or we will break it. Sure, the niche will be important but *we* will select it. And certainly our employees will be important, but *we* will choose the people we hire (and the people we fire). And, of course, our products (or services) will be important, but *we* will have the final word in defining them. Everything that happens within our business will have our own personal stamp on it. Nothing will be outside of our grasp.

Today's venture capitalists have for many years understood the same lesson that Sam Walton's banker learned in the course of that meeting. The small-business owner is the number one determinant of his or her company's success or failure.

Chapter 4

Turning Your Ideas into Plans

. . . .

In This Chapter

▶ Writing mission statements

▶ Writing business plans

▶ Updating business plans

. . . .

*A*fter you decide to start your own business, you need to embark on your first meaningful hands-on task: developing and writing your business plan. But before you get started, it is important that you write a mission statement to set the stage for the plan.

Your Mission — As You Choose to Define It

A *mission statement* is a written, easy-to-remember sentence, a short list of bullet points, or a paragraph illustrating your business's goals and purpose in life. Mission statements come in many sizes, shapes, and forms, but they all have one common purpose: to guide you and your employees in making the critical decisions that affect the direction of your company. Additionally, your mission statement should identify your company to outsiders — your customers, your vendors, the media, and others.

To give you an idea of how well-developed mission statements identify the businesses behind them, we invite you to mix and match the following companies with their mission statements:

Company	Mission Statement
1. Disney	A. "To give unlimited opportunity to women."
2. Boeing	B. "To solve unsolved problems innovatively."
3. 3M	C. "To make people away from home feel that they're among friends and really wanted."
4. Mary Kay	D. "To make people happy."
5. Marriott	E. "To push the leading edge of aviation, taking on huge challenges doing what others cannot do."

Our guess? You didn't have much trouble coming up with the following matches:

- Disney: "To make people happy." (How easy is this to remember?)

- Boeing: "To push the leading edge of aviation, taking on huge challenges doing what others cannot do." (A tad fluffy perhaps, but definitely challenging, especially at a time when the competition is briskly nipping at Boeing's wings.)

- 3M: "To solve unsolved problems innovatively." (No restrictions to the range of niches here. No wonder its products range from fishing line to sealing tape to Post-it Notes.)

- Mary Kay: "To give unlimited opportunity to women." (And it has done exactly that — for women *and* for men. Countless new businesses over the years have emulated their networking approach to sales.)

- Marriott: "To make people away from home feel that they're among friends and really wanted." (This mission statement says what the company is trying to do; at the same time it provides guidelines to its employees on how to deal with customers.)

Okay, so we're not really sure whether these are the companies' official corporate mission statements, their goals or unofficial guidelines, or simply quick phrases their CEOs use when talking to management expert James C. Collins, who reported these in the November 1997 *Inc.* magazine. But we think that, if these aren't their official mission statements, they ought to be.

In the following pages, we help you write *your* mission statement.

Writing your mission statement

And what about your business? How should your mission statement read?

- If you were to own a bookstore, would your mission statement state "to sell books" or "to increase the educational and enjoyment levels of customers?"

- If you were to own a contracting business, would your mission statement read "to build houses" or "to provide affordable building solutions for customers?"

- If you were writing a how-to book for small-business owners, would your mission statement read "to write a 400-page business book that will sell for $19.99" or "to provide readers with solutions to their business problems and suggestions for taking advantage of their business opportunities?"

Notice the common inference in all of these mission statements to the key word *solutions*.

Every successful company these days is in the business of providing solutions to its customers' problems, which means the question you need to answer when creating your mission statement is, "What solution do I provide and what must I do to make sure that the solution I provide is consistently and economically delivered?"

Also, be sure to give yourself plenty of room to grow (within your niche) when developing your business's mission statement. When the bookstore owner in the example above defines the business as "education and enjoyment," the owner leaves open the option to sell CDs or tapes, rather than just books. The contractor has the option to build garages, barns, and outbuildings, in addition to homes. The writer retains the option to develop CDs or tapes, not to mention to consult or hold seminars.

Keeping your mission in people's minds

After your company is up and running, you should display your mission statement in the following places:

- On the wall in the most visible place in your business, as a constant reminder to you, your employees, and your customers.

- In the executive summary section of your business plan (discussed in the next section).

- On the first page of your employee manual, if your business is large enough to warrant one (we discuss such manuals in Chapter 13).

Your Business Plan: Don't Start Up without It

You say you don't need a plan?

Sure, and neither did Wrong Way Corrigan, Alice in Wonderland, and Dr. Livingstone (who presumed to know where he was going) as he disappeared into the African bush, as well as tens of thousands of other folks who get lost along their way. If you prepare a well-defined plan and stick with it, and if you update your plan as you proceed, point A will lead to point B, rather than point Q or no-point-at-all. And so it is with your business.

Furthermore, if ensuring that you're traveling in the right direction isn't enough reason to prepare a plan, talk to some of the people in the business of loaning or investing money (see Chapter 5). These folks won't even think about doling out their cash unless you include a business plan as a part of the package. And it had better be a humdinger of a plan, at that.

A business plan serves two distinct and separate purposes: to serve as your road map and to attract loans or investments.

The business plan as a road map

Bankers, venture capitalists, and other folks who see a lot of business proposals have learned that viable ideas are a dime a dozen — the idea itself won't make or break a business; the person behind the idea and the idea's execution hold the key. So how do you show the business plan reader what kind of person is behind the idea? And where does the execution of that idea begin?

In the business plan. Sure, the business plan begins its steady march to obsolescence the same day the ink is dry — things happen fast in small business. However, while the business plan itself is of obvious importance, of even more importance is the process. A well-thought-out business-plan-writing process asks the right questions, forcing the preparer to think through the solutions at the outset and minimize the chance of major problems, instead of having to crisis-manage them later on.

An example of this is the "Risk" section of the business plan. Most entrepreneurs do not see the risks inherent in starting a business, as optimism and a half-full glass rule the day. Having to write the "Risk" section, however, forces the entrepreneur to not only itemize the risks but, where possible, explain how he or she intends to manage them.

If you value time, money, and pleasantness of experience, you wouldn't take a trip to a new destination without first consulting a map, would you? Why should running your business be any different?

The business plan as a tool for financing

Lenders and professional investors read a business plan as much to learn about the preparer as to understand the business. They look for thoroughness, professionalism, and attention to detail in the plan, in addition to the presentation of a credible scenario for running a successful business. After all, thoroughness, professionalism, and attention to detail are the same traits they want to see in the person responsible for managing the money they invest in or lend to the business. What better early indication of these characteristics than the business plan?

The sophisticated investor has learned from experience — horses don't win races; jockeys do. The jockey is you, the preparer, and the business plan is the first official indication of the kind of work you can do.

Question: "What do finding a mentor, locating financing, and writing a business plan have in common?"

Answer: "They are all a pain in the posterior."

Jim counsels aspiring small-business owners (wannabes) for the SCORE organization (discussed in Chapter 3). Whenever one of those counseling sessions threatens to exceed the time he has allotted for it, Jim has learned how to bring the meeting to a close.

"Harry," he says, looking the wannabe straight in the eyes. "Go home and write your business plan and then give me a call. We'll go over it together."

More often than not, that's the last time Jim hears from Harry, because business plans take lots of time to prepare well and are not to be confused with an afternoon at the beach. Similar to successfully locating the right financing and finding the right mentor, however, developing a successful business plan separates the potential doers from the dreamers.

By and large, only the truly committed take the trouble to prepare a business plan. You find some exceptions, of course; some potential small-business owners have enough of their act together to carry a good business plan in their head. And, yes, some of those business owners have gone on to achieve great success. But you'd have a hard time convincing us that these same business owners couldn't have accomplished even greater success and avoided some early mistakes if they had taken the time to record and refine their ideas in a tangible business plan.

Those of us who spend time with our noses in other people's businesses have long ago learned the lesson here: The depth of early commitment directly correlates to the owner's chance for success. And a well-thought-out business plan demonstrates the depth of commitment necessary to end up at the helm of a successful small business.

Writing Your Business Plan

How detailed should you make your plan? A simple, more short-term focused plan (ten pages or so) is adequate if say, you're a home office business and the plan is for your benefit alone. However, if you intend to expand your business, hire employees, and even open multiple locations, then your plan should cover the long-term issues more extensively and thus be lengthier (20 to 50 pages). Finally, no matter what size or direction you contemplate for your business, if you intend to look for outside investors, an even more complete business plan is necessary.

Whichever length you decide upon, your plan can always be added to and/or upgraded. Later on, after you've completed the plan and your business (surprise, surprise!) takes off to unplanned heights, you will have plenty of opportunities to rewrite.

Several additional pointers on the actual writing of the plan:

- ✔ Always double space.

- ✔ Each part (Description of Business, Management Summary, Marketing Plan, and so on) should start on a new page. Within each section (Mission Statement, Summary of the Business, Legal Description, and so on), the text can be continuous but be sure to make significant space breaks between each section.

- ✔ Feel free to change the wording or add titles to the sections. No two businesses are exactly the same.

- ✔ While the order of parts should be maintained, the order of the sections within those parts can be varied.

Here we give you a suggested format for your business plan. Whether you use this particular format or adapt one of your own, your business plan should address the issues listed.

Part I: Description of the Business

Part I is intended to provide the reader with an overview of the business. After reviewing the part, the reader should understand exactly what business you're in, its legal entity, and how your business intends to differentiate itself from its competitors.

A. Mission statement

As described earlier in this chapter (see "Your Mission — As You Choose to Define It").

B. Summary of the business

This category answers the basic question: What business am I in? You should precede this summary with a one-sentence definition of exactly what the business will do or does, the same to-the-point definition you'll ultimately use to explain your business to everyone from bankers to customers to cocktail party acquaintances.

If you can't define the business in one sentence, something is wrong with your definition.

The concept of your business doesn't have to be unique or extraordinary. Electricians, tax preparers, and computer consultants will always be in demand. You need to commit more to running your business efficiently and wisely than to providing a new and unique product or service.

Even if your concept has been around for a while, you can put a new twist on it. Suppose you're a veterinarian, but you recognize that more than a few people in your area are too busy to bring their pets to your office for treatment. Thus, you might create a new business, say, Vet on Wheels. You also have the option to run your veterinarian business the traditional way, while offering quality services at a competitive price. Plenty of room in the pet care industry exists for both.

C. Legal description

Is your business a Sole Proprietorship, Partnership, C Corporation, S Corporation, or Limited Liability Corporation? (See complete details on these in Chapter 5.)

What business do you really want to be in?

Jim recently started his fifth small business, called "The Advisory Board" (TAB), to organize small-business owners into teams, and then facilitate monthly board of adviser meetings for its members. TAB members (12 to a team) use those monthly meetings to solve their problems, get feedback on their ideas, and receive support from their peers.

At the first meeting of one of Jim's TAB home-office teams, a woman (we'll call her Kate) presented her critical issue. She designed, manufactured, and sold custom, hand-painted kitchen and bathroom tile, but was spending most of her time performing the manufacturing functions (hand-painting the tiles) with little time left to design new products and gain new customers.

"Kate," one member of her team inquired, "did you go into business to become a tile painter?"

"No," Kate replied. "I started the business because I wanted to be a tile designer and sell my designs across the country."

"Then you should be designing, selling, and marketing your tile, not painting them," another team member suggested. "Farm out the manufacturing and do the design, sales, and marketing yourself."

You could see a light go on inside Kate's head. Right there in front of her newly formed "board of advisers," she made the decision to make a major change in the focus of her business. Now, she spends her days designing, marketing, and selling her products, while an outside vendor handles the production.

The lesson for you? Don't wait for someone else to ask, "What business do you really want to be in?" Ask yourself the question and then answer it in your business plan.

D. Competitive edge

You must answer the following questions to communicate how you intend to differentiate your company from your competitors:

- ✔ **Who are your competitors and what (in your opinion) is currently their competitive edge?** Here you want to identify your competitors' strengths so that you can, in the early stages of your business anyway, avoid directly competing against them. If, for instance, you are considering entering the soft drink business, you wouldn't want to confront Pepsi head on in the "sweet cola" niche.

- ✔ **What are your competitors' weaknesses?** By identifying their weaknesses, you open the opportunity to hit 'em where they're the most vulnerable. Pepsi Cola again? You'd be better off to try a canned coffee drink (such as is popular in Asian countries), a niche where Pepsi's brand isn't nearly as strong.

- ✔ **What will distinguish your products or services from those of your competitors?** This distinction doesn't have to be something new and unique. Simply doing something better usually suffices. If you're operating a lawn-care business, for customers who use your services throughout the grass-cutting season, you could trim their bushes at no charge as a customer loyalty bonus.

✔ **Service, quality, and price — which of the three do you intend to emphasize?** Remember, you can't be all things to all people. Where do you intend to position your product in the marketplace? Do you intend to be the top service and quality provider within your niche or do you intend to concentrate on the low end of the niche by focusing mainly on price? (Remember, you can find a number of positions in every marketplace, so there should be plenty of room for you if you do what you do better than those you compete against.)

Also, it is extremely difficult, if not impossible, for most small businesses to be the "low-cost" player in a niche. In most cases, the small business should focus on service and quality, and leave the low pricing to someone else.

Part 2: Management

The management section is the most important of all business plan categories in those cases where you intend to use the business plan as a vehicle to raise money. Intelligent investors recognize that the success or failure of a business will hinge on the quality of the management team. Begin the management section with biographies of the principal members of your business: the president, vice president, sales and marketing managers, board members, and so on. Be accurate in outlining their backgrounds in three or four paragraphs, and remember the prudent investor checks references. You should, incidentally, pay the most attention to the section pertaining to the person making the most difference to the business: You!

Be sure to include in the descriptive paragraphs such information as education, prior positions, and noteworthy achievements. Remember, you are selling your management team to the reader; don't leave out the important elements.

If you use the business plan only as a road map and not as an inducement for investment, the management summary is less important. Putting the qualifications and employment histories of the major players on paper, however, may help you to better think through whether the players fit well together and make a complete team.

Part 3: Marketing plan

The marketing plan portion of the business plan provides the reader with an overview of the industry in which your business competes, a description of your business's potential customers, and how you intend to sell, distribute, and promote your product or service.

A. The industry at large

In this section of the plan, you need to provide an overview of the industry (within the geographical area you expect your business to cover) by answering the following questions:

- ✔ How competitive is the industry?
- ✔ What are the growth opportunities?
- ✔ Who are the industry leaders?
- ✔ Where are the niches in addition to yours?

The answers to these questions can usually be obtained from speaking with people at your industry's trade associations. Another reliable source would be those who are already in the industry, such as a manufacturer, a wholesaler, or a manufacturer's rep.

Research model companies

If your business provides products or services similar to those offered by others, identify one, two, or three of your successful competitors that seem most similar to what you'd like your company to be like. Which of these companies do you want to emulate? In what areas can you improve or differentiate your offerings?

Even if you have an innovative and unique concept, you must identify those companies in related and even dissimilar fields to find those you want to mimic. (Never underestimate the value of mimicry; most successful entrepreneurs are inveterate copycats.)

For the model companies you examine, answer the following questions:

Why did they choose their location?

How do they promote their services and products?

What types of customers do they attract?

What are their revenues, expenses, and profitability?

How have they grown and expanded over time?

What are their plans for the future?

How can you determine all this? Ask the model company's customers or become a customer yourself (before you open your own doors, of course). Or better yet, talk to the vendors that are common to your two businesses. Most vendors, in an attempt to be a "friend" to their customers, will spill more beans than they should about their customers.

B. Identify potential customers

If your business sells to consumers rather than to other businesses, consider the gender, age, income, geographic location, marital status, number of children, education, living situation (rent or own), and the reasons they might want your product or service. Which of these demographics represent your target customer?

On the other hand, if you sell to businesses, you must understand similar demographic issues that relate to them. What types of businesses will buy your product and services? Who within those businesses will be the ultimate decision makers and how can you reach them? What problems of the ultimate decision makers will you solve with your products or services?

C. Geography

Identify your primary geographical focus; that is, where do you expect your customers to come from? Will your customer focus be within local markets? Statewide? National? International? Clearly, your advertising and other promotions will be quite different if you're marketing overseas as opposed to simply your hometown.

D. Distribution

How do you plan to get your products or services to the marketplace? Describe your role in the industry and your distribution plan. Are you a manufacturer? Service provider? Wholesaler? Retailer? Will you utilize a direct sales force? Manufacturers' reps? Catalogs? Telemarketing? Direct mail? Explain how you intend to create and organize your distribution system (see Chapter 9 for the information you will need in order to answer these questions).

E. Advertising

You need to identify how you can best reach your potential customers. Will it be via newspaper, radio, TV, magazines, direct mail, Internet, or telemarketing? Which are most economically feasible within your budget? What internal programs or external agencies can you use? (See Chapter 9 for more about advertising.)

F. Public relations

Public relations is the art of keeping your name before the public in a positive way other than through paid advertising. Good public relations is always the best and most economical way to get the word out about your products and services because it often results in free publicity that can expand awareness of your product.

The good news is that the best public relations resources are usually free; the trick is to get the attention of the writer or reporter who can do you the most good when your competitors and, indeed, just about everyone else in the business world, are trying to do the same thing.

This section of your business plan should answer the following questions:

- ✔ What techniques will you use to avail yourself of public relations?
- ✔ What is your business's "hook" and why will it interest the general public?
- ✔ How can you tap your network of friends to get a public relations referral?

For example, in the restaurant business, one of the best public relations hits is a favorable write-up in the local newspaper. You can find, within your community and in other media outlets, many similar and effective public relations resources. Consider participating in career day at a local school, sponsoring a runner in a charity marathon, or designating a portion of a road or highway to be maintained by your business. And don't forget the simple press release, alerting the community to worthwhile achievements of your company and its people. See Chapter 9 for more about public relations.

G. Pricing

You need to explain your short-term and long-term pricing strategy. Include information on costs and profit expectations, along with a thorough review of your competitors' pricing.

When pricing your products, always consider the current competitive climate first. Research the pricing of similar services or products in the marketplace, and then price your product accordingly. Don't make the mistake early on of pricing your products based upon some predetermined profit margin that you or your accountant would like to achieve. Price instead on what your competitive research (primarily talking to customers) determines the market will bear.

And don't be afraid to sell your services or products at healthy margins when the opportunity presents itself. Rest assured, it won't last forever. (For more on pricing, see Chapter 9.)

H. Sales terms and credit policies

A sale is never complete until you deposit the proceeds safely in your business account. With this in mind, you need to spell out the terms of the sale and the conditions governing the payment before you make your first sale. For more on this subject, see Chapter 9.

Part 4: Management plan

Part 4 could also be entitled "Operations." This part outlines the nuts and bolts of keeping the doors open — the day-to-day solutions to the operational issues of the company. The scope of the management plan covers a wide range of functions, from dealing with employees to purchasing from vendors to maintaining your company's accounting records.

A. Employees

Many small businesses are one-person operations. So much the better for those of you who fall into this category — you have none of the headaches of hiring, motivating, training, and firing. You only have to worry about you, which should be no small project in itself.

However, for those of you who plan to have employees, you need to answer the following questions in this section of the business plan:

- ✔ How will you assemble your team, by leasing your employees or by hiring them outright?
- ✔ Where will you find the employees you intend to hire yourself?
- ✔ What benefits will you offer them?
- ✔ What motivational incentives will you use?
- ✔ Will you assemble an employee manual?
- ✔ Will you offer a retirement plan?
- ✔ Will there be down-the-road opportunities for ownership for key employees?
- ✔ How will you train your employees?

See Chapter 13 for a discussion of these employee issues.

B. Compensation

Too many small businesses hire their first employees without first devising an overall compensation plan. Such an oversight inevitably leads to a lack of uniformity in compensation, which in turn results in uncertainty and dissension among your employees. It's a given that your employees will compare wages over lunch or around the water cooler. When employees perceive that you're not compensating them fairly relative to other employees and that you haven't communicated an objective reason why, don't be surprised to see a line begin to form outside your office.

For purposes of the business plan, you need to objectively define the basics of your compensation plan for hourly, salaried, and commissioned employees. You need to include bonus plans and perks. (For more on compensation plans, see Chapter 14.)

C. Vendors and outside resources

What vendors and outside resources do you intend to use? How do you plan to kick off your relationship with key vendors? Vendor accessibility is an important issue in many industries. Frequently, the best vendors don't open their line of products to every customer, especially the new kid on the block with no history, no prior connections in the industry, and an anemic balance sheet.

D. Accounting and/or bookkeeping

Answer the following questions when describing who will take care of your accounting and bookkeeping duties:

- Will you hire an experienced bookkeeper? CPA? Controller? Chief financial officer?
- Do you intend to computerize your accounting system?
- What accounting software package will you use?
- Do you plan to outsource your bookkeeping or accounting? What resource will you use?

For those businesses that intend to use the business plan as a tool to invite a loan or an investment, this section is particularly important. The smart lender or investor wants to be sure that the financial responsibilities of running the business are in good hands. This is especially true when the entrepreneur isn't particularly strong on the financial side of business.

Part 5: Risks

You, as well as potential lenders and investors in your business, will care and should care a great deal about the risks in your business. The better you understand them, the better able you'll be to anticipate them, minimize them, and keep your business in business.

Risks are inherent in every business, and yours will be no exception. Identify those risks. Be candid and thorough in describing your risks. Investors and lenders look for honesty here, not avoidance. They know how to recognize the difference.

Risk: You've got to see it to beat it

You must recognize risk before you can face it. Mary, an experienced small-business veteran, was asked to serve on the board of a local nonprofit agency that was having serious financial problems. Its recently fired executive director had, over a period of years, spent hundreds of thousands of the agency's dollars on cars, vacations, and even a second home. The agency faced serious financial problems; not only had it lost money to the crooked director, but due to the resulting adverse publicity, many of the nonprofit's sources for donations began drying up.

Before agreeing to accept the position, Mary asked the current board chairperson for a current business plan; that is a plan on how the nonprofit expected to turn around its financial problems. (To the nonprofit's credit, it had prepared one.)

Following an interview with the executive director and the chairman, she turned down the board position down.

"The business plan read like an ad-agency marketing brochure," she later explained. "All it talked about was the wonderful opportunity for the agency to make a difference, the terrific future of the nonprofit's cause, and the need for such a charity in the local community. It was as if their cash flow problems, their image, and their publicity problems didn't exist.

"My interview with the executive director and the board chairman was more of the same," Mary continued. "A good break here, a

random event there, and everything was bound to come up roses. Try as I did to change the subject and discuss the immediate risks that faced the agency and their need to confront them, neither the director nor the chairperson would face up to the risks that currently faced the agency. Failure was right around the corner, yet they refused to acknowledge it, much less do anything about it.

"You know," Mary laughed, "one of the things I love about small-business owners is their unbridled optimism. Their glasses are always half-full; there is nothing they can't do, given a little time and a lot of hard work. That's the good news! The bad news is that there has to be the voice of the devil's advocate somewhere in the back of a successful business owner's head. Devil's advocates preach risk, and risk is very much a part of being in business.

"The experiences of this nonprofit are a perfect example," Mary concluded. "If you refuse to recognize the risk in the beginning, you're eventually going to be blindsided by it."

When asked what she looked for in the nonprofit's turnaround plan, she replied, "A good turnaround plan is not that different from a good business plan. I would look first to the people issue, that is, what is the nonprofit going to do to replace the departing executive director and how do they intend to motivate and upgrade their current staff. After that I would want to know what they intend to do to solve their image problems. Communications is, of course, the key."

Part 6: Financial management plan

Your good idea is likely to turn into your worst nightmare if you don't examine or fail to be realistic about the financial side of your business. If you're one of those creative types or a mover and a shaker who hates to work with numbers, you may decide to blow off the financial part of the business plan. Doing so, we're sorry to tell you, could cost you, at the minimum, the dollars that you need to grow your business; at the maximum, it could cost you the very existence of the business itself.

Before you launch your business, you should first do the research you need to come up with the financial figures we describe here. We not only suggest that you do these projections; we also suggest that you make this process mandatory, especially if you need to seek outside financing.

You should do your projections on a spreadsheet (Lotus 1-2-3, Excel, and so on). If you don't know how to use a spreadsheet, we suggest you either learn (from computer training companies in your community or good books on the topic) or have someone do it for you. And if you don't understand the difference between a profit & loss statement and a balance sheet, we suggest you see Chapter 11. Spreadsheets and financial statements are tools that every successful small-business owner should eventually understand. You can learn how to use them now or later — we suggest now.

You need to consider these three types of financial statements when compiling your business plan:

A. Pro forma profit-and-loss statement

A pro forma *profit-and-loss statement* is a "projected income and expense plan" and it summarizes your estimated revenue and expenses over a given period of time. The accuracy of your profit-and-loss pro forma depends on the quality of the assumptions you make. If you make good assumptions going in, then you can expect meaningful results. An important part of the value of preparing a pro forma profit-and-loss statement is that it forces you to think through the questions that you need to answer to arrive at the assumptions you make.

You should prepare your profit-and-loss projections for the first three years of your business (unless you're seeking venture capital funding, in which case five years may be required). Anything longer requires too many far-out, hard-to-make assumptions. Compute the first year's pro forma on a month-to-month basis, and the second and third years on a quarterly basis.

For the small-business owner who doesn't know how to read financial documents, much less prepare them, we suggest that you pick up a copy of Eric's *Investing For Dummies* (IDG Books Worldwide, Inc.) or take a good class in how to read financial statements at a local college. Also, most, if not all, of the computerized business plan software packages include financial projection templates.

B. Balance sheet

The *balance sheet* measures your business's resources (assets) and obligations (liabilities) at a particular time. This balance sheet concept is important to understand and, incidentally, is just as relevant to your personal financial situation as to your business one. As a matter of fact, those of you who will apply for a loan at a financial institution almost certainly will have to submit a personal balance sheet.

Although we recommend balance-sheet projections for every business, they are especially relevant for those businesses that have significant noncash assets tied up in such categories as inventory and accounts receivable.

As with the profit & loss statement, you need to prepare a projected balance sheet for the first three years of business; project the first year on a monthly basis; and the second and third years on a quarterly basis.

C. Cash-flow projections

Cash flow is the amount of cash that moves through your business in the form of receipts (representing an increase in cash) and expenses and capital expenditures (representing a decrease in cash). Cash flow is the practical side of the accounting equation, representing the cash required to keep your business operating on a day-to-day basis. Don't confuse cash flow with *profitability,* which measures the results of the entire operation of the business (of which cash is only one important part) over a given period of time. Profitability provides the benchmarks for measuring the effectiveness of your operations, but cash flow pays the bills.

As a prospective business owner, you should project the business's cash needs before going into business so that you know how much money you need to raise. As with profit-and-loss and balance-sheet projections, you should project cash flow needs for the first three years of the business. For more information on cash flow, see Chapter 11.

Before doing your financial projections

✔ Ask your tax advisor (if you're working with one) to show you examples of similar financial projections from other business plans to use as a guideline.

✔ Don't bother projecting more than three years out; the assumptions you must use will be too vague. (Exception: Some outside investors may require five-year projections.)

✔ Thoroughly identify the assumptions you make. The garbage-in, garbage-out theory is alive and well when applied to projecting financial results. The conclusions you reach will be no better than the quality of your assumptions.

✔ In the likely event that you don't know at first how to produce the pro forma profit-and-loss statement, balance sheet, and cash flow projections, you can

- Hire a tax advisor.
- Hire a business plan consultant (most larger cities have them).
- Purchase a business plan software package.
- Learn to use spreadsheet software and do the projections yourself.

Business plan software

It's only a matter of time. Someday, someone will develop a software package that will take out the garbage or read the Sunday paper, thereby allowing us to watch the game of the week uninterrupted. Don't laugh; a gazillion software packages are out there and developers are making more as we speak. Of that gazillion, more than a few are designed to help you prepare your business plan.

Getting started with a business plan software program is as easy as being approved by yet another credit card company: All you have to do is shell out $50 or $100, boot up your computer, and begin filling in the blanks. Okay, so completing a software-driven business plan won't exactly be a cakewalk; we're not talking a true-and-false format here, but the preparation will be one heck of a lot easier than creating the plan from scratch. But will it be as effective?

Not a chance, if you get lazy and use canned solutions to complicated problems and don't do your homework.

For starters, remember that it is you, the owner, who will ultimately determine the fate of your venture. No matter how slick your business plan's package, it can't substitute for a determined, enthusiastic owner. Automation is an aid, not an answer. Only you can search for the answers — and then, only if you ask the right questions.

The primary problem with business plan software is that its fill-in-the-blank mentality can diminish its preparer's creativity. Plug in a generic form and watch for a generic business plan to evolve, one that looks strangely similar to a myriad other plans. Make no mistake about it — a sophisticated investor can spot a canned plan a mile away. Be warned.

Furthermore, whether you intend to use the business plan as a sales tool or as a planning mechanism, the stifling of creativity inherent in canned programs is its own worst enemy. You just follow the steps; you don't think for yourself. Because creativity (along with hard work) is what ultimately sets your business apart from the competition, tread carefully if you're considering business plan software.

Using the best of business plan software is, of course, far better than drafting a lousy plan yourself. It does save time and makes sure you don't forget any major issues. Also, you can use its boilerplated financial projections to help you through the forecasting process, bearing in mind that you should ultimately gain the skills required to complete the financial projections yourself.

Keeping Your Plan Current

Guarantees are dangerous in small business, but we can make two without hesitation:

✔ The progress of your business will deviate from your original plan.

✔ Your business will change dramatically over the years.

Deviation and change are constants in this sometimes roller-coaster endeavor, but deviation and change are why many of us selected this career in the first place.

To make the necessary adjustments in response to this deviation and change, you must keep your business plan current. How? Take a day away from the office and the phone every 6 to 12 months and dissect the important portions of your business plan — particularly those involving staffing, marketing, distribution, and product development — and answer the following questions:

✔ Has the business developed according to plan within each of these areas (staffing, marketing, distribution, and product development)? If not, why?

✔ In areas where the business hasn't developed according to plan, do you want to get back on track?

✔ What adjustments will you make in each area to get back on track?

✔ Given the passage of time, where do you want your business to be a year from now, and how and what changes will you make to support that new direction?

Then work away at making your changes to the plan, remembering that, if those changes have a financial impact on your business (and most important changes will), you must also apply the changes to the pro forma profit-and-loss statement and to your balance sheet and cash-flow projections.

A significant change in bottom-line income will obviously impact key balance sheet numbers, which in turn will affect such key ratios as debt to equity and the current ratio. (See Chapter 11 for an explanation of these terms.) Extreme variations in these ratios influence your credit lines, your relationships with lenders and vendors, and your long-range plans for capital expenditures and new hires.

Creating a business plan is a one-time experience, but keeping it up to date is an ongoing task, not unlike the relationship between starting a business and maintaining one.

Chapter 5

Financing, Ownership, and Organizational Options

* *

In This Chapter

▶ Determining the amount of money you'll need to launch your business

▶ Assessing how, and where, to finance your business

▶ Deciding about partners and/or shareholders

▶ Selecting the legal entity that works best for you

* *

*W*e hope you are figuring out where you want to go with your small business as you read this book. Assuming that you've decided to commit to the journey, it's time to begin making some decisions about how you're going to get there. In this chapter, we help you determine how much cash you need to get started, where you can find that cash, whether you'll be traveling alone or with others, and what kind of vehicle you'll be driving to get there.

Determining Your Initial Cash Needs

You have two basic methods with which to finance your start-up:

✔ **Bootstrapping:** The internal generation of start-up financing, using primarily the owner's personal resources, and sometimes complemented by investments or loans from family, friends, and relatives.

✔ **Outsourcing:** The external generation of financing for both start-ups and for ongoing business needs, using outside resources such as banks, angels, and venture capitalists (which are defined later in the chapter).

Not only is bootstrapping a more likely source of funds than outsourcing, but also outsources aren't likely to give you the money you need unless they see that you've done your bootstrapping first.

Whether you bootstrap the financing of your business or whether you finance it using money from outsiders, you must first estimate your cash needs:

- ✔ Bootstrappers should estimate their needs to minimize the chances of running out of cash, which could lead to the failure of the business and loss of all the invested capital.

- ✔ Outsourcing agencies or other capital resources will require that you have solid projections of your future cash needs.

If you do end up obtaining outside capital, nothing shouts inexperience like having to go back to your source and ask for more money. Looking for a sure-fire way to raise a red flag in front of your banker or investor? Tell him or her you made a mistake in forecasting and you need more capital than you had originally asked for. Whether you'll get your capital the second time around is up for grabs, but one thing is for certain: You'll get increased scrutinization. Bankers and investors don't like oversights and mistakes, especially when it comes to issues dealing with their money.

The obvious solution? Plan for enough capital in the beginning. Just as remodeling work on a home almost always takes longer and costs more than expected, many entrepreneurs find that their start-up costs more than they originally expected. That's why you need to allow yourself sufficient time to investigate, reflect upon, and estimate the costs associated with starting up your chosen business.

First, you must understand that your business's initial cash requirements will include not only *one-time start-up costs,* but also *working capital* and a *reserve.* Here's a further description of each of these three requirements:

- ✔ **One-time start-up costs:** Start-up costs include such one-time expenses as legal fees, licenses and permits, deposits, furniture and fixtures, inventory, leasehold improvements (remodels or additions to the store or office space you rent or lease), signage, and everything you need to initially open for business.

- ✔ **Working capital:** Working capital includes what you need to keep open for business, including such ongoing, everyday expenditures as replacement inventory and raw materials, accounts receivable, hiring of employees, and the general operation of your business until such time as you become consistently profitable and can fund operations out of internally generated cash flow. Don't forget to include debt payments — both interest and principal — when arriving at this figure. (Although principal payments are not an expense, they do represent a reduction in available capital.)

> ✔ **Reserve:** The reserve is, as the word indicates, an amount consisting of enough capital to overcome forecasting mistakes and/or make up for variances from budget. If you end up having neither forecasting mistakes not budget variances, then give the *Guinness Book of World Records* a call. You'll have just set a new world's entrepreneurial record!

If you've completed your profit-and-loss statement, balance sheet, and cash flow projections as discussed in Chapter 4 ("The Business Plan"), the following exercise should be simple. If you haven't, the exercise that follows will be a headache, so do yourself a favor and complete Chapter 4 now!

This worksheet is designed to help you estimate your business's capital requirements:

Estimated Capital Requirement Worksheet

I. Add up all one-time preopening costs such as legal fees, licenses and permits, deposits, furniture and fixtures, inventory, leasehold improvements, signage, insurance, and so forth (your "one-time start-up costs")   _____

2. Add your projected early-month consecutive losses from your profit-and-loss statement. Be sure to include debt payments, both interest and principal (the first part of your "working capital")   _____

3. Add the anticipated purchase of assets from your balance sheet for the first year: equipment, inventory, furniture and fixtures (the second part of your "working capital")   _____

4. Add lines I, 2, and 3, and then add 25 percent of the total (your "reserve"*)   _____

Total Capital Requirements   _____

*Note: The percentage required by this reserve figure will vary depending on the experience of the person or persons starting and running the business. The more experienced the entrepreneur, the less the reserve will have to be; the less experienced, the higher it will have to be.

This "Total Capital Requirements" figure represents the amount of capital your business will require from all sources before start-up. After you determine how much capital you need, the even harder work begins — finding it.

Bootstrapping: Using Your Own Resources

Not only is bootstrapping a more likely source of funds than outsourcing, also outsources aren't likely to give you the money you need unless they see that you've done your bootstrapping first. If your small-business start-up is like most others, you probably don't need outside capital.

How important is bootstrapping in the overall picture of financing start-ups? Well, every year *Inc.* magazine publishes the Inc. 500, a listing of fast-growing small businesses in the United States. The most recent list of fast-growers included a smattering of miscellaneous data concerning those companies, including the portion started at home (50 percent), the average capital required to fund the typical start-up ($25,000), and the percentage of founders who started their business in the same industry as they had previously worked (60 percent).

Also included in the recent *Inc.* magazine listings was a table showing the source of original financing for 396 respondents from those Inc. 500 companies. The information in that table is reproduced in Table 5-1:

Table 5-1	Where the Money Came From
Resource Tapped	*Percentage of CEOs Who Tapped Resources*
Personal savings	79%
Family members	16%
Partners	14%
Personal credit cards	10%
Friends	7%
Bank loans	7%
Angels	5%
Mortgaged property	4%
Venture capital	3%
Other	8%

* The total exceeds 100 percent because some CEOs tapped more than one resource.

An interesting note here is that the nonbootstrapping resources, such as banks, angels, and venture capitalists (which we explain in the section on outsourcing), are a minor factor on the overall list. Meanwhile, the bootstrapping sources emerge as the clear-cut winner in the start-up financing competition, even for this exclusive list of fast-track, rapid-growth companies.

The fact that bootstrapping is so pervasive and works so well makes sense if you think about it. First, what better way to instill discipline and to make things work efficiently than to have a limited supply of funds? Second, because you care deeply about risking your own money or that of family or friends, you have a powerful incentive to work hard and smart at making your business succeed.

So take heart if you think that you need vast sums of cash to start a small business or if you have been turned down (perhaps more than once) by outside sources of funding. As you can see from Table 5-1, the entrepreneurial traits of hard work, perseverance, and yes, good old-fashioned scrounging will help most of you locate the money that you need to start your business.

Bootstrapping is the unchallenged king of start-up financing!

Profiles of bootstrappers

Bootstrappers come in all sizes, shapes, and forms. Some prefer to conduct their growing businesses alone, some jump from start-up to start-up, and some make the transition from small business to large business.

Here are profiles of several typical bootstrappers:

- ✔ **Eric:** Before Eric set out to start his financial counseling business, he kept his expenses low enough to save about half of his employment earnings, which provided a nice nest egg to finance his business start-up. While living in Boston and still single, Eric shared apartments with anywhere from two to four roommates to keep his rental expenses quite low. As he made the transition into his entrepreneurial endeavor, Eric worked half-time for four months so that his salaried income didn't completely disappear.

- ✔ **Jim:** Jim's fourth business (all four were bootstrapped) was started to provide a needed service to his sporting goods business. He purchased a screen printing company from its owner for $10,000, moved the business out of the owner's basement, and funded its growth from the revenues of the sporting goods business until the screen printing company was profitable and could stand on its own. He sold the business when its revenues reached $25 million.

- ✔ **Ted Waitt:** Ted quit college to take a job selling PCs, and then, as so many bootstrappers do, quit that job to start his own company. Using his grandmother's nest egg as collateral, he borrowed $10,000 to start a business in his father's South Dakota barn. That business would later become Gateway 2000, one of the nation's leading computer manufacturers with revenues in the billions.

These examples point out the typical pattern of bootstrapping. The start-up capital is provided by the founder and/or family and friends. Subsequent growth is funded by either profits from the business, money from outside resources (banks, shareholders, and so on), or a combination of both.

Bootstrapping sources for financing

Bootstrapping, as the above examples point out, begins at home. If you're like us and the majority of entrepreneurs, here's how you may go about locating the funds you need to finance your start-up:

1. **Take stock of your assets and liabilities.**

   As we discuss in Chapter 2, you should get your personal finances in order and determine where you stand in terms of common important goals such as retirement planning. Only then can you begin to determine what portion of your assets you might feel comfortable using in your business.

2. **Assuming your parents and family are financially able to help, reluctantly and oh-so-gingerly approach them.**

   This resource is appropriately known as *relationship investing* or *relationship lending.* Although relationship investing is a widely used resource for raising money (16 percent of the *Inc.* 500 CEOs used it), it is also the most dangerous. Telling the bank to write off its loan is one thing; telling a close relative that you've lost her nest egg is quite another. The good news is that you will work that much harder to succeed; the bad news is that the investment could damage relationships. Proceed with great care and be clear with family and friends as to the risks, including the risk that they could lose their entire investment if your business gets into trouble!

3. **Ask friends, as the next logical step, especially those friends who can bring expertise to the table along with their money.**

   Be aware, however, that the risks involved when borrowing money from friends are similar to the risks when borrowing from family. The downsides can be just as painful.

4. **If Steps 1, 2, and 3 still aren't enough, you'll need to start looking for a, gulp, partner (or partners).**

   We talk more about the role of partners later on in this chapter. Suffice it to say here that partners are a roll of the dice — make a good roll, and your business will prosper beyond what it could with you alone; make a bad roll, and your problems could be multiplied.

5. **When all else fails, look to the outside resources, even though you know their track record for funding start-ups is not very good.**

   You'll look for angels first, before heading for the banks, the SBA, and SBICs (we explain these all later). If your idea or concept is compelling enough, you may even inquire about venture capitalists.

After you've tapped out your own resources but before you begin probing family and friends, you should remember to tape the *Golden Rule of Bootstrapping* to the middle of your forehead and then take a long look in the mirror. In the event that you haven't come across it yet, the Golden Rule of Bootstrapping states the following:

> *"Do not do unto others until you've done unto yourself," or, stated in words that apply specifically to your search for capital, "If you aren't willing to risk your own money, why should anyone else?" especially family and friends!*

The purpose of the Golden Rule of Bootstrapping is to make sure that you, the bootstrapper, don't even think about asking your family, friends, and relatives for money before you've contributed yourself. The first question family and friends inevitably will ask is, "How much of your own money are you investing?"

These are some of the most common places to find bootstrapping capital:

- ✔ **Savings, investments, and salable assets:** This is always the first place to look. Theoretically, all you are doing here is simply transferring your assets from one investment (your savings account) to another (your new business). Okay, so you are increasing your risk by a quantum leap, but you are also increasing your opportunity for reward.

- ✔ **The family and friends network:** Be sure to make your "relationship loans" as official as possible — always create a promissory note complete with fixed interest rate (at least 1 percent over prime to avoid IRS scrutinization) and include cast-in-stone payback terms. Consult a lawyer when larger loans (in excess of $10,000) are required.

- ✔ **Life insurance:** If you own life insurance policies with a cash value, you probably shouldn't, because term life insurance is a far better deal (see Chapter 2). Consider cashing in such policies and putting that money to far better use — your business. Remember, however, that you may owe some income tax on accumulated interest (in excess of the premiums you paid) inside your life insurance policy.

   Ask yourself if you really need life insurance at all. If you have no financial dependents, then you won't need it to replace your income should you pass away. If you do indeed need life insurance, however, secure good term life coverage *before* you cancel/cash in your current policy. Otherwise, your dependents will be in trouble if you pass away after you've canceled your current policy but before you've secured new coverage.

✔ **Credit cards:** Credit cards provide expensive money, perhaps, but easy money as well. No personal guarantees here, no bankers looking over your shoulder; just sign your name and get on with the business at hand. In the increasingly competitive credit card market, interest rates on some cards are around 10 percent, so be sure to shop around rather than simply accumulating a balance on whatever platinum-hued card that currently happens to be in your wallet.

✔ **Home equity:** Proceed with extreme care when borrowing against home equity. A misstep could cost you the roof over your family's head. Don't even consider this option until you've thoroughly reviewed your overall personal financial situation (see Chapter 2).

Outsourcing for Your Capital Needs

As you can see by referring to Table 5-1 earlier in the chapter, outsourcing institutions — banks, the Small Business Administration (SBA), Small Business Investment Companies (SBICs), angels, venture capitalists — are not a primary resource for start-up capital. This is because most of these outsourcers are looking for either significant collateral and operating history (banks and the SBA) or a business in an industry with uncommon opportunities for return on investment (venture capitalists). Meanwhile, angels are the most versatile of the outsourcing resources, but they are also the most difficult to find. We talk about each of these resources later in this section.

Outsourcers, with the possible exception of SBICs, have a well-deserved role in the financing world; that role just doesn't happen to be at the start-up stage. After your business has matured and has a track record, then the outsourcers can become a more important part of the financing game for your business.

The first thing you will want to know when considering which outsourcer to use is: Are they loaning you money (banks, SBA, and others) or are they investing their money (venture capitalists, sometimes angels, and the like)? Or, stated another way, will they be a creditor or will they be a part owner?

Outsourcing resources fall into two general categories: banks and, er, nonbanks.

Banks

Contrary to the popular opinion that bankers enjoy turning down prospective borrowers, bankers are in business to lend money. This means that every time bankers sit down in front of a prospective borrower, they hope that what they are about to see is a deal that will work. After all, no loans means no income for the bank, and no income means no marble columns and without marble columns what will hold up their gold-inlaid ceilings?

Make no mistake about it, banks are in business to lend money. And to make money, banks *play the spread* — charging you more to use their money than they paid somebody else (namely, depositors) to get it.

Most banks do not make start-up loans to small-business owners, unless the owner's collateral is such that it will cover 100 percent of the loan. Examples of such collateral include real estate (including home equity) and liquid stocks and bonds.

A bank's primary role in the small-business lending arena is funding growth, for example, financing the expansion of a small business that has a track record. Most banks can offer a wide variety of creative loan packages designed to finance the existing small business. These loan packages include the following financing possibilities.

Asset-based financing

Asset-based financing is a general term describing the situation whereby a lender accepts as collateral the assets of a company in exchange for a loan. Most asset-based loans are collateralized against either accounts receivable (money owed by customers for products or services sold but not yet paid for) or inventory. Accounts receivable is the favorite of the two because it can be more quickly converted into cash. Banks will only advance funds on a percentage of receivables or inventory, the typical percentages being 75 percent of receivables and 50 percent of inventory.

For example, using these percentages, if your business has $20,000 in receivables due from customers and $40,000 in inventory, the bank would loan you 75 percent of $20,000 (which equals $15,000) and 50 percent of $40,000 (which equals $20,000). The total of the two ($35,000) would then be available for you to use as working capital.

Line of credit

A *line of credit* involves the bank's setting aside designated funds for the business to draw against the ebb and flow of cash as needs dictate. As line-of-credit funds are used, the credit line is reduced; conversely, when payments are made, the line is replenished.

An advantage of line-of-credit financing is that no interest is accrued unless the funds are actually used. Ironically, the best time to arrange for your business's line of credit is when your business is doing well and you need the money the least. Why? Because that's when getting approval from the banker for the line of credit will be easiest, and you'll qualify for the best loan terms.

Just because you don't presently need money is no reason not to establish a line of credit (a "line" doesn't cost anything if you don't draw against it). Establish your credit line when things are going well; sooner or later, if you're like most small businesses, you'll someday need some money.

Letter of credit

A *letter of credit* is a guarantee from the bank that a specific obligation of the business will be honored. Letters of credit are most often used to buy products sight unseen from overseas vendors. The bank generates its income in these situations by charging fees for making the guarantee.

Floor planning

Floor planning is another form of asset-based lending in which the borrower's inventory is used as collateral for the loan. Car dealerships often use floor planning as their primary financing tool.

New trends in bank financing

What a difference a decade makes! It seems like only yesterday when bankers would ask prospective small-business borrowers for, at the very least, four guarantees, three years of tax returns, two sets of pro-forma profit-and-loss statements, one business plan, and a partridge in a pear tree. Then the bankers would politely (well, sometimes) suggest that you call them back in 30 days to set up an appointment for your next interview. This appointment would only be a formality because bankers weren't really interested in making business loans, but they would subsequently suggest that you come back when looking to finance your next automobile.

Fast forward to today: The times they are a-changin'. Increasing numbers of banks offer as a part of their small-business sales pitch:

✔ Two easy pages of applications to fill out. That's all. Just two.

✔ No tax returns required on loans up to $50,000.

✔ No business plans. Period.

What's the catch?

The catch is that you and your business must have an acceptable credit rating and a solid financial history if you are going to be approved. The reason the bank can offer such quick turnaround time with so little paperwork is the sophisticated information systems that exist today. Your banker can plug your Social Security number and/or your business's Employer Identification number into a computer; in a short period of time, out will come your entire personal and business credit history. In effect, banks have decided that rather than to try to judge you and your business on what you are going to do in the future, they will make their decisions based on what you've done in the past. It's a lesson that applies to just about everything people do — past performance is a good indicator of future behavior.

This is not to say that every bank in your hometown is as aggressive and consumer-friendly and technologically wired as those banks we're describing above. You can still find plenty of banks around that are standing in the wings watching and wondering how long this "fad" will last. But this new attitude is not a fad; it appears to be a trend, especially now that banks are finally understanding how to harness the powers of technology to better serve their customers.

What's happening here is that the banks are finally waking up. It's about time. The future of economic growth is in the small-business sector.

Nonbanks

Banks do not have a lock on the small-business lending market. When it comes to financing a loan for an existing business, you have a number of other options. Investment brokerage firms and major business conglomerates are becoming more important players in the small-business lending market.

Most nonbank lenders find their niche by specializing in a specific category of loan, such as leasing or asset-based financing. Leasing companies (you can lease your business's equipment or furniture and fixtures), for example, are the most common nonbank financing resource, with 25 percent of small businesses availing themselves of some sort of leasing financing. Leasing, in case you've never done it, is basically a rental — you pay a monthly fee for the use of an item and at the end of the lease term, you return the item to the company which leased it to you.

A compilation of non-bank resources follows.

The Small Business Administration (SBA)

An SBA loan is a loan made by a local lender (bank or nonbank) that is, in turn, guaranteed by a federal agency called the Small Business Administration (SBA). The SBA provides its back-up guarantee as an inducement for banks to make loans that otherwise may be a little too risky from a banker's perspective. Only in rare cases does the SBA actually provide the money itself.

SBA loans usually provide longer repayment terms and lower down payment requirement ratios than conventional bank loans. They are available to most for-profit small businesses that do not exceed the SBA's parameters on size (which can vary depending on the industry). SBA loans can be used for a number of reasons including (in infrequent cases) start-up monies, if you have sufficient collateral in long-term, tangible assets, such as real estate, machinery, and equipment.

Getting an SBA loan is not a slam-dunk occurrence; to the contrary, the agency is extremely selective about whom it approves. Take a look at the primary criteria the SBA looks for when considering guaranteeing a loan:

- The owner must have invested at least 30 percent of the required capital and be willing to guarantee the balance of the loan.
- The owner must be active in the management of the business.
- All principals must have a clean credit history.
- The business must project adequate cash flow to pay off the loan, and the debt/net worth ratio must fall within the SBA's approved guidelines.

SBA loans have a reputation for being cumbersome and subject to enormous red tape. This reputation had been deserved in years past, but technology has made inroads everywhere, even in the government. The SBA's "LowDoc (low documentation) Program," for loans under $100,000, processes loan requests in less than 48 hours and requires that the borrower fill out only a one-page application form. Other documentation the borrower can be expected to furnish when applying for an SBA loan in excess of $100,000 will include a personal financial statement, three years of tax returns, and three years of financial projections.

To find a local bank or nonbank institution that works with the SBA, look in the Yellow Pages for SBA "Approved Lending Sources" (ALS) or call the SBA at 800-827-5722. If you're on the Internet, see www.sbaonline.gov for a listing of other SBA loans that may work for you.

Small Business Investment Companies (SBICs)

SBICs are privately owned, quasi-venture capital firms organized under the auspices of the SBA. SBICs either lend money to, or invest money in, small businesses primarily within their local area. Categorized as "Federal Licensees" (meaning the federal government has given the SBIC its stamp of approval), SBICs either fund start-ups or provide operating funds with which to expand existing businesses. Through their relationship with the SBA, they are also able to offer particularly favorable terms and conditions to "disadvantaged businesses."

Hundreds of SBICs operate around the country. To learn more about them, call the SBA or check out the SBA's Web site or contact a nearby Small Business Development Center (discussed in Chapter 3).

Certified Development Companies (CDCs)

Another program of the SBA, the CDC program (also known as the *504 Loan Program*), provides long-term (10- and 20-year), fixed-rate loans for small business. This program focuses on financing fixed assets such as real estate (land and buildings). CDCs work with a local lender; typical financing may include 50 percent from the local lender, 40 percent from the CDC, and 10 percent down from the small business being helped. The asset being purchased acts as the collateral.

Several hundred CDCs exist nationwide. For the CDC nearest you, call the SBA or visit the SBA's Web site and inquire about the 504 Loan Program.

Angels: Investors with heart

Angels are individuals, usually ex-entrepreneurs who are experienced enough to understand and live with the risks they take, with money available to lend or invest. The angels' motives may vary: Most seek to increase their net worth, some want to help aspiring entrepreneurs, and some simply crave being a part of the action.

Angels come in many forms: Some fly in flocks (angel organizations or investment groups), some solo, some look for a piece of the company's ownership (equity), others to lend (debt). Almost all angels demand personal involvement, however, and in many cases, the know-how an angel can bring to the table is worth more than the capital itself.

Angels are like the highway patrol — the time that you need them the most for help is when they are the most difficult to find (not nearly as easy to find as when you're exceeding the speed limit). Movements are afoot, however, to make the identity of angels more accessible. According to the Yellow Pages Publishers Association, "Angels" will be a Yellow Page heading in most telephone books in coming years (along with "psychic life readings" and "body piercing").

Meanwhile, the SBA has instituted ACE-Net, which stands for the Angel Capital Electronic Network. Find ACE-Net on the Internet (ace-net.sr.unh.edu) and you'll discover a mix-and-match format designed to bring together aspiring small-business start-ups and "accredited small-business investors." The "accredited small-business investor" must have a net worth in excess of $1 million or net income in excess of $200,000.

For those of you who wish to find an angel in your own backyard, your state or city may have an angel-matching program. Ask local bankers, accountants, financial advisors, or lawyers for their input on how to find a local angel-matching program; call your local Chamber of Commerce; or call your state's Department of Commerce.

Venture capital

Venture capital firms and organizations offer cash in exchange for equity in start-up companies, so they are, in effect, an organized version of angel investing. As opposed to more conservative sources of capital, which look closely at a business's past performance and its collateral before handing out cash, venture capital firms focus primarily on future prospects when looking at a business plan. Thus, venture capital is useful for a few sophisticated businesses in higher-risk, higher-reward industries. Venture capital firms look for the possibility of hefty annual returns (30 percent and more) on their investments in order to offset the losses that are sure to occur within their high-risk portfolios.

It is the rare small-business start-up that is in a position to take advantage of venture capital financing. The typical venture capital firm funds only 2 percent of the deals it sees, and that 2 percent has to meet a wide range of investment criteria such as highly attractive niches, sophisticated management, potential for high return — criteria that the typical small-business start-up cannot begin to meet. Don't be disappointed at not qualifying for venture capital funding. As this chapter details, many other, more appropriate financing resources exist for small businesses.

One angel's investing criteria

Angels do their investment thing for a number of reasons, ranging from greed to boredom to altruism. The best angels we know, however, are those who invest not because they are looking to make money, but because they enjoy the thrill of the start-up and working with aspiring entrepreneurs. One such fellow is Norm Brodsky, who was featured in a July 1997 article in *Inc.* magazine.

Brodsky, who views himself as much as a mentor as he does an angel, lists four basic rules for the angel investor:

Rule #1: Invest in people who want your help, not your money. Brodsky is looking for people who will listen. If they aren't ready to listen and are unwilling to take an old pro's advice, Brodsky sees no compelling reason to get involved.

The lesson for you: Angels are usually ex-entrepreneurs with deeply ingrained ideas on how to create and build a business. Be willing to use their ideas and suggestions or you'll probably lose the angel. The flip side, of course, is to be sure that an angel's view of the world and your business mission match. No investment is worth compromising your principles and vision over.

Rule #2: When possible, go it alone. Independence is, and always will be, one of the entrepreneur's primary traits, in Brodsky's mind anyway. Entrepreneurs need to have things done their way, not someone else's way.

The lesson for you: One angel is preferable to a team of angels. In general, Brodsky believes that the "too-many-cooks-spoil-the-broth" principle is at work here. In some situations, however, more than one angel may be preferable — for example, when one angel doesn't have enough cash to meet the business's growth needs or where one angel may add flavors to the broth that the other angel doesn't.

Rule #3: Take a majority stake (become a partner) until your investment has been paid. Preservation of capital is of the utmost importance to sophisticated angels. They know that if they don't preserve it, they won't have it to invest again.

The lesson for you: Expect your angel to be demanding on the issue of ownership; he wants a voice in the direction of the business. He or she needs to have control, at least until it is obvious that the business is going to be successful and that the investment goals will be achieved.

In the end, of course, if you don't have enough money to go it alone and it may be the angel who makes the difference whether your business gets off the ground, he or she will have great influence over the ultimate terms. We suggest, however, that you not give up the controlling equity in your company (51 percent) unless it's absolutely, positively your last course of action in obtaining financing. The amount of equity to be ceded is always negotiable — try to hold out for at least 51 percent for yourself.

Rule #4: Retain the right to force a payout (payback including interest) of the loan or investment. A business's profitability does not necessarily foretell a payout, unless it is specified in the agreement. Although the profitability of the business is important to the angel, the payout of the loan or investment is even more important. Success without a return is not success; it is only grounds for disagreement.

The lesson for you: Expect your angel to demand in writing a payout that would come from earnings, even though you'd prefer to spend or invest the cash elsewhere.

Minority funding resources

The resources for low-income and minority funding (which in many cases is defined to include women-owned businesses) are many. Look to the following for starters:

- ✔ The National Bankers Association in Washington, D.C. (NBA) represents minority-owned banks that target loans to minority-owned businesses. For the nearest member bank in your area, call the NBA at 202-588-5432.

- ✔ Most states have an agency that provides one-stop assistance on financial services for small businesses. Check the library or the phone book for such an agency in your state, and then ask about state-operated minority funding resources.

- ✔ On the federal level, the Small Business Administration can help direct callers to local organizations that can, in turn, help locate low income and minority funding opportunities. Call the SBA at 800-827-5722 for the resource nearest you.

- ✔ The U.S. Commerce Department's Minority Business Development Agency funds Business Development Centers nationwide whose function is, in part, to help minority-owned start-up businesses. Call 202-482-1015 for more information.

Ownership Options: Going It Alone versus Partners and Shareholders

In theory, all businesses have three ownership options:

- ✔ Privately held with the founder being the only shareholder
- ✔ Privately held, sharing ownership with partners or other shareholders
- ✔ Publicly held, meaning that shares in your company are available to the general public via the stock market

In reality, of course, most businesses only have the first two of these options — going it alone or having partners or minority shareholders. Very few businesses have the management, resources, and appeal needed to go public, either at the start-up stage or in the course of the business's growth.

There is no right or wrong answer as to which of the three options you should use, but there is a right or wrong way to determine which works best for you. At the heart of making that decision is . . . you guessed it . . . you! You are the primary ingredient that will determine which of the three options will best work for your business. Your criteria will include the kind of person you are, the way you communicate, the way you delegate, and the manner in which you work with people.

The kind of business you intend to start also can be a factor. If, for example, you intend to start a high-tech manufacturing business, you may find that the key employees you desire will demand some ownership (such as stock options; see Chapter 14) as part of their compensation package. On the other hand, if you intend to go into the consulting business, sole ownership is the likely ticket for you.

The role of business incubators

A business incubator is, quite simply, a building that is divided into units of space, which are then leased to early-stage small businesses. The result is a collection of offices and small warehouses filled with businesses (most likely in the light manufacturing, service, or technology sectors) that have one thing in common: They are businesses in the early stages of development. Each of the businesses has problems and needs that are similar, and each is in need of a variety of help, ranging from technical assistance to shared business opportunities to a simple pat on the back. Attesting to the benefits that incubators offer is the fact that today more than 500 incubators are operating in North America, up from only 15 in 1980.

Business incubators are not intended to provide permanent homes to their client businesses but rather to provide them with a temporary nurturing environment, until such time as the business is financially healthy. Upon reaching more predictable profitability, the incubated business can then be expected to "graduate" and move on to a typical office or warehouse building.

The advantages of working in a business incubator environment are many; here are but a few of the most important ones:

✔ **Financing:** Most incubators offer some kind of access to capital. We should mention here that incubator companies are carefully screened; thus, a business that has been accepted into an incubator offers somewhat of a stamp of approval on the business in the eyes of potential lenders and investors. Also, angels tend to hover around business incubators, so acceptance into one is a sure-fire way to get in touch with the local angel community.

✔ **Shared opportunities:** Sales leads, new business opportunities, strategic alliances — all are part of an incubator's offerings.

✔ **Shared business services:** A number of important business services can be found inside an incubator, including but not limited to telephone answering, bookkeeping services, access to fax and copy machines, and a wide variety of services and equipment that would otherwise require outlays by the start-up business.

✔ **Affordable rents and flexible real estate:** Rental costs are often a bit below market, and the sizes of the offices and warehouses vary widely, thereby affording clients more flexibility.

✔ **Networking with peers:** Imagine a collection of small-business owners, people like you, in every workspace. Being a small-business owner doesn't have to be lonely.

Our recommendation? Consider a business incubator right from the get-go, unless yours is a business that depends on a geographic location that the incubator can't provide. To find the small-business incubator nearest you, call the National Business Incubation Association at 740-593-4331 or visit its Web site at www.nbia.org.

The following sections offer a brief discussion of the pros and cons of each of the three ownership options.

You as the one and only owner

Sole ownership is always the least conflictive and most popular of the three options for starting a company, assuming that you have access to the necessary funds to launch your business, industry knowledge, and energy to make a go of the business by yourself. Sure, the leverage and financial benefits that partners and shareholders bring to the table can be worth their weight in potential opportunities, but decision-making in shared ownership situations requires consensus, and consensus can take so much time. Besides, consensus doesn't always represent *your interests,* and when your name is on the dotted line, *your interests* should be at or near the top of the reasons for making decisions.

Being the only owner has the following *pros:*

✔ Being the only owner is generally easier, quicker, and less expensive. No lawyers are required to write partnership agreements and help determine answers to all of the questions that partnership agreements require. (More on this subject later in this chapter.)

✔ The profits belong solely to you.

✔ You have no need for consensus. Your way is the only way.

✔ You don't waste time catering to the often-aggravating demands of shareholders. There's no possibility of shareholder lawsuits.

Being the only owner also has the following *cons:*

✔ You have no one to share the risk with.

✔ Your limited skills will have to make do until you can hire someone with complementary skills.

✔ Single ownership can be downright lonely. Many times, you will wish you had someone with whom to share the problems and stress. Of course, if you have good friends and/or a strong marriage partner, these people can be a source of support.

Still confused as to whether you want to go it alone or share ownership? Take this quiz to help with the decision:

1. **Do you believe that you need a partner?**

   Do you absolutely, positively need a partner? For cash? For knowledge? If you do, that settles the issue; if you don't, continue with this quiz.

2. **Are you capable of working with partners or shareholders?**

   Will you have a problem sharing the decisions and the profits as well as the risks?

3. **Does your business fit the multiple ownership profile?**

   In other words, does this business have room for two partners, and is it a business that has the growth potential to support two partners? Will a partner have an important role in the organization? Would his or her complementary skills enhance the business's chance for success?

4. **What are the legal requirements of multiple ownership?**

   (Read the remainder of this chapter, and then consult with an attorney if you still have questions.) Can you live within these legal parameters?

5. **What do you have in common with other business owners who have opted for multiple ownership? Where do you see conflicts?**

   Ask your banker, accountant, or attorney for the names of other business owners who have opted for multiple ownership. Interview those owners. Get their feedback on the list of pros and cons.

6. **What's the likelihood of finding a partner with complementary skills and a personality compatible with yours?**

   This will depend on how wired into the business community you are and the line of work you're going into. If you have a lot of business contacts and know exactly what you want, finding a partner may be easy. More typically, it is not.

After you answer these questions, you should have enough information to make the decision. Make your own list of pros and cons. Will your business have a better chance of success with just you at the helm, or are other skills immediately needed? Take your time. Remember, if you opt for multiple ownership, you'll live with the decision for a long time. If you elect sole ownership at the start, however, you can always seek partners later if you see the need.

Sharing ownership with partners or minority shareholders

As discussed earlier in this chapter, partners make sense when they can bring sorely needed capital to the business and add complementary management skills. Unfortunately, partners also present the opportunity for turmoil, and, especially in the early stages of a business's growth, turmoil takes time and costs money — items most small-business founders lack.

If you're one of those rare individuals who is fortunate enough to have found the right partner, then go for it; work out a deal. We've seen this proven many times over: A partnership in the right hands will outperform a sole proprietorship in the right hands, any day.

Having *minority shareholders* (any and all shareholders who collectively own less than 50 percent) can also make sense, especially after the business is out of the blocks and has accumulated value. The most common methods of putting stock in the hands of employees include stock option plans, bonuses, and Employee Stock Ownership Plans. See Chapter 14 for more details.

Here's a warning based on our personal experience: Minority shareholders can be a pain; they have legal rights that often run counter to the wishes of the majority. Because majority shareholders are ceded the right to make the final decisions, courts have determined that minority shareholders must have an avenue of appeal. Thus, minority shareholders, particularly in our litigious society, sometimes look to the courts whenever they feel their rights of ownership are being violated. Unfortunately, shareholder suits are a sign of the times.

As a result of this potentially tenuous relationship, you should always involve an attorney when inviting minority shareholders to the party, and you should always include a buy-sell agreement in the deal. In the event that the relationship doesn't turn out to be what all parties expected, buy-sell agreements establish procedures for issuing, valuing, and selling shares of the company, including how to determine the value of shares when one or more of the owners wishes to cash out.

Occasionally, especially where venture capital financing is involved, the founder of the business may find himself or herself working for majority shareholders. Fortunately, this situation presents itself very rarely, because the typical small-business founder has already proven that taking orders from others is not exactly one of his or her inherent strengths. We've found that, on the infrequent occasions when this situation does occur, more often than not, the founder of the company is the first one to go when the going gets tough as the chief financiers step in to protect their investment. That's why we strongly recommend that you find a way to retain majority control.

Going public: Cashing in

No question about it, the lure of liquidity and the possibility of interest-free capital can be overpowering to the small-business owner, especially after years of personally guaranteeing debt, scraping for money, and living on a reduced (or no) salary. Many small-business owners at one time or another fantasize about going public, yet very few businesses ever make it. Several reasons exist for this, the first and foremost of which is that the stock markets are highly selective; they only function for businesses that have outstanding track records and that meet particular hurdles.

Here's what it takes to get your stock listed on the major U.S. stock exchanges:

✔ **National Association of Securities Dealers Automated Quotation system (NASDAQ):** NASDAQ has approximately 5,000 listed companies ranging from small emerging firms to large firms such as Microsoft. Listing requirements include either a pretax income of $750,000 or market value of all shares totaling at least $1 million, 40 or more shareholders, and net assets of at least $4 million. There are approximately 28,000 other companies in the over-the-counter market, but these companies are so low-priced and/or infrequently traded that they are not listed on NASDAQ. (In case you care — and it's okay if you don't — NASDAQ is an electronic network that allows brokers to trade "over-the-counter" from their offices all over the country.)

✔ **The American Stock Exchange (AMEX):** The AMEX lists more than 800 companies, which are typically midsized firms. It is the second largest stock exchange in the United States. Listing requirements include a pretax income of at least $750,000 and either 500,000 shares publicly held with a minimum market value of $3 million or 250,000 shares held with a minimum market value of $2.5 million.

✔ **The New York Stock Exchange (NYSE):** The NYSE is the largest stock exchange in the world in terms of total volume and value of shares traded. It lists more than 2,000 companies, which tend to be among the oldest, largest, and best-known American corporations. To be listed on the NYSE, a company must annually earn at least $2.5 million before taxes and must have at least 1.1 million shares of stock outstanding with a market value of at least $18 million.

In truth, however, going public is not everything it's cut out to be. Hidden downsides abound that are easily overlooked. Although the capital raised may be interest-free, it is by no means hassle-free. You'll find that the army of outside shareholders that comes with going public, in concert with the Securities and Exchange Commission (SEC), requires an avalanche of public filings. Liquidity? Yes. The public business is liquid, but at what cost to management's time? And, in public companies, every shareholder, customer, media person, and competitor can peer into your financial records and ask you those questions that you may not have the time or the desire to answer, and they will learn things that you really don't want them to know.

In short, going public only works for a sophisticated, chosen few, so don't waste a lot of time now fantasizing about being the CEO of a public company. Given the entrepreneurial characteristics of the vast majority of us who typically decide to start businesses, public companies and small-business owners are like a size 9 shoe on a size 10 foot.

The Entity Decision: Should You Incorporate?

Before we discuss the variety of legal entities available to you, we must first pass on one piece of overriding advice. Today's high cost of legal consultations notwithstanding, this entity decision is one time when consulting a lawyer usually makes sense. (Also, as we discuss in Chapter 19, quality legal software and books are lower cost options.)

No other business will be exactly like yours. No other small-business owner's needs, motivations, and financial background will be exactly like yours. The entity options we describe in the upcoming sections are only intended to serve as guidelines. Although the entity decision you make will not necessarily be forever (your legal framework can and may change as your business changes), the choice you make now is bound to have significant short-term financial and legal implications — implications that will far exceed the cost of any up-front legal fees.

Three basic categories of legal entities are available: unincorporated, corporations, and limited liability companies. Of the more than 22 million legal entities operating in the United States, just over 6 million are corporations and limited liability companies, meaning that the remaining 16 million or so (approximately 72 percent) are unincorporated (sole proprietorships and partnerships).

The first decision that you must make, in the process of determining which legal entity to adopt, is "to incorporate" or "not to incorporate." After you have made that choice, if your decision is to incorporate, your choices are then to become a "C Corporation," a "Subchapter S Corporation," or a Limited Liability Corporation (LLC).

In the following sections, we discuss the factors involved in your decision to incorporate or remain unincorporated and your options within each category. Be sure to research all aspects of this issue, as a host of tax, liability, and administrative issues should be considered before you decide.

Unincorporated options

The preponderance of small-business entities are unincorporated for any number of valid reasons (such as the cost and complexity of the incorporating process; we talk about that process later in this chapter). Should you decide to remain unincorporated your business will automatically become either a sole proprietorship or, if you have a partner or partners, a partnership.

Sole proprietorship

If you are a typical small-business owner, especially one of the home office variety, your first consideration should always be the sole proprietorship, which is generally the simplest and least costly way to structure a business. Simply open your door, hang out your shingle, and zap, zap, you're a sole proprietorship. Little muss, little fuss, and little paperwork.

So why doesn't everyone become a sole proprietorship if it's so simple? The primary reason is the personal liability issue. The sole proprietor is personally liable for the business and puts his or her nonbusiness assets at risk. If you have selected an industry in which the chances for liability are high (consulting, for example) you should at least consider the option of incorporating.

Most people decide to open their businesses using their own name as the principal owner. If you decide to use a fictitious name or a trade name, however, you'll need to file a "Certificate of Conducting Business Under an Assumed Name" with your state or local town/city/county clerk. You can obtain these forms from good self-help law books; the filing fee for this form is minimal.

Other important characteristics of the sole proprietorship include

- ✔ Sole proprietorship status is limited to a single owner or a married couple.
- ✔ Taxable income is subject to both income and self-employment tax (see Chapter 16).
- ✔ Business losses may offset income from other personal sources subject to certain limitations (see Chapter 16).
- ✔ Some states allow protection of personal assets from business risks by owning them jointly with a spouse or by transferring them to a spouse or children. (Check with an attorney or your state's attorney general's office.)
- ✔ Insurance is available to cover some of the risks of a sole proprietorship. (Check with associations that are appropriate for your profession; also check with local insurance agents who specialize in working with small-business owners.)
- ✔ Termination of the business is easy for the sole proprietorship, especially compared to all the legal ramifications required when terminating something like a C Corporation. When putting an end to a sole proprietorship, simply close the doors and (assuming that you have no outstanding creditors) walk away.

Partnerships

Similar to a sole proprietorship, a "general partnership" can also be initiated by simply opening the doors. In a partnership, all partners are personally liable for their obligations to the partnership.

The downside of a partnership is that the partners can be held personally liable, as with sole proprietorships. Because of this liability issue, partnerships can be particularly sticky relationships unless the partners are capable of resolving disagreements amicably.

In addition to the standard partnership (also known as a "general partnership"), you can create a business entity known as a "limited partnership" — a combination of at least one general partner and one or more limited partners. The limited partners are only liable to the extent of the cash and/or property they have contributed to the partnership; the general partners are liable for everything else. The general partner is the managing partner; the limited partners are passive investors only.

A partnership may include two or more partners and is similar to the sole proprietorship — little paperwork is required in the formation stage. The individual partners are taxed on their percentage of the partnership income; therefore, the partnership itself, similar to the sole proprietorship, does not pay taxes.

We strongly recommend that you prepare a Partnership Agreement when you make the decision to involve a partner or partners. Although such an agreement is not legally required for a partnership to conduct its business, we recommend its preparation in order to outline what happens should various and inevitable problems or issues arise, such as one partner wanting out of the business or the need for the infusion of new capital in unequal contributions by the partners. The partnership agreement should include the following specifics:

- ✔ **The duration of the partnership:** Generally, a partnership agreement's duration is "in perpetuity." You may have reasons why one partner or another may specify that the agreement will lapse, such as when a business reaches a certain size or when profits are available to repay one partner's initial investment.

- ✔ **The time or money each partner will contribute:** The time and money contributed will rarely be the same throughout the duration of a partnership. When an unplanned difference between the two exists (for example, one partner works longer hours than the other or one partner contributes new money to the company while the other does not), you must find a way to equate the disparity.

- ✔ **The methods for making business decisions:** Generally speaking, someone has to have the final word in the likely event the partners have disagreements.

- ✔ **The sharing of profits and losses:** Normally, profit sharing (as well as loss sharing) will be in concert with the percentage of ownership. However, you may have occasions when one partner will receive more than the other. These occasions, which should be spelled out in the Partnership Agreement, may include new responsibilities, new investments, or new workloads.

- ✔ **The determination of when to distribute profits:** Partners' wishes on this issue are not always consistent; one partner may wish to take money out of the partnership and the other may wish to leave the money in to help the company grow.

- ✔ **The dissolution or restructuring of the partnership in the event of death or disability of a partner:** Sooner or later, death and/or disability is going to happen, and when it does, you must have a way for determining the valuation of the partnership for estate or cash-out purposes and for redefining the ongoing business.

In the absence of a partnership agreement, the division of ownership, profits, and liabilities among partners will be legally assumed to be equal, regardless of whether some partners have contributed more assets or time than others to the business.

Incorporated business entities

A corporation is considered a legal entity of its own; thus, its owners (shareholders or stockholders) are not personally liable for the business's liabilities, losses, and risks. Shareholders can come and go, but, unlike a sole proprietorship or a partnership, the business will continue to exist in spite of any change in the corporation's ownership.

Generally speaking, the decision to incorporate is usually made either as a result of the business's growth and the issues that accompany that growth or when the personal tax considerations of one or more of the owners warrant incorporation. The desired benefits of making the incorporation decision are usually the following:

- ✔ Shielding the company's principals from personal liability. Consider whether the type of business you're getting into or are already in has high potential for lawsuits.

- ✔ Providing an opportunity to raise capital by selling stock.

- ✔ Providing an opportunity to more quickly and easily transfer ownership from one shareholder to another.

- ✔ Allowing for the adoption of a variety of employee benefits (such as the corporation's ability to fully tax deduct employee health and disability insurance premiums paid) not available to other types of unincorporated entities (see Chapter 14 for a discussion of benefits).

Every corporation should execute a buy-sell agreement, which usually involves the assistance of an attorney competent in this area. Among other things, the buy-sell agreement dictates how a person's shares of stock will be handled if that person retires from the business, becomes disabled, or dies. This *exit strategy* issue is one of the most overlooked potential problems among entrepreneurs.

Given the benefits of incorporating, you may assume that you'll find significant disadvantages to incorporating, otherwise everyone would do it. Correctamundo! The primary disadvantages of incorporating are

- The cost and hassle of the incorporation procedure and complying with the public agencies (federal and state agencies) that oversee corporations.

- The hassle and potential liability from shareholder lawsuits involved in dealing with shareholders.

- The "double taxation" that occurs in a C Corporation when dividends are paid. When corporations earn profits, those profits are taxed at the corporate level. If some of those profits are then paid in dividends to company shareholders, company shareholders also must pay income tax on the dividends, hence the term "double taxation."

If you decide to incorporate, you have two kinds of corporations to consider, the C Corporation and the Subchapter S Corporation. We discuss each in the sections that follow.

C Corporations: The norm

Most big businesses and some small corporations elect C or regular corporation status, primarily because of their need for the liability protection that C Corporations offer. Because of their size and the public nature of their business, these large corporations do not qualify for either Subchapter S or Limited Liability Company status.

A C Corporation is taxed as an entity separate from any of the individuals comprising it, and all the profits of the business are taxed at the corporate level. And, if some of those profits are paid in dividends to the corporation's shareholders, the shareholders are obligated to pay ordinary income tax on those dividends. The result of this is the so-called "double taxation" status of corporations.

As with the other types of corporations, C Corporations are expensive and time-consuming to create. The process includes the owners of the business (the shareholders and stockholders) agreeing on the following:

✔ The name of the business

✔ The number of shares of stock the company can sell, the class of stock, and the book value

✔ The number of shares the owners will buy

✔ The amount of money (or other assets) the owners will contribute to buy shares of stock

✔ The directors and officers who will manage the corporation

The act of incorporation can be expensive, especially from the perspective of a budding entrepreneur with limited cash and few or no customers. The cost of incorporation depends upon the state in which you incorporate. Costs range from about $100 to approximately $1,000 for incorporation fees, and the corporation must pay an annual tax that varies by state. These costs do not include attorney's fees or any other fees that may crop up.

Filings can take from a few days to several weeks, again depending on the state and who is handling the process within that state. In some states, filings can take up to two months because they must be reviewed by the secretary of state and county officials.

Subchapter S Corporation: Liability protection

Named after the Internal Revenue Code section that allows it, Subchapter S is the corporation of the "little folks" — smaller companies that need the liability protection it affords but don't have the issue of multiple shareholders to worry about. Subchapter S status is reserved for businesses with no more than 75 shareholders. Both new and existing businesses may elect to adopt Subchapter S status.

When would you consider an S Corporation? As with a C corporation, an S Corporation provides the liability protection, but unlike a C Corporation, it avoids the double taxation status by allowing the income of the corporation to pass through to its owners/shareholders. The major difference between an S Corporation and a C Corporation or a LLC is that the S Corporation income is subject to only one tax, the personal income tax.

S Corporation status is the usual choice of small-business owners who make the decision to incorporate for liability purposes. This is especially true for start-up businesses because early-stage losses can be offset against one's personal income.

You should consider a number of other issues before deciding to create a Subchapter S Corporation. These issues include

✔ **Personal tax considerations:** If you are in the highest personal tax bracket already (don't you wish!), you may benefit from leaving the majority of your business's earnings in the company, thus paying the corporate tax rate, not the personal rate.

✔ **Profitability expectations of the business:** In the start-up years, if you are like most small businesses, you can expect your business to lose money. In this case, opting for Subchapter S status is advisable, so you can offset your business losses against your personal income. In later years, as your business becomes profitable, paying taxes at the corporate rate instead of the personal rate becomes more advantageous, so you'd switch to C Corporation status.

The election of Subchapter S status has many other varied ramifications. We strongly recommend that an attorney or qualified tax advisor help you to make this decision.

Limited Liability Corporations: A hybrid invention

The Limited Liability Corporation (LLC) is the new kid on the corporate block. The IRS officially awarded the LLC favorable tax status in 1988; since then, all 50 states and the District of Columbia allow this unique entity. An LLC is a hybrid entity. It combines the benefits of a corporation with those of a partnership:

✔ Like a corporation, investors in an LLC do not face personal liability for the debts or obligations of the LLC.

✔ Like a partnership, the LLC is afforded favorable tax treatment because the income and losses of the business flow through to the individual investors, who are called members, and are reported only once on each investor's personal income tax return.

Another advantage of an LLC is its flexibility. Unlike an S Corporation, an LLC can be structured to allocate the profits of the business differently among the various members, while at the same time preserving the flow-through tax treatment. An LLC has the added advantage over a partnership of providing the members with limited liability. The relationship of the members in an LLC is controlled by an operating agreement, a document not unlike a Partnership Agreement. The operating agreement can be quite complex. LLCs are relatively new, so we recommend that you consult an attorney with significant experience in establishing LLCs for small businesses like yours to help in making the decision whether or not an LLC can work for your business, and to help draft the operating agreement. Be careful to find an attorney who really understands the ins and outs.

Part II
Buying an Existing Business

The 5th Wave   By Rich Tennant

OUT OF BUSINESS

Main Street CHINA SU

"What made you think you were the one to own and operate a china shop, I'll never know."

In this part . . .

Wait. You say you're considering buying an existing business? Great! But you still have work to do. This part explores the advantages and disadvantages of buying an existing business, and helps you determine what kind of business to buy and what you should pay for it, as well as tax implications, potential employee issues, and a process for moving forward.

Chapter 6

Identifying the Right Business to Buy

In This Chapter

▶ The pros and cons of buying a small business

▶ The skills you need when buying a small business

▶ Your business-shopping criteria

▶ The best resources for generating leads

▶ Franchises and multilevel marketing companies

As sometimes happens in life, those who end up buying a business end up doing so as a result of some outside force or circumstance that propels them in that direction. Consider the case of David, a veterinarian who had worked for nearly a decade for two different practices. In the last practice, the owner agreed to offer David 10 percent of the practice after David had worked there for a number of years.

Over time, however, the owner engaged in various legal maneuverings that allowed him to wiggle out of the offer. David became dejected and upset; he'd been a loyal and highly competent employee over the years. His customers enjoyed working with him and requested his services when scheduling future appointments. David couldn't understand how the owner could treat him so poorly despite his years of excellent service to the business. David couldn't see and understand that the owner was greedy and unethical because David was neither.

The silver lining to this story was that this horrible experience was the catalyst David needed to go into business for himself. Instead of building a practice from scratch, however, David bought an existing practice. And he's glad that he did. David hit the ground running with the established practice, yet through his energies and talents, he made the practice bigger and better. Today, David is a contented small-business owner and a multimillionaire to boot.

Why Buy?

After it is created, a business can have a life of its own. The umbilical cord to its creator can be cut, and the business can pass through the hands of various owners. In some cases, a great small business can outlive its original owners — assuming, of course, that subsequent owners have the necessary management skills.

Every year, hundreds of thousands of small businesses change hands. Why? For the same reasons that many people purchase an already-built home instead of building from scratch. Because building a home or a business takes a lot of time and work, with lots of potential for problems.

We don't mean for you to take this analogy too far. After all, you can start most small businesses without drawing on your carpentry skills. However, as with buying an existing home, you may find that the advantages to buying someone else's business outweigh the advantages of building one yourself.

In the following sections, we discuss reasons why you may prefer to buy rather than build.

You want to reduce start-up hassles and headaches

Running a business is always a juggling act, but you often have more balls in the air during those start-up years than at any other time in the life of the business. Beyond formulating a business plan, you have to develop a marketing plan, find customers, hire employees, locate space, and possibly incorporate. Although you still need a game plan when buying an existing business, many of these details have already been done — if it's a good business.

Consider the learning curve for the type of business you're thinking of purchasing. Buying an existing business makes sense especially if the business is complicated. For example, purchasing a business that manufactures an intricate product makes more sense than purchasing a house-painting business, which doesn't require much more than the necessary tools and equipment and painting know-how. By contrast, unless you yourself have built the product the company manufactures and understand the intricacies of the production process, starting such a business from scratch is quite risky and perhaps even foolhardy.

You want to lessen risk

In situations where a business has an operating history and offers a product or service with a demonstrated market, some of the risk in the company is removed. Although no investment is a sure thing, the risk should be significantly lower than the risk involved in a start-up. Looking at historical financial statements also helps you make more accurate financial forecasts than you can with a start-up venture.

As we cover in detail in Chapter 7, you must do your homework; you have to inspect carefully the business you're considering buying and its financial statements. You can't take at face value how the business appears on paper or in the flesh, because more than a few business sellers have been known to dress up the books and the business to hide problems and flaws.

You can increase profits by adding value

Some business owners don't see the potential for growth or don't want to grow their businesses. They may be burned out, content with their current earnings, or simply ready to retire. Finding businesses that have the potential to improve operating efficiency and expand into new markets is not difficult. Relative to finding undervalued stocks or real estate when investing in those markets, it's easier for a business-minded person to find small companies that are undervalued relative to the potential they have to offer.

However, just because you think you see potential to improve a business, never, ever pay a high price based on your expectations of being able to add to that value. Even if you're correct about the potential, why should you pay the current owner for the hard work and ingenuity you plan to bring to the business? If you're wrong, you could grossly overpay for the business. Always offer a fair price based on *the value of the business at the time you purchase it* (we explain how to arrive at this figure in Chapter 7). Then you can realize the rewards of your improvements after you make them.

You want an established cash flow

One of the biggest question marks involved in starting a business from scratch is estimating the new business's cash flow. (We discuss cash flow in detail in Chapter 11.) Will the business generate cash quickly, or will it take a long time? How long will it take to collect payments from customers (receivables)? How long will it take to sell inventory? How quickly will your sales be established? With new businesses, estimating these figures is fraught with potential for wide margins of error.

Not so when buying an existing business. The previous owners have already answered most of these questions. Assuming you don't walk in and make immediate, glaring changes to the business's products or operations, the cash flow pattern should continue. As a small-business owner, you'll find it reassuring to have a predictable cash flow. You and your family, your banker, and other investors will deeply appreciate it. Conversely, unpredictable cash flow is troublesome and will keep you up at night.

If you buy a business rather than do a traditional start-up, borrowing money from banks and raising money from investors should be easier for you. Lenders and investors rightfully see more risk with a start-up than with an established enterprise with a good track record. And for the amount they invest, investors usually demand a smaller percentage of ownership in an existing business than in a new business.

You don't have a good business idea

We've said it before: You don't need a novel idea to go into business for yourself. Plenty of successful small-business people enjoy running a business, and it doesn't much matter whether they sell tires or trim trees.

If you know you want to own a business, but you lack an idea for a product or service to sell, chalk up another good reason to buy an existing business.

You want to open locked doors

In certain businesses, you can enter geographic territories only as a result of buying an existing business. For example, suppose you want to own a Ford dealership within an hour of where you currently live. If Ford is not granting any more new dealerships, your only ticket into the automobile industry may be to buy an existing business in your area.

You're not a great salesperson

Perhaps you're not terribly good at selling (maybe because you dislike it). Buying an existing business gives you a stable of customers, which means you don't have to recruit them yourself. Then, if you can provide quality products or services and meet customers' needs, you can see your business grow through word-of-mouth referrals.

In the long term, your lack of sales ability could wreck even an established business. How? All businesses, even those that don't desire growth, need to add new customers if only to replace those who inevitably leave. If you can't sell (or figure out how to sell to new customers), your business eventually may die. Be sure to hire people with the necessary selling skills and also be sure to read the relevant sections in this book about gaining and keeping customers.

Why NOT Buy?

Of course, you can find many downsides to buying an existing business. Similar to the advantages, the relative weight of these disadvantages depends largely on your personality and available resources.

You dislike inherited baggage

When you buy an existing business, the bad comes with the good. All businesses have their share of the bad. The business may have problem employees, for example, or it may have a less-than-stellar reputation in the marketplace. Even if the employees are good, they and the culture of the company may not mesh with your direction for the company in the future.

Do you have the disposition and desire to motivate your employees to change or to fire employees who don't want to change? Do you have the patience to work at improving the company's products and reputation? All these issues are barriers to running and adding value to a company. Some people enjoy and thrive on such challenges; others toss and turn in their sleep at night with such pressures. Think back on your other work experiences for clues as to what challenges you have tackled and how you felt about them. If you haven't done so already, take the quiz in Chapter 1 to help you assess your workplace likes and dislikes.

You're going to skimp on inspections

If you think buying a company is easy, think again. You must know what you're buying beforehand. So you need to do a comprehensive inspection, perform due diligence, kick the tires, whatever you want to call it (see Chapter 7). For example, you need to rip apart the existing business's financial statements to ascertain if the company really is as profitable as it appears and to determine its financial health.

After you close the deal and transfer the money or duly record the IOUs, you can't turn back. Unless a seller commits fraud or lies (which is difficult and costly for a buyer to prove in a court of law), it's "buyer beware" when the quality of the business you're buying is the issue. In Chapter 7, we cover all the homework you need to do before you decide to buy.

The right and wrong reasons for buying a business

Jeff (not his real name) was a successful electronics wholesaler. As Jeff approached the age of 50, he and his wife began to think more and more about where they might spend their retirement. As is typical of many Midwesterners fed up with the long and dreary winters, Florida came to mind.

During a winter vacation in Naples, Florida, Jeff was idly thumbing through the classified ads when he noticed a business for sale in the wholesale electronics industry. His curiosity got the better of him; he visited the company and talked at length with the owner. Before you could mutter the words *spring break*, Jeff had purchased the company with one-third of the purchase price in cash and the balance borrowed as a long-term loan.

Jeff's primary reason for buying the business? To give himself and his family a chance to travel to Naples on the company expense account, mixing golf with business during those cold Midwestern winters. "A great way to ease into retirement," he told his friends.

Fast forward two years. The Naples business was foundering badly. Apparently, many of the company's customers had been "relationship customers" with the previous owner, and now that he was gone, so were they. (It didn't help that Jeff was only around three months out of

the year, and the company's efficiency suffered accordingly.) Additionally, Jeff discovered that managing his new employees had little in common with managing Midwestern employees. Meanwhile, the business was hemorrhaging money.

Six months later, Jeff reluctantly closed the company's doors by transferring the remaining inventory to Minneapolis, taking a $250,000 hit to his bottom line in the process. A hefty price to pay, he admitted, for a few rounds of wintertime golf and some tax deductions.

In the end, Jeff's business failed because he purchased it for the wrong reasons. He didn't purchase it because he had a passion for his customers, or because he had an urge to make a difference for his employees, or because he had a driving need to create something meaningful, or for any strategic business reason. He purchased the business to get away from Minnesota winters and for some meager tax deductions, which, Jeff can tell you in retrospect, isn't nearly enough.

You should have compelling reasons to buy a business (such as those we discuss earlier in this chapter). As Jeff learned the hard way, golf in Florida and travel tax deductions just aren't enough.

You lack capital

Why do a lot of people start a business instead of buying one? Because they simply don't have enough cash to buy one. Existing businesses have value, which is why you generally need more money to buy a business than to start one. Although you may feel like you're more the business-buying than the business-starting type, if you don't have the necessary dough, and if you can't find investors to provide it, then your avenue to business ownership may be decided for you, regardless of the avenue you'd prefer.

You can't handle lower potential returns

If you purchase a proven business and run it well, you can make good money. In some cases, you can make lots of money. But you generally have less upside and potential for hitting it really big when you buy, rather than start, your own business. Those who have created the greatest wealth from small businesses are those who have started them.

If you buy a business, you still have plenty of potential profits and wealth to make, just not as much. And, besides, how many millions or billions of dollars do you really need?

You don't get the satisfaction of creating a business

Whether it nourishes their souls or simply gratifies their egos, entrepreneurs who build their own businesses get a different rush than those who buy someone else's. Certainly you can make your mark on a business you buy, but doing so takes a number of years. Even then, the business is never completely your own creation.

What Should You Have Before You Buy?

Not everyone is cut out to buy an existing business, and we're not just referring to those who don't have enough money. In fact, you can purchase a good small business with little or, in rare cases, with no money down.

Buying a business requires lots of work. However, successfully running the business day in and day out is much harder for most people than finding and buying a business. Some succeed wildly at running a business they buy; others fail miserably. So what, then, are the traits common to people who successfully buy and operate an existing small business?

Business experience and training

First, you should have business experience and background. If you were an economics or business major in college and took accounting and other quantitatively oriented courses, you're off to a good start.

If you have worked on business-management issues within a variety of industries, you also may have the proper background. Consultants who work as generalists get such training. However, one danger in having done only consulting is that you're usually not on the front lines where most of the serious business operational battles take place.

If none of the above apply to you, we're not going to say that you'll fail if you decide to buy a business, but the deck is stacked against you. If you don't have a business background and work experience, you may still succeed. However, you more likely may simply survive. And your prospects for outright failure are relatively high.

We strongly encourage you to get some hands-on experience, which is more valuable than any degree or credential you earn through course work. You'll find no substitute for real live experience in marketing to and interacting with customers, grappling with financial statements, dealing with competitive threats, and doing the business of business.

If you want to own a computer repair service, go work in one. If you want to run a jet ski rental business, go work in one. Try to wear as many hats in the business as the boss allows. Consider the experience as paid, on-the-job training for running a business.

We're not saying that you should avoid academic work. You may, in fact, have to get a certain credential to do the work that you want to do, such as an M.D. if you want to practice medicine. If you don't need a specific credential, taking selected courses, as well as reading good business books can boost your knowledge.

Down payment money

To purchase a business, as in purchasing real estate, you need to make a down payment on the negotiated purchase price. In most cases, you need to put down at least 25 to 30 percent of the total purchase price. Bankers and business sellers who make loans to business buyers normally require such down payments to protect their loans. Small-business buyers who make small down payments are more likely to walk away from a loan obligation if the business gets into financial trouble.

For example, consider what happened with Jim's fourth business, which he sold for 33 percent of the sales price in cash and the balance on a ten-year loan. Two years after the sale, the buyers declared bankruptcy, leaving Jim holding the bag on the remainder of the loan, which was more than 60 percent of the purchase price. Had Jim not required a down payment at all, he would have been stuck with nearly all of the loss; on the other hand, had he required 50 percent down, he would have lost significantly less than he did.

If you lack a sufficient down payment, try asking family or friends to invest or lend you the cash (see Chapter 5 for more on *bootstrapping options*). You can also set your sights on a less-expensive business or seek out business sellers willing to accept a small down payment.

If you find a business for sale in which the owner wants less than 20 percent down, you may be on to something good. Be careful, though — owners willing to accept such small down payments may be having a difficult time selling because of problems inherent in the business or simply because they've overpriced the business. Smart sellers want to maximize the amount of the down payment. Your intent as a buyer should be to keep the down payment to a minimum (subject, of course, to obtaining favorable loan terms), thereby retaining as much cash as possible to use in operating the business.

You can purchase many existing small businesses with a loan from the seller. Also, check for loans from banks that specialize in small-business loans. For further financing recommendations, see Chapter 5.

Succeeding with less money down

We know two people who made hefty profits with businesses they bought with small down payments. We don't want to mislead you into believing that it's easy or that anyone can do it, but it can be done.

First, Ken purchased an off-site file-storage company from an older owner who wanted to retire. The business did about half a million a year in sales and had allowed the owner to earn a decent living. After working for a year at a low salary, Ken gained the trust of the owner, who sold Ken and his partner the business for just $20,000 down, which represented less than 5 percent of the $550,000 purchase price. Ken and his partner had lots of great ideas about how to grow and build the business, and they did just that. Within seven years, after acquiring another area business and opening another location, sales and profits mushroomed, and the partners' stake in the business was worth about $7 million.

If you think Ken's story is extraordinary, check out Kyle's. He worked as an investment banker and discovered how to borrow large sums of money through selling high yield (junk) bonds. Kyle and a business partner purchased a company that manufactures musical instruments. With $250,000 down, Kyle and his partner bought the business for $95 million. (In other words, they financed $94.75 million of the $95 million purchase price!) In case you don't have your calculator handy, that's a down payment of less than one-half of 1 percent! Kyle's stake in the company is now worth tens of millions of dollars. Despite pulling off these smashing successes in their early 30s, both Ken and Kyle had excellent backgrounds to prepare them. Kyle, a Stanford MBA, had worked as a management consultant and investment banker. He also loved musical instruments and knew how to structure deals with little money down. Ken, also a Stanford MBA, had a background as a financial analyst and had done lots of research into the off-site file-storage industry.

Above all else, it pays to be persistent, patient, and willing to spend some time on things that don't lead to immediate results. You need to be willing to sort through some rubbish to find the keepers. If you're a person who needs immediate gratification in terms of completing a deal, you may become miserable as you search or end up rushing into a bad deal. Try breaking the process into steps to provide more success points and give yourself time for clear thinking.

How Do You Find Good Businesses?

Be realistic as you set out to find a good business to buy. Give yourself plenty of time; haste makes for lost money if you purchase a business without thinking through what you want and taking the proper steps to buy a good quality business for a fair price.

If you limit your search time to nonbusiness hours, finding a good business can easily take a year or two. Even if you can afford to search full time, you can still expect to spend several months on the prowl.

Name your preferences

Lots of businesses are for sale. To conduct an efficient search, you need to set some preliminary criteria. Although you don't have to define every precise detail of the business you want to purchase, a few well-chosen parameters help focus your search and keep you from spinning your wheels.

Although everyone has a different set of business-shopping criteria, here are some general issues that most wannabe small-business buyers will want to nail down:

✔ **Industry:** We highly recommend focusing on some specific niches in industries that interest you or that you know something about. Focusing helps you conduct a more thorough search and turns up high-quality companies. In addition to the industry knowledge you bring to the table, the knowledge you accumulate in your search can pay big dividends during your years of ownership.

If you have a hard time brainstorming about specific industries, here's a trick to jump start your cerebral synapses. Take a walk through your local Yellow Pages. Listed alphabetically are all the businesses known to exist in your area. Remember that a separate Yellow Page directory exists for businesses that sell mainly to consumers, while a "business-to-business" yellow book lists businesses whose customers primarily are other businesses. Look at either or both, depending upon the types of businesses in which you're interested.

You also may want to buy a business in a sector that is experiencing fast growth so that you, too, can ride the wave. Check out *Inc.* magazine's annual Inc. 500 list of the fastest-growing smaller companies in America.

✔ **Lifestyle:** The type of lifestyle you want your small business to provide can narrow your search significantly. If you're going into small business because you'd like to work from home, for example, then you obviously don't want to buy a retail store. Also, consider how big an income you want or need to generate.

✔ **Size/purchase price:** Unless you can cleverly craft a deal with a low down payment, such as those discussed in the sidebar "Succeeding with less money down," the money you have to invest in a business constrains the size of business you can afford.

As a rule, figure that you can afford to pay a purchase price of about three times the amount you have earmarked for the business. For example, if you have $30,000 in savings, you should look at buying a business for $100,000 or less. Because many business sellers overprice their businesses, you can probably look at businesses listed at a price above $100,000, perhaps even as high as $150,000 because you can probably negotiate to buy such businesses for less. Don't invest all your money in the purchase as you may need some money to finance the day-to-day operations of the business.

✔ **Location:** If you're rooted to a location already and don't want to move or have a long commute, the business's location further narrows the field. Although you may be willing to consider broader territory — maybe even nationally if you're willing to relocate — evaluating businesses long distance is difficult and expensive. Unless you want a highly specialized type of company, try to keep your search local.

✔ **Opportunity to add value:** Some buyers want to purchase a business with problems that need fixing or with untapped opportunities. For most people, managing a business is enough of a challenge. As with real estate, most people are happier leaving the fixer-uppers to the contractors. However, some businesses without major problems offer significant untapped potential.

After you define your shopping criteria, you're ready to go to the marketplace of businesses for sale. We recommend typing up your criteria on a single page so that you can hand it to others who can put you in touch with businesses for sale.

Generate leads

Break out your Sherlock Holmes cape and magnifying glass. Finding a good business to buy is a lot more like detective work than shopping at the mall. Be prepared to turn over a lot of stones and to follow a lot of tracks, many of which may lead to dead ends. Here are some proven resources for generating leads in your search for a business to buy.

Peruse publications

If you focus on specific industry sectors, you may be surprised to discover all sorts of specialty newsletters and magazines. Just think of the fun you can have reading publications like *Marine Store Merchandising, Piano Technicians Journal,* and *Diaper Delivery Service Business Guide!* Specialty publications get you into the thick of an industry and also contain ads for businesses for sale or business brokers who work in the industry.

A useful reference publication that you can find in public libraries with decent business sections is the *Small Business Sourcebook* (Gale). Organized alphabetically, this reference contains listings of publications, trade associations, and other information sources by industry.

Conducting literature searches of general interest business publications helps identify articles on your industry of interest. The *Reader's Guide to Periodicals* and online computer searches at your local library can help find the articles. Larger local newspapers in your area also contain classified ads of businesses for sale.

Network with advisors

Speak with accountants, attorneys, bankers, financial advisors, and business consultants who specialize in working with small businesses. These advisors sometimes are the first to learn of a small-business owner's desire to sell. Advisors can also suggest good businesses that are not for sale but whose owners may be worth approaching anyway.

Knock on some doors

If you're a homeowner and someone came to your door and said they were interested in buying your home, you'd probably say that you're not interested in selling. If the interested buyer said they really liked the type of property you had and were willing to pay a good price, the person may get a little more of your attention, but you'd still likely turn him away. But if you, as the homeowner, were considering selling anyway, you would be all ears, especially if you think you can sell directly and save paying a broker's selling commission.

Some business owners who haven't listed their business for sale are right now thinking about selling. So if you approach enough businesses that interest you, you'll find some of these not-yet-on-the-market businesses.

Why would you want to go to this trouble and potentially bother business owners? Simple. You increase the possibility of finding the right business. You may also get a good deal on such a business. You can negotiate with the seller from the beneficial position of not competing with other potential buyers.

Instead of calling on the phone or knocking on the business's door, start by sending a concise letter of introduction that explains what kind of business you're looking for and what a wonderful person you are. This demonstrates that you're investing some time into this endeavor. By all means, follow up by phone a week or so after you send the letter.

Consider enlisting business brokers

Some sellers list their businesses with business brokers. Just as a real estate agent makes a living selling real estate, a business broker makes a living selling businesses.

Business brokers generally sell smaller small businesses — those with less than $1 million in sales annually. These businesses tend to be family-owned or sole proprietorships, such as restaurants, dry cleaners, other retailers, and service firms. Approximately half of such small businesses are sold through brokers.

If you don't have your heart set on buying a particular type of business — a doughnut shop, for example — one advantage of working with brokers is that they can expose you to other businesses you may not have considered. Brokers can also share their knowledge about some of your ideas — like the fact that you need to get up at 2 a.m. to make doughnuts if you buy a doughnut shop. Still want to buy one?

Most business brokerage firms sell different types of businesses. Some firms, however, specialize in only one industry or a few industries.

The pitfalls with working with brokers are numerous:

- **Commission conflicts:** Brokers are not your business advisors; they are salespeople. That fact doesn't make them corrupt or dishonest, but it does mean that their interests are not aligned with yours. Their incentive is to do a deal and do the deal soon — and the more you pay, the more they make.

  Business brokers typically get paid 10 to 12 percent of the sales price of the business. Technically, the seller pays this fee, but as with real estate brokers, the buyer often pays, too. Remember, if a broker isn't involved, the seller can sell for a lower price and still clear more money, and the buyer is better off, too.

- **Undesirable businesses:** Problem businesses are everywhere, but a fair number end up with brokers. The reason: The owners had trouble selling them on their own.

- **Packaging:** This problem relates to the previous two potential pitfalls. Brokers help not-so-hot businesses look better than they really are. Doing so may involve out-and-out deception, but more typically it involves stretching the truth — that is, omitting negatives and hyping potential. (Owners selling their business themselves may do these things as well.)

You (and your advisors) need to exercise due diligence on the business you're thinking of buying. Never, ever trust or use the selling package a broker prepares for a business as your sole source of information. Unscrupulous brokers, as well as unscrupulous sellers, can stretch the truth, lie, and commit fraud.

✔ **Access to limited inventory:** Unlike a real estate broker who typically has access, through a shared listing service, to almost all the homes currently for sale in a particular area, a business broker can only tell you about his office's listings. (Confidentiality is an issue, as a shared listing service increases the number of people who can find out that a business is for sale and the particulars of the sale.)

If you plan to work with a business broker, use more than one. Working with a larger business brokerage firm or one that specializes in listing the type of business you're looking for can maximize the number of possible prospects you see. In some areas, brokerages pool listings to allow access. Florida, for example, has a state association of business brokers that share listings. However, even in areas like Florida, some larger brokerages opt not to be included because they benefit less by sharing their listings.

✔ **Few licensing requirements:** Unlike real estate agents in most states, the federal government doesn't regulate the business brokerage field and requires no official licensing. Approximately 20 states require real estate licenses of business brokers who operate in their states. This licensing requirement may seem odd, and it is. States don't know which department should monitor business brokers. Real estate seems logical to some state governments, because some of the selling process (getting listings and working on commission) is similar. Real estate transactions or leases are also part of many business deals. Some states allow those with securities brokerage licenses to operate as business brokers. The majority of states have no requirements — anyone can hang out a shingle and work as a business broker.

You can find business brokers in the Yellow Pages under "Business Brokers." Ads for businesses for sale may lead you to a broker as well. You can also ask tax, legal, and business consultants for good brokers they may know. If you've found a broker you think you'd like to work with, check references from other buyers who have worked with the broker. Be sure that the broker works full time at his profession and has solid experience. Some business brokers dabble in it part time and make a living other ways.

When evaluating brokers, ask for the names of several buyers the broker has worked with in the past six months. Ask for buyers of businesses in your field of interest, so that brokers can't simply refer you to the three best deals of their careers. Also, check with the local Better Business Bureau and any state regulatory department (for example, real estate, attorney general, department of corporations) that oversees business brokers to see if complaints have been filed against the brokerage.

Should You Consider a Franchise?

Among the businesses that you can purchase are franchises. Some companies expand their locations by selling replicas, or *franchises,* of their business. When you purchase a franchise, you buy the local rights within a specified geographic area to sell the company's products or services under the company's name and to use the company's system of operation. In addition to an up-front franchisee fee, franchisers typically charge an ongoing royalty.

As a consumer, you've likely done business with franchises. Franchising is a huge part of the business world. Companies that franchise — such as McDonald's, H&R Block, Century 21, Subway, and FootLocker — account for approximately $1 trillion in sales annually. Purchasing a good franchise can be your more expensive but relatively safer ticket into the world of small-business ownership.

Franchise advantages

Unlike buying other businesses, when you purchase a franchise, you don't buy an existing enterprise. Although the parent company should have a track record and multiple locations with customers, you start from scratch if you purchase a new franchise. (You can purchase existing franchises directly from owners interested in selling.) As the proud owner of a new franchise, you don't have customers. As with starting any new business, you must recruit your customers.

So why would you want to pay a good chunk of money to buy a business without customers? Actually, you should consider purchasing a good franchise for the same reasons that you would purchase other good, established businesses. A company that has been in business for a number of years and has successful franchisees proves the demand for the company's products and services and that its system for providing those products and services works. The company has worked the bugs out and hopefully solved common problems. As a franchise owner, you benefit from and share in the experience that the parent company has gained over the years.

Franchises offer two additional advantages that most other small businesses don't:

- A larger and successful franchise company should have brand-name recognition. In other words, consumers recognize the company name and may be more inclined to purchase its products and services.

  Some consumers feel more comfortable getting a muffler repaired by franchiser Midas Muffler than hunting around in the Yellow Pages and calling the local Discount Muffler World or Manny's Muffler Bazaar. The comfort of dealing with Midas may stem from the influence of its advertisements, seeing some of its hundreds of locations nationwide, recommendations of friends, or their own familiarity with Midas's services, perhaps in another part of the country. They also figure that if the company can be in business successfully in so many locations, it must be good.

✔ Another advantage of owning a franchise is the centralized purchasing advantages that it offers. As you would hope and expect from a corporation made up of so many locations, Midas can buy its mufflers at an extremely low price. Such volume-purchasing generally leads to bigger discounts to customers and bigger profit margins to franchise holders. In addition to possibly saving franchisees money on supplies, the parent company can take the hassle out of figuring where and how to purchase supplies.

Franchise disadvantages

Franchises are not for everyone. As with purchasing any other small business, pitfalls abound in buying franchises. Some of the more common problems that you should watch for include the following:

✔ **You're not the franchise type.** When you buy a franchise, you buy into a system that the franchiser has created for you. People who like structure and following established rules and systems more easily adapt to the franchise life. But if you're the creative and free-wheeling sort who likes to experiment and change things to keep life interesting, you'd probably be an unhappy franchisee.

Unlike starting your own business in which you may get into the game without investing lots of time and money, buying a business that ends up not being what you want can be a more expensive learning experience. For example, you may discover you don't like being on the phone and dealing with the public after shelling out good money to purchase a travel agency franchise.

✔ **You're required to buy overpriced supplies.** Centralized, bulk purchasing through the corporate headquarters is supposed to save franchisees time and money on supplies and other expenditures. Some franchisers, however, attempt to make big profit margins through large markups on the proprietary items that they contractually obligate franchisees to buy from them.

✔ **The franchise is unproven.** One of the problems with buying a franchise is that you're not buying an ongoing, established business complete with customers. If the concept has not stood the test of time and survived the experiences of other franchisees, you don't want to be a guinea pig as the first franchisee. And some franchisers are more interested in simply selling franchises to collect the up-front franchise money. Reputable franchisers want to help their franchisees succeed so that they can collect an ongoing royalty from the franchisees' sales.

✔ **The franchise is a pyramid scheme.** Unscrupulous, short-term focused business owners sometimes attempt to franchise their business and sell as many franchises as quickly as possible. Some even have their franchisees sell franchises and share the loot with them. Everything becomes focused on selling franchises rather than operating a business that sells a product or service intended to satisfy customers. In rare cases, franchisers engage in fraud and sell next to nothing, except the hopes of getting rich quick.

What About Multilevel Marketing Companies?

A twist, and in many cases a bad one, to the franchising idea is *multilevel marketing* (MLM) companies. Multilevel marketing is designed to replace the retail store as a conduit for selling certain products. Advocates of the MLM maintain that, when given identical products, the one sold face to face (without the cost of maintaining a storefront and hiring employees and paying insurance) is less expensive than the same product sold in a store. Additionally, MLM advocates believe that it makes more sense to buy a product from someone you know and trust rather than from a clerk behind a retail counter.

Sometimes known as network companies, MLMs can be thought of as a poor person's franchise. For those weary of traditional jobs, the appeal is obvious. Work at home, part time, no employees, no experience necessary, and make big bucks. We've heard claims that you can make tens of thousands of dollars per month for just a few hours per week.

Representatives for an MLM, who are treated as independent contractors, work to solicit new customers as well as to recruit new representatives, known in the industry as your *down line*. The big selling point is that you make money not only off your own customers but also off the business that your recruits bring in.

Beware of the pyramid

The trait of MLM that leads to its all-too-frequent excesses is that everyone can get in for very little money up front; thus, everyone does get in. And we do mean everyone — hence, MLM's shaky reputation.

The problem is that the worst of the MLMs are the equivalent of a pyramid scheme. They offer no legitimate service or product and exist solely to "sign up" as many reps as they can before someone realizes that the castle has been built on a cloud — at which point they take the money and run.

Be skeptical of multilevel marketing systems, especially if the company promises outrageous incomes for very little work. Also, be wary if the MLM is a lot more interested in telling you how to sign up new recruits than how to sell its products. That's a red flag for a pyramid scheme.

Finding the better MLMs

Legitimate MLMs, such as Mary Kay, put as much emphasis, if not more, on the products or services they offer, and they don't claim that you'll make a killing without working hard to find new customers. Although not shy about advertising the big earnings its successful salespeople make, Mary Kay doesn't hype the income potential. Local sales directors typically earn $50,000 to $100,000 per year, but this income comes after many years of hard work. Mary Kay rewards top sellers with gifts, such as the infamous pink Cadillac.

The ingredients for Mary Kay's success include competitive pricing, personal attention, and social interaction, which many stores don't or can't offer their customers. "We make shopping and life fun . . . we make people look and feel good," says one of Mary Kay's sales directors.

Mary Kay encourages prospective reps to try the products first and host a group before they sign up and fork over the $100 to purchase a showcase of items to sell. To maximize sales, Mary Kay representatives are encouraged to keep a ready inventory because customers tend to buy more when products are immediately available. If reps want out of the business, they can sell the inventory back to the company at 90 cents on the dollar originally paid, a good sign that the company stands behind its product.

Remember that due diligence requires digging for facts and talking to people who don't have a bias or reason to sell to you. Do the same homework that we recommend in Chapter 7 when thinking about buying a franchise. Assume that an MLM company is not worth pursuing until your immense due diligence proves otherwise.

Quality multilevel marketing companies make sense for people who really believe in and want to sell a particular product or service and don't want to or can't tie up a lot of money buying a franchise or other business. Just remember to check out the MLM company, and remember, you won't get rich in a hurry, or probably ever.

Chapter 7

Making a Successful Offer to Buy

● ●

In This Chapter

▶ Doing a pre-offer evaluation

▶ Crafting an offer sellers will love

▶ Negotiating strategies

▶ Due diligence

▶ Assessing what needs changing

● ●

*I*n the American legal system, a person is presumed innocent until proven guilty beyond a reasonable doubt. When you're purchasing a business, however, you should assume, until proven otherwise, that the selling business owner is guilty of making the business appear better than it really is.

We don't want to sound cynical, but more than a few owners out there try to make their businesses look more profitable, more financially healthy, and more desirable than they really are. Don't trust your gut on this one.

Consider Katie's unfortunate story. Katie made a gut-level decision when she decided to buy a restaurant from a silver-haired, distinguished-looking gentleman named Max. Well-dressed, well-educated, well-traveled, and well-versed in his wines, Max charmed the socks off Katie, flattering her about how successfully she could run his restaurant (his French accent didn't hurt either).

Max's "fact sheet" on the business was also impressive. It showed, over a period of several years, steadily increasing revenue and even more rapidly increasing profits for the restaurant. In the 12 months before the negotiations, the restaurant grossed in excess of $500,000 and had pretax profits of about $150,000.

A wine collector and food connoisseur, Katie had always dreamed of running her own restaurant. But she wanted no part of the grunt work of a start-up: developing a complete menu from scratch, negotiating a lease on a good location, advertising for and interviewing prospective employees, and so on. However, with a recently received inheritance, Katie could now afford to bypass the start-up stage and purchase an established restaurant such as the one Max offered for sale.

After just a couple of offers and counteroffers, Katie slapped down cash for the whole business. Max turned over the restaurant, soon thereafter hailed a cab for the airport, and headed for a retirement cottage in the south of France.

The first few months, business seemed a little slower than Katie had anticipated, but, overall, things seemed to be going okay. But by the end of the first year, Katie found that she had some serious problems.

First, expenses were higher and revenues lower than Max's historic financial statements had indicated they would be. For the first full year under Katie's ownership, the restaurant grossed around $300,000, which, after expenses, was just barely enough to break even.

Second, Katie ended up with lease problems. In her tenth month of ownership, the owner of the building that housed Katie's restaurant politely informed her that the restaurant's lease was about to expire; when it did, he was going to increase the rent 300 percent. Katie couldn't believe it. Max never mentioned that the lease was about to expire, or that he had negotiated a rate well below market value a long time ago and that it was bound to jump up when it did expire.

To make a long story short and to spare you the agonizing details of what Katie discovered in the ensuing months and years, Katie's restaurant eventually sucked her into personal bankruptcy. As it turns out, when Max was preparing the financial statements for Katie, he exercised quite a bit of, how shall we say it, advertising license.

Katie was never able to track Max down in France. If she had found him, she could have tried to sue him for misrepresenting the business's profitability. Of course, that's probably why Max did such a good job covering his tracks.

Although somewhat extreme, problems of the magnitude left hidden in Katie's restaurant are not that unusual among businesses for sale. Don't expect the business seller to point out the cracks in the foundation; you've got to hunt for them yourself. Until you prove to yourself beyond a reasonable doubt that negative surprises don't exist, you should not go through with a business purchase.

Evaluating a Small Business for Sale

As we discuss later in the chapter, smart buyers build plenty of contingencies into a purchase offer for a small business, just as you do when buying a home or other real estate. If your financing doesn't come through or you find some dirty laundry in the business (and you're not buying a laundromat), contingencies allow you to legally back out of the deal. However, knowing that you'll draft all purchase offers with plenty of contingencies shouldn't encourage you to make a purchase offer casually. Making an offer and doing the necessary research and homework is costly, both in time and money.

Before you make an offer to buy a small business, you should do some digging into the company; you can save yourself a lot of headaches, time, and money. And you'll minimize your chances of mistakenly buying a problematic business or overpaying for a good business.

Before making an offer for a business, you'll want reasonably clear answers to the important questions discussed in the upcoming sections.

What is the background of owners and key employees?

A business is usually only as good or bad as the owners and key employees running it. Ethical, business-savvy owners and key employees generally run successful businesses worthy of buying. Unscrupulous, marginally competent, or incompetent business owners and key employees are indicative of businesses that you should avoid.

Just as you wouldn't (we hope) hire employees without reviewing their resumes, interviewing them, and checking employment references, you should never consider making an offer to buy a business until you do similar homework on the owners and key employees of the business for sale. Here's a short list of information we suggest gathering as well as suggestions on how to find it:

- **Business background:** Request and review the owner's and key employee's resumes, remembering that some people may fabricate or puff up information on that piece of paper. Are the backgrounds impressive and filled with good, applicable business experience? Just as you should do when hiring an employee, be sure to check resumes to make sure the information they provide is correct. Glaring omissions or inaccuracies are a strong negative message as to the kind of people you are dealing with.

- **Personal reputations in the business community:** Sometimes we forget what a small world we live in. Yes, we know how many billions of people are crowding various parts of this planet. When we say, "this world," we're referring to the small geographic and work/professional communities to which we belong. Any business that's been up and running for a number of years has had interactions with many people and other companies. Take the time to talk to others who may have had experience dealing with the business for sale and ask them their thoughts on the company's owners and key employees. Of course, we shouldn't need to remind you that you can't always accept the statements of others at face value. You have to consider the merits or lack thereof of the source.

✔ **Credit history:** If you were a banker, we hope you wouldn't lend money to anyone without first assessing their credit risk. At a minimum, you would want to review a person's credit history to see how good they've been at paying off, on time, money they've borrowed. Even though you won't be lending money to the business seller you're speaking with, we think you should check his credit records. Why? Well, a problematic credit record could uncover business problems the owner had that he may be less than forthcoming in revealing.

✔ **Key customers:** The people who can usually give you the best indication of the value of a business for sale are its current customers. Get a list of the company's top five to ten customers, and ask them the following questions. In general, how is the company perceived by its customers? Does it deliver on time? Are its products or services comparable to what its competitors offer? Does it have a culture of integrity? What does the company do best? What does it need to improve?

✔ **Key employees:** On those occasions when the employees of the business for sale are aware of what is going on, always be sure to interview them and get their slant on the condition of the business. You also want to know whether they will remain as employees under the new ownership. (If Katie, in the earlier example, had interviewed the restaurant's employees, she surely would have learned about Max's character and credibility shortcomings, and maybe even had an insight into the false revenue figures he presented.)

Why is the owner selling?

If you've followed our advice earlier in this book, you should have a good sense as to what type of business you're in the market for. Just as you can't thoughtfully buy a home until you define what attributes you're looking for in a community (for example, good public schools, reasonable commute to your job, proximity to family, and so on) and a house (for example, architectural style, number of bedrooms and bathrooms, square footage, and so on), you should likewise have your shopping criteria already developed for the business you hope to buy. You should also be scouring the marketplace using the suggested resources we provide in Chapter 6 for maximizing your chances of finding a good small business for sale of the type you desire.

After you find a potentially attractive business for sale, the serious work begins. First, try to discover why the owner is selling. Small-business owners can be selling for a reason that shouldn't matter to you — such as they have reached the age and financial status where they simply want to retire — or they may be selling for reasons that should matter to you — such as the business is a neverending headache to run, it's not very profitable, or competition is heating up.

Just because an owner desires to sell for some negative reason shouldn't scare you off from buying the business. If the business has a low level of profitability, quite possibly the current owner hasn't taken the proper steps (such as cost management, good marketing, and so on) to boost its profitability. You may very well be able to overcome hurdles the current owner can't. But before you make a purchase offer and then commit to following through on that offer, you absolutely, positively should seek to understand many aspects of the business including, first and foremost, why the current owner wants out.

Here's how to discover why the current owner is selling (where appropriate, get the current owner's permission to speak with these people):

- ✔ **Chat with the owner.** Okay, so this isn't a terribly creative, Sherlock Holmes-type method, and yes, we know that many sellers aren't going to be completely candid about why they are selling, but you never know. Besides, the answer you get from the owner can be verified against what other sources tell you about the owner's motivations to sell.

- ✔ **Chat with the business owner's advisors.** As we explain later in this chapter, in the course of evaluating the worth of the business, you should be speaking with various advisors, including those you hire yourself. Don't overlook, however, the wealth of information and background that the current owner's advisors have. These advisors may include lawyers, accountants, bankers, and/or the business's own board of advisors or directors.

- ✔ **Chat with industry sources.** Most industries are closely knit groups of companies, each one knowing, in general, what's going on with the other businesses in the same industry. Most importantly, the vendor salespeople who call on the industry can be a terrific source for information. Sure, they may not be totally frank, but your job is to read between the lines of what they have to say. (They generally won't out-and-out lie to you either. They are aware that you could be their next customer.) Also, the business's current customers usually have a good idea of why a business is for sale; they can provide you with the information you need to determine whether the current owner is selling from strength or from weakness.

In your discussions with and investigations about the current owner, also reflect upon these final, critical questions: How important is the current owner to the success of the business? What will happen when he or she is no longer there? Will the business lose key employees, key customers, and so on?

How to tell if a seller is motivated

Imagine that you are in the market to buy a home. In the course of touring houses for sale in a neighborhood you'd like to live in, you discover two houses — one on Elm Street and the other on Oak Street — that meet your wish list of criteria. Both houses have the right amount of space and good-sized yards, and are located on quiet streets. In all other respects, the two houses are pretty darn similar and your analysis of comparable house sales in the neighborhood indicates that each house is worth about $190,000.

The Elm Street house is priced at $229,000, while the Oak Street house is priced at $199,000. The owner of the Oak Street house has already had the house inspected, has provided a copy of the inspection report, and has offered to correct the problematic items in the report at his cost. You also notice that the Oak Street house has been cleaned up both inside and out and looks ready to move into.

Now, assuming you like both houses equally well, which house would you be more interested in

making an offer on? It should be no contest. Clearly, the Oak Street house owner is more motivated and serious about selling. You can tell this not only from the more realistic asking price he has put on his house but also from all the time, effort, and money he has put into getting his house ready to sell.

So, when you're shopping for a small business to buy, you should be looking for similar ways to identify a motivated seller. Just as with real estate, a fair portion of sellers of small businesses aren't serious or motivated about selling. And just as with some house sellers who don't need to sell, some small-business owners stick a high price on their business and are willing to sell only if some sucker comes along and is willing to (over)pay.

Other small-business owners aren't really emotionally ready yet to part with their "baby." If you follow our advice in this chapter, you won't be anyone's sucker because you'll know how to value a business for sale and how to identify whether the owner is motivated to sell.

What kind of company culture are you buying into?

When you buy a small business, you're adopting someone else's child. Depending on the strength of its already-formed personality and how it meshes with yours, you may or may not be successful in molding that business into your image.

Larry was an MBA from one of the nation's top business schools. He thought he could make a bundle of money buying a small manufacturing company and running it better than its current owners. With his blue chip education and background as a consultant to similar businesses, he thought running the company would be easy. So, Larry purchased the company with a 35 percent down payment of the purchase price.

Larry's first task was to clean house of the "deadwood," as he referred to it. No, he wasn't talking about taking care of neglected landscaping on the company's grounds. Instead, he was referring to firing key employees so he could replace them with people who would better measure up to his high standards.

Larry made his downsizing decisions after just a couple of weeks on the job. Larry didn't seem to know (or perhaps didn't care) that the company had a history of respect for its employees built into its culture. Even during slow economic times, previous management hadn't let people go but instead scaled back hours of operation.

Not surprisingly, after nearly 20 percent of the staff was gone, Larry had earned himself the reputation as the "grim reaper." In short order, he came be known as the stupid grim reaper. Why? Because many of Larry's new hires couldn't do the jobs as well as the previous job holders who had been fired.

The original staff that remained, not surprisingly, feared for their jobs, thought Larry was a callous nincompoop, and worried about the future of the company. Many of the best remaining employees had updated their resumes and were actively seeking employment elsewhere.

Gradually, most of the good employees who had survived Larry's initial bloodlettings quit as the company went into a financial tailspin. Larry still owns the company, but he's at the helm of a severely wounded ship. If he tried to sell the company, he would lose all (and more) of his original investment. Although Larry thought that getting an MBA from a top business school was costly, this real world school of hard knocks education has cost him a couple hundred thousand dollars so far, in terms of his lost investment, not to mention the costs he inflicted on his fired employees.

So what is the point of this story? What should Larry have done differently?

✔ First, buying and running a company isn't as easy as people like Larry may think. An MBA from a top school and specific work experience don't come close to guaranteeing success when buying and managing a business. Larry should have maintained the company as it had been run until he studied its real strengths and weaknesses, knew the business well enough to recognize the skills needed of given employees, and could formulate an informed plan to move the company forward. Preconceived notions rarely withstand the scrutiny of day-to-day operations.

✔ Second, before buying the company, Larry should have taken the time to understand the company's culture. Changing employees may not be impossible in the company you buy, but changing the culture, especially in such a short period of time, is a dangerous and too-often-fatal endeavor. Cultures are a sensitive business asset and should not be treated lightly. He should have spent more time both before he bought the business as well as after his purchase in assessing and thinking about the company's culture.

What do the financial statements reveal?

We explain in Chapter 11 the ins and outs of the various financial statements — such as the balance sheet and income statement (also known as the profit-and-loss statement) — that you'll find in your typical small business. If you're unfamiliar with those statements, you should familiarize yourself with them now; otherwise, you're going to be at a huge disadvantage in evaluating businesses for sale. The following sections explain what to look for and what to look out for in the income statements and balance sheet.

The income statement (P&L)

A company's profits are simply revenues less expenses. Revenues are the money that the company receives from its customers as payment for its products or services.

Expenses are the company's costs of doing business. Just as much of your personal income or revenue goes toward income taxes, housing, food, and clothing, company expenses use up much and sometimes all of a company's revenue.

Audited and unaudited financial statements

In your initial evaluation of a potential business to purchase, you will be handed (at your request) the company's financial statements. Some business owners will be reluctant (usually due to concerns about confidentiality or because they may not be convinced yet that you are a serious buyer) to release too much financial data.

You may be asked to sign what's called a non-disclosure agreement (NDA), which typically asks you to legally bind yourself to keep confidential any information that the company shares with you. NDAs are fine as long as signing one doesn't tie your hands from evaluating similar businesses for sale, including those that compete with the one under consideration.

If the financial statements you're handed haven't been independently audited by a reputable accounting firm, be extremely cautious in assuming accuracy and honesty in the statements. In our story that opened this chapter, had Katie demanded that Max's financial statements be audited by a reputable accounting firm, she would either not have bought the company, or she would not have paid out the high price that she did.

And, don't take the financial statements at face value simply because they are audited. The accountant who did the audit could be incompetent or chummy with the seller.

An excellent way to uncover inflated profitability as reported on the financial statements that the current business owner shares with you is to ask the seller for a copy of the business's income tax returns. Owners are more likely to try to minimize reported revenue and maximize expenses on their tax return to keep from paying more tax.

We explain later in this chapter, in the "Due diligence" section, how to properly review a company's financial statements.

When considering buying a business, take the time to examine the following issues on the company's income statement:

- **Change in revenues over time:** Examining at least the last three to five years of income statements, you'd like to see a steady or accelerating rate of growth in a company's revenues. If a company's revenues are growing slowly, that raises the important question, "Why?" Is it because of poor service or product performance, better competitor offerings, ineffective marketing, or an owner who is financially set and unmotivated to grow the business? Now's the time to find out.

- **Revenues by product line:** For companies with multiple divisions or product lines, ask for the revenue details of each product line. Find out what's spurring, or holding back, the company's overall growth. One red flag is businesses that were acquired but don't really fit with the company's other business units. Some larger small companies that are struggling to build revenues sometimes try to "enter" new businesses through acquisition but then don't manage them well because they don't understand the keys to success in those businesses.

- **Revenues by individual stores:** With retail stores, such as a picture-framing enterprise that has multiple locations, examine the revenues on a store-by-store basis. If the business has been opening new sites, also determine the change in revenues coming from opening new locations versus the change at existing locations. A company can show overall revenue growth by simply adding new stores while the existing locations may actually be experiencing declining revenues.

- **Expense detail:** To help you identify which expense categories are growing and which are shrinking over time, take a look at the expense categories for the past three to five years and calculate what percentage each category is of the company's revenue. As a well-managed and financially healthy company grows, expenses as a percentage of revenues should decrease. Not all expense categories necessarily decrease. Research and development, for example, may be expanding in a company awash in revenues.

- **The bottom line:** The net result of revenues increasing faster than expenses is a fatter bottom line (the last line of the income statement sheet that indicates profits or losses). When you examine how a company's profits change relative to total revenue received, focus on operating income. Sometimes companies experience one-time events that can change profits temporarily.

Even healthy, growing businesses can get into trouble if their expenses balloon faster than their revenues. Well-managed companies stay on top of their expenses during good and bad times. Unfortunately, it's easier for companies to get sloppy during good times. So, don't be fooled into thinking that all is well in financial land just because a company's revenues have been increasing.

- ✔ **The owner's salary and bonuses:** Of utmost importance when computing the profitability of any business is the determination of how much money the owner is (or has been) taking out of it. The profitability of the business may look large at first glance, but the owner may be paying himself little in order to fatten the bottom line. Or the converse may also be true. The owner may be taking out excessive salary and bonuses, minimizing the business's profitability in the process.

- ✔ **Other expenses:** Also, thoroughly examine other expense items, such as automobile expenses, club memberships, and travel and entertainment for insight as to how the business has spent its money in the past. You may unearth fat which, if you're successful in cutting, could almost immediately improve your bottom line as the new owner.

The balance sheet

A balance sheet is a snapshot-in-time summary of a company's assets and liabilities. This report is typically prepared as of the last day of the company's fiscal year-end, which for most companies is December 31. Some companies have a fiscal year that ends at a different time of the year.

The assets section of the balance sheet summarizes what the company holds or owns that is of significant value. The liabilities section details what the company owes to others. Here are several key things to look for and to look out for when reviewing a company's balance sheet:

- ✔ **Accounts receivable (a.k.a. "receivables"):** This is money that is owed to a company for products or services already sold but not yet paid for. As companies grow, so too typically do their receivables. Be on the lookout, however, for accounts receivables growing at a faster rate than the company's revenues (in other words, its receivables are becoming a larger portion/percentage of the company's revenues). Bloated receivables may indicate that the company is having problems with the quality of its product or pricing. Dissatisfied customers pay more slowly and/or haggle for bigger discounts. Out of proportion receivables may also indicate that the company's customers are having financial problems of their own.

- ✔ **Property and equipment:** All companies require some equipment such as office furniture, computers, and so on, also known as *fixed assets*. Manufacturing companies also own machinery for making their products. Equipment becomes less valuable as it becomes more obsolete over time. This *depreciation of fixed assets* is charged against profits by the company as a cost of doing business each year. Thus, even if a company ceases buying new equipment, this entry on the balance sheet can gradually decrease as the depreciation is subtracted from the value of the equipment.

If a company hasn't been periodically upgrading its equipment, you could get stuck buying a company needing lots of costly new equipment purchases. Should the company's balance sheet indicate a continual decline in the bookkeeping value of the company's equipment, beware that the company may simply be deferring new equipment purchases. Inspect the company's equipment and talk with others familiar with the type of business so that you can understand how out-of-date the equipment in the business really is and how much you're likely to expend on replacement equipment down the road if you buy the business.

✔ **Inventory:** The balance sheets of manufacturing and retail companies should detail inventory, which is simply the cost of the products that have not yet been sold. As a business expands over time, inventory should follow suit. However, beware if you see inventory increasing faster than revenues because this may signal several problems, including customers scaling back on purchases, poor management, or an obsolete or inferior product offering.

✔ **Accounts payable:** When companies purchase supplies, equipment, or products for resale for their business, they generally have a period of time in which to pay the bills. Similar to inventory and accounts receivable, accounts payable (which is on the liability side of a company's balance sheet) usually increases in tune with a company's increasing revenues. If accounts payable is growing faster than revenues, it may or may not indicate financial trouble. The increase may simply be good financial management (the slower a company is with paying bills, the longer the funds are in the corporate accounts drawing interest). On the other hand, if the company is struggling to make ends meet, an accumulation of accounts payable can occur and can be an early warning sign of financial trouble.

✔ **Debt:** Debt is money that the company has borrowed and must some-day pay back. Footnotes to the financial statements generally detail the terms of the debt, such as when the debt is to be paid back. In Chapter 11, we detail some important ratios and calculations that can assist you with sizing up the amount and type of debt a company is carrying.

✔ **Other assets:** This catch-all category is for the other assets of the company and can include some stuff that will make your eyes glaze over. For example, companies keep a different (yes, this is legal) set of books for tax purposes. Not surprisingly, companies do this because the Internal Revenue Service (IRS) allows, in some cases, more deductions than what the company is required to show from an accounting standpoint on its financial statements. (If you were a company, wouldn't you want your shareholders, but not the IRS, to see gobs of profits?) The benefit of deferring taxes is treated as an asset until the IRS gets more of its share down the road.

✔ **Goodwill:** One of the assets that doesn't show up on most companies' balance sheets is their goodwill. Companies work hard through advertising, product development, and service to attract and retain customers. Name-brand recognition is a term you sometimes hear. Companies can't put a value on the goodwill they've generated, but when they purchase (acquire) another firm, some of the purchase price is considered goodwill. Specifically, if a company is acquired for $100 million yet has a net worth (assets minus liabilities) of just $50 million, the extra $50 million is considered to have gone to goodwill. This goodwill then becomes an asset, which, similar to equipment, is depreciated or amortized over the years ahead.

What are the terms of the company's lease contracts?

A soon-to-expire lease at a low rate can ruin a business's profit margins (poor Katie earlier in this chapter had this problem with the business she bought). With a retail location, the ability to maintain a good location is critical as well.

What are the "off balance sheet" assets worth?

The value of a company's assets includes not only tangible items, such as equipment, but also "soft" assets, such as the firm's name and reputation with customers and suppliers, customer lists, patents, and so on.

If you're seriously interested in making an offer on a particular business, you need to do some assessment as to whether the current customers of the business will still buy from the business after you take it over.

You should also assess the quality of the key employees. How about the business's relationships with suppliers? Also check out the competition — does it seem formidable?

Questions to ask key employees include: What do you like the most about your company? What do you like the least? How do you see the future of the company? Can the products or services be improved? What would be the number one improvement you'd make if you owned the business?

Questions to ask suppliers include: Does the company pay its bills on time? Do you get an inordinate amount of returns from them? Compared to other companies in the industry, how does the company treat its suppliers — as partners or as a necessary evil? If you could change one thing about the company, what would it be?

Check comparables — that is, what similar locations lease for — to see if the current lease rate is fair and talk to the building owner to discover his plans. Ask for and review (possibly with the help of a legal advisor) the current owner's lease contract. Pay extra careful attention to the provisions of the lease contracts that discuss what happens if the business is sold or its ownership changes.

Special issues when evaluating a franchise

As we discuss in Chapter 6, buying a reputable franchise can be a good way into the small business world. No matter what type of franchise you're buying, do lots of homework before you agree to buy. The following sections describe steps to take and questions to ask when evaluating a franchise.

Don't skip any of these steps when evaluating a franchise opportunity. You may be most tempted to cut corners when reviewing a franchise from a long-established company. Don't. You may not be right for the specific franchise, or perhaps the "successful" company has been good at keeping its franchisee problems under wraps.

Thoroughly review regulatory filings

The Federal Trade Commission (FTC) requires all franchisers to issue what is called the Uniform Franchise Offering Circular (UFOC) at least ten days before a prospective franchise buyer writes a check or signs a document to purchase. We recommend that you ask for this valuable document well before that deadline if you're seriously interested in a particular franchise.

Don't be put off by the size of the UFOC. Read the document cover to cover. The UFOC contains such valuable information as

- The names and addresses of the ten geographically closest franchisees to the one you may buy, as well as a list of franchises that were terminated, not renewed, or bought back by the company. Speaking with franchisees for whom things did not work out may help you uncover some aspects of the business that are turnoffs for you. Now is not the time to stick your head in the sand about possible problems or drawbacks of a given franchise — it's better for you to find out those downsides now rather than after you've plunked down a chunk of your money, borrowed lots more, and gone through lots of work to buy a franchise.

- Disclosure of pending or settled litigation, as well as a detailing of potential or actual troubles between franchisers and franchisees.

- The employment background of the senior management of the franchiser.

- The costs to the franchisee of purchasing a franchise, as well as required inventory, leases, and other costs.

Evaluate the motives of the franchisers

A good franchising company should want to check you out almost as much as you should want to check it out. Successful franchisers don't want to sell a franchise to someone who is likely to crash and burn and tarnish the good reputation they've worked so hard to build. These companies know that their interests are aligned with yours — they make more money from ongoing royalties if they sell franchises to solid franchisees who are determined to be successful. Are the franchisers looking for a long-term business partner or simply the fast sale of another franchise?

Observe closely how the franchising company interacts with you. Be wary if the franchiser seems more interested in selling franchises than in finding and helping the most-qualified franchisees succeed. Obviously, franchising representatives will be generally enthusiastic about their company. But a fine line exists between enthusiasm and a hard sell.

Run in the opposite direction if a franchiser tells tales of great riches from just a small investment of your time and money. Run extra fast if the franchiser is pressuring you into making a quick decision to buy and is evasive about providing detailed information about the business. And if the franchiser doesn't want to give you the UFOC, sprint.

Interview lots of franchisees

Interview as many of the company's franchisees as is practical — both current owners as well as those who quit or were terminated (who should be listed in the UFOC). Skip the list of references eagerly provided by the franchise company; go to the lists of franchisees provided in the UFOC. Ask the franchisees what their experiences, both good and bad, have been with the parent company. Those franchisees for whom things didn't work out are generally more forthcoming about the warts of the system, but you should also try to identify whether some of these people were poor fits.

Conversely, active franchisees are more likely to see things through rose-colored glasses, if, for no other reason, than to reassure themselves on their decision to buy a franchise. If active franchisees are dissatisfied, steer clear. Observe which franchisees are happiest and most successful and see if you share their business perspectives and traits.

Understand what you're buying and examine comparables

Most reputable franchises require you to plop down a chunk of cash to get started. Home office-based service businesses may charge a $25,000 up-front franchise fee, compared to the several hundred thousand to a million dollars required for the brick-and-mortar locations of established franchisers, such as McDonald's. Additionally, ongoing franchise royalties run about 3 to 10 percent of gross revenue. The UFOC should detail all the up-front costs.

What are you receiving for these payments? Is the system and name brand really worth this fee? What kind of training will you receive? What kind of corporate headquarters management assistance is provided? What programs are in place to foster communications with other franchisees?

Few franchises are unique. Compare the cost of what a franchise is offering to the cost of purchasing franchises from different companies in the same business. For example, if you're considering the purchase of a franchise from Wendy's, compare the terms and offerings to those of McDonald's and Burger King.

If you look at the "best" franchises in a particular business and think, "Hey, I can do this as well or better and at less cost on my own," remember that you don't have to buy a franchise. Consider the start-up alternative. Be realistic, though, because many hidden costs — both out-of-pocket financial costs and costs in the form of lots of time — are involved in starting a business from scratch. And the franchise has a head start in name recognition and customer base.

Check with federal and state regulators

Franchises are generally regulated at both the federal and state level. The FTC regulates nationally, and the state-level regulatory agency is usually called something like the "department of corporations" or the "attorney general's office." Check with these regulators to see whether complaints about a franchiser are on file.

The UFOC should also detail pending litigation against the company by disgruntled franchisees. You may also want to check with the Better Business Bureau in the city where the franchising company is headquartered to discover whether anything is on file.

Investigate the company's credit history

Just as you have a personal credit report on file, every business has a credit report that shows how the company has dealt with payments and debts owed to suppliers and creditors. This credit report is a good indicator of how well the franchiser maintains its business relationships.

Analyze and negotiate the franchise contract

If your digging has made you feel more, rather than less, comfortable with the franchise purchase, you now need to get down to the nitty-gritty of the contract. Franchise contracts are usually long, tedious, and filled with legalese. Read the contract completely to get a sense of what you're getting yourself into. Have an attorney experienced with franchising agreements review the contract as well.

In addition to the financial terms, the franchise contract should specify how disputes are to be handled, what rights you have to sell the franchise in the future, and under what conditions the parent company can terminate the franchise. Make sure that you can live with and be happy with the non-financial parts of the contract.

Remember that almost everything is negotiable. (This is especially true with the lesser-known franchisers that are in the early stages of their business growth.) Although some companies offer their best deal up front and refuse to engage in haggling, others don't initially put their best terms and conditions on the table, hoping that you'll simply sign and accept the inferior terms and conditions.

Making an Offer to Purchase a Business

As we've cautioned before, don't make an offer on a business unless you've done plenty of soul-searching and research as to the type of business you want and the merits and drawbacks of the specific business under consideration. Granted, you can build a number of contingencies into an offer, just as you can for a real estate offer, allowing you to back out of the deal if you find something wrong.

But, again similar to the real estate world, making an offer is still making a commitment to a certain amount of money and a large amount of time, both of which are nonrefundable if the deal goes sour. Small-business deals require lots more time and money in the early stages of the buying process, so you don't want to enter into the deal-making stages lightly.

Assembling an all-star advisory team

Ask yourself this important and hopefully revealing question: "How many businesses have I purchased in my lifetime?" If you're like most people we know, the answer is a big, fat zero.

Now, you're a smart person as evidenced by the fact that you knew to buy this book to help fill gaps in your small-business knowledge. And we, as your humble authors, have high hopes that you'll gain a wealth of practical insights and knowledge by reading what we've worked to provide in this book. However, and this is a most important however, we think you will benefit from retaining the services of experts with lots of small-business deal-making experience. We cover in Chapter 8 how to find good experts in each of the following disciplines:

✔ **Tax advisor:** A good portion of a small-business deal revolves around picking apart company financial statements and structuring a deal that makes sense from the standpoint of taxes. Hence, you should hire a qualified tax advisor.

✔ **Attorney:** Buying a business involves legal contracts, so you'll also want to have a good legal advisor on your small-business purchase team.

✔ **Small-business consultant:** (Optional) If you can find an experienced and knowledgeable small-business consultant, he or she can also help you with assessing and valuing possible businesses that you may buy.

And, if you've been searching for businesses through a small-business broker (which we discuss in Chapter 6), he or she should become part of your team as well.

Negotiating a good deal

To a certain degree, negotiating is a skill that comes with experience. As we discussed in the last section, good advisors can help you inspect what you're buying and look for red flags in the company's financial statements. Advisors can also help structure the purchase to protect what you're buying and to gain maximum tax benefits.

To get the best deal, you need to do a number of things well, the first of which is to put a value on the business under consideration.

Resources for valuing (determining the worth of)

When you first begin exploring businesses for sale, you won't know what a given business is really worth. Thus, you will be at great risk of overpaying for a given business, considering your lack of knowledge. However, with time and the right resources and investigative work, you can get a good handle on what a given business is really worth, which may or may not be close to the listing price the owner has chosen for it.

You can start by taking a cue from smart home buyers and real estate investors: In order to find out how much a property is really worth, they consider comparable sales — that is, what other similar properties have sold for. Compared to business buyers, however, home buyers have it relatively easy. Real estate transactions are a matter of public record; small-business sales are not. You've got to do extra sleuthing to find the specific price and terms of comparable businesses that have sold. In a moment, we'll share our top picks for resources that provide such comparable small-business sales information.

Multiple of earnings and book value

Many methods exist for valuing a business. Some are unnecessarily complicated; others won't provide you with sensible answers. For example, some advisors and business brokers advocate using a multiple of revenue to determine the value of a business — that is, if a business has $300,000 in revenues, it might be valued at $600,000 (a multiple of 2). However, revenue is a poor proxy for profitability. Two businesses in the same field can have identical revenue yet quite different profitability due to the efficiency of their operations, the pricing of their products and services, and the types of customers they attract.

Other measures are more exact. So, without further ado, we list our preferred valuation measures for small businesses:

- **Multiple of earnings:** When you compare the sales data for comparable companies to the one you're interested in buying, pay close attention to what *multiple of earnings* these businesses sold for; that is, divide the price the business sold for by its annual earnings (profits) to arrive at a figure that will give you the *multiple of earnings* (also known as the *price-earnings ratio*) of that transaction.

  When the multiple is low, say 3 to 1 (meaning if the business had earnings of $50,000, it sold for $150,000), this means that the buyer and seller did not have great expectations for the business's future earnings. However, when the multiple is high, say 12 to 1 (earnings of $50,000 and a selling price $600,000), the buyer's and seller's expectations of future earnings are correspondingly high. Remember that future earnings are what will provide the return on the buyer's investment; therefore, the higher the buyer expects those potential earnings to be, the more he or she is willing to pay for the business.

  Small, privately held businesses, however, typically sell for a lower multiple of earnings than larger companies in the same line of business. The reason: Small companies are less well-established and riskier from an investing standpoint.

- **Book value:** In addition to looking at the sales price of other businesses relative to earnings, you can also consider the value of a company's assets. The *book value* of a company is the company's assets less its liabilities, which is the same as the net worth of the business that comes from its balance sheet (assuming that the values for the assets and liabilities on the balance sheet are accurate; see Chapter 11 for more on balance sheets). The figures that go into determining book value should be checked carefully to ensure that the underlying asset values and liability accounts are correct.

Of the two approaches, each of which has advantages as well as imperfections, the multiple of earnings approach is superior to the book value method. After all, what you are purchasing when you buy a business is not primarily its assets but rather its ability to generate profits (earnings). Some businesses, such as a consulting firm, have little in the way of tangible assets — the personnel may be the firm's greatest asset, and valuing that is difficult. Because the determination of a price-earnings multiple figure is based on an income-generating formula, it is a better indicator than the book value approach, which measures only the difference between assets and liabilities.

Business appraisers

Business appraisers make a living estimating the value of businesses. If you're serious about buying a business and your initial investigation suggests that the seller is committed and serious about selling the business, you should consider hiring an appraiser. Although the fees they charge will vary depending on the size and complexity of your prospective business, for the typical small business you can usually figure at least several thousand dollars for an appraisal.

Tax advisors, lawyers, and business consultants who specialize in working with small businesses may be able to refer you to a good business appraiser. The Institute of Business Appraisers (561-732-3202) can provide you with a list of association members in your area. Also, let your fingers do the walking — check the business-to-business Yellow Pages in your area under "Appraisers – Business."

Businesses you've explored that have sold

If your search for a business to buy lasts months or perhaps years, keep track of similar businesses you've considered that eventually sell. These sales provide valuable comparables because you have seen the business up close and obtained details about the company's financial position that give you a valuable perspective in assessing the eventual sale.

Obtaining the final selling price of a small business can be challenging. You can try asking the ex-owner. Other options include speaking with advisors who are involved in such deals and business brokers. For more details on these sources, keep reading.

Advisors who work with comparable companies

Business consultants, attorneys, and tax advisors you work with can assist you with pinning down sales data for companies comparable to the one you're considering buying. The challenge is to find advisors who have knowledge of and experience with small businesses in general, as well as businesses similar to the one you're thinking of buying.

If you do end up buying a small business, you'll benefit from having good advisors on your team. Should an advisor not be able to cite business deals that he or she has worked for companies such as your prospective one, you need to find another advisor. Ultimately, when you're going to hire an advisor for tax, legal, or business advice, be sure to check references. You could also ask the advisor for a comprehensive list of business deals (including purchase or sale price and industry) that he or she has been involved in over the past year.

Research firms and publications

Because it can be difficult to find the details on similar companies which have sold, wouldn't it be helpful if a service compiled such information? Well, you may be happy to know that some companies do publish comparable sales information or conduct searches for a fee (some public libraries with extensive business sections carry some of these publications):

- *Bizcomps* is an annual publication that provides sales price, revenue, and other financial details for businesses sold. This compendium of sales information is available for different major regions of the United States (Western, Central, and Eastern editions). A national edition provides sales information for larger manufacturing, wholesale, and service businesses. Call 619-457-0366 for a sample of this publication. Each directory sells for $98.

- *Financial Studies of the Small Business* is an annual directory published by Financial Research Associates (FRA) that provides balance sheet and income statement comparisons for small companies. Call 941-299-3969 to receive a background package on this directory, which sells for $97.

- *Business Valuations by Industry* is a two-volume directory that contains a wealth of information on public company transactions in each selected type of business covered. Thus, this reference publication serves two purposes. First, it contains comparative information on the prices others have paid for companies, which can assist you in valuing similar businesses. (Remember, though, as we point out earlier in the chapter, larger public companies, because of their relatively greater stability and, hence, lower risk, generally sell for a higher multiple of earnings than smaller, privately held companies.) Second, the industry-specific data this publication provides can help you gain further industry-specific knowledge.

Trade publications

As we recommend in Chapter 6, trade publications can help you learn more about a particular industry and how to value companies within that particular industry. Most publications are willing, typically for a small fee, to send you past articles on the topic.

Business brokers

If you're already working with a business broker (salesperson who lists small businesses for sale and who works with buyers as well) or looking at businesses listed for sale through business brokers, the broker should be able to provide a comparable market analysis of similar businesses that the broker's office has sold.

We'd like to think that we don't need to say this, but such an "analysis" may be less analytic and more sales-oriented than you want. Business brokers earn commissions based upon a percentage of the selling price of the business that you may buy through them. The commissions may range anywhere from 2 to 12 percent, depending on the size and complexity of the deal.

Also, understand that business brokers generally have access to sales data only on the small number of similar businesses that their particular office has sold. Unlike real estate agents, business brokers who work for different brokerage firms in a given community don't share their sales data with one another.

Finally, before enlisting the services of a broker, be sure to check his or her references carefully, especially given the fact that business brokers are in a virtually unregulated business requiring no specific credentials or educational training to enter.

Purchase offer contingencies

When you make an offer to buy a home, you should make your purchase offer contingent upon obtaining mortgage loan approval, satisfactory inspections, and the property seller holding clear title to the home. By the same token, when you make an offer to buy a business, you should likewise make your purchase contingent upon similar issues, including the following:

- ✔ **Inspections and due diligence:** Your purchase offer for a business should be contingent upon a complete review of the company's financial statements and interviews of key employees, customers, and suppliers. You should be allowed to employ whomever you like to help you with these evaluations.

  You may also want to defer paying a portion of the purchase price for 6 to 12 months. Some items may not be verifiable until after the deal closes, and you'll want to make sure that everything is as the owner/seller claimed. We give you more details on this process in the next section.

✔ **Financing:** Unless you're paying cash for the full purchase price of the business, another condition of your purchase offer may be an acceptable seller-provided lend. Sellers can be a great financing source, and many are willing to loan you money to purchase their business. Seller financing is quite common in small-business purchases.

Be sure to compare the terms that the seller is offering to those of some local banks that specialize in small-business loans (we outline in Chapter 5 your best sources for financing). In the purchase offer, you should specify the acceptable loan terms, including the duration of the loan and the maximum interest rate. Should interest rates rocket up before your loan is finalized, you don't want to be forced to complete your deal at too high an interest rate.

✔ **Noncompete clause:** You don't want to buy a business only to have the former owner set up an identical one down the block and steal back his previous customers. To avoid this unpleasant possibility, be sure that your purchase offer includes a *noncompete clause,* which should state something along the lines that the seller can't establish a similar business within a certain nearby geographic area for the next so many years.

You may also consider asking the owner, as part of the deal, to make himself available to consult with you, at a specified hourly rate, for 6 to 12 months to make sure that you tap all of his or her valuable experience, as well as to transition relationships with key employees, vendors, and customers. To further align the selling owner's interests with yours, also consider having a portion of the total purchase price dependent on the future success of the company.

✔ **Limited potential liabilities:** When you buy a business, as we discuss earlier in this chapter, you buy that business's assets and liabilities. Some potential liabilities aren't going to show up on a company's balance sheet and could become a thorn in your side. Make sure that the seller is liable for environmental cleanup and undisclosed existing liabilities (debts).

Conduct legal searches for liens, litigation, and tax problems. Your attorney should do this for you.

Allocation of the purchase price

When you pay $300,000 for a business, you're not simply paying $300,000 for the business. You're paying $60,000 for the inventory, $40,000 for the name, $50,000 for the company equipment, and so on.

No matter how you determined the purchase price, it must always be broken down, or allocated, among the assets of the business and other categories. This requirement applies whether you set the price of the business by determining the value of its assets (such as the multiple of earnings method) or by some other method. Although this stuff makes accountants giddy and may cause your eyes to glaze over, snap to attention when the subject comes up, because how you structure the purchase can save you tens of thousands of dollars in taxes.

When you're ready to buy, good tax advisors will tell you that you'll generally want to allocate much of the purchase price to the assets of the business because such assets can generally be depreciated (written off for tax purposes) over a few years. However, the seller of the small business may, for tax reasons, want to allocate as little to the assets as possible. So expect some negotiating on this issue.

The purchase of the business and allocation of the purchase price among business assets must be reported on IRS Form 8594. Make sure that you do so because if you don't, the penalty is stiff — up to 10 percent of the amount not reported.

Due diligence

So you've spent months searching for the right business to buy. Then, after you've found one that fits your fancy, you may very well spend weeks negotiating an acceptable deal. Now, just as you're about to stumble across what you think is the finish line . . .

. . . you realize you've got several miles left to go in this marathon.

Time to get out the microscope and really pick nits. Time to play devil's advocate and assume that you've got problems to uncover. Before you go through with the deal and fork over the dough, you have a last chance to discover hidden flaws. All businesses, of course, have their warts, but better for you to uncover them now so that the purchase price and terms reflect those warts.

Is the business as profitable as the financial statements indicate? Will the business's customers remain after a change in ownership? What lease, debt, or other obligations will you be assuming when buying the business? You should answer these and other important questions through what is known as "due diligence."

As we explain earlier in this chapter, in the section, "Assembling an all-star advisory team," you should be working on your small-business purchase with experts who can assist you with putting together a good deal. These same experts also will form your due-diligence team.

In addition to the homework we recommend in the section titled "Evaluating a Small Business for Sale" at the beginning of this chapter, read over the following sections that list some additional due-diligence steps for you to perform before even making an offer.

Income statement issues

The following steps relate to income statement issues:

- ✔ **Have an experienced small-business tax advisor review the company's financial statements.** He or she will know what to look out for. Just be sure to agree on a budget for the cost of his or her services (and, therefore, the time he or she will spend).

- ✔ **Adjust for one-time events.** If necessary, factor out one-time events from the profit analysis. For example, if the business got an unusually large order last year that is unlikely to be repeated and hasn't been the norm in the past, you should subtract this amount from the profitability analysis.

- ✔ **Check the owner's compensation.** Examine the owner's salary to see whether it's too high or low for the field. Owners can pump up the profitability of their company in the years before they sell by reducing or keeping their salary to a minimum or by paying family members in the business less than fair market salaries.

- ✔ **Consider how the building expense will change.** You should also consider whether the rent or mortgage expense will be different after you buy the business. (Remember Katie's example at the start of this chapter?) This change clearly affects the profitability of the business.

- ✔ **Factor in financing costs.** Consider what will happen to profits when you factor in the financing costs from borrowing money to buy the business.

Legal and tax issues

The following steps relate to legal and tax issues:

- ✔ **Look for liens.** Check to make sure that no liens are filed against assets of the business and, if you're buying real estate, that the property title is clear. A competent attorney can help with this tedious and important legal task.

- ✔ **Get proof that taxes are all paid.** Get the seller to provide proof certifying that federal and state employment, sales, and use taxes are all paid up.

Moving into Your Newly Bought Business

If you've made it through the searching, researching, negotiating, and closing phases, you're now a bona fide small-business owner. Congratulations and welcome to your new business! You've completed a lot of challenging and important work and should feel proud of yourself.

After your deal is closed, remember to do the following tasks as soon as possible:

- ✔ **Disclose ownership transfer.** Notify creditors of the transfer of ownership. In counties where the company does business, you should publish a transfer of ownership notice in a general circulation newspaper. If you omit this step, unsecured creditors can come after your business if the previous owner had outstanding debts.

- ✔ **Write a business plan and mission statement.** Having researched the industry and evaluated in detail the business you bought, writing a good business plan should be relatively painless. Doing a good business plan, however, will take some time and thinking, which will benefit you and your business in increased sales, reduced costs, and happier employees. Should you ever seek outside capital from a banker or investor, you'll also need a good business plan. We explain how to do your business plan and mission statement in Chapter 4.

- ✔ **Plan the company's finances.** Going forward, you need to have a good handle on the revenue, expenses, and cash flow of your business. Your business should have a budget in place, and you should forecast future needs for capital. See Chapters 5 and 11 for details.

- ✔ **Consider the entity/legal form of organization.** Just because the business you bought was structured as a sole proprietorship or corporation does not mean that such a legal entity makes the most sense for you. We provide the framework for you to think through this important decision in Chapter 5.

- ✔ **Spend lots of time thinking about your customers.** Without good customers who buy profitable products and services and who pay their bills on time, you won't have a viable long-term business. And, even the best of businesses will lose customers for a variety of reasons beyond the business owner's control. So don't skimp on understanding your customers' needs, what makes them buy your company's wares, and what their ongoing customer service needs are. Completing your business plan should help clarify many of these vital issues, as will reading Chapters 9 and 10.

✔ **Get to know your employees.** Employees who liked the previous owner(s) will take time to warm up to you. Some employees will fear for their jobs or may worry about a change in ownership leading to reduced job satisfaction. Err on the side of doing more *listening* to your employees rather than always being the one jabbering about all your grand plans. The employees contain a wealth of knowledge about the business from which you can learn, and the better you listen, the more the employees will grow to respect and like you. Also be sure to evaluate the employee benefits package and compensation structure (see Chapters 13 and 14), which may not make the most sense. Don't make rash changes in this area, especially if you're thinking about reducing benefits and/or compensation. Early, negative changes can have ugly long-term consequences.

✔ **Walk, don't run.** Don't make huge changes your first day, week, or even month at the helm. Take your time to learn the culture of the business, the needs of its customers, and the idiosyncrasies of its vendors before you attempt major changes. Employees, customers, and vendors don't like quick change, especially when the person behind the change is new and relatively unknown.

✔ **Consult the prior owner.** Don't expect that you will know everything there is to know about running your new business. No matter how much better a business manager you may think you are than your predecessor, he or she has certain knowledge and skills that you don't have. Don't let your ego stand in the way of asking the previous owner to help you.

✔ **Work with a good tax advisor.** You don't want to fall behind in your taxes or the required filing of myriad tax forms, or you'll have a nasty surprise in the form of an unexpectedly large tax bill. The tax advisor who helped you with evaluating your business purchase may be able to recommend a tax advisor you could work with at least during your first year of business ownership. See Chapter 16 for more details.

Much like a first-time home buyer moving into a newly purchased home, your euphoria at owning your business may quietly slip into anxiety when you more fully realize that your work is just beginning. Relax, take deep breaths, and use the time-tested method of breaking a big task into lots of little manageable ones. Also, rest assured that if you have taken our advice from Chapter 6 and this one, and have done your homework before buying your business, you should have a business that doesn't have major problems, a business that you have the skills to run well.

Part III
The Keys to Running a Successful Small Business

The 5th Wave   By Rich Tennant

"Well, there's another caravan that didn't stop. Now will you let me add salted dates to the menu?!"

In this part . . .

Small-business ownership is really one never-ending exercise in problem solving. This part is designed to help you resolve a small business's most compelling problems, including "the care-and-feeding" of customers, improving sales and increasing profitability, using advertising and publicity, developing strategies for pricing and distribution, and keeping tabs on the all-important profit & loss statement.

Chapter 8

The Owner as Jack or Jill of All Trades

. . . .

In This Chapter

▶ Handling the details of start-up

▶ Determining which tasks you want to outsource

▶ Establishing a bookkeeping system that works best for you

▶ Controlling your expenses

▶ Dealing with people outside your business (bankers, consultants, lawyers, and so on)

. . . .

*I*n the beginning, you as owner will perform all of your start-up's chores, or at least you will personally see that they get done. Well, all the *important* chores anyway — those chores that will, down the road, either make you or break you if they aren't done correctly.

More often than not, however, much of those early-stage duties is grunt work, the not-so-exciting-to-entrepreneurs stuff that doesn't involve dealing with customers, or creating new products, or generating much-needed cash. Instead, it's that yawn-inducing stuff like appeasing the government, developing a bookkeeping system, and covering-your-behind-in-the-event-of-adversity. You know — the kind of stuff that, if it doesn't get done, will come back to haunt you someday.

The Nitty-Gritty Details of the Start-Up

We're assuming here that the big-picture tasks of the start-up, many of which we discuss in earlier chapters of this book, have been completed. Such obvious tasks as writing a business plan, finding a mentor, determining the legal entity that works best for you, locating financing, and developing the product or service. Now you must dive into the nitty-gritty details.

Buying insurance

We're talking here about liability: auto, fire, theft, business interruption, and so on. Insurance is an expense that never goes away and generally increases every year. Making things worse is the fact that, if you are like most entrepreneurs, after the original policies are signed, you'll file the policies away and won't consider reshopping them to get a better price for long periods of time because you're so busy running your business. This means that the expenses related to insurance policies will be etched on your profit-and-loss statement for long periods of time. Don't even think about entrusting the creation and negotiation of your initial insurance package (and the creation of the costs related to it) to anyone else.

In most cases, insurance is a necessary expense, not unlike a host of other necessary expenses such as rent, telephone, and salaries. In some cases the justification for insurance is the owner's logic; in others, the insurance is required by an outsider — a bank or a property-leasing company. For example:

- **Theft insurance:** Sooner or later someone is going to steal something of value from you. (That someone incidentally, is likely to be an employee.) Our recommendation: If you're in the high-ticket retail or wholesale business (automobiles, appliances, and the like), buy theft insurance. Otherwise take your chances until you're profitable, especially in the early stages of your business.

- **Property damage insurance:** In addition to the physical property you own, rent, or lease, property damage insurance also covers your inventory. Similar to homeowner's insurance, property damage insurance is often required by the terms of a lease or by the terms of a bank loan. Our recommendation: If you're in a service business without a lot of expensive equipment and you are leasing or renting in an office building, take your chances if your lease will allow it (until you are profitable). Otherwise, buy it.

- **Liability:** No telling what might happen on your business premises in these litigious times. Our recommendation: Buy it. Get enough to protect at least twice your net worth.

- **Business interruption:** Business interruption insurance covers the possibility of your business being interrupted by any number of random events, most of them natural disasters. Business interruption reimburses you for the profits you don't make during your downtime. Our recommendation: In a business's early stages, there usually isn't much business to interrupt. Spend your money elsewhere. However, this situation (hopefully) will change. When it does, business interruption insurance is a "must" buy. We talk about workers' compensation insurance in the next section, as the state-mandated program has complicated requirements.

Workers' Compensation Insurance

Workers' Compensation is payment for state-mandated insurance that provides benefits to employees injured on the job in the form of medical expense reimbursement and replacement of lost wages. Workers' Compensation is a state-mandated, no-fault insurance system and, when you have employees, is a hefty expense on the profit & loss statement.

Shop around for an insurance agent (referrals from satisfied small-business customers is usually the best indicator), set up a meeting with him or her along with a representative of the state, and learn what it will take to keep your *experience modification factor* at a minimum. (The experience modification factor is a numerical expression of a company's accident and injury record compared with the average for the firm's industry. A high experience modification factor equals high cost.)

In addition to the experience modification factor, job classification also plays an important role in determining the cost of your Workers' Compensation Insurance. Each employee (or job) in your small business is assigned by the state a particular rating — and subsequently a particular premium — based on the estimated level of risk involved in the performance of that job. (The higher the job classification the more it will cost you; the lower, the less. Argue for the lower; the classification criteria is often fuzzy.) Myriad job categories exist to choose from, and you'll find a lot of overlap between various jobs. Your business can waste a bunch of money if your employees aren't properly classified. Don't take this classification process lightly.

Workers' Compensation Insurance is a state-run program. For further questions on the subject, ask your insurance agent for the telephone number and address of the applicable state agency.

Paying federal, state, and local taxes

Federal taxes (income, Social Security, unemployment, excise) come in a mind-boggling array, as do state and local taxes (income, real estate, sales, and assorted other special levies depending on your industry). For more on the nuts and bolts of taxes affecting your small-business, see Chapter 16.

When short of cash (don't kid yourself, sooner or later, it's bound to happen), make sure that you pay what you owe the government, even if you have to put off paying your private vendors. Governments, especially the federal one, have an enormous array of collection tools at their disposal, are not given to negotiation and compromise, and have the right to extract a dear price (in the form of onerous penalties and interest rates) from those who don't meet the letter of the law. We strongly recommend you faithfully pay your taxes on time.

Negotiating leases

Unfortunately, reading, understanding, and creating a lease is for lawyers, not lay people. Pay them their two hundred bucks and don't get locked into any long-term leases with the lure of free rent or equipment use.

Long-term leases are a no-win situation for the small-business owner: If your business grows, it will outgrow the long-term lease, and you'll pay a higher price for its cancellation; if your business doesn't grow, you'll pay an even greater price to get out of the lease.

In essence, any lease for more than two years can be considered "long term." Many landlords will offer you long-term leases (three to five years) with all sorts of exotic discounts; don't be lured into taking them unless you can afford to pick up the final three years on your own. When leasing space as a start-up, aim for two-year leases, three years as an absolute maximum.

Maintaining employee records

The day you hire your first employee is the same day you must create and begin maintaining your first employee-personnel folder. Keep a running written record for every employee, covering such issues as employment agreements, performance reviews, business goals, commendations, and, of course, reprimands.

These records come in handy when managing and motivating your employees. Such key managerial and motivational tools as goal-setting and performance reviews require that you keep detailed employee records for these tools to work. (For more information on these two subjects, see Chapter 13.)

Also, assuming that you employ living, breathing human beings, you can also count on the fact that, sooner or later, you will have conflict with one or more of those living, breathing human beings — conflict that in the worst case can end up in court. When this occurs, the party who can back up his claims with the most information usually prevails. Don't you be the one who is handicapped by poor record-keeping and documentation.

Getting licenses and permits — city, state, and federal

Almost all businesses require filing certain licenses and obtaining of particular permits. We cover all this in detail in Chapter 15.

Check signing

Unless you have a spouse as your bookkeeper, always sign your business's checks yourself, until such time as you can turn the signing over to someone that you can absolutely, positively trust.

Checks represent cash, and from the day you hang out your shingle until the day you close your doors, cash will be the lifeblood of your business.

Deciding What Tasks to Outsource

We define *outsourcing* as delegating services you don't want to do or don't have time to do to someone (not an employee) who can usually do them better and faster.

Outsourcing is a buzzword that has surfaced only in recent years, but the concept itself is not new. Businesses have been "outsourcing" in one form or another for many years. The story of Kate, the tile-designer who outsourced the manufacturing of her painted tiles (see Chapter 4), illustrates a typical outsourcing scenario. Ditto the business that utilizes manufacturers' reps for selling its products or the business that subcontracts its accounting or legal services. These folks are all outsourcing.

Typical small business jobs which are outsourced

Take a look at this list of small-business functions that are most frequently outsourced:

- ✔ **Accounting and bookkeeping:** Accounting (the beginning-to-end process of collecting financial data, generating financial statements, and preparing tax forms) and bookkeeping (the collecting-of-financial-data function only) provide the gamut of outsourcing opportunities; you can, for example, hire someone to do *all* of your accounting and bookkeeping or you can hire someone to do *only* your payroll or *only* your financial statements or *only* your tax returns. Because the typical entrepreneur is not usually well-versed in accounting and bookkeeping skills, our suggestion here is that these functions be among the first to be considered for outsourcing.

✔ **Human resources:** As your company grows, the various functions of human resources should be next in line for outsourcing consideration. (A testimony to this fact is that 8 out of 10 of America's 400 fastest-growing companies outsource some or all of their human resource needs.) Human resources includes a wide variety of nonproduct, non-customer, nonsales related issues such as

> New-employee hiring procedures
>
> Policies and procedure manuals for employees
>
> Payroll and related information-gathering systems
>
> Employee training on human resource issues
>
> Employee training on a wide variety of sensitivity issues, such as ethics and sexual harassment

✔ **Manufacturing:** Again, the story of Kate, the designer in Chapter 4 who outsourced the manufacturing of her tiles, is typical. The manufacturing process for most products is expensive, time-consuming, and extremely detail-oriented. For many entrepreneurs, especially the "creative and sales types" who typically gravitate to this career, the outsourcing of manufacturing makes a lot of sense.

Even if your business is manufacturing, there may be some elements of your product that would lend themselves to outsourcing their manufacture to sub-contractors. Even behemoth manufacturers such as General Motors subcontract a good deal of their work.

✔ **Sales:** Outsourcing sales is certainly the most potentially dangerous of the outsourcing options but one that is used by some businesses, including those who employ manufacturers' reps. We say "potentially dangerous" because it is difficult to impart to outsiders the enthusiasm and knowledge necessary to most effectively sell your business's product or service. Sales is definitely the last of the responsibilities to consider outsourcing, although doing so is made to order for some small businesses. (For more on the subject of manufacturers' reps, see Chapter 9.)

Questions to determine what to outsource

And now for the $64,000 question: How do you determine which services to outsource and which to retain in-house? Every business and owner is different of course, but you need to answer these questions before making the decision:

✔ **Can I better manage my available cash if I outsource?** The answer here will primarily depend upon how much cash you have available. For example, by outsourcing the manufacturing process, you avoid the costs associated with maintaining an inventory of raw materials and hiring manufacturing employees. Or by outsourcing your sales functions, you avoid the costs associated with maintaining a sales force. The less cash you have, the more outsourcing you will be forced to do.

✔ **What do I do best?** If you are like Kate, designing is what you do best. Because time is finite, why spend a lot of time doing the things you don't do well (such as bookkeeping) when those duties can be farmed out, thereby leaving you with more time to do the things you do well?

✔ **Will the cost of the outsourcing service include a product (or service) whose quality is better than what I can produce at that same cost?** Given the fact that the best outsourcing sources are almost always specialists in their area of expertise, in almost every case, the answer to this question will be yes. Of course, if you don't find a good specialist, you shouldn't outsource until you do.

✔ **What do I enjoy doing the most?** We can guarantee you this; if you choose to keep your bookkeeping or human resource functions in-house, you will, over the years, end up spending no small amount of time dealing with issues related to these functions. Think about it: Is this the way you want to spend your time?

In the final analysis, the decision whether or not to outsource will be primarily based on the last point above (what you enjoy spending your time doing). In Kate's case, she chose to outsource the manufacturing but keep the sales function in-house because she preferred to design and sell her products rather than manufacture them.

Why You Need a Good Accounting System

If this were a perfect world, you wouldn't need an accounting system — you'd simply let your checkbook do the talking. You'd pay your bills and deposit your receipts, and whatever was left over at the end of the year would represent your profit. How simple (and inexpensive) such a procedure would be.

Alas, this isn't a perfect world, and your checkbook only does the talking when measuring one of your assets (cash). Furthermore, your checkbook only measures today's cash; it doesn't give you the foggiest idea of what tomorrow's or next month's cash balance will be. Will you have enough cash in the bank to pay the month's end bills, to meet next Friday's payroll, or to pay the quarterly tax payments that come due in 30 days? Who knows? The checkbook isn't talking.

The problem here is that your business's checkbook can't do any of the following things:

- ✔ Keep score (of anything but cash)
- ✔ Give you the information you need to pay your income taxes
- ✔ Give you the percentages and ratios you need to help you manage your business
- ✔ Give you the information you need to value your business

Like it or not, accounting is one of the most important functions of running your business. Whether or not you intend to eventually out-source your accounting or do all of the work yourself, at the start-up stage, it demands your undivided attention.

Which accounting system should you use?

Every entrepreneur has three options to consider when determining which accounting system to employ. The first option (this decision is to be made before opening your business's doors) is to outsource the accounting services (as described earlier in this chapter). The second is to employ an in-house *manual* bookkeeping system. The third is to use an in-house *computer-based* accounting system. A discussion of the manual and computer-based options follows. In Chapter 16, we provide advice on how to hire good tax and bookkeeping assistance.

Manual bookkeeping systems

Maintaining a manual bookkeeping system is certainly the quickest and easiest of the two in-house options. All you have to do is visit your local office supply store, purchase one of the many "manual bookkeeping ledger and journal" systems available (the entire package should cost less than $25), and voilà, before you can mutter the words "green eyeshades," you're a bookkeeper. You won't need to buy an expensive computer or the software to go with it; the only accessories required are a #2 pencil or a pen and, depending on the complexity of your business, no small amount of your (or someone else's) time.

After you purchase your manual system, follow the step-by-step directions inside the ledgers and journals to perform a relatively uncomplicated, connect-the-dots bookkeeping process.

During the course of your fiscal year, make your entries in the general journal pages (*journals* are where you make the entries; *ledgers* are where you total the journal entries). The manual system you will buy will include both definitions of each of the following categories (disbursements, receipts, and adjusting entries) and examples. Such journal entries will include

- ✔ Your disbursements according to their expense and/or capital account category
- ✔ The receipts (income) of your business
- ✔ Various period-ending adjusting entries designed to record such items as depreciation, accrued taxes, and accrued payroll

At the end of the year, complete your journal entries summarizing the year's activity. Then, if you prefer, you can turn your journals over to a tax advisor, wait for 30 days, and be rewarded with a professionally prepared profit-and-loss statement, a balance sheet, and the balance due for your year-end tax payment. If, on the other hand, you are that special entrepreneur who actually enjoys the bookkeeping process, you can expand the manual bookkeeping process to include the year-end preparation of your profit-and-loss statement, as well as the balance sheet, leaving only your taxes to be computed by a tax practitioner.

And finally, in those cases where your business is a relatively uncomplicated sole proprietorship or partnership, you may make the determination to carry the manual process through preparation of Schedule C of IRS Form 1040 and on into the preparation of your income taxes.

The sky's the limit — except when hampered by your time and patience — as to how much of your own bookkeeping and taxes you perform yourself. The primary issue to consider when determining how much, or how little, of your accounting you should do is how best to utilize your time.

In addition to the general ledger and journal functions previously described, most manual bookkeeping ledger and journal systems also include the forms you need to maintain such subsidiary records as monthly payrolls, schedule of accounts receivable, schedule of accounts payable, and inventory worksheets.

The low cost associated with a manual bookkeeping system is not the only good news that stems from selecting this option. Another advantage of a manual system is that you learn the basics of the standard double-entry accounting systems from the ground up, a skill that will hold you in good stead as your business grows. (See the sidebar on accounting definitions if you need more information about double-entry accounting.)

The bad news is that the manual-entry system, especially when your business has a lot of activity, can be extremely time-consuming, and time is money in the small-business world. Also, the information that you collect manually won't always provide you with the depth of financial data you need for making your business decisions. Finally, manual bookkeeping is more prone to human error than are computer-based systems.

Computer-based systems

If you already have a computer, using it to accomplish your bookkeeping and accounting functions probably makes sense. Although the least-expensive computerized software package available is a tad more expensive than a comparable manual system, the computerized system, if properly used, should save you time, provide you with more information, and establish a base for you to grow into a more sophisticated system as your business (hopefully) expands.

You can consider four categories of computerized systems when shopping for your first accounting package, remembering that the system you ultimately decide to install will depend upon the size and complexity of your business. A description of the four categories follows, along with several basic questions and a collection of tips intended to help you make the final choice.

Category #1: Quick and easy

Category #1 includes those quick-and-easy accounting systems used by many families, as well as by small businesses. The cost of these Category #1 systems is usually in the neighborhood of $50. These systems are basically an electronic checkbook register with the capacity to categorize expenses and generate both profit-and-loss statements and balance sheets. Most Category #1 systems also include the capability to electronically pay bills.

Examples of Category #1 accounting software packages include Quicken and Microsoft Money.

The primary shortcoming with Category #1 systems is that the software allows for the deletion of bookkeeping entries, so if you're interested in providing an audit trail for you or your accountant, you should not purchase a Category #1 package. An *audit trail* enables you to track every dollar of income and expenses, thus making theft much more difficult. (Audit trails are required in all publicly held companies.) For this reason, most accountants do not recommend Category #1 systems to small-business owners who have prospects of future growth — these owners will eventually require the security that audit trails provide.

A collection of accounting definitions

In the interest of assisting those of you interested in learning a manual system (or for that matter, for those of you interested in understanding the basics of accounting no matter what system you use), we include the following definitions of key accounting terms you need to know:

Fiscal year: A fiscal year is the specific 365-day period that you have chosen to begin and end your accounting period. Most businesses must choose a calendar year as their fiscal year; in other words, their year begins January 1 and ends December 31. (All personal service businesses are required to use a calendar year, as are all partnerships and sole proprietorships.) Some corporations, LLCs and Subchapter S corporations may elect to use a fiscal year other than the standard calendar year; for example, many retailers choose not to end their fiscal year on December 31 because they are still too busy winding up their holiday season. As a result, they may select a non-calendar fiscal year of February 1 through January 31 (or any such 365-day period).

Double-entry accounting and bookkeeping: All accounting and bookkeeping "systems" are double-entry. For each entry made on the expense side, an offsetting entry must be made on the income side. Every plus must be accompanied by an offsetting minus, or in accounting-speak, every debit to one account must be offset by a credit to another. Because of this double-entry aspect, such systems are always self-balancing. (The total debits will always add up to equal the total credits, hence the term "Balance Sheet.")

Single-entry record-keeping: Single entry record-keeping can best be illustrated by the example of your personal checkbook — one entry, and the transaction is completed. Single-entry record-keeping systems are not self-balancing (your checkbook doesn't balance until you've reconciled it to your statement). Cash register tapes and the maintenance of internal ledgers are other examples of single-entry record-keeping systems.

Cash-basis accounting: A cash-basis bookkeeping system records income at the time it is received and deducts expenses at the time they are paid. In effect, the date of the check and/or the deposit determines the date of the applicable bookkeeping entry. Most sole proprietorships and partnerships use the cash-basis accounting system because it is easier to understand and requires fewer year-end adjusting entries. However, you get much less useful information with which to manage your business.

Accrual-basis accounting: Accrual-basis accounting records income at the time it is earned and deducts expenses at the time they are incurred. The IRS requires that businesses that have inventory use the accrual system. As a result, most corporations use the accrual system. If you have an option, consult with a tax advisor for advice as to which system will work best for your business.

When your business is small, is going to remain small, and you will be the only person writing the checks, Category #1 systems may be satisfactory for you.

Category #1 systems also do not include payroll systems. If you plan on eventually having employees and don't want to figure your payrolls or write your checks manually, your next choice would be to spend another $50–$100 and upgrade to Category #2.

Category #2: Plus payroll and inventory

For about $100, Category #2 systems will provide a number of services that Category #1 systems will not. For example, Category #2 systems can perform the following functions:

- ✔ Compute, write, and compile, employee payroll.

- ✔ Track and age receivables and payables. (*Receivables* represent the monies owed to you by your customers; *payables* represent the monies you owe to your vendors; *aging* means determining the amount of time your receivables have been due to you or your payables have been due to your vendors. For more on the aging of receivables, see Chapter 11.)

- ✔ Establish customer receivable ledgers. (These are the ledgers that are, in effect, your customer's "statements.")

- ✔ Maintain a basic inventory system.

The primary disadvantage to Category #2 accounting software programs is that, similar to Category #1, the system does not provide an audit trail.

Examples of Category #2 accounting software packages include QuickBooks, Cash Flow, and Manage Your Own Business (MYOB).

Category #3: Marching the audit trail

Category #3 programs provide their owners with all the benefits that Category #2 systems provide, as well as the audit trail necessary to the business in which someone other than the owner will be writing checks and maintaining the books. Additionally, Category #3 systems allow for multiple users: the bookkeeping department, the accounts receivable department, the inventory department, and so on. Prices vary, depending on the horsepower required, but are generally in the range of $200 to $700.

Examples of Category #3 accounting software packages include BusinessWorks, AccPac, BPI, and Peachtree Accounting.

Category #4: Modular power

Unlike the software packages described in Categories #1, #2, and #3, which are purchased in a single package, Category #4 systems are purchased in modules.

Separate Category #4 modules include these components:

- ✔ Basic system manager (the module that manages all the other modules)
- ✔ General ledger (the chart of accounts)
- ✔ Accounts receivable
- ✔ Accounts payable
- ✔ Payroll
- ✔ Inventory
- ✔ Job costing (a system that allows you to compute the exact cost of each of your products or services for pricing purposes)

The cost of each module is approximately $500, but the total price for a complete system can begin at $2,000 and run all the way up to $10,000, depending on the bells and whistles selected. Category #4 programs are extremely flexible and can support many types of accounting issues and business processes.

Examples of Category #4 accounting software packages include Great Plains, Dynamics, AccPac Plus, and MAS-90.

Category #3 and #4 programs overlap to some degree. A few of the #3 programs come with modules, thus making the choice between the two even more complicated. We recommend consultation with a computer software professional if you are unsure which programs would work best for you.

Determining the system that's right for you

When it comes time to decide which software package to purchase, you'll first want to ask yourself the following questions:

- ✔ What characterizes your business? Will you have inventory? Do you expect your business to significantly grow within the next year? Who will be maintaining the books and writing the checks? And the most important question of all: Do you intend to follow our advice on using financial reports to manage your business? Or is your bookkeeping solely for the purpose of collecting information to later get your taxes done?

- ✔ How many employees will you have on your payroll? Do you expect this number to expand significantly within the first two years?

- ✔ Do you intend to sell your products on the Internet? (If so, look at Category #4 systems that have the capability to handle these electronic commerce transactions.)

The answers to these questions should help you narrow your choice. The following collection of tips should assist you in making the final decision:

- Don't waste your time purchasing and learning a system that you're going to outgrow in six months or a year.

- Don't buy a system that you think will take you three years or more to grow into. That's too far out to accurately project. Buy a system that you believe will work for you for the next two years or so.

- When purchasing a software system, in addition to considering the system itself, consider the company behind the package you're buying. Criteria should include the support that the company provides, the history of its program updates (as a general rule, better companies provide more frequent updates), and the future of that company (will it be around to provide upgrades in future years?).

- In the likely event that you can't answer these questions yourself, call the company (most have a toll-free number on the package) and ask the direct questions yourself.

- Find out whether someone locally is trained to provide implementation and support services for the product you are considering. Look in the Yellow Pages, ask an accountant, or call the manufacturer.

- If you suspect you are a Category #3 or Category #4 customer, buying several hours of computer accounting consulting may be a worthwhile investment. Rates range from $50 an hour on up.

Companies grow. Even if you think you want a Category #1 software package now, chances are you will be in the market for an upgrade soon enough. The additional investment required to switch software packages is not really the issue. The real damage comes from the time and staff retraining required to effect the switch of the software.

The lesson here? When in doubt, buy the highest category that you can afford and that you can picture yourself using within the next two years.

Controlling Your Expenses

You have only three ways to increase your business's profitability (for more on this subject, see Chapter 11):

- Increasing sales (in which case, a percentage of those sales *may or may not* have a positive impact on profitability)

- Increasing prices (in which case, the entire amount of the increase *will* have a positive impact on profitability assuming that you don't lose customers due to the price increase)

✔ Decreasing expenses (in which case, the entire decrease *will* have a positive impact on profitability).

In other words, you'll find a one-to-one leverage factor at work on your bottom line profits when you increase prices or cut expenses. This is why the successful small-business owner always looks to the expense and pricing categories first when in a profitability crunch: Results can be instantaneous, and the impact is usually dollar on dollar.

Whether starting a new company or running an existing one, you must always remember that controlling expenses is a cultural issue, and cultural issues begin at the top. This means that many of your employees are going to emulate you; if you have overstuffed chairs in your office and overpriced secretaries in your foyer, your employees are likewise going to demonstrate a penchant for spending unnecessary money. We're talking about the old "lead by example" trick here.

Whenever we walk into a business's lobby or reception area and are greeted by the gurgle of cascading waterfalls and the sight of bronze sculptures, we are reminded again of Sam Walton and Wal-Mart. Linoleum floors and metal desks were the order of the day at Wal-Mart's corporate headquarters in Bentonville, Arkansas. No wonder they could underprice and outperform such longtime competitors as Sears or J.C. Penney, whose overhead included the cost of maintaining their corporate offices in the towering skyscrapers of Chicago and Dallas.

Fixed versus variable expenses

Two kinds of expenses need controlling; the first is fixed and the second is variable. Fixed expenses do not fluctuate with sales; they are usually negotiated in the start-up stage and then are left to their own devices until the original negotiations lapse and it is time to renegotiate them. Such periods may be anywhere from one year to five years.

Effective control of these fixed expenses, which include such categories as insurance, rent, and equipment leases, requires that the small-business owner assure that she is always the person who does the up-front negotiating. Fixed expenses should be skillfully negotiated, because once they are established, it will typically be a long time until renegotiation comes around. That cost is then fixed, and you can do little about it.

Variable expenses are those expenses that fluctuate with sales — as sales go up variable expenses will go up as well (and vice versa). The determination of the prices to be paid for variable expenses can be delegated, all the while remembering that the responsibility for controlling them, in the early stages of a business anyway, should always be with the owner. He should approve all purchase orders and sign all checks that relate to variable expenses.

As the company grows, the responsibility for controlling expenses may be delegated to other responsible individuals inside the company. However, the owner may still choose to maintain control by signing the checks and questioning the invoices that support those checks.

A key to controlling expenses is keeping your employees cost-conscious: If the employees know that you or other key managers are conscious of costs and will question unreasonable or unnecessary expenses, then they will be motivated to contain them. Incentives are also an often-used tool for cutting costs — give your employees a reason (bonus, perks, recognition) to look for unnecessary costs and they're sure to find them.

Always be aware that the 80-20 rule is alive and well when it comes to expenses. In this case, the 80-20 rule says that 80 percent of your wasted expense dollars can be found in 20 percent of your expense categories. For businesses that have a number of employees, the wages and salary category is usually the largest and thus the most often abused.

We don't mean to say that expenses shouldn't be challenged in every category. Quick and easy dollars can usually be found by rooting around in such expense accounts as utilities, travel, insurance, and of course, the compost heap of them all, the miscellaneous expense account.

And finally, remember that effective expense control is not only a profitability issue; it is also an important element for controlling cash flow (see Chapter 11). Because lack of cash is usually the number one symptom of a small business's impending failure, how better to begin building a solid foundation than by controlling your company's expenses?

Zero-based budgeting

Budgeting, a.k.a. *forecasting,* is the periodic (usually annual) review of past financial information with the purpose of forecasting future financial information. For those of you who completed your business plan, you have, in effect, prepared your first budget when you forecasted your profit-and-loss statement. The only difference in preparing a budget for your ongoing business is that you will now enjoy the advantage of having yesterday's figures to work with.

Incidentally, this process of budgeting is one that should apply not only to your business, but also to your personal finances as well, especially if you have trouble saving money. If you aren't currently budgeting your personal revenues and expenses, what better way to prepare yourself for running a business than to first begin at home.

In your small business, you have two ways to budget expenses from year to year. The first — the easy way — is to assume a percentage increase for each expense category, both variable and fixed. For example, say that you decide that your telephone expense (a variable expense) will increase by 5 percent next year, your rent (a fixed expense) will remain the same, and your advertising and promotion (a variable expense) will increase by 10 percent. Whoosh, a few multiplications later, and you've budgeted these expenses for the course of a year. How easy can budgeting get?

Zero-based budgeting, on the other hand, makes the assumption that last year's expenses were zero, and begins the budgeting process from that point. For example, this budgeting formula assumes that your supplies expense account begins at zero; thus you must first determine who consumed what supplies last year, who will be consuming them this year, and how much will be consumed. Then you must determine what price you will pay for this year's supplies. In this manner, zero-based budgeting forces you to annually manage your consumption at the same time that you are annually reviewing your costs. What better way to run a business?

The effect of zero-based budgeting is that no longer will you include prior years' mistakes in the current year's budgets. For example, when budgeting telephone expenses for the year, instead of increasing it by a flat percentage, zero-based budgeting demands that you make sure that your prior year's bill was the lowest it could be. This will force you to determine who is using your phones for what kind of activity and also to reprice your rates with telephone carriers. Instead of forecasting a 5 percent increase, you may well end up projecting a 5 percent decrease.

Far too many small businesses do not budget expenses at all. Furthermore, of those small-business owners who do, few use zero-based budgeting, despite its many advantages. Not budgeting is truly one of the most expensive mistakes the small-business owner can make. Sure, zero-based budgeting may take more of the owner's time, but it can pay big dividends in increasing bottom-line profitability — at home or at your business.

Managing Vendor Relationships

Some management gurus say that the customer is at the top of a small business's pyramid, an approach which preaches that every small-business owner's number one priority is to keep the customer happy.

We take a different approach to who belongs at the top of that pyramid. We acknowledge the importance of the customer, but we believe that you — the entrepreneur — and your employees belong at the top of the pyramid and that you deserve the number one priority status. This is because the entrepreneur and her employees are the people who make the products or provide the service that the customer stands in line to consume. No product or service worth waiting for? No customer!

Whichever viewpoint you favor, one thing is for sure: A small business's most *underrated* priority is the vendor (supplier). Think about it, without a good vendor, what would happen to your business? You own a computer retail store? Where would you be without Compaq and Hewlett Packard and Microsoft on your shelves? A restaurant? Where would you be without a reliable baker, meat supplier, and fresh vegetable resource to depend on? An upscale department store? Where would you be without Calvin Klein and Elizabeth Arden? Every successful business owner has learned the importance of having a cadre of loyal vendors standing behind his business.

Yet few small businesses have the muscle or the clout to demand such vendor loyalty, which means that they must build strong vendor relationships the old-fashioned way — by earning them. The following tips provide information on how to earn favored-customer relationships with your vendors:

✔ **Don't nickel-and-dime your vendors to death.** Agree on the details of your business arrangement (price, delivery, terms) and then try to work within the parameters of those arrangements for the agreed-upon period of time. (Occasional exceptions will exist.) And whatever you do, don't use the lowball pricing of the latest-vendor-on-the-street as leverage against the longtime-reliable-vendor unless you're prepared to lose or greatly annoy the longtime-reliable one.

✔ **Pay your bills on time.** Pay your bills in the designated period of time and you'll always maintain favored-customer status. After all, isn't this what you expect of *your* customers?

✔ **Save your special favors for when you need them.** Don't cry wolf on requests for out-of-the-ordinary service; save those requests for crunch time.

✔ **Treat your vendor's representatives (sales or customer service employees) as you want your own employees to be treated.** The Golden Rule is alive and well when it comes to maintaining vendor relationships.

Vendors incidentally, especially the good ones, can provide you with more than just a product or service. They can also provide training to both your employees and on some occasions, your customers — a form of assistance that the typical small businesses can never get enough of. For example, in Jim's sporting goods business, the manufacturers of many of the products the company sold (fitness products especially) offered both on-site and off-site training programs at no charge. Be sure to ask your vendors what training programs and/or aids they offer, and don't be afraid to take advantage of them.

Not every prospective vendor will measure up to your standards, by the way. Be sure to check out your new vendors carefully, especially when they don't have a reputation or a track record. You can accomplish this inspection by touring their facilities, by requesting customer references, or by asking them for a financial statement (always the best way to know for sure that they'll be around for awhile).

The overriding point here is that it takes a unique combination of human beings to create a successful business: you, your employees, your customers, your vendors, and a variety of outsiders (see the next section, "Dealing with People Outside of the Business"). No matter which of these you consider the most important, the others all have their role in building your successful business.

Dealing with Bankers, Lawyers, and Other Folks Outside Your Business

In earlier chapters of this book, we discuss the loans bankers make, the entities lawyers initiate, the government agencies that interact with the entrepreneur, and the financial statements that accountants generate. But we haven't discussed the people themselves who are behind all of that activity.

So what's so important about all those outside folks? Heck, if you had things your way you wouldn't need most of them.

Sorry, but you won't always have things your way.

The small business grows or dies depending upon the relationships developed between the owner and her employees and the business and its customers, vendors, and a variety of outsiders. This section is intended to help you understand the outsiders you must deal with, with the intention of helping you successfully manage the relationships that evolve.

Bankers

Ask the typical small-business owner what he thinks about bankers, and you'll usually get a reaction somewhere between a roll of the eyes and a hair-tearing tantrum. Bankers get a bad rap from the small-business community.

When bankers say no, they are only doing what they're bred to do — protect their depositors' money. For example, we know of a banker who will, as part of his spiel to would-be borrowers, say, "I treat my bank's money as if it belonged to my parents." What this banker is really saying here is, "If there's a hint of a risk, you'll have to find your money elsewhere." After all, most of a typical bank's depositors *are* someone's parents or grandparents.

Recognizing risk

What this translates to is that bankers don't like to take big risks; that's a key part of their job description. Think about it: If bankers were creative and optimistic and prone to take risks, they wouldn't be bankers. They'd be like us. Entrepreneurs. We all have our roles in a capitalistic system. Being safe and conservative just happens to be theirs.

Make no mistake about it; start-ups are the riskiest of risks, which is the reason bankers don't usually consider financing them, unless the collateral is right. Meanwhile, especially in recent years, a variety of small-business lenders have appeared on the scene, and today a number of viable alternatives exist for finding start-up capital.

Working with your existing banker

Although bankers may not play an important role in the start-up, after the business is up and running, their role can become more crucial, especially when the maturing small business experiences rapid growth. Growth often requires operating capital in the form of outside financing, which is where the bankers come in. (On occasion, of course, the entrepreneur might go back to his original source for that operating capital; more typically, however, it is provided by bank loans.)

We think you'll find this collection of tips on how to work with your banker helpful:

✔ Help your banker do his job. Call him more often than he calls you — not with just the good news, but also with the bad. Bankers don't like surprises, especially bad ones.

✔ Always ask for more money than you think you need. A little insurance never hurt anybody, and you usually won't get everything you ask for anyway. Besides, going back to the well a second time can be difficult as well as embarrassing.

✔ Prepare in advance for your banker's visits. These aren't social calls your banker's paying on you; he's kicking your tires. Include an agenda and a tour of your facilities, and then review your financial results before he asks you for them. Finally, follow up your banker's visit with a letter outlining your discussion and thanking him for his time.

✔ Face up to the fact that you're probably going to have to personally guarantee (legally obligate your personal assets as collateral) the loan. After all, you're asking your banker to, in effect, deposit his firm's money into your business. If you were in your banker's shoes, wouldn't you ask for a guarantee too? (Remember, however, that your guarantee is only one of many issues that is up for negotiation when you're borrowing money. Try to use your guarantee to get an offsetting concession in the contract.)

✔ Don't lose sight of the fact that a bank's services, like everyone else's, are negotiable. The rate it quotes, the collateral it requires, and the terms it outlines are usually up for grabs, and what you settle on will depend on the strength of your bargaining position. Don't blindly accept everything it offers and do be sure to shop around among various banks that do small-business lending.

✔ Be prepared to answer the bank's tough questions, especially where your assets are concerned. Bankers will want to know more about such hard assets as inventory, receivables, and equipment than you ever thought possible. But remember, that's their insurance. They need to know, and the better your business looks to them, the better your negotiating position will be when the time comes to work out the terms of the loan.

And finally, remember that bankers and their conservative, close-to-the-vest ways are a fact of life. You can learn to live with them, or you must face life without being able to borrow their money.

Lawyers

Lawyers used to be like FBI agents: You were aware that they existed, and sometimes you even met one, but you never had occasion to deal with one. Lawyers practiced their trade on someone else. Never on you.

Today, lawyers are like pets. Everybody seems to have one.

If you worked for General Motors, for example, lawyers would be part of the overhead — a fixed expense, similar to rent and depreciation and the CEO's limousine driver.

But small-business owners don't work for General Motors. To you, lawyers are a large, additional expense. Lawyers' fees redirect your hard-earned cash, resulting in capital expenditures that must be put on hold, new employees that cannot be hired, trade shows that must be skipped. Additionally, spending time with them takes time away from work and results in lost efficiency on the job.

The problem with committees

Several years after Jim purchased General Sports Corp., the largest bank in Minneapolis granted his business its first line of credit. The relationship between Minneapolis's biggest bank (at the time) and its scrawniest entrepreneur (at the time) proceeded smoothly for the next several years, thanks to General Sports's profitable operations and the bank's capable account executive who handled the account. The account executive, who had become Jim's friend, knew everything that went on inside the business; Jim saw to that.

One day, the account executive stopped by unexpectedly to say goodbye (he had been promoted) and to pass on the news of a new bank policy: Jim's loan application must now be approved by "the committee." It seems that General Sports's borrowing needs had exceeded some magic level and now required three loan-officer signatures instead of one. Jim was assured that this new procedure was only a formality.

A year or so later, the inevitable happened. "The committee regrets to inform you," the voice on the telephone began. And so ended the relationship between Jim and the biggest bank in town.

Jim and General Sports eventually survived, thanks to hard work and a relationship with a neighborhood bank. And as Jim's companies have grown over the years, he's learned to live with banks' committees. Although the formula is simple (you depend on facts and figures and not on trust), the enactment is difficult and usually runs against human nature. Against Jim's, anyway.

The problem, as Jim sees it looking back on the incident, is that committees don't spawn relationships; individuals spawn relationships. Jim has learned the hard way that he would rather do business with a living, breathing human being than a committee, any time.

Consulting a lawyer has a time and a place. Lawyers provide protection (often against other lawyers) and force you to make plans to guard against the downsides that your entrepreneurially optimistic natures often overlook.

Yes, lawyers definitely have a time and a place. The place is always in the *lawyer's* office — you can't afford to pay a lawyer to travel to *your* office — or on the phone, and the times are as follows:

- ✔ When forming your corporation or LLC
- ✔ When taking in a partner or partners
- ✔ When creating shares of stock in your company — for you and for others
- ✔ When signing a lease, contract, or binding agreement
- ✔ When buying or selling a business
- ✔ When dealing with someone else's attorney on a conflictive issue
- ✔ When creating an employee handbook

✔ When designing employee bonus programs that result in company ownership for the employees

✔ When dealing with a situation that could result in expensive litigation (such as terminating a long-time employee)

No matter how much you want to avoid the expense of consulting with a lawyer, you're going to need to consult one at the start-up stage and on occasion throughout the life of your business. When these occasions present themselves, follow these suggestions on how best to find and utilize your lawyer:

✔ When you absolutely, positively have to find a lawyer, don't shop price. Shop quality *and* price. As with cars and quarterbacks, lawyers differ greatly in how they perform, and that difference usually translates into winning or losing. Check references closely.

✔ Get a quote on your prospective lawyer's hourly fees and ask for an estimate of the total tab in advance. The estimate may not hold up, but they will know that you're watching.

✔ Always ask for your invoices to be itemized. A lump sum invoice includes only time and rate, while an itemized invoice includes the date and time of each segment of work, the specific subject of each charge, and then the rate. An itemized invoice also indicates work that was done by others — paralegals, for example — their rates and charges for related materials.

✔ Don't let lawyers chitchat about golf and *Monday Night Football* if their meters are running.

✔ Lawyers are human beings too, which means they are not always right. They work in a gray profession, not a black-and-white one. The power of logic, theirs and yours, working in unison with their knowledge of the law, will play a significant role in your business. You are capable of logic too. Don't be afraid to use it in their presence. If a lawyer won't listen to you, ditch 'em.

✔ Lawyers are no different than employees, accountants, and anyone else you hire to provide a service. Don't be afraid to fire them when they fail to perform up to your expectations.

Tax advisors

Tax advisors, like lawyers, are professionals too. The services they provide aren't rooted in conflict, but it can be equally annoying to hire and pay them.

The role of tax advisors, in essence, is to provide you with the information you need to pay your taxes, make tax-wise business decisions, keep score of your progress, and help you manage your business. We cover the hiring of tax advisors in Chapter 16.

Consultants

Hiring a consultant is akin to playing wild-card poker, meaning that fate will be a factor in determining whether or not you select the right one. That is not to say your success or failure is entirely in fate's hands, because the more effort you put into the hiring process, the better your chances will be to do the job right.

Consultants can provide a wide array of services. Several of the areas where consultants can help the most include computer and information systems, tax issues, sales, and marketing.

You will find more than one way to use and pay consultants. Some consultants offer their clients advice only; other consultants dive head-first into their client's business and get their hands dirty. Some consultants are paid by the hour, others by retainer (a fixed fee every month). It all depends on what you want and what you can afford.

We've collected these lessons on how to get the most out of your consultant:

- ✔ **Lesson #1:** Engage a consultant as if hiring a key staff employee. Network to find the best one and always check references carefully, being careful to avoid consultants who have had only big corporate (as opposed to small-business) experience. Despite what they'll tell you, most don't understand what running a small business is like. Hire only consultants with lots of small-business experience.

- ✔ **Lesson #2:** Whatever you do, don't hand over to your consultants the responsibility to make key decisions. Also, never bet the house on the suggestions they make. Make your consultants prove themselves on smaller issues before you make the bigger changes they're recommending. And never forget that you're in charge.

- ✔ **Lesson #3:** Offer no long-term contracts. Build in a quick-exit option in the event that you don't get what you expected.

- ✔ **Lesson #4:** Understand that the ultimate cost of engaging ineffectual consultants can be measured only in part by their fees. Add misdirection, upset employees, and time lost, and consultants are capable of running up monumental tabs in surprisingly short periods of time.

- ✔ **Lesson #5:** Don't hesitate to show consultants the door when they aren't doing the job.

Governments

If only entrepreneurs would understand that the government is often an uncontrollable random event, like a fire or a flood or a competitor moving next door. This is especially true of the federal government, where the small-business owner may find it quite difficult to so much as talk to those officials who are the actual decision-makers, let alone to get their problems resolved.

So, come to terms with the fact that you'll sometimes have to comply with the government's unwieldy and often unfriendly rules and regulations. Don't antagonize unfriendly government employees — they can make your life miserable. Do what needs to be done to satisfy the sometimes disagreeable government employees, treat the agreeable ones like you'd want your own employees to be treated, and don't shoot the messenger — most government employees are only trying to do their job. In Chapter 15, we offer lots of helpful advice for dealing with government regulations.

Thinning out the herd

Back in the early 1980s, runaway inflation ruled the land. The Federal Reserve System (lovingly known as The Fed) decided that something had to be done to contain this silent but evil economic killer. Paul Volcker, the head of the Fed in those days, believed that the best way to fight inflation was to raise interest rates.

Over the next two years, U.S. interest rates spiraled crazily upward. And upward. Until, lo and behold, they topped out somewhere in the neighborhood of 20 percent, give or take a percentage point or two. What this meant for the hapless small-business owner who needed to borrow new money, or whose interest rate on current borrowings floated was that she was paying 21 or 22 percent interest on borrowed funds. Try booking that kind of interest expense for a year or two and see what it does to your profit & loss statement!

A friend of ours (we'll call him Don) was in the retail and wholesale appliance business at the time, with a warehouse full of inventory and a ledger full of receivables. Receivables and inventory, as every small-business owner knows, are the two most voracious gobblers of cash on the balance sheet, and each time Volcker would edge the discount rate up another point or so, the profits of Don's business would take another hit.

Fast forward two years. Interest rates had plunged back to the single digits again, inflation was tamed, and economic serenity ruled the land. Oh, yes, and Don's doors were still open, although a significant number of his competitors had closed. Those lofty interest rates, it turned out, had placed a premium on efficient business practices, and those who couldn't control their inventory, collect their receivables, and otherwise run a profitable business had paid the ultimate price. The herd had been thinned, so to speak.

What turned out to be fatal for Don's competitors turned out to be beneficial for Don. With so many of his competitors out of business, an expanded market was available to him.

Instead of spending his time moaning about "those stupid bureaucrats" and feeling sorry for himself as his profits were eaten up by interest payments, Don kept his eye on the basics of running his business: managing inventory, collecting receivables, and doing the things that make customers and employees happy.

The lesson here? Learn to react to a sometimes small-business–unfriendly government the same way Don did — by turning today's problems into tomorrow's opportunities.

Chapter 9

Defining a Marketing Strategy: Product Development, Promotion, Sales, Distribution, and Pricing

. . . .

In This Chapter

▶ Defining marketing

▶ Sharing ideas on inexpensive promotions

▶ Selling benefits rather than features

▶ Setting up a distribution system

▶ Pricing your products or services

▶ Getting your products and services sold

. . . .

*C*lose the door, turn off the phone and stereo, and put on your thinking cap; it's time to discuss marketing and the process that defines it. For marketing is, after all, the facet of your business that is going to separate your product or service from the hundreds (or is that thousands?) of competing products or services in the marketplace. And yet marketing is typically either number one or number two on the list of the small-business owner's most difficult skills to master. (Managing employees is the other.)

The process of marketing is often misunderstood by the typical small-business owner; nevertheless to be a successful marketer requires a number of make-it-or-break-it skills that, more than any others, will separate the mediocre (or failed) company from the long-lived or fast-track ones. The importance of marketing as a business skill is witnessed by the fact that some less-than-stellar products and services are quite successful thanks to first-class marketing efforts (McDonald's *doesn't* have the best hamburgers in the world), but rarely are first-rate products successful through inadequate marketing efforts.

Marketing Illustrated; Marketing Defined

Before we discuss the five basic components of the marketing process, you should first understand the true meaning of the word "marketing," as well as the true meaning of two other words that are sometimes confused with it: sales and distribution. The definitions are as follows:

- ✔ **Marketing:** Marketing is the manner in which product development, sales, promotion, distribution, and pricing are bundled together into an overall plan designed to deliver your company's products or services to the marketplace and hence to the ultimate customer.

- ✔ **Sales:** Sales is a component of the marketing process whereby your company, either directly or indirectly, contacts, convinces, and contracts with customers to purchase your products or services.

- ✔ **Distribution:** Distribution defines the channels (such as retailers, wholesalers, or catalogs) that are used in the sales process.

In large corporations, the senior executive in charge of marketing is always in a pivotal position in the success or failure of the business. In a small business, however, the marketing function usually rests with the owner.

These five key components make up the marketing process: product development, promotion, sales, distribution, and pricing. The rest of this chapter explains these five elements and includes tips and suggestions aimed at helping you develop your marketing skills.

Product and Service Development

For most entrepreneurs, product and service development is the most enjoyable part of building a business. Whether refining an existing product or service or inventing a brand-spanking new one, many of us hang out our shingles in the first place because we believe we have a valuable product or service to offer. We love the nuances of our product or service and are forever looking for ways to redefine and expand it.

Eric is an excellent example of how product and service development can define the direction of a small business. From his work in the corporate world, Eric understood the financial services industry from the inside, and he sought to take that knowledge to help people improve their personal financial situation. He looked forward to developing new services and was forever tinkering, refining, and adding new twists to existing ideas in the financial services industry. For him, developing new services to offer his customers was fun and interesting and something he never tired of.

Eric's initial service was personal financial counseling. Because he enjoyed teaching, he soon began teaching personal finance courses through the University of California at Berkeley.

Eric also was beginning to write for a variety of newspapers and magazines and was hard at work on a book proposal. Today, somewhat to his surprise, Eric's writing takes most of his time, whereas in the early stages of the business, Eric had envisioned reaching more people and growing his business through his financial counseling practice.

Jim's second business had a similar growth pattern also resulting from the development of new products. His retail and wholesale sporting goods company spawned a screen-printing operation as he strove to add new lines of products. (His sporting goods company wanted to be able to number and letter the athletic jerseys it sold to teams.) Fifteen years later, that simple product development idea had grown into a stand-alone $25-million business.

Despite the fact that too many small businesses go about product and service development in haphazard ways, a defined process exists. That process goes something like this:

1. **The idea**

   The idea itself is hatched by someone, not necessarily the entrepreneur. No matter where it comes from, however, it is always "championed" by the entrepreneur.

2. **Evaluation**

   The idea is evaluated by the entrepreneur and those responsible for product development, with particular attention to such issues as profit potential, ease of manufacturing (where applicable), competition, and pricing.

3. **Opportunity analysis**

   The product or service is presented to a few, select customers in an attempt to ascertain the size and scope of the potential market.

4. **Product development**

   Assuming that the idea has been evaluated, the opportunity identified, and the project is still a go, the time has come to develop the product or service. Time to dot the i's and cross the t's in preparation for the next step.

5. **Test marketing**

   This is the time to test the (hopefully) completed product or service with a few specific customers, with the intent of working out any bugs, in preparation for the product's introduction to the marketplace.

6. Introduction to the marketplace

This is the time to begin the advertising program, the press releases, and the training of the salespeople responsible for selling the new product or service.

Not every idea is going to turn into a workable or profitable product or service. You need to be critical and tough as you proceed through these steps, especially when you reach the second step — the evaluation process. Be sure to ask the following questions:

✔ Do you have the staff and the cash to back the idea?

✔ Does the idea fit your product line, mission statement, and values?

✔ Is it already being offered by the competition and, if so, is your idea distinctly better or more competitive than theirs?

Make sure that you can answer "yes" to these three questions before moving on to the opportunity analysis stage. The product development process is expensive, and you're better off cutting your losses early in the process rather than later.

New product ideas can come from a variety of sources, including vendors, trade magazines, and of course, employees. Unquestionably, however, the majority of new product ideas come as a result of talking with and listening to customers. After all, customers are the people who are most familiar with the use of the product or service, and customers will, in most cases, be the same people who will ultimately consume them. The alert small-business owner's ears should always be open for customer ideas, no matter how off-the-wall they may appear to be. Or, when your employee is doing the selling, your ears must always be open to those in contact with your customers.

The illustrious *...For Dummies* series was, in fact, inspired by a prospective customer's comment. John Kilcullen, CEO of IDG Books Worldwide, Inc., the publishing company that produced this book, overheard a bookstore conversation about computer books in which the customer was frustrated at not being able to find a basic computer book that could answer even the dumbest questions.

Promotion: Getting Out the Word

Promotion is the process of informing potential customers about your company and its products and services and then influencing them to purchase what you're selling. Promotional activities include word-of-mouth advertising, networking, media advertising, and publicity.

Some of your promotional efforts will be undertaken to directly generate sales, while others will aim to educate, inform, and plant the seed for future sales.

Before you invest in any promotional effort, you must first determine your objective. With advertising, for example, a company owner may fault an ad for not generating results, failing to realize that the ad never included any kind of *call to action* to begin with. If you want to make the phone ring, your ad better give a good reason to call, and it better have a prominent presentation of your phone number. On the other hand, if you're looking for foot traffic, you have got to put forward a time-sensitive, compelling reason to visit your business, such as a one-time discount or the appearance of a VIP.

To put it in one sentence: Know your objective and craft your messages accordingly.

Networking

Networking is the process of connecting with people in order to make good things happen. Networking offers a host of benefits to those who partake in it, the two most obvious being the opportunity to promote your products or services and the opportunity for you to learn from your peers. These two benefits are the primary reasons that organizations such as the Chamber of Commerce, the Rotary, and Toastmasters exist.

But wait. Before you run out and join your local business organizations, think about using the networks you already have. Your friends, your relatives, your alma mater, your church, your children's school, and the social organizations you belong to are all viable networks. With a little priming (proactivity on your part), many of your existing networks will be happy to give your product or service a try. All you have to do is initiate the priming.

This priming can come in many forms — a telephone call, a flyer in the mail, or even a casual mention during a conversation following a school event. All these are viable parts of the network priming process and all are available at very little cost.

You can improve your network priming with these tips:

- ✔ Make a list of the networks you currently have. How many are being sufficiently primed? For those that are not, what can you do to prime them?
- ✔ At the beginning of every year, make a goal for yourself to add one more network to your current inventory.

> ✔ Make sure that you have a professional-looking business card and don't be shy about handing it out.
>
> ✔ Be sure to follow up every networking opportunity. A telephone call or a letter the next day will remind your networking prospects of your business, in addition to giving them the impression that you go about managing it professionally.
>
> ✔ Remember that networking works both ways. Help another small business within your network, and you can usually expect that the other business will eventually help you. Such is the basis for successful networking.

Be thoughtful and careful when networking the people you know. People are busy and bombarded daily (aren't you?) with tons of advertising and solicitations. The last thing most people want is to be accosted by a pushy salesperson in what they thought were the friendly and safe confines of a school or church. Start with a low-key approach: Assemble a one-page summary or a simple flyer of your company's products or services, and mail them to people you know.

Word-of-mouth: The power of referrals

What do you think when you hear a radio spot that says the Greasy Spoon Cafe serves the best burgers in town, but five minutes later, a friend tells you that it's Danny's Diner that really serves the best burgers? Who are you going to believe — the radio ad or your friend?

If you're like most people, you'll believe your friend. After all, radio ads are scripted and paid advertising. Not so with friends; they have no script and generally no agenda, which makes them a credible resource. Such is the power of word-of-mouth referrals.

The problem, of course, is that you can't dictate the script of a referral the way you can with a radio ad. If Danny's hamburgers aren't up to snuff, Danny's would be better off if his customers kept their mouths shut. Word-of-mouth referrals tell it the way the customer sees it, not as the owner would like him to see it.

And so it is with you and your business: You must first make sure that your burgers are tasty before you start asking for referrals. After you know they're tasty (your customers will be the judge), however, the time is ripe to open the referral floodgates. Referrals are just another reason of many why you should do a top-notch job providing your product or service, as well as following up with more service. If you take care of your customers in the early stages of your business's life, the referrals from those satisfied customers should take care of you and your business in the future.

Wouldn't it be nice if all of your satisfied customers would immediately jump on the phone and begin telling the world how wonderful your products and services are? Think of the steady stream of unsolicited customers you'd have, without having to go to the trouble (and the expense) of working with the advertising department of a newspaper or radio station. Unfortunately, however, most customers aren't disposed to passing on referrals, not without encouragement anyway. You must do some of the encouraging.

Every time you serve a satisfied customer, follow up the sale either by calling the satisfied customer or asking her to fill out a feedback card, making sure the transaction went to her satisfaction, and ask for one referral. Then, assuming that referral turns into a sale, do it again six months down the road.

Another suggestion on how to encourage your customers to provide referrals: Whenever a new customer does business with you, ask how he heard about you. When the customer replies that he has been referred to you by say, Harry, make sure that the next time Harry stops by, he gets a sincere thank you and possibly a discount or a freebie. You are thereby rewarding Harry's behavior, not necessarily a new trick in the motivational game, but an effective one.

One final advantage of word-of-mouth promotion: You don't have to hire an ad agency or media consultant to do the job for you; you can do it yourself. The price is right.

Media advertising

Our definition of *advertising* is a program of paid messages designed to inform and educate large numbers of prospective consumers on the features and benefits of your product or services. Although the ultimate long-term purpose of advertising is, of course, to persuade the consumer to purchase your product or service, some short-term advertising strategies may focus on the development of name recognition only.

Good advertising is about repetition. Mention Federal Express, and people remember "When It Absolutely, Positively Has To Be There Overnight." M&Ms are remembered for the slogan "Melts In Your Mouth, Not In Your Hand."

Note that none of these slogans was implanted in your mind via a one-shot advertising blitz or a slogan-of-the-month effort. Those well-known brands became well-known in part because they invested heavily in advertising; and then kept their messages focused and consistent.

Almost certainly, the companies mentioned previously view their advertising as an important investment instead of a dreaded expense. When you can afford to budget the kind of money necessary to put a repetitive message in front of your prospective customers, you too should view it as an investment.

Because you're not a large company, you can't afford to spend buckets of money on media advertising. That's why we highly recommend that, in the early stages of your business where cash is generally scarce, you focus on networking and referrals as well as other low-cost advertising tools to get your first customers in the door. When you are ready to venture out into the world of paid advertising, use one of these three methods of developing your advertisements to get the best results in a cost-effective manner:

✔ You can create your ads in-house, either by writing them yourself or by hiring an employee who has advertising and creative talent. Hiring a creative employee makes sense if you have a fairly small advertising budget or if you have access to franchise or supplier ad materials that simply need to be customized for delivery to the media. Make sure however, that when your ads are done in-house, serious editing is performed on everything that goes out your door. Mistakes or misspellings in advertising materials reflects poorly on the advertiser.

✔ You can work with freelance copywriters, designers, media buyers, or other resource professionals. You, or someone in your company, serves as the point person in corralling available talent to create your advertising materials. Contract projects on an as-needed basis, and maintain responsibility for continuity, accuracy, and timeliness.

✔ You can hire an advertising agency to handle all of your advertising needs. This way, instead of calling a designer when you need a trade booth, a copywriter when you need an ad, or a direct-mail house when you want a mailing, you turn to a single resource. A good agency should review your entire communications needs, create a single campaign, and produce all the materials that you need to prepare the message that works best for you. Yes, you pay for the expertise and service, but you free yourself for other activities. Also, assuming the agency you select is a good one (check references carefully), your advertising program will give you a bang for your bucks.

To find the advertising resource that's right for you, watch, read, or listen to media (radio, TV, magazine, newspaper), select the ads you like, and then call the business that's doing the advertising and find out who produced or assisted in producing the ad. Or simply network with other small-business owners who have advertised and ask questions to determine who and what worked for them. Also network with your vendors, your customers, or within your business organizations. Be sure to check your prospective advertisers' credentials and get firm quotes on the cost of their services.

Successful advertising requires plenty of focus. Focusing on the proper consumer demographics is important. If, for instance, you are selling opera star Placido Domingo recordings and advertising on a Country & Western radio station, you're focusing on the wrong audience. Make sure that your message focuses on the benefits your product offers, not necessarily on its features.

The following media options are the most widely used for spreading your message:

Yellow Pages

Small businesses, especially locally based small businesses, *are* the Yellow Pages. This medium of advertising virtually was created for, and belongs to, hometown retailers and service suppliers. Looking for a hardware store, a candy shop, or somewhere to rent a tux? Many prospective customers will head for the Yellow Pages first.

Generally speaking, if your small business is looking to advertise and if your clientele is primarily local, consider the Yellow Pages first. The relatively low cost of ads in the Yellow Pages allows smaller businesses to compete with the bigger ones. Best of all, ads in the Yellow Pages have an extended shelf life; they can be found next to most people's telephones for at least a year or more.

Be creative with your ad, and remember that bigger (which the Yellow Pages sales rep will push for, thanks to the commission) isn't necessarily better. In the Yellow Pages, your ad will be placed right there with all your direct competitors. Your ad needs to set you apart from the rest of the pack. Also remember that oftentimes there may be more than one category for your product or services. (Suppose that you sell screen-printed T-shirts. You could be listed under T-shirts, Advertising, or Screen Printing.)

Newspapers

In general, newspaper advertising requires less cash outlay than most other forms of advertising. Most ads are black and white, so production costs are low. Newspaper ads are great for specific geographic targeting (such as zoned advertising, in which areas of town are targeted for specific advertising content in news sections tailored to them). Most large metropolitan newspapers offer community sections with advertising targeted at local customers.

Newspaper ads have a relatively short life span, don't offer the same quality of reproduction that other print advertising tools do, and are oftentimes quickly scanned by their readers.

Radio

Radio, along with magazines, can better target a specific demographic group. Also, similar to newspapers, radio focuses on a specific geographic area. Want to sell acne cream in Albuquerque? Then, buy commercial time on the local hard rock station.

Additional advantages of radio advertising are that it allows for short lead times, and can be targeted to people in their cars. Also, if speedy reaction is what you're looking for, radio advertising is a proven answer. Studies indicate that approximately 75 percent of the responses to radio advertising occur in the first week after being aired.

That same immediacy, however, is also the downside of radio advertising. If your prospects are not tuned in at the exact moment that your ad airs, you're out of luck. That's why radio advertisers use the term "frequency" when planning their schedules. They aim to have the same ad run over and over, often on several stations in the same market area, hoping to catch the attention of the prospective customer at least a few times.

Television

Television takes radio advertising one step further, adding video to the audio, thus making more impact on the listener. TV also adds prestige to the business doing the advertising, although not without significant costs. Finally, similar to radio ads, good television ads can evoke a speedy response.

Television ad buys — the buying of time to present your ads — come in two packages: *network* buys and *spot* buys.

Network buys of time are megabuys. When you hear that a 30-second spot for an ad shown during the Super Bowl costs $1 million, that's a network buy, which means that the advertiser is placing its ad on the entire network and reaching its entire viewership of millions during the Super Bowl.

Spot buys, on the other hand, are local time buys. Even within the Super Bowl, for example, some ad time slots are left free by the network for use by local stations. Those ads will be priced based on the size of the audience reached by the local station and the time slot — the time of day the ad runs.

As with buying radio ad spots, television ad buys, especially those on a local basis, usually involve a frequency strategy, that is, the ad is intended to be viewed frequently over relatively short periods of time. TV ads also work best when the message is clear, fairly simple, and entertaining.

The cost for producing a television ad can run the gamut. You can have the local station assemble a simple 30-second ad relatively inexpensively, you can have an ad agency produce the ad (the same ad agency that does your print advertising), or you may be able to produce the ad yourself. Look at what the other advertisers in your category are doing, and be sure that your ad ranks right up there with the best of the kind.

After your ad is produced and you're ready to buy time slots on the local station, approach the scheduling process with your facts in hand. Know the age, gender, and programming preferences of your customer prospects. Then either your station representative (the salesperson representing the TV station) or your media buyer (the ad agency that is putting together your ad program) can show you the viewer demographics and other viewing patterns for various programs to help you select a schedule that will target the right audience. Discuss your overall strategy with your media buyer, making sure that he or she also understands your budget constraints.

Magazines (local and national)

The primary benefit of magazine advertising is that the advertiser can target specific audiences, as opposed to newspaper ads where anyone and everyone may be the reader.

Run an ad in *Scientific American,* and you'll attract one kind of audience; place an ad in *GQ,* and you'll reach another. An additional advantage of magazine ads is that they have a longer life than the other media, as magazines are often passed from reader to reader. Compare this longer-life benefit to radio or TV, whose ads are gone after their broadcast cycle.

If you are a manufacturer, for example, a magazine for your trade can offer a rare degree of consumer-targeting potential. Readers of trade magazines are more than likely potential consumers; in many cases, readers will peruse a trade magazine with the specific intent of studying its ads. See Chapter 6 for information on a reference book entitled *Small Business Sourcebook* (Gale), which includes lists of trade publications for all types of businesses.

The downside of magazine advertising is that it is a high-budget item relative to the other media, especially if you're using high-profile publications. The cost of a full-page, full-color ad in a national magazine can easily hit five figures.

A few other interesting notes on magazine advertising:

✔ You must plan your magazine ads well in advance. Often, magazine ads must be submitted more than two months before the publication hits the mailbox or newsstand.

✔ Cross your fingers when it comes to placement of your ad. Everyone wants front-of-the-magazine-right-hand-page placement, but at some magazines you may stand in line behind those long-standing, multiple-page advertisers who have built up clout with the magazine over the years. If you're an infrequent advertiser, you may be placed in less-desirable space.

✔ The more upscale the magazine, the more expensive the space. Plan accordingly.

Online advertising

An increasingly viable option for many small businesses today is a company Web site. Web sites are relatively inexpensive to establish (several hundred dollars and up) and maintain.

One distinct advantage of online advertising is that it "levels the playing field." Smaller companies can compete with the big boys by building a professional Web site and maintaining it diligently.

Like other advertising media, the success of a Web site will be determined by how many people are introduced to your company and how frequently your message falls on their eyes. Following are several tips on how to build a strong Web presence and how to keep your Web customers coming back for more information:

✔ **Up-to-date content:** Your Web site information should be updated on a regular basis so your visitors have an incentive to come back. You are looking for repeat visitors here.

✔ **Functionality:** A wide variety of Internet tools are available to take your business beyond a basic Web presence, enabling you to communicate and collaborate with both customers and potential customers. Ask your local Web site designer for a list of these tools.

✔ **Easy navigation:** Keep the look and the layout clean. If information is difficult to come by, if the flow of your site is not intuitive, or if the font or the background makes information difficult to read, visitors will move on to the hundreds of other choices on the Web.

✔ **Differentiation:** Your site needs to stand out by being creative with both the text and the graphics. Once visitors arrive you need to make sure they understand what it is that makes your site (and your products or services) different from the crowd.

Other advertising vehicles

A wide range of other, usually less-expensive advertising options are available. That range includes such media as billboards, buses, and other transportation-oriented media, as well as such less-professional advertising tools as flyers, posters, and handbills.

A wide variety of advertising options are available to every small-business owner. We recommend you research the various media carefully, making your decisions methodically after studying all the alternatives. Ultimately, the target of your message, the depth of your pocketbook, and your own expertise will determine the medium that's best for you.

Publicity

Publicity, in effect, is "free advertising." Typical examples include feature stories and product (or service) announcements published in either print or broadcast media. Publicity is especially effective as a promotional tool because people (specifically, prospective consumers) give more credibility to what they read or hear when it comes from news sources, whereas their belief in advertising messages understandably is often tainted with varying degrees of suspicion.

The downside to free publicity, of course, is that similar to word of mouth, you can't control what is said about your company or your product or service. Make sure that what you are about to publicize can withstand the sharp eye of media scrutiny. After all, members of the media know that to maintain their credibility they must present the facts as they really are, not as you say they are. They have been trained to be suspicious.

Media resources that can offer the publicity you're looking for include local newspapers, business periodicals, TV and radio stations, and magazines. Don't limit your search for free publicity to only the business-oriented outlets; oftentimes, exposure in the news or human interest stories will be of more benefit. Generally speaking, more consumers read or listen to news and human interest stories than to those media outlets that focus only on business people.

The news release

One tool of publicity is the news release. A *news release* is a notification sent to appropriate newspaper, magazine, and radio and television editors and/or reporters. Send most news releases about your business to the business editor or business reporter; in some cases, however, you can send them to the editor of a specific area, such as sports or lifestyle. News releases are appropriate for such occasions as the opening of a new store, the introduction of new products and services, or the procurement of an important new customer or key employee.

A secondary publicity tool is contacting an appropriate editor or reporter and advising her of your unique story (the more unique the story, the better the chance of the media picking it up). The best way to determine the appropriate editor or reporter is to look at the bylines on newspaper or magazine public interest articles that are about companies similar to yours or listen for the name of the reporter on public interest radio or TV stories.

The hook

In most cases, you need some sort of a *hook* to attract publicity. A hook is the characteristic that makes you or your product or service "unique" and of "publicity value." Examples of hooks include a restaurant where the waiters are intentionally rude to its patrons (it also happens to serve the best Italian food in town), the gas station that gives newspapers to its customers with every fill up, and the antique shop with goats in its lobby for visitors to feed. A secondary advantage of having a hook is that it makes your attempts to find publicity easier. A bona fide hook will interest the media in your story, as the media writer will perceive it as something of interest to the readers or viewers.

How about your business? What exactly is *your* hook? Have you thought about this question? If you can't think of a hook, perhaps you need to do some thinking about your overall approach to marketing. Everyone can use a hook, whether you're looking for free publicity, writing a radio commercial, or handing out flyers on the street corner. If your business doesn't have a hook, you should develop one.

Hooks incidentally, don't have to be as "exotic" as goats in the lobby. Hooks can be as simple as a bowl of Tootsie Rolls next to the cash register, follow-up telephone calls to thank your customers for their business, or happy birthday cards to your best customers.

Here are some additional tips on how to develop "free advertising" for your business:

- ✔ Write an article for your local newspaper on a subject that relates to you or your business. If the article is well-written and has a special hook, it could bring you the publicity you seek.

- ✔ Give talks or teach classes about your profession or business (or hook) to local groups such as the Chamber of Commerce, Rotary Club, civic associations, and other groups.

- ✔ Hire a public relations firm — PR firms are to publicity what ad agencies are to advertising. (Their fees are similar, too!)

Finally, whenever appropriate, remember to send a photo of yourself (and of your event, if there is one) along with any publicity requests. Photos tend to personalize the request and give the reporter someone to relate to. Make sure, however, that the photos you send are of professional quality, as you and your business will be judged accordingly.

Distribution: Moving Products into Channels

Distribution is the *channel* that moves your product or service to the ultimate consumer. Distribution channels vary within the same industry and apply to all businesses. No one right or wrong way exists to distribute your products; you can, however, almost always find a *best* way.

Two basic categories of distribution exist, depending on whether a middleman comes between the manufacturer of the products (or the provider of the services) and the consumer. Direct distribution occurs when no middleman is involved; indirect distribution involves a middleman.

Jim's fourth business, for example, manufactured imprinted sportswear. The distribution channel that his company selected was indirect distribution, whereby his salespeople sold the company's products to both small and large retail businesses, and those retailers added the price of their services to the products and resold them to the consumer.

Meanwhile, competing companies within Jim's industry selected other distribution channels. Some sold directly to the consumer; mail-order sales companies are a good example of direct distribution. Others may include direct-response advertisements in magazines and television. Today, the Internet is also a direct distribution option. One manufacturing company in Jim's industry even established retail outlets of its own, in addition to maintaining its own sales force — companies can choose more than one distribution channel.

Each distribution channel has evolved for a reason, and each has its strengths and weaknesses. Following is a discussion of the various distribution options.

Product distribution versus service distribution

You'll see an identifiable difference between the distribution of products and the distribution of services. We spend the majority of this section discussing the channels of product distribution, as that process is usually much more complicated than is service distribution. A service business uses one of two basic distribution options: direct or indirect. The vast majority of service businesses use the direct distribution channel, that is selling their services directly to the consumer with no middleman. The computer-repair company, for example, sells its services directly to its customers, with the process resembling that involving a plumber, an electrician, or a tax preparer. Direct, one-on-one, seller-to-buyer interactions are the order of the day.

Occasionally, a middleman is involved in service distribution. Agents are the most typical example of middlemen, with typical examples including those small-business owners who sell such personal services as writing, speaking, and entertaining. Independent agents contract to work for their clients (writers, speakers, entertainers) in business arrangements with those who employ them.

Direct distribution of products

Similar to the direct distribution of services, the direct distribution of products involves establishing one-on-one relationships with the buyer, without passing any middlemen along the way. We discuss examples of this direct distribution channel for products in the following sections.

Retail

What better way to avoid a middleman and be close to your customer than to physically interact with him in a retail environment? Knowing your customer is tantamount to any small business's success, and a retail distribution system offers a perfect vehicle for doing just that. Retail chains like The Gap have chosen to sell their products through "direct distribution."

Another advantage of retail distribution is that you retain the entire markup on your products. Still another advantage is that, in most cases, you don't have the expense of maintaining charge accounts because retailing is primarily a cash business. Establishing charge accounts (accounts receivable), which we discuss in Chapter 11, is like lending money to your customers; thus charge accounts are an extremely expensive way of selling products or services. (Yes, credit card charges — VISA, MasterCard, American Express, and others — may not be *immediate* cash either, but they do represent a dependable stream of cash, and you don't have to worry about collecting them. You do, of course, pay a slight fee for these privileges.)

The disadvantage of retail distribution is that the costs of maintaining and staffing a retail store are high. Also, because you can't have your eye on the till and the door all the time, retail is susceptible to theft of both cash and products.

Direct mail

The increasing popularity of direct-mail advertising is by no means accidental and shows no signs of slowing down. Direct mail refers to the mailing of flyers and advertisements directly to a targeted audience. The success and/ or failure of any direct-mail campaign is usually tied to the quality of both the mailing list and the promotional piece itself.

One of direct mail's advantages is its capability to directly target and reach qualified prospects whether they want to be reached or not. Another key advantage of direct mail is that, given the sophistication of today's mailing lists, you can target your programs to exactly the demographics you choose. Looking for a list of potential customers with two or more children who own their own home and have an annual income in excess of $100,000? No sweat. You can purchase a list and do the mailing yourself. Or you can employ a firm that will do it all for you.

One disadvantage of direct mail is the relatively high cost per contact. The cost-per-thousand of direct mailings is significantly higher than the cost-per-thousand to reach newspaper or magazine readers via advertising. The difference, of course, is that — if your mailing list is good — every recipient represents a *qualified prospect* (someone who fits your demographic projections of who is most likely to want your product or service), whereas only a fraction of your advertising contacts may be qualified. A secondary disadvantage of direct mail is that many consumers simply do not like businesses that use the direct-mail medium; thus you can alienate potential customers.

This collection of tips gives you some ideas on how to develop your own direct-mail program:

- ✔ Collect existing direct-mail pieces that you like, and use them as examples for your own design. Contact the business who did the mail piece, and find out how it was done and who did it.

- ✔ Concentrate on solving your customer's problems, not on selling him products. People don't want to pop pills; they want to increase their energy, so if your vitamins can help them do that, tell them so.

- ✔ Purchase or rent your list by interviewing several different list companies. (Look in the Yellow Pages under "Mailing Lists" and/or call your trade magazine reps and inquire about their subscription lists.) Costs should vary from $25 to $75 per thousand names.

- ✔ Consider using a self-mailer where possible, thereby saving the cost of an envelope.

- ✔ Stick with it; don't give up after the first mailing. Many consumers need to see the same message several times before they react.

- ✔ When you intend to follow-up the mailing with a phone call, stagger your mailings.

Finally, be sure to maintain a complete record of the results of your mailing, detailing the number of responses and the number of orders that result. Don't set your goals overly high — a 2 to 3 percent response rate on a first-time direct mailing is usually considered good.

Mail order catalogs

Mail order catalogs have enjoyed a leap in popularity as the American shopper does more and more of her shopping from the comfort of the home. Catalogs can be expensive to produce and mail but remember, the alternative is opening a retail store, which is very expensive. Companies such as Lands' End and L.L. Bean are examples of businesses that have built a loyal customer base using the catalog distribution channel.

Make no mistake about it, however: Catalog selling is an expensive channel, especially for start-ups. Creating and mailing a top-notch catalog (if you can't afford a top-notch catalog, you probably don't belong in this distribution channel) can run into the tens of thousands of dollars. Initial outlays include the charge for obtaining mailing lists, the costs of creating and developing the catalog, and the mailing expenses. And don't forget the additional cost (and risk) of maintaining enough inventory to be able to ship your orders within a reasonable amount of time.

Internet sales

Certainly the new kid on the block, Internet selling is, depending on whom you talk to, either the most exciting invention since sliced bread or little more than another fad like the hula hoop. In essence, Internet sales are another form of catalog sales; you simply dial up the company's Web site, click around until you find the items you are looking for, plug in your credit card number, and wait for the package to arrive by mail. Distribution via the Internet is easy on the shopper (no dodging traffic or fighting crowds) and easy on the vendor (no mall rent or expensive mailing lists). Incidentally, this relatively inexpensive way of reaching customers also allows Internet prices for most products (except for those which are quite costly to ship) to be competitive.

Internet selling works best for the small business when you have an off-the-beaten-path product that can't be found anywhere else. One company we know sells, via the Internet, car-mounting brackets for carrying fly rods on the top of automobiles. A national magazine recently published an article about a man who successfully sells emus over the Internet!

Indirect distribution

Indirect distribution defines the process whereby consumer products or services first pass through a middleman before reaching the consumer. Examples of indirect distribution include the following.

Retailers

Traversing the aisles of a Wal-Mart or Kmart store, you find that every product on its shelves is from a manufacturer somewhere that has opted for this secondhand retailing method of indirect distribution. After all, Wal-Mart and Kmart aren't in business to manufacture products. Instead they are there to do what they do best: *Sell* them.

The advantage of selling to retailers is that you only have to deal with one, or a few, customers — the retailer's buyer(s) — which simplifies the distribution process immensely.

This one-stop selling process enhances the *relationship selling* process, that is, the establishment of a relationship between the vendor and the customer. (For more on "relationship selling," see "Sales: Where the Rubber Hits the Road" in this chapter.) In this case, the relationship would be between the manufacturer's salesperson and the retailer's buyer. Meanwhile, it is virtually impossible to develop relationships when you are dealing with thousands of customers.

One distinct disadvantage of selling your products to retailers, especially those with multiple stores, is that they often use the size of the orders they place as leverage to become extremely demanding on such issues as price, delivery, and packaging. And, yes, on payment-related issues, too. Jim's sportswear company had included a number of the nation's largest retailers as its customers. Many would drag payments out for up to 60 days and demand a variety of invoice reductions whether Jim's company had agreed to them or not. Retailers, especially the larger ones, are able to keep their prices low for a reason, and more often than not, that "reason" comes at the expense of their vendors.

Wholesalers/distributors

Wholesale distribution is a perfect example of how the middleman process works. The typical wholesaler/distributor buys large quantities of products from manufacturers, breaks them down into manageable quantities, sometimes repackages them, and then offers them to the consumer in manageable, bite-sized pieces. Examples of wholesalers include plumbing and electrical-supply businesses whose primary customers are contractors and grocery wholesalers, whose primary customers are grocery and convenience stores.

Wholesale distribution exists for two reasons:

- ✔ Many manufacturers don't want the hassles associated with selling to consumers and smaller customers; after all, their expertise is in manufacturing, and that's what they want to specialize in.

- ✔ The consumer values having her products immediately available to her — she wants to see, touch, and feel the product before she buys it and will pay a premium for the privilege.

  Even in cases where a consumer can buy directly from the manufacturer, he will often opt for the convenience of buying locally, which also gives her someone to return the product to if it falls short of expectations.

The line between retail and wholesale has become blurred as several large retail/wholesale chains (Sam's, Costco) have emerged. Although these companies present themselves as "wholesalers to small business," they are in truth discount retailers, offering their products to anyone who can pass himself off as a business. The line between discount retailers and wholesalers is blurry; wholesalers usually sell their product only to businesses that resell it while discount retailers sell to the general public.

Repackaging

Another common example of indirect distribution is *repackaging:* that is, selling your products to another manufacturer or a developer of related products who offers them to their customers in another form. An advantage of repackaging is that, in most cases, the sales and marketing functions are left to the customer, allowing you to concentrate on the manufacturing part of your business. The disadvantages are that your profit margins are likely to suffer and you are likely to be overly dependent on one customer, the repackager.

You often see examples of repackaging in the grocery business where grocery store chains include on their shelves generic products with their name on the container of a product that someone else has manufactured. Many juices, frozen foods, and health and beauty aid products have been repackaged.

Deciding on distribution

We presented the preceding examples of direct and indirect distribution as a review of the options available to you. No easy answer exists to the question of which distribution channels would be best suited to your business. Our suggestion, as you set about determining the answer to this question, is to make the following lists as a starting point:

- ✔ List the distribution channels that your competitors are using. Rank the list with the most successful businesses at the top.

- ✔ List the channels that you can afford.

- ✔ List the channels that your research and intuition tell you will be successful in your industry five years from now.

Now compare the three lists, add a pinch of common sense, and determine the distribution channel that you prefer. Then gear up to meet the needs of that channel.

Whatever you do, don't lock yourself into any one distribution channel forever. Today's technologies are changing distribution. Remember, small business is about staying flexible — whatever distribution channel or channels you select should be subject to ongoing review.

Pricing: A Matter of Cost Plus Value

Someone once made the observation that pricing is two-thirds marketing and one-third financial. This statement goes against the grain of common sense, which suggests that nothing could be more financial than price. But if your pricing is not right, your marketing plan, no matter how well crafted, won't get off the ground. Prices too high? Your product won't sell. Prices too low? Your product may sell, but your company won't be profitable. The price, as the TV game show proclaims, must be right.

Still confused about the relationship between pricing and marketing? Think about the advertisements you see for special "Sales" and for one-time "Price Reductions." Why do you think businesses cut their prices — in effect lowering the profit margins on their products or services?

The answer? To attract more customers. That's marketing!

Thus, we present the basic discussion of pricing in this chapter because it's such an integral part of your overall marketing package. We talk more about the financial aspects of pricing in Chapter 11, in our presentation on the key elements of profitability. For now, however, we want you to think of price as a marketing issue.

To properly understand the role of pricing, we must first define the word *margin.* Margin is the difference between your cost to produce your product or service and the price for which it can be sold. If your widget costs your company $2 to manufacture and you sell it for $3, your margin is $1. Or, presented in terms of percentages, you have made a profit of $1 on that $3 sale, in the process providing you with a margin of 33 percent ($1 divided by $3).

Margins vary widely depending on the industry, so we can't give you guidelines about what margins to expect for your specific business. The margins on grocery items, for example, are relatively low, ranging typically from 5 to 10 percent. Meanwhile, the margins on computer software are relatively high, beginning at 20 percent and moving forever upward from there.

The six factors to consider when developing your pricing strategy

First, a word about "pricing strategy." Every business needs an overall strategy to guide it in making its pricing decisions. This means you'll need to "plan" your pricing strategy, as opposed to letting it evolve. Pricing should not be a decision you make on a day-to-day basis, but rather an extension of an overall plan.

For example, you may decide (by planning) to be the lowest-priced company in your niche, thus attracting customers who think they are getting a bargain by frequenting your business. Or you may want to have the highest prices in your niche — high prices send messages of quality and distinction to some customers. (Witness art galleries, fine wines, or Brooks Brothers shirts.) You may want to sell some of your products at a low price (known as loss leaders) in order to attract customers who will then buy other products at higher prices.

By contrast, if you owned a public utility, the formula for computing your prices would probably be to first determine your costs; then a regulatory agency would step forward and dictate your pricing based on those costs. This method of computing price is known as *cost-based pricing* and, unfortunately, is used by too many small-business owners as their only criterion for establishing price.

Because you don't (or so we're assuming anyway) own a public utility, you have the flexibility to determine your prices any way you see fit. With this flexibility in mind, read this discussion of the six factors that you need to consider before you can arrive at your pricing strategy:

Your marketing objectives

Marketing objectives will vary with the product or service you are selling. If, for example, you have a new product to introduce, your short-term objective may be to gain market share and preempt competition, in the process making your product well-known to the consumer. So your normal prices may be discounted over the short-term in order to achieve these long-term objectives, with profitability being shunted to the background. Discounted prices cannot go on forever, however, because sooner or later you won't have an ongoing business to provide them.

Another marketing objective may be to sell slow-moving inventory. Similar to the example of new product introduction, this objective also dictates short-term discounted pricing.

Be careful, however, not to get in the habit of continually discounting prices, unless that is, you want to be perceived as a discount retailer. One business maxim states that "if you lowball (discount prices) in the beginning, you'll lowball forever."

Most of the time, your marketing objective should be to maximize profit on your products without losing (too many) sales in the process. This is the objective that should dictate your long-term pricing decisions.

Cost to produce the product (or service)

Cost is the total of all the expenses involved in your product or service — not only direct costs, such as wages and salaries directly involved in the product, materials, and freight-in — but also indirect costs, such as administration, accounting, and sales.

Knowing the direct and indirect costs of your product is important in determining its *break-even point,* or the price below which you cannot sell your product without incurring losses. Cost is one barometer of your break-even point but should never be the primary determinant in the pricing process.

The process of determining your break-even cost is quite simple — assuming, that is, that your accounting system is capable of gathering the necessary figures (see Chapter 11 for more on accounting systems).

Here's how to determine your break-even cost:

1. **Determine the *direct cost allocation* for each product or service.**

   To do this: Add all the direct costs (those *directly* involved in its manufacture — wages specifically involved in the product or service, materials, and incoming freight) associated with that particular product or service during a specific accounting period (preferably one month, no more than one quarter).

   Divide the total amount of direct-cost dollars by the total number of products manufactured or services provided during that period.

2. **Determine the *indirect cost allocation* for each product or service.**

   Add the total dollars of your indirect costs (those *indirect* general and administrative costs that cannot be specifically tied to a product) for that period. Divide that number by the total number of products or services you provided in that period.

3. **Add the direct cost allocation to the indirect cost allocation.**

   The result is your break-even cost.

Anything above the break-even cost represents your profit on that product or service; anything below it represents your loss.

If you offer more than one product or service, this process of determining a break-even point for each product or service can become complicated. The sophistication of your accounting system will determine whether or not you gather enough information to make the many assumptions you'll need to make in order to arrive at an accurate break-even cost for each product or service. (See Chapter 11.)

Customer demand

The relative ease or difficulty in selling your product or service to the customer should play an important part in the pricing decision. What's the ratio of product on the market to supply available?

You see this factor at work every day as you watch gasoline prices at the pump fluctuate due to supply and demand factors. Although the price pressures in other industries may not be as readily apparent to the public as they are in the gasoline business, all industries are subject to similar supply and demand factors.

Comparative value to customer

Just as beauty is in the eyes of the beholder, so is the value of a product. In addition to knowing what your product is worth in your eyes, you also need to understand how much your product is *perceived* to be worth in the eyes of your customers.

The most obvious example of how the concept of perceived value works is in products related to the arts — paintings, sculptures, and yes, even books. Unlike generic products (such as aspirin and T-shirts) where the price seldom varies, the value of art-related products varies depending on the customer's perception. A painting may be worth $1,000 to John and only $1 to Mary. The difference is perceived value, which can be defined as the value the customer places on a product or service regardless of the posted price.

Competition

Who is your competition, and what is the price point of their products? How comparable are those products to yours? What is their product's perceived value compared to yours and what factors affect their perceived value?

Be sure, when comparing your product to that of your competitors, to include all of the criteria involved, not just the price. Additional criteria can include but not be limited to delivery, strength of brand name (image), quality, after-sales service, guarantees, and return and trade-in policies.

To determine the answer to these questions, you must first kick your competitors' tires by visiting the stores where their products are sold or picking up the phone and asking questions. Ask the buyers and/or the consumers such questions as why they purchased the product, what is their perception of the relationship between value and price, would they pay more for it if they had to, what do they like most about the product, and what do they like the least about it?

Then walk the store aisles; compare prices in the same product and those related to it. In short, do whatever it takes to piece together your competition's pricing strategy.

You can bet your balance sheet that, if your competitor is a successful company, it has an identifiable pricing strategy, and its components are there for you to figure out. Only a lack of research will keep you from determining what that strategy is.

Substitute products

Are substitute products available, products that are not the same but would serve the same purpose? (If your product is popcorn, for example, pretzels are a substitute product.) How much do those substitute products sell for? Should your product sell for more or less? How much more or less?

Again, comparative shopping is the only way to learn the answers to these questions.

Deciding on price

After you understand the factors that go into making your pricing decisions, and you've done your comparative shopping, you need to pull all the pieces together to make the pricing decision.

We explain in this section how to make pricing decisions both for introducing a new product or service and for updating your price list for existing products or services.

Pricing new products or services

When introducing new products or services, you have three options. You may choose any one of the following three, depending on your predetermined pricing strategy:

- ✔ **Premium pricing:** Premium pricing is when you set your price higher than the competition or, in the event that you have no competition, higher than your usual profit margins. In this way, you skim the market, in effect appealing to the customers who are most motivated to pay a high price for products based on perceived value. Premium pricing may limit your unit sales, but it will also increase your profit margin.

    This strategy is most successful when you have unusual, one-of-a-kind products (art galleries, and so forth) or provide hard-to-get services where your pricing strategy can be to create a high perceived value.

- ✔ **Market penetration:** This choice involves lowering your price to undercut competition, with the intent of gathering market share (the percentage that you own of the total available market) and making your otherwise unknown product known. This pricing strategy is designed to attract those customers who purchase products dependent upon their price.

✔ **Meeting the competition:** This pricing decision is, as the name implies, designed to meet the price of your competition, thus encouraging the customer to compare your product or service to your competitor's, feature by feature, benefit by benefit. Before adopting this pricing decision, however, you should make sure that your product or service can withstand the comparison and that you can offer a competing low price without threatening your survival.

Updating prices of existing products and services

Reviewing and altering prices is an ongoing procedure and not a once-year-occurrence. Before attempting to price existing products, you must first divide your array of products or services into one of the following three categories:

✔ **Specials and loss leaders:** These are the products that are priced close to cost or below cost in order to attract customers to your products or services. In this manner, you expect to build traffic and generate sales in other, more profitably-priced categories. In the hardware business, for example, light bulbs are often priced as loss leaders by their manufacturers in order to build the brand's name and develop business in other, less competitive categories. Unlike the lowball pricing of the market penetration option described earlier, loss-leader pricing can be a long-term strategy.

✔ **Standard or branded items:** These are the staples of your industry, the products that can be and often are comparison-priced from one company to the next. These products are usually well-known and widely available and thus must be sold at moderate profit margins.

✔ **Specialty or proprietary items:** These are the branded items that the consumer can't get anywhere else. Because of their uniqueness, you can usually sell these items at higher margins.

Unfortunately, no formula helps you price your products, but we hereby provide a workable technique:

1. **First, determine your break-even price — the price below which you cannot make a profit.**

   If yours is an existing business and you are generating accurate financial figures, you can use the formula presented in the "Cost to produce the product (or service)" section as presented earlier in this chapter.

   If yours is a start-up business without existing financial figures, you can accomplish this by using the following *cost-based method for determining prices.* Take the projected cost of the item; add the gross margin that you know you need to be profitable (go back to your profit-and-loss projections in your business plan in the event you've forgotten what this gross margin is); then determine the minimum price that you must charge. For example, if the cost of your product is projected to be $10 and the gross margin that you are projected to require to break even is 25 percent, then you need to sell that product for at least $13.33.

(*Note:* To arrive at this $13.33 figure, you divide the cost of the item by the complement of the gross margin you require. In this case, the cost is $10 and the complement of 25 is 75. Thus, $10 divided by 75 equals $13.33.)

Learning the lessons of pricing by trial-and-error

Remember Jim's wholesale and retail sporting goods business we've mentioned in Chapter 3 and throughout this book? Because the retail store was located in icy Minnesota, hockey was an important part of the company's business. So skate sharpening was included in the store's wide variety of products and services.

Skate sharpening bordered on being a ritual for the store's predominately young hockey-playing customers. They would come to the store accompanied by their parents, hand over their skates for sharpening, and wait. While waiting, they would browse the store (the kid-in-a-candy-shop concept), purchasing a hockey stick here or pointing out a prospective Christmas present there.

The year was 1970 and skate sharpening prices were 50 cents per pair. Jim settled on this price partly because it was a "nice, round figure" and partly because it was the price competitors charged. Because the actual cost of sharpening computed to only 15 cents, the 50-cent price provided a handsome profit (relative to cost) of 35 cents, or a profit margin of 70 percent.

Two years later Jim's company, for reasons unremembered (but probably related to a change by a major competitor), doubled the price for skate sharpening to $1. Guess what?

No change in demand. Absolutely zippo. Meanwhile, every penny of that price increase went into the store's profitability (85 cents instead of 15 cents), and the margin increased to 85 percent.

Today, the same skate sharpening is priced at $2.50. Although Jim is no longer involved in the business, he knows that costs haven't increased anywhere near that much. His successors have learned the lessons of pricing well:

✔ Don't figure your prices only on cost. In this case, customer demand and perceived value allowed profit margins unheard of in other store products.

✔ Don't price all your products or services using the same criteria. Different products can bear different profit margins. Although the hockey skates themselves would only bear a 20 percent profit margin in those days, skate sharpening was entirely different. Every product has its own unique margin tolerance.

✔ Increase your margins on the small (and necessary) purchases. The 1972 sporting goods customer evidently saw no difference between paying 50 cents and $1 for the skate-sharpening service.

2. **From what you know about the overall marketplace, the competition, and the substitute products available, determine the maximum price for which you believe you can sell the product.**

   You now have a minimum price and a maximum price; the price to settle on probably lies somewhere in between. Review the six pricing factors, and the answer will come.

Prices must not be cast in stone; they can and should change as market conditions change (think of gasoline prices, as noted earlier in the chapter). You can't always change prices, but remember that pricing is primarily a marketing strategy; as markets change, so must your strategies for capturing those markets.

Sales: Where the Rubber Hits the Road

Jim spent the majority of his business career in Minneapolis. One of that city's most successful entrepreneurs, Curt Carlson (known for Radisson Hotels, TGIF Restaurants, Carlson Travel), coined a phrase years ago that Minneapolis business veterans know by heart: "Nothing happens until a sale is made."

What is Curt really saying here? Is he saying that a company's marketing functions are more important than the product or service itself? Is he saying that a mediocre product or service in the hands of an outstanding marketing and sales staff will result in more sales than an outstanding product in the hands of a mediocre marketing and sales staff? Is he saying that a product or service, no matter how good it may be, will live or die based on the merits of the marketing and sales staff?

Yes, that is exactly what he is saying.

Going in-house, or not in-house; that is the question

Face it; someone has to sell your products or services — as good as they may be, they can't sell themselves. The question then becomes: Who should that selling-someone be?

- ✔ Should the seller be you, an employee hired by you, or a team of employees hired by you? (These are examples of an in-house sales force.)
- ✔ Or should the seller be an outsider, someone who is already calling on your potential customers with related products? (These are also known as manufacturers' representatives.)

The following sections are designed to help you make that decision.

Using an in-house sales force

The term "in-house sales" represents, as the name implies, a sales force whose members are direct employees of the company whose products they sell. In-house salespeople are usually hired, trained, and compensated by the company itself. Thus, their mission is to sell only the company's products.

The advantage of hiring and maintaining your own sales force is that you can exert direct control over your salespeople, and they can direct all their energies toward selling your products or services. The disadvantage of an in-house sales force is that you are picking up 100 percent of the expenses involved in employing and deploying your salespeople; therefore, you must be able to find enough sales potential within any given geographical area to support the salesperson assigned to it.

An interesting note about sales is that several of the nation's largest retailers (Wal-Mart and Kmart, for example) specify that they will only deal with salespeople who are *employees* of their vendors. In other words, no manufacturers' reps are allowed. Wal-Mart and Kmart want to be sure they are dealing directly with their vendors and not through an intermediary.

Most in-house salespeople today are compensated on a commission basis. You'll find a wide variety of ways to pay those commissions; for more on this subject, see Chapter 13.

Using manufacturers' representatives

Manufacturers' reps (also called independent agents) are independent salespeople who carry a collection of products from different manufacturers and get paid a percentage of every sale they make. The collection of products they choose to sell is usually aimed at customers within a given industry.

For example, the rep who calls on photography stores will pitch products such as film, tripods, and scrapbooks. A varied bag to be sure, but all are designed for the photography shop customer. The collection of products from any one manufacturer is called a *line,* and a rep may have anywhere from 1 to 30 lines of products in his bag. (Always ask how many lines your rep is carrying; the more lines in his bag, the less attention yours will get.)

Manufacturers' reps are paid only for what they sell (in other words, straight commission) and often cover, depending on the density of population, a large geographic territory. The commission they charge will vary with the product and the areas they cover; it can range anywhere from a low of 5 percent (sometimes less on high-ticket sales) to 25 percent. Some reps are part of a firm; others work on their own.

The primary advantage of using manufacturers' reps is that you do not have the out-of-pocket expense of maintaining a sales force: no salaries, benefits, or travel expenses. Because the reps are paid solely on commission, if they aren't selling your products or services, they aren't getting paid. Period.

Also, because reps can spread their costs over a number of manufacturers' lines, they can cover a wide geographical area for minimal expense. Networks of manufacturers' reps, both individuals and firms, cover every state in the nation; you can pick and choose until you find the combination you need. Thus, you can have nationwide distribution without the corresponding high expenses.

Reps also can make "small ticket" (low price tag) sales as a result of their ability to spread their time and expenses over a number of products. This means that, when you have a small-ticket product, your reps can afford to sell it to customers in outlying areas, whereas your own sales staff, with only one manufacturer's products in their bag, could not afford to make the sale.

The primary disadvantage of hiring manufacturers' reps is that you lack control over your reps' activities. After all, you aren't employing them; they are employing themselves.

Remember, manufacturers' reps, like all salespeople, have only a designated amount of time in front of each customer. The products the reps choose to sell during that designated time depend upon their perception of how easily they can sell a given product, as well as how much commission they can generate from the transaction.

If your product or service is well-established and relatively easy to sell, and your customer base is widespread, a manufacturers' rep may work the best for you. In these cases, the reps will be sure to pull your product out of the bag during the course of a sales call. On the other hand, if you have a relatively new product or one without an established customer base, manufacturers' reps may not give your product the time or attention it needs.

Another disadvantage of manufacturers' reps is that, due to the reps' distance from and noninvolvement in your day-to-day business, they cannot possibly know your product as well as an in-house sales staff, especially if your product is technical in nature.

In short, you sacrifice control for expense when you employ a manufacturers' rep in lieu of your own sales force. Neither right nor wrong, the decision depends on your situation.

The following itemized equations can help you decide what will work best for you:

- ✔ Easy products to sell, limited finances = manufacturers' reps
- ✔ Difficult products to sell, adequate finances = your own sales staff
- ✔ Small ticket item, wide territory = manufacturers' reps
- ✔ High ticket item, small territory = your own sales staff

Where do you find manufacturers' reps? Look in your industry's trade magazines or visit a trade show and ask for the Manufacturers' Rep bulletin board. Or call the Manufacturers' Agents National Association (714-859-4040) and ask for the latest directory containing names of manufacturers' rep organizations around the country. (Your library may also have this directory.)

Becoming a sales-driven company

First, a disclaimer. A sales-driven company is not a team of employees whipped into a frenzy by the scent of a sale. Rather, a sales-driven company is a company that recognizes, as the main heading of this section implies, that the rubber does meet the road when it comes to the sale. These companies have learned that the sales function is the most important element of them all in turning products or service into profits.

Today's owners and leaders of sales-driven companies know that to be truly sales-driven, every employee — from the person who answers the telephone to the one who drives the truck — must understand the three overriding principles of a sales-driven company:

✔ **Sales-driven companies sell solutions, not products.** Product-driven companies focus on the product, which is only a part of the solution. Meanwhile, sales-driven companies focus on the entire solution, which is what the customer is really seeking. The result is that the company that provides solutions builds relationships with its customers, while the company that sells products only sets itself up to be undersold by its competitors.

✔ **Sales-driven companies sell benefits, not features.** One sure sign of a sales-driven company is the manner in which salespeople are perceived by the other employees. Because salespeople are the voice of the customer and because they are responsible for making the sale — without which "nothing happens" — salespeople in sales-driven companies are held in high esteem. They are perceived as the leaders and movers and shakers of the business team, the people who make things happen. And yes, they are usually paid more than the other employees.

✔ **Sales-driven companies build relationships; they don't just sell products or services.** It used to be the typical business's primary sales goal would be to "get the order." Everything that the company did was in response to that goal. If the salesperson wrote the order the sales call was a success; if she didn't the call was a failure. And so it went through the company, the emphasis was on getting the goods out of the door.

No more. Today the sales-driven business's primary sales goal is to establish a relationship with the customer. Relationships come from solving problems and not from shipping products (or delivering services). The goal then is for all employees to understand the value of the relationship with the customer, and do whatever they can to foster that relationship. If it involves the customer returning a product that was ordered incorrectly, then so be it. This is how relationships are built.

It matters not, incidentally, whether it is you, your employees, or your manufacturers' reps who are dealing with the customer. Every employee in the business chain, from customer service to the shipping department, must be in tune with the relationship-building principle.

Today's successful companies have learned this lesson well: You can put a price on a product or service, but you can't put a price on a relationship.

Understanding the Business Triangle

To be a successful sales-driven company, the small-business owner must first create a mindset within the company that everyone must be a winner in the sales transaction, the customer included. To understand how to develop this concept within your company, take a look at the Business Triangle.

The Business Triangle

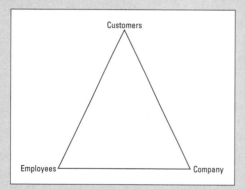

The Business Triangle represents the relationship between the three principals of the business: the company itself, its employees, and the company's customers.

When the three sides of the triangle are equal and stable, a balanced triangle results, one that is unlikely to teeter or fall. However,

when one side is significantly longer or shorter than the other two, the triangle, and thus the relationships among its principals, becomes unbalanced and precarious.

The length of each side of the triangle is determined by the benefits that each party derives from the relationship. Because those benefits are measured against expectations, take a look at what each of these three parties expects from a business relationship:

Business Triangle Expectations

> **The customer expects:** Solutions to problems and promises kept regarding quality, delivery, and pricing

> **The employee expects:** Fair wages, reasonable job security, and courteous treatment

> **The company expects:** Fair profit, good professional reputation, and opportunity for continued growth

Your job as a small-business owner is to make sure that you and your employees understand how this Business Triangle works and then work to see that the three legs remain balanced. The overriding principle here is that, in the long term anyway, nobody wins unless everybody wins.

Chapter 10

Keeping Your Customers Happy

. . . .

In This Chapter

▶ Knowing that satisfied customers are long-term profitable customers

▶ Examining customer defections

▶ Practicing good customer service before, during, and after the sale

▶ Dealing with unhappy and difficult customers

. . . .

A huge factor in your business's long-term success will be not only attracting but also retaining and satisfying your customers. As a small-business owner, you may very well be on the front lines of dealing with your business's customers. However, if you have employees, they will likely be dealing with customers as well. Therefore, our advice in this chapter for providing excellent customer service must penetrate all people in your organization who have any impact on customer satisfaction.

Whether you're starting your own business or buying a business, if you upset and disappoint your customers through lousy products or services, poor follow-up, or overbilling, you're going to have an uphill struggle on your hands.

Although it has been said that the level of customer service in many American businesses leaves much to be desired, only a foolish business owner today would assume that unhappy customers will continue to tolerate poor service or buy products that don't perform. If you and your employees don't satisfy your customers' needs, consider these likely unpleasant occurrences:

✔ **Competitive threats:** Now more than ever, customers have many options for buying what your firm has to offer. For the vast majority of businesses, competition is intense at the global, national, state, regional, and local level. It's only a matter of time before your unhappy customers become your competitors' newest customers.

✔ **Negative word-of-mouth:** Even worse than losing your dissatisfied customers to the competition is "negative word-of-mouth," whereby your unhappy customers talk and tell others not to buy your products and services. Furthermore, your competitors will happily recount to whoever will listen the negative stories they've heard from your disgruntled customers.

✔ **Potential lawsuits:** And, if losing customers and tarnishing your business's reputation aren't enough, disgruntled customers can initiate (gasp!) lawsuits. Even if the suing customers don't prevail in court, you could face large legal bills and suffer further damage to both the profitability and the reputation of your business.

The Keys to Retaining Good Customers

As the owner of a small business, you should want to keep your customers happy. We're not talking happy here in a spiritual or global sense — after all, you can't be responsible for your customers' home lives and careers! However, you can have an enormous impact upon your customers' satisfaction with your company's products and services. This section of the chapter provides you with some keys to keeping your customers satisfied.

What is a good customer?

Some small-business owners believe that all they have to do is build a quality product or develop a quality service, entice someone to purchase it — in other words, create the demand — and then deliver the goods. Whereupon, poof!, after the goods are delivered, the party on the receiving end immediately becomes a customer.

Nothing could be further from the truth. Although developing the product or service, creating the demand, and delivering the product or service may initially create the customer, it takes much more than that to maintain a successful two-way customer relationship.

Webster's Dictionary defines a customer as *someone who buys from, or patronizes, a business regularly.* To us, this definition is not comprehensive enough. Your business doesn't want just anyone as a customer — to qualify as a good customer, you want customers who

✔ Purchase your product or service

✔ Pay you for it

✔ Enable you to make a profit

✔ Make repeat purchases and refer others

If any one of these conditions (especially the first three) is not met, then your "customer" is not really a good customer. If the customer you are doing business with wants your product or service but is unwilling to pay you for it, or is willing to pay you for it but not at a price that allows you to make a profit, then he is not a good customer. Let him go to your competitor.

And one more thing. You've perhaps heard the expression, "The customer is always right." Well, we would modify this expression to say that the customer is always right as long as the customer is a good customer, as previously defined. If, on the other hand, the customer is not a good customer, he or she may not always be right.

Get it right the first time

During the 1970s and 1980s, the big U.S. auto manufacturers (Ford, Chrysler, GM, and AMC) made a major mistake — they ignored the competitive threat of foreign automakers. Despite having a relatively small market share in the early 1970s, the foreign auto manufacturers had intensely loyal customers. Why? Because the best foreign automakers made quality cars that rarely had problems. And, when the rare problem did occur, they provided excellent service.

The domestic automakers had a huge market share coming into the 1970s but, unfortunately, were upsetting customers left and right. The Detroit auto manufacturers were able to keep their costs low and profits high in part by producing sub-par cars. Sure, their cars looked nice on the auto dealer's lot, but after a short time in use, many of the U.S.-manufactured cars developed far more problems than their foreign equivalents. And, to add insult to injury, U.S. auto customers didn't get particularly good customer service when they brought their cars in for needed tune-ups and repairs.

The chief bean counters and the management of the major U.S. automakers weren't considering the bigger picture when they analyzed their companies' financial statements during the 1970s. These companies were too focused on their short-term profitability and weren't considering the after-sales service that was required as a result of their initially shoddy products.

Not surprisingly, the U.S. automakers lost tremendous market share at the expense of the best foreign automakers during the 1970s and 1980s. In fact, one of the big four U.S. automakers — Chrysler — nearly went bankrupt and was saved only because of a government bailout.

In the long run, the Detroit automakers learned the hard way that getting your product right the first time is less costly and more profitable than retrenching to play catch-up. Customers aren't stupid, and if you continually sell them shoddy merchandise (especially when better merchandise is available from other sources), they won't come back the next time they're in the market for the products and services you have to offer. What's more, they'll tell others of their lousy experience with your company.

Although the major U.S. automakers ultimately got their act together in the 1990s and have stopped the erosion of market share, they still feel the financial pain from the millions of customers they alienated and lost to foreign competitors in the two preceding decades. As a small-business owner, remember that if you don't get your product right the first time, you may not have a second chance. Although the large automakers had enough cash reserves built up to weather the storm, the typical small-business owner does not.

Keep offering more value

Getting your product or service right the first time isn't enough in the long run. As with life itself, the business world keeps changing. Due to the ever-present threat of competition, resting on one's laurels is foolish — and perhaps fatal.

Suppose that you're a dry cleaner and a new dry-cleaning technology is introduced that allows dry-cleaning establishments to get their work done 20 percent faster and 30 percent cheaper. If you fail to take advantage of this improvement in your industry, you may discover the hard way that your competitors have implemented this new technique. As your competitors cut prices and reap greater numbers of customers and profits, you lose business and experience shrinking profit margins.

So, in addition to initially developing a top-notch quality product or service for your customers, you should regularly examine how you can offer even more value — improved products and services at the same or lower cost. If you don't, competitors who faithfully do this will gradually eat your lunch.

Company policy is meant to be bent

Put yourself in the following situations:

- You're an electrical contractor who needs material to complete a job. Your electrical wholesaler tells you that he has a "backlog in the order-entry system" and can't process your order right now, so you'll have to come back tomorrow to place your order.

- You recently purchased an automobile, but the radio doesn't work. You take the car back to the dealership, and the service department informs you that the radio specialist is on vacation and that your radio won't be repaired for a week.

- You are a regular customer at a dry cleaner. It's Wednesday and you need your tuxedo dry cleaned by Friday night. Sorry, the dry cleaner informs you, it won't be ready until Saturday because of the firm's three-day turnaround policy.

What are the common threads here?

The first common thread is that the electrical wholesaler, the auto dealership, and the dry cleaner apparently have a cast-in-stone set of rules and regulations that dictate the way they do business, and they won't bend those rules to solve a customer's problem. The second common thread is that all three businesses are in danger of losing a good customer.

Short-term profit-maximizing behavior can kill long-term profitability

In business schools and economics courses all across the world, eager business students are taught to maximize profits. However, in the quest for higher and higher profits, some companies cut corners. In addition to perhaps lessening the quality of their products and services, some companies do things that clearly are not in their customers' best interests.

Just as the major U.S. automakers got into trouble by not producing high-quality cars, some major U.S. investment brokerage firms did significant long-term damage to their own businesses by engaging in short-term profit-maximizing behavior.

Prior to May 1, 1975, retail brokerage firms (companies that act as brokers in the buying and selling of securities such as stocks, bonds, and mutual funds for their customers) had their commissions regulated. Regulation was great for the industry (but not for their customers) because the commission rates were high and brokerage firms didn't have to compete with one another on price as companies do in nearly all other industries.

The world changed for securities brokerage firms and their customers when the Securities and Exchange Commission deregulated brokerage commissions in 1975. Interestingly, many of the old-line brokerage firms, such as Merrill Lynch, Prudential, Smith Barney, and E.F. Hutton, gradually raised their prices.

Gradually too, however, upstart discount brokers, such as Charles Schwab and Quick & Reilly, offered big commission discounts. These firms paid their brokers on salary rather than commission, which not only saved the brokerage firm money (a savings that could be passed on to their customers), but also eliminated the conflicts of interest inherent when securities brokers work on commission.

During the late 1970s and early 1980s, the discount brokers chipped away at the old-line brokerage firms' share of the marketplace. Some of the old-line brokers responded by finding a short-term solution to the profit pressure they were feeling: Jumping on the bandwagon of selling newfangled investments such as limited partnerships (LPs) to their customers. The appeal to the brokerage firms of peddling LPs was the huge up-front commissions of 8 to 10 percent or more of the amount invested. Never mind that the customer who bought an LP had little chance of earning a decent return due to the high commissions and the levying of high ongoing management fees.

In the short term, sales of LPs did boost brokerage firms' profits. In the long term, however, as customers learned for themselves what crummy investments LPs were, brokerage firms that sold lots of LPs began losing customers. And the most disgruntled LP owners participated in lawsuits against the brokerage firms.

By viewing their association with their customers as a one-night stand rather than a long-term relationship built on trust, the old-line brokerage firms' pursuit of short-term profits tremendously damaged the long-term health and profitability of their businesses. The leading discount brokerage firms and mutual fund companies reaped the benefits and captured a huge portion of the dissatisfied customers who left the old-line firms.

In the small-business world, you need to take a long-term view on your customer relationships; otherwise your business may not be around in the long term.

Flexibility is paramount in any organization, but it is especially important in your small business, where service can set you apart from the larger companies. If a customer has a problem but you have a rule or regulation preventing you from resolving that problem, then forget the rule or regulation. Bend it. Skirt it. Find a loophole in it.

In the situations listed earlier in this section, the electrical wholesaler should give the contractor his material today and run the transaction through his order-entry system tomorrow. The automobile dealership should take the customer's car and have it fixed somewhere else if it can't do it in its own shop. And the dry cleaner should put the customer's tuxedo in front of someone else's order, no matter what its operations manual dictates.

These are the moments of truth in any business — the times when what the business says it will do conflicts with what the business actually does — the times that differentiate the business that *says* the customer is king from the business that *acts* as if the customer is king.

This isn't to say that you should always provide extra service casually or for free. In some situations, you may want to charge more for a special service. Consider this when you look at your pricing strategy. Also, you don't want to tell your employees to feel free to break all the rules at any time; that's the road to chaos and lack of profits. But flexibility helps keep customers happy and coming back. Let your managers and employees know that you stand behind this philosophy, and you'll empower them to always provide good customers with top service.

Learn from customer defections

The costs of acquiring a new customer are huge. After spending the marketing effort and dollars needed to secure a new customer for your business, you want to keep that customer loyally patronizing your business for many years to come. If you experience much customer turnover, your cost of doing business will rise significantly as you try to attract replacement customers. Customer turnover can indicate some major problems with your company's products or services and customer service.

The value of customer loyalty

Frederick Reichheld is a management consultant who specializes in understanding, and working with corporations on, customer loyalty. He is the author of *The Loyalty Effect: The Hidden Force Behind Growth, Profits and Lasting Value* (Harvard Business School Press). Reichheld's research and work have produced the following powerful insights and facts:

✔ The average company today loses half of its customers in five years.

✔ The typical Fortune 500 company has an average annual real growth (that is, growth in excess of the rate of inflation) of 2.5 percent. If these companies retained just 5 percent more of their customers each year, their real growth would triple to 7.5 percent.

✔ A 5-percent increase in customer retention in a typical company generally translates into an increase in profits of more than 25 percent. In some industries, good long-standing customers are worth so much that reducing customer defections by 5 percent can double profits.

Clearly, retaining customers — particularly your best customers — has an enormous bottom-line impact. Given how important and valuable retaining customers is, you may think that if a business were losing many of its customers, it would seek to understand why and to correct the underlying problems. Well, if that were the case, then customer loss wouldn't remain as high as it does in as many businesses as it does.

Reichheld has found in his work and research that, not surprisingly, many businesses don't learn from their customer losses. "Psychologically and culturally, it's difficult and sometimes threatening to look at failure too closely. Ambitious managers want to link their careers to successes; failures are usually examined for purposes of assigning blame rather than detecting and eradicating the systemic causes of poor performance," says Reichheld.

Tracking customer defections

The good news for you, the small-business owner, is that you don't have to be concerned with bosses and organizational politics when addressing the problem of customer defections. You are The Boss. However, it is a natural human tendency to spend more time chasing and celebrating success rather than stopping long enough to investigate and learn from your failures and losses.

Make a commitment to tracking the customers that you lose and asking why. (This is the customer equivalent to the exit interview that you do with departing employees.) Knowing that you've lost customers is not enough; you must learn why you lost them. Many businesses don't even know what customers they've lost, and it's rare that a business takes the time to discover why. But doing so can help keep you in business and help keep your business growing.

Consider, for example, the auto oil change business that Eric used to frequent about one mile from his home. The business boasts that you can get your oil changed within 10 minutes and be on your merry way.

On a visit to the establishment, Eric pulled into the entrance and got out of his car. He then proceeded to be ignored for the next 10 minutes — not because the business was so busy but rather because the people who were checking in new customers moved at a snail's speed, and one employee even spent several minutes on a personal phone call.

When it was Eric's turn to be checked in, the employee who checked him in was rude. Eric left the car to have the oil changed and went to do some shopping nearby rather than sit in the poorly ventilated, exhaust-infested garage. Upon his return, Eric had to wait another 10 minutes because, although his car had finally been serviced, the paperwork wasn't completed. The same employee who checked Eric in took another 15 minutes to get the paperwork done, and the employee was again unfriendly and surly.

Throughout this poor service experience, Eric didn't utter a word of complaint, but guess which oil change shop he bypassed the next time his car needed an oil change? A gas station that was just one-quarter mile from Eric's home started offering oil changes, which were about 20 percent less costly than the last place Eric had used. The attendant who checked Eric in at the service station was friendly and polite, and the car and paperwork were ready when promised.

A popular and politically acceptable action within a business is to celebrate successes rather than to examine failures. However, as a small-business owner, you'll learn far, far more by examining your failures and making positive changes to correct them. Take the time to examine customer defections and their underlying causes. You need to make it part of your company's culture that you don't expect employees to be perfect, so making mistakes won't necessarily lead to an employee's immediate firing. However, you should show little tolerance toward employees who repeatedly drive away good customers from your business.

Customer service is part of what your customers buy

All businesses have products or services to sell. And sometimes businesses get too focused on those products and services, giving short shrift to the accompanying customer service that customers expect.

Maybe you can't readily define the term *customer service,* but we'd bet that you know what it is when you get it or don't get it. For example, we'd bet that you recognize customer service in a company you do business with when

✔ Its telephone operator (or at least its telephone system) connects you with your party quickly and efficiently.

✔ Its bookkeeper politely explains a question you have on an invoice.

✔ Its shipping clerk quickly traces your order and tells you exactly when to expect it.

✔ Its salesperson gets back to you quickly with the quotes and delivery schedules you requested.

In each of the situations just described, the customer is having his or her problem solved, which is, after all, the definition of customer service. Customer service = Solving your customer's problems.

Sometimes larger companies have distinctly identified *customer service departments* — a person or group of persons whose sole purpose it is to solve customer problems. In these cases, all customer telephone calls requiring information are routed through the customer service department.

In smaller companies, however, many — perhaps even all — employees are involved in customer service. In the examples previously cited, the telephone operator, the bookkeeper, the shipping clerk, and the salesperson are all providing customer service. If you, the boss and grand poobah, get involved in solving a customer's problem, then you too are in customer service. The same is true for the janitor or the night watchman.

Have you ever heard the following response when you ask an employee of a business that you frequent for help? "I'm sorry, but that's not my department." In a business — large or small — where the value of customer service is recognized, the correct response to the preceding question would be: "Let me find the solution for you." The solution may ultimately rest in the hands of another employee, another department, or even another business, but the customer now knows that someone is solving his problem.

The challenge is for your employees to understand that they are on the job to solve your customers' problems. Instead, they may believe (because this is the way their job description reads) that their role is simply to answer the telephone or keep the books or ship products or sell services. Although each of these functions accurately describes the employee's activities, these functions don't define the reason that employees exist.

Your employees exist, just as you — the owner — exist, and just as your entire company exists, for one reason and one reason only: To solve your customers' problems.

Smart business owners know that customer service (and the accompanying problem solving) begins before a sale is made, continues during the sale, and continues long after the sale is complete.

Customer service before the sale

Consider the last time you bought something, whether a car, groceries, a medical exam, or a haircut. With each of these purchases, you interacted with the business provider before you committed to buy the product or service.

Think back to the last time you bought a car. If you're like most of us, you probably have some bad memories about slick salespeople who accosted you the moment you walked onto the auto dealer's lot and then spent more time selling rather than listening and educating. The salesperson wasn't trying to solve *your* problem — figuring out which car to purchase. He was trying to solve *his* problem — how to make a fat commission that would meet his next mortgage payment. Because of such poor customer service, you may very well have turned around, checkbook in hand, and taken your business elsewhere.

If you're scheduling a doctor's appointment, you may experience how politely and flexibly you're treated when arranging a time for you to come in. But when you arrive for your appointment, you are greeted and asked to wait before you see the doctor — and the wait stretches on and on. Although you're less likely in this circumstance to walk out if you don't like how things are going, we know people who have walked out of a doctor's office never to return again after waiting more than 45 minutes beyond the scheduled appointment time without a word from anyone. Think about it; whose problem is that doctor solving when he or she makes you wait for 45 minutes? Not yours, that's for sure.

When a person buys a product or service, part of what can close the sale or blow the deal is the quality (or lack thereof) of customer service before the moment a customer decides to buy. When a person is in the market for a product or service, the customer service before the sale is crucial to making or breaking a deal. When a person schedules an appointment, such as with a physician, he's not just buying that person's expertise — he's also buying "proper care and handling" before the service is provided. When a person enters your store, she wants it clean and well-maintained and conveniently arranged. It's all customer service.

Customer service during the sale

After a customer commits to buy a product or service, the customer service must still continue. After the doctor arrives in the examination room, you'll pay close attention to how well he listens to you and his demeanor toward you. If the doctor is abrupt, a poor listener, and arrogant in asserting his opinion, rather than showing a willingness to discuss options and consider your needs, you may choose to find another physician.

Likewise, if you've decided to buy a car, you won't be overjoyed if it takes several hours to complete the transaction. Even though you may be happy with the selection of the car, the hassle in getting on your way may make you less glowing in your recommendation to others about buying from the same dealership.

Just because customers decide to buy your products and services doesn't mean that you should stop working at satisfying them. When a customer forks over the dough for your wares, she most rightfully expects a high level of service. If you don't meet the customer's needs for service at this point, even if the sale goes through, you may lose repeat business from this customer, and you may lose the opportunity for referrals to other customers.

Customer service after the sale

After a customer has purchased your company's products or services and is on his merry way, your relationship with that customer, at least as it relates to that transaction, isn't over. Customers may have follow-up questions that need to be answered, or they may have problems down the road with your products or services.

If you or your employees treat your customers as if they are bothering you and you aren't attentive to after-sales service, again you could turn off such customers from making more purchases and referring others to your business. Poor follow-up and after-sales service will communicate to your customers that after you've got their money, you don't really care what happens to them.

In some businesses, you must be careful not to give away valuable support that you can and should charge for. For example, if follow-up exams or appointments are to be expected, you need to either build the cost of those expected services into your up-front pricing or set a pricing schedule for the cost of the follow-up. Be sure that at the time customers buy from you, they know the cost of such follow-up work.

Remember that customers aren't just coming to your business for your products and services. The attentiveness to your customers' needs — before, during, and after the sale — that comes with what you sell is also an integral part of the package. Treat your customers as you would a good friend. As with the products and services you sell, be sure to solicit feedback (possibly from a formal survey) from your customers as to the quality of the customer service that your business offers them.

Some customers, of course, begin complaining at the drop of a hat. Although some may be justified in their complaints, others complain simply because that's the type of people they are. Know how to tell the difference. And that brings us to the topic of our next section — dealing with the inevitable less-than-satisfied customers that every business encounters.

Dealing With Unhappy (and Difficult) Customers

You can have the best products and services, offer the fairest prices, and provide the greatest customer service in town, and you're still going to end up with unhappy customers. We all know from our personal and professional experience that some people are seemingly impossible to please.

Keep in mind that you have your own way of doing things, that yours is not a perfect product or service, and that you can't meet your customers' needs and expectations *all* the time.

How you handle complaints — both justified as well as unjustified ones — is vital to the long-term reputation and health of your business. Here is our time-tested advice for dealing with your unhappy and sometimes troublesome customers.

Listen, listen, listen

We all would like to believe that we are terrific listeners. The reality is that most of us aren't, and even those of us who are good listeners have moments when, for any of a variety of reasons, we don't listen well. We get busy and stressed out with the competing demands on our time from work, family, friends, daily chores, and obligations. We all have days when we're tired, not feeling well, or have been on the receiving end of bad news or bad experiences.

Another impediment to good listening is that we may be convinced that a given customer is simply being a troublemaker. As with all personal relationships, however, our preconceived notions (dare we call them prejudices) about others can keep us from hearing an unhappy customer's legitimate and real concerns and reasons for being dissatisfied.

So, before you (or one of your employees) lose your temper with a complaining customer, take a deep breath and put aside your opinions about the situation and your preconceived notions about the customer and his right to be unhappy. Stop and listen. Try to ask about and care about discovering why and what the customer is unhappy about. Different people, not surprisingly, get upset about different things. You have no way to know and understand what's upsetting a particular customer until you take the time to ask and truly listen.

To ensure that you have really heard what your upset customer has said, paraphrase the concerns that you've heard and tell the customer that you are sorry that he is unhappy with how things have gone for him. (Recognize that this is not an admission of wrongdoing or guilt on your part if you're worried about landing in court and being sued for product liability.)

The key to understanding your customers' complaints (and the key to understanding your employees' complaints) is your ability to put yourself in the complainer's shoes. After you've made this transition (learned how to view your business through the eyes of a customer), you will find that you can solve your customers' problems the vast majority of the time.

Develop a solution

When a customer complains, remember that he is complaining because he isn't satisfied with the deal that he got. The next step, after listening to the customer's complaints, is to develop a solution that addresses the complaints.

You have two ways to arrive at a solution. First, you can propose a solution yourself and then wait for the customer to come up with a solution that she thinks is better; second, you can ask the customer what solution she would propose and then see how it compares to what you can do.

The advantage of asking the customer for the solution is the same as with any other form of negotiation (which, after all, is what is going on in this situation). Always let the party of the second part make the opening offer. After that, you know exactly where you stand and what you have to do to satisfy him or her.

Imagine the benefit you can derive when the customer's solution is clearly inferior to what you were about to offer. In such a circumstance, the opportunity suddenly exists for you to take an unpleasant situation and turn it into an opportunity to strengthen the complaining customer's loyalty to your business.

Only when the customer doesn't have, or refuses to come up with, a solution, is it time for you to propose one. For example, suppose that you run a professional service business and you're responsible for missing a customer's appointment, either because of a scheduling mistake or because you're behind schedule and the customer simply couldn't wait any longer. By listening to the customer, you quickly determine that the customer is really angry about having been stood up when he had taken valuable time out of his workday and ended up without accomplishing what he set out to do.

Your solution to ease the customer's unhappiness could go something like this:

✔ Apologize for the time he wasted.

✔ Ask for his recommended solution.

✔ If he doesn't already have a solution, offer a discount, perhaps 15 or 20 percent off the appointment price when he reschedules.

✔ When the customer returns for the rescheduled appointment, be absolutely certain that he is seen on time and provided the best possible service.

Now, suppose that your company sells products, and a customer comes in to say that your product broke and it stinks. In this case, you could offer a replacement product, fix the broken one, or offer the customer a refund. If you're highly certain that the customer misused the product that subsequently led to the breakage, then you've got a dilemma on your hands. You'll have to make the decision whether this person adheres to your definition of what a customer should be.

Even in those situations in which you determine that this person is not what you consider to be a good customer, try to make the parting of your ways as harmonious and conflict-free as possible. It's okay if an unmanageable customer doesn't do business with you anymore; it's not okay if he goes away angry and tells others what a lousy service or product your business offers.

If you would like to delve into more details about what makes for good customer service, we highly recommend reading *Customer Service For Dummies* by Karen Leland and Keith Bailey, published by IDG Books Worldwide, Inc.

Chapter 11

Minding the Financials: Cash Flow, Costs, and Profitability

● ●

In This Chapter
▶ Grasping the concept of cash flow
▶ Reading and understanding financial statements
▶ Understanding the key elements of profitability
▶ Controlling your costs
▶ Managing your accounts receivable and inventory

● ●

*B*usiness, no matter how you shake it, is about people. It's about the things that people make and buy and sell, the manner in which people work and interact together, and even the reasons that people get out of bed and go to work in the morning. Let's face it, without people there would be no one to do business and no one to do business with.

But although people drive the business of doing business, money fuels the engine. That money can be counted and compiled and presented in a number of different ways — ways that, in the right hands, can provide a steady flow of financial information with which to accomplish a number of key business functions. Those key business functions are

✔ **Maintaining bookkeeping information:** This includes keeping records of physical inventories, monies due from others (accounts receivable), and monies due to others (payroll and accounts payable).

✔ **Paying taxes:** Federal, state, and local governments not only require that the business pay taxes, but also that you keep records to back those payments.

✔ **Keeping score:** In order to know whether you're winning or losing, you need to keep track of the results of doing business.

✔ **Providing a management information tool:** Information fuels the decision-making process, and the more information the small-business owner has, the better his or her decisions can be.

This chapter is about collecting and using financial information. Although we discuss three of the four functions mentioned here (the subject of taxes is dealt with in Chapter 16) in the course of this chapter, our primary emphasis is on the use of financial information as a management tool — information that you can use to manage your cash flow, increase your profitability, and improve your chances of staying in business for the long haul.

Cash Flow — the Fuel That Drives Your Business

To pay your bills you need to manage the money/cash you have both going out and coming in — your cash flow. Before you can have cash flowing out, it is necessary to have cash flowing in. When your cash flows out before it flows in, your business will be in big trouble.

To understand the concept of cash flow, you need first to distinguish between two oft-confused terms: cash flow and profitability. Their definitions follow:

- ✔ **Cash flow:** An operating term describing the movement of money (cash, checks, electronic debits and credits) in and out of your business.

- ✔ **Profitability:** An accounting term meaning the capability of your business to generate more sales dollars than the cost of operating expenses.

To understand the difference between these two terms, you must first understand that when a business is profitable, profits do not necessarily accumulate in the form of cash. Instead, they can take the form of an increase in other noncash assets such as inventory, accounts receivable, equipment, or real estate. Yes, those profits may once have been in the form of cash, but somewhere along the line the owner has made the decision to shift that cash into something else — purchasing additional inventory or buying a piece of equipment, for example. In this manner, a business can be profitable, but short of cash.

Although an increase in cash is only one of the many possible results of profitability, it is by far the most important result, because cash fuels the operation of your business. If you've chosen to spend too much cash on purchasing inventory and equipment, or you've been too slow in collecting your accounts receivable, you may not be able to pay your vendors and compensate your employees. After all, you can't pay them with inventory or equipment! Sorry, vendors and employees want cash.

Ironically, some profitable businesses have gone bankrupt because their owners made the wrong choices when allocating the cash they receive. Instead of accumulating it, they (knowingly or unknowingly) accumulated other nonliquid assets, and then, lo and behold, the bills came due and the cupboards were bare.

Your business's bank account (or money market fund) is the obvious measure of today's cash. Do you have enough money in it to pay today's bills and meet today's payroll, and will you still have money left over when the day is done? If so, your cash flow is ensured — for today anyway.

The difficulty comes in projecting tomorrow's cash flow. Because every business has to be concerned with more than just what's happening today, projecting tomorrow's cash flow is an important and necessary task. To do that, you need to consider questions like the following:

✔ Will you have enough cash to meet next Friday's payroll?

✔ Will you have enough to pay that big vendor invoice that's due the following Monday?

✔ How about the bank loan payment, the upcoming utility bills, the real estate taxes that come due at the end of the month? Will there be enough money in the checking account when the time comes to pay them too?

Questions like these, and the answers they beg, point out the need for preparing *cash flow projections* — forecasts of how much cash you'll have over a given future time frame. Some businesses project cash flow for 30 days out, some for 180 days, and some even for an entire year in advance.

In order to effectively project cash flow, you must first polish up the old crystal ball, because you are about to make a number of important predictions. For example, you must predict your future sales, the rate at which you'll collect the money that's due you, the dollar amount of your upcoming payrolls, and the dollar amount of vendor invoices to be paid in the next day, week, 30 days, 180 days, even 365 days. The better your predictions, the more accurate a forecast you can prepare.

Table 11-1 shows a sample format for making cash flow projections:

Table 11-1	Cash Flow Projections
Period of time (days, weeks, months, and so on)	_____
Current cash (checking account and petty cash account)	$ _____
Add expected cash sales for time period	$ _____
Add expected receivable collections for time period	$ _____
Subtotal	$ _____
* Less disbursements	
Payroll	$ _____
Taxes	$ _____
All other Accounts Payable	$ _____
Total = Expected cash balance at end of time period	$ _____

You can prepare your cash flow projections for one day out, one week out, one month out, one year out, or any combination thereof. Predictions for longer time periods, while more useful, are also likely to be fuzzier and less accurate than your predictions for shorter time periods. We recommend that you make your cash flow projections for at least six months out, and then update them at least once each month, always staying six months out. That way you'll spot problem periods earlier and be able to adjust to them more quickly.

A disclaimer here. Although it's true that most start-up small businesses will keep their cash flow projections in their head and will not go to the trouble of generating cash flow projections from one day to the next, it is important that every small-business owner understand the concept behind measuring cash flow. No matter how small or uncomplicated your business happens to be, cash is key.

Most accountants have a preformatted "cash flow projections" worksheet available for their clients to use. Whatever you do, if you don't thoroughly understand this concept of cash flow, read this section again. Cash flow is one of the most important (and least understood) financial concepts that a small-business owner must know.

And yet, don't let cash flow intimidate you — the concept is as simple as the concept behind maintaining a checkbook — something most of us have been doing for years. Cash flow is nothing more than a few new wrinkles on an old, familiar face.

Getting to Know Your Financial Statements

Whether manual or computer-based, the accounting system you use is designed to generate two financial statements: the Profit & Loss Statement (or the Income Statement) and the Balance Sheet. Both of these statements are generated at the end of a business's accounting period, usually monthly, quarterly, or annually.

We recommend that your financial statements be prepared as frequently as possible, with monthly statements usually being the most useful. If your accounting system allows you to generate your financial statements internally, we suggest you generate your statements monthly. If monthly statements are impossible for some reason, quarterly statements will do, but don't fall into the trap that many businesses do by generating your statements only once or twice a year. Remember, these financial statements function primarily as a management tool, and you shouldn't go 365 days without paying attention to the information they provide.

The following two sections discuss in detail the Profit & Loss Statement and the Balance Sheet.

The Profit & Loss Statement

The Profit & Loss Statement (P & L) measures the *results of operations* of a business over a given period of time — typically a month, a quarter, or a year. In effect, the P & L adds all the revenues of the business and subtracts all the operating expenses, thereby providing its user with a figure representing what's left: the profits. (If the total expenses exceed the total revenues, the business would have a loss instead of a profit.)

In Figure 11-1, we reproduce a sample P & L statement to help you understand how to construct one and how to effectively use it in managing your business.

You can use a wide variety of formats in presenting a P & L Statement. The four-column format that we use in Figure 11-1 is the one that we recommend for both the Profit & Loss Statement and the Balance Sheet. This four-column format lets you quickly and easily compare each of the three key figures (Prior Year, Budget, and Current Year). The fourth column measures the percentage increase or decrease (in parentheses) between the current year and prior year.

Big Spenders Corp.
Profit and Loss Statement
For the year ending December 31, 1998

	Prior Year	Budget	Current Year	Percent Compared to Prior Year
Sales (revenues)	$450,000	$475,000	$500,000	11%
- Cost of goods sold	$200,000	$210,000	$225,000	12.5%
= Gross margin	$250,000	$265,000	$275,000	10%
Expenses				
Wages and salaries	$75,000	$77,000	$97,000	29%
Rent	$50,000	$52,000	$54,000	8%
Selling expenses	$55,000	$58,000	$61,000	11%
Telephone	$10,000	$11,000	$11,000	10%
Utilities	$10,000	$11,000	$11,000	10%
Total expenses	$200,000	$209,000	$241,000	15%
Net income (pretax)	$50,000	$56,000	$41,000	(32%)

Figure 11-1:
Sample Profit & Loss Statement showing good news.

Notwithstanding the initially confusing appearance of a typical P & L, the process used in arriving at its net income conclusion is not difficult to understand. Follow its construction through these five easy steps:

1. **Begin with your gross sales.**

   In Figure 11-1, the current year amount is $500,000.

2. **Subtract the cost of the goods that were included in those sales.**

   The figure used in the example is $225,000.

3. **What's left is gross margin on those sales — the gross income before subtracting expenses.**

   Our example shows this figure to be $275,000.

4. **Now subtract all the operating expenses incurred during that accounting period, including all selling, and administrative expenses.**

   You see $241,000 as this figure in the example.

5. **The number left over is — how easy is this? — net income.**

   Ta-da! $41,000!

As you can see, the trick is not so much in assembling the P & L, rather it is in retaining and retrieving all the figures that go into it. In essence, the better the business's accounting system, the easier this process will be. (See Chapter 8 for more on accounting systems.)

Deciphering important information from a statement formatted like this is easy.

- ✔ Go to the net income figure under the Current Year column — the P & L number that every small-business owner is most interested in. Using the percentage in the adjacent column, you can quickly determine how profitable the Big Spenders Corp. was compared to the previous year. (Profits were down by 32 percent.)

- ✔ A quick glance at the top of the statement reveals that the profitability decrease was not due to sales, which were up by 11 percent, nor was it due to gross margin, which was up by 10. Recalling our discussion on profitability earlier in this chapter, you can then assume that the problem must be related to expenses.

- ✔ Moving down the expense column, you see that wages and salaries are up by 29 percent. This means that, although sales have increased by 11 percent and the gross margin is up by 10 percent, the whopping increase in wages and salaries has caused a problem. A quick comparison to the wages and salaries budget column reveals that the 29 percent increase was *not* budgeted; therefore, whatever has happened was not planned. You can then delve into the wages and salaries account to determine what caused the problem.

Some companies may include an additional three columns on the P & L. These three columns would be columns for the percentage of the total for the Prior Year, Budget, and Current Year categories. For example, using the sales total as 100 percent, every figure in the rest of the chart would represent a percentage of that total. Thus, in the Big Spenders Corp. example, the percentage of the Total column for the current year would reveal a gross margin of 55 percent ($275,000 divided by $500,000), wages and salaries to sales of 19 percent ($97,000 divided by $500,000), and net income to sales of 8.2 percent ($41,000 divided by $500,000). The only disadvantage of adding these three columns is that it clutters up the P & L and makes it more difficult to read.

After you have your P & L prepared in this easy-to-read, four-column format, you'll find it relatively easy to determine what your business has done and where it currently needs to improve. For example, as a result of comparing three of the columns, the P & L allows you to quickly answer the three questions that define any business's profitability:

- ✔ Have you controlled your costs? For Big Spenders Corp., the answer is no.
- ✔ Have you maintained or improved your margin (the difference between what it costs you to produce your product and the price you charge for it)? In this example, yes.
- ✔ Have you maintained or increased sales? In this example, yes.

Although the answers to these three questions are a significant help in managing your business, the answers are not the only information the P & L provides. See "Turning the Numbers into Action," later in this chapter, for even more uses of the figures generated by the Profit & Loss Statement.

The Balance Sheet

The second of a small-business's important financial statements is the Balance Sheet, which provides a snapshot of a company's financial position at any given point in time. As with the P & L, the concept behind a Balance Sheet is not complex. Quite simply, the Balance Sheet is a list of what the business owns (assets) less what the business owes (liabilities), with the resulting difference being what the business is worth (net worth). This net worth figure is also commonly referred to as _book value_.

In Figure 11-2 we reproduce a sample Balance Sheet to help you understand how this important financial statement works.

We have prepared this example in the same four-column format we used in the P & L. This format is designed to make quick and easy work of the comparison of Prior Year, Budget, and Current Year figures. Although we suggest that you consider this format when preparing your own Balance Sheet, we should note that the vast majority of businesses don't "budget" their balance sheet but operate successfully.

In our example, Big Spenders Corp. completed its 1998 fiscal year with an increase in net worth of $41,000 over the prior year. This is the same $41,000 of profit reported by the Profit & Loss Statement in the earlier example. By comparing the Current Year column on the Balance Sheet with the Prior Year column, you can readily determine what has happened to the mixture of assets and liabilities during the course of the year; in other words, how Big Spenders Corp. management decided to allocate the company's resources.

To give you a further example of how easy it is to glean information from this four-column Balance Sheet format, take a look at the Percent Compared to Prior Year column. You will quickly note that, although the total current

Big Spenders Corp.
Balance Sheet
For the year ending December 31, 1998

	Prior Year	Budget	Current Year	Percent Compared to Prior Year
Assets				
Current Assets				
Cash	$25,000	$35,000	$5,000	(80%)
Accounts receivable	$50,000	$55,000	$55,000	10%
Inventory	$50,000	$55,000	$85,000	70%
Total current assets	$125,000	$145,000	$145,000	16%
Fixed assets				
Land, buildings	$100,000	$95,000	$95,000	(5%)
Furniture & fixtures	$50,000	$47,000	$47,000	(6%)
Equipment	$50,000	$47,000	$47,000	(6%)
Total fixed assets	$200,000	$189,000	$189,000	(5.5%)
Total Assets	$325,000	$334,000	$334,000	
Liabilities				
Current liabilities				
Accounts payable	$75,000	$69,000	$80,000	6.7%
Short-term notes payable	$10,000	$10,000	$10,000	—
Total current liabilities	$85,000	$79,000	$90,000	6%
Long-term liabilities				
Mortgages payable	$70,000	$65,000	$65,000	(7%)
Long-term notes payable	$45,000	$0	$20,000	(55%)
Total long-term liabilities	$115,000	$65,000	$85,000	
Total Liabilities	**$200,000**	**$144,000**	**$175,000**	
Owner's equity (net worth)	$125,000	$190,000	$159,000	27%
Total Liabilities & Net Worth	**$325,000**	**$334,000**	**$334,000**	

Figure 11-2:
Sample
Balance
Sheet
showing
how the
owner
decided to
allocate
resources.

assets did not change appreciably, two of the categories within the current asset category did — cash and inventory. The cash account as of December 31 is only $5,000, while inventory has ballooned to $85,000. Sometime during the course of the year, a larger inventory was built up, depleting the company's cash reserves in the process.

A quick look at the Budget column confirms the fact that this inventory accumulation was unplanned and unbudgeted. (Incidentally, this is a typical example of how a company can be profitable and still get into financial trouble). As evidenced by this Balance Sheet, Big Spenders Corp. currently has $90,000 in short-term liabilities, but only $5,000 available in cash.

The only other percentage on this sample Balance Sheet that attracts immediate attention is the 55 percent decrease in long-term notes payable. Sometime during the course of the year, management decided to retire a portion of its long-term debt — a decision that, in light of its present cash shortage, they would now probably like to reverse.

As discussed previously, the P & L is designed to analyze profitability issues: sales, margins, and expenses. The Balance Sheet, on the other hand, answers an entirely different question: How did you allocate your resources? Did you decide to allocate your dollars to inventory, to paying off loans, or to accumulating cash? The business owner makes hundreds of asset-allocation decisions over the course of the year; the Balance Sheet tells the story of those decisions.

Turning the Numbers into Action

Here's an exercise that every small-business owner should attempt: Try figuring out exactly how much money it costs to produce your financial statements every year. Go ahead, we dare you! Add up the wages and salary costs of the people responsible for collecting the data, the depreciation of the accounting hardware and software involved, and the cost of any outside services you contract (tax preparers and advisers, and so on). Now add the figures together and what do you have?

You have one very expensive process for determining how much income tax you have to pay, that's what you have — especially if that's all you use your financial statements for!

On the other hand, if you use your financial statements as a management tool, the picture changes. In some cases, your financial statements may even pay for themselves if the actions you take as a result of the lessons they provide result in good management decisions.

For example, in the Big Spenders Corp. Profit & Loss Statement, had the business owner plugged the salary increases into the budget in advance of making them and been fully aware of the impending negative impact on the company's profitability, he may have given second thoughts to this decision. Ditto with the Balance Sheet example, where the owner made the decision to increase inventory and pay off his long-term loan. Had he plugged those figures into his Balance Sheet budget he would have understood the impact these decisions would have on his Cash account and would probably have seriously altered those decisions.

Such is the power of using financial statements and budgets. They allow you to see the results of your decisions — before you make them!

Getting your money's worth from your financial statements

Ed owned a successful construction company. In business for 15 years, Ed's company employed 20 people, did several million dollars in yearly sales, and appeared to provide a comfortable living for Ed. During the course of a meeting between Ed and Jim, who was a consultant with Ed's company at the time, Ed confided that he had been embarrassed by a question the bank had asked when he recently inquired about a loan.

"They asked what my current ratio was," Ed said sheepishly. "And I not only didn't know the answer, I didn't know where on my financial statements to find it."

As it turned out, that wasn't all Ed didn't know about his financial statements. He also didn't know where to find his return-on-sales, or how to determine his days-in-accounts-receivable, or how to compute his debt-to-equity ratio. And he didn't have year-to-year comparison figures with which to properly compare his Profit & Loss Statement and Balance Sheet line items. In short, Ed didn't know how to read his financial statements, much less utilize the information that was on them.

Unfortunately, Ed is typical of many small-business owners who use their financial statements for little more than keeping score and paying taxes. Ironically, Ed employed a $40,000-a-year controller, which means he was paying $40,000 (plus another $10,000 or so for miscellaneous related expenses) to maintain his books, keep score, and pay the business's taxes. Not much of a return on a $50,000 investment!

Just as a baseball coach uses a host of batting and pitching statistics to make his important decisions, so should every small-business owner use the statistics that the business generates to help make important decisions. After all, you wouldn't consider coaching a baseball team if you didn't understand and know how to apply baseball statistics, would you?

Why should running a business be any different?

Your business's key ratios and percentages

Before we take the numbers generated by the P&L and Balance Sheet and turn them into meaningful management tools, we need to make two overall points about the numbers, ratios, and percentages that come from those financial statements:

- ✔ **Comparisons work best.** Numbers, ratios, and percentages are most useful when compared to other numbers, ratios, and percentages. This means that your company may have what appears to be a respectable percentage of net profit on its sales, but if that percentage is less than it was during the same period the preceding year, danger may lie ahead. Numbers are most effective when they can be used to identify trends, and identifying trends always requires a comparison of numbers over time.

- ✔ **The industry matters.** Acceptable numbers in one industry may not be acceptable in another. Industries vary widely as to the numbers they generate. For example, if you are in the software business, you may be disappointed with a 15 percent profit return on your sales dollar (we explain what that means later in this chapter). If you are in the grocery store business, however, you'd probably be ecstatic with a 5 percent profit return on sales.

If you don't know the acceptable ratios and percentages in your industry, contact your trade association. Most trade associations can give you the benchmark ratios and percentages that you need to know to compare your own business to industry averages. *The Small Business Sourcebook* (Gale), which we recommend in Chapter 6, should list associations for your profession.

We strongly advise that you learn how to extract these ratios and percentages from your financial statements by yourself, rather than depending upon your bookkeeper or tax advisor to do so. The process of doing it yourself gives you a better idea of where the numbers come from and how to use the financial statements for other ratios and percentages that may be meaningful to your own individual business.

Although any one of these ratios or percentages alone will not give you all the information that you need to become a sophisticated financial manager, the knowledge of how they all work together will make you much more effective.

In the following sections, we explain seven of the most commonly used percentages and ratios.

Return on sales (R.O.S.)

Return on sales is a percentage determined by dividing net pretax profits (from the P & L) by total sales (also from the P & L). The resulting figure represents that portion of the price of your product that you make on every dollar of sales; thus, it measures your company's overall efficiency in converting a sales dollar into profits. R.O.S. very much depends upon what type of business you operate.

The R.O.S. is an excellent figure on which your employees can focus and increase their motivation to improve company profits. It's relatively easy to track, easy to understand, and easy to explain. Some businesses use this percentage as a companywide scorecard to help their employees understand how the business makes money, motivating them in turn to do their part in assuring profitability.

Return on equity (R.O.E.)

Return on equity is a percentage determined by dividing pretax profits (from the P & L) by Equity/Net Worth (from the Balance Sheet). The resulting figure represents the return on the dollars that you have invested in your business (your *equity*).

Over a period of time (no less than three years for most businesses), if your return on equity isn't higher than 5 percent or thereabouts (which is the average return on money invested in such secure investments as short-term high-quality bonds and money markets), you may want to consider selling your business and investing the proceeds in a bond or money market. Your return would be similar, your risk smaller, and the work easier. (This example assumes that you are in business to "make money." If, however, you are motivated by something else — creativity, growth, independence — or if you simply like owning your own business, you may be happy enough despite the fact that you could make a similar or better return elsewhere.)

Note: Both R.O.S. and R.O.E. are impacted heavily by what the owner decides to take out of the business in the form of salaries, bonuses, and benefits. Obviously, the more taken out, the less the R.O.S. and R.O.E. percentages will be.

Gross margin

Gross margin is a percentage that is determined by subtracting your Cost of Goods Sold (from the P & L) from total Sales (also from the P & L). This figure represents your business's effective overall markup on products sold, before deducting your operating expenses.

How good your gross margin is depends upon your industry, your business, and what you're selling.

Trend is especially important here. Over a period of time, you'd like to see an increasing rather than decreasing gross margin.

Quick ratio

Quick ratio is the ratio that is determined by dividing current assets (from the Balance Sheet) by current liabilities (also from the Balance Sheet). The resulting figure measures your business's *liquidity* (the ability to raise immediate cash from the sale of its assets); thus, this ratio is of great interest especially to your lenders and investors.

The higher the quick ratio (4-to-1, 5-to-1), the more liquid the business. As a general rule, any Quick Ratio in excess of 2-to-1 is considered healthy; anything less is questionable.

Again, trend is especially important here. Over a period of time, you'd like to see an increasing rather than decreasing quick ratio.

Debt-to-equity ratio

The *debt-to-equity ratio* is determined by dividing equity/net worth (from the Balance Sheet) by debt/total liabilities (also from the Balance Sheet). The resulting ratio indicates how much of the business is owned by the owners of the business (represented by equity/net worth) and how much is owned by its creditors (represented by debt/total liabilities).

As a general rule, 1 to 1 is considered healthy; anything less, questionable. To further illustrate this point, refer to the Big Spenders Corp. Balance Sheet. You will note that Big Spenders Corp. owes its creditors and debtors $175,000 (its total liabilities), while the company's net worth is $159,000 (the owner's equity). This means, in effect, that as of the date that this Balance Sheet was assembled, Big Spenders Corp. creditors and debtors had $16,000 more dollars working for the company than the owners did (the difference between $175,000 and $159,000), which means its debt-to-equity ratio was slightly less than 1. If the owners needed another loan to make ends meet, they would have a hard time showing that their financial stake in the company justified another loan.

Keeping the debt-to-equity ratio within the 1 to 1 parameter as outlined above is of paramount importance to the small-business owner. For example when the debt-to-equity ratio falls below 1 to 1, such cash-draining options as adding inventory, hiring new employees, or buying new equipment should be put on hold until the ratio becomes banker-friendly.

Inventory turn

Inventory turn is the number of times your inventory "turns over" each year. The number is determined by dividing your Cost of Goods Sold (from the P & L) by your *average inventory*. If your beginning inventory was $100,000 and your ending inventory was $150,000, then your average inventory would be $125,000.

The figure that results from dividing the average inventory into your Cost of Goods Sold shows how well you are managing your inventory. The higher the number, the more times your inventory has turned — a situation that is always preferable.

The number of times your inventory turns is highly dependent upon the industry and your role in it (manufacturer, wholesaler, retailer). Typical inventory turns can range anywhere from 5 to 20 times a year.

Number of days in receivables

The *number of days in receivables* is determined by first computing your average sales day. An *average sales day* can be computed by dividing your total sales for the period (from the P & L) by the number of days in that period (for a year, use 365).

After you have computed the average sales day, divide that number into your current accounts receivable balance (from the Balance Sheet). The resulting figure will give you the number of sales days in your receivables — that is the average length of time between selling a product or service and getting paid for it.

Generally speaking, anything less than 30 days sales in receivables is excellent; anything between 30 and 45 is acceptable; anything over 45 is cause for concern.

Managing Your Inventory

Aside from cheating the IRS or squealing on the Mafia, the accumulation of excess inventory is the quickest and easiest way we know to get into trouble. Excess inventory and its long list of hidden horrors are sure to turn a healthy business into an ailing one.

Unlike getting rid of employees who aren't performing, you can't give inventory that isn't performing a pink slip and send it out the door. Nor can you step up your collection effort with your inventory, as you would do with your slow-moving receivables, and expect it to turn into cash. Nonperforming inventory just sits there, collecting dust, at the same time that you are paying interest on the money you've invested in it.

Yes, sometimes inventory disappears, but not always in the manner intended and not always in exchange for a customer's money. Inventory can disappear in a number of unsatisfactory ways, including internal theft (by your employees), external theft (by your customers), and at the hands of the most lethal killer of them all — obsolescence.

If inventory is an integral part of your business, use these tips to effectively manage it:

- ✔ Prevention of inventory accumulation starts with the person doing the purchasing. The more information that person has, the better his or her purchasing decisions can be.

  - Make sure that you buy the best inventory-tracking software available, as inventory's past performance is usually the best indicator of how it will perform in the future. A good small-business tax advisor should be able to counsel you on which software is best for you. (If you aren't computerized, ask your accountant to help you develop a manual system.)

  - For those considering entering the retailing business, make sure that you include a point-of-sale program (a system that makes adjustments to inventory as a result of cash register transactions) that is sophisticated enough to capture the information needed for you to accurately track your inventory.

- ✔ Divide your inventory into small, manageable pieces. Pay especially close attention to those pieces where you have the most financial exposure. Remember, inventory is subject to the 80-20 rule: You usually get about 80 percent of your sales from 20 percent of your inventory units. Pay special attention to tracking that 20 percent. And start considering which of the slow-moving 80 percent you may want to discontinue selling.

- ✔ Make sure that you have a workable system and qualified employees in place at the inventory handling corners: shipping and receiving. Most inventory disappearance problems can be identified at one of these two positions. In the event your inventory system is manual, ask your tax advisor to help you establish a workable system — most experienced tax practitioners have dealt with the inventory problem on numerous occasions.

- ✔ Take frequent physical inventories. Count the items in your inventory and compare your physical count to your financial records. This procedure will tell you whether you're having inventory-shrinkage problems and, if so, how significant they are. Also, if you have divided your inventory into small, manageable pieces as suggested earlier, then if you are having shrinkage problems, you can more readily determine where the shrinkage is occurring.

  We suggest that most businesses take a thorough physical inventory at least twice a year, preferably four times.

- ✔ When selecting suppliers, don't simply settle on the supplier with the lowest price. Include delivery time and shipping dependability at or near the top of your criteria. After all, the shorter the delivery time and the more dependable the vendor, the less of that vendor's inventory you will have to carry.

Finally, we have some good news on the subject of inventory. The opportunities to improve profitability by the efficient handling of it are endless. Inventory isn't gray, like marketing, or in the future, like sales; it is here, today, on your shelves, available to touch and feel and count. As a result of its on-your-shelf physical presence, the increased efficiency of handling inventory can have an immediate impact on both profitability (the less inventory you write off the more profitable you will be) and cash flow (the fewer dollars you have invested in inventory the more cash you'll have in your bank account).

As Sam Walton (his company, Wal-Mart, pioneered many inventory-handling techniques over the years) proved so many years ago, if you are one of those businesses that can learn to handle inventory properly, the world is yours for the asking. Walton knew that availability of product would become increasingly important in the days of increased competition and on-time delivery expectations. Those who can provide inventory immediately without shrinking it (having portions of it disappear), and who can ship it immediately without losing it, will be able to write their own tickets to business success.

Collecting Your Accounts Receivables

Banks aren't the only institutions in the business of lending money; most small businesses lend money, too. The primary difference between the two, however, is that when banks lend money to their customers (known as loans), they charge interest; when small businesses lend money to their customers (known as accounts receivable), they usually don't.

Think about it. When customers buy your product (except those of you whose businesses deal only in cash), you usually give them 30 days to pay the invoice. That's 30 days when the customer not only has your product but also retains the cash that is due you — the same cash that could otherwise be used to reduce your debt, pay your bills, or earn interest in your money market account.

Every successful small business needs someone dedicated to the collection of its accounts receivable. In the early stages of the business, that someone is almost always the entrepreneur or founder. In later stages, that responsibility may be delegated to a bookkeeper, controller, or CFO (Chief Financial Officer). But whoever that person happens to be, he or she must be passionate about collecting the monies that are due the business by first politely following up with the slow pays, then relentlessly pursuing them, and then, when all else fails, hauling the deadbeats off to court.

Today's business culture places the customer on a pedestal, and well it should. After all, someone has to purchase your products or services. But that word *customer* is incomplete; the correct phrase should be *paying customer*. Today's successful entrepreneurs know that a customer is not a desired customer until he or she has paid the bill.

Finding customers likely to pay

This collection of tips on how to find, and do business with, "paying customers" should be helpful to you:

✔ **Understand that not everyone is a desirable customer.** Only those customers who pay their bills within a time frame that allows you to make a profit are desirable customers. Don't bet the house on a hot-shot customer who promises big sales; make sure that the customer can also pay.

✔ **Use a credit application.** Design and use your own credit application. Ask one of your vendors to use theirs as a sample. Make sure that every potential customer fills one out before you ship the first order or provide the first service.

✔ **Ask for a financial statement.** Don't be afraid to ask for a financial statement before shipping to a first-time customer. Can you imagine a bank lending you money for your business without first asking for a financial statement?

✔ **Evaluate every applicant.** Ask yourself these questions about every prospective customer who submits a credit application:

- Does this applicant have the ability to pay?

- Has he or she indicated by his or her past actions a willingness to pay on time?

- Can you make a reasonable profit on sales to this account?

If the answer to any of these questions is no, feel free to wave goodbye to the prospective sale.

✔ **Check credit.** You can bet that your good vendors checked on your credit; you should check on your customer's, too. Remember, the granting of credit is a privilege; in effect, you are lending money to the person requesting it. Grant credit like the banks do — with extreme care.

✔ **Establish terms.** No sale should be made without first establishing credit terms. Terms should work for both parties, but remember that when a customer wants you to carry his receivables for long periods of time, that's your signature on the bank's guarantee. Your bank won't back off its terms; why should you?

Managing your accounts receivables

After you have properly established your accounts receivables, you need to figure out how to manage them. Use this collection of suggestions to help you do just that:

- ✔ **What gets measured gets attention.** Outstanding receivables should be *aged* (the process of computing the number of days that every receivable has been outstanding) at least once a month. Create an aging list that sits on the entrepreneur's desk as a constant reminder of who's in control of a large amount of the company's cash. An acceptable age of a receivable (in most industries anyway) is 30 days; danger signals should appear after a receivable exceeds 45 days.

- ✔ **The older the receivable, the less likely to pay.** Don't wait until your receivables are over 90 days old to kick in your collection procedures. Do it while the invoice is still warm (no more than 45 days).

- ✔ **Utilize a carrying charge or interest charge.** Why shouldn't you charge interest on overdue balances? After all, you are expected to pay a carrying charge when you exceed *your* payment terms (review your MasterCard or Visa agreement if you have any doubts on this one). Don't charge anything less than 12 percent. A relatively high interest rate will assure that you get the overdue account's attention.

- ✔ **No pay, no ship.** Don't continue to ship to customers who don't pay in accordance with your terms. Your good vendors won't ship to you if you don't abide by their terms.

- ✔ **Use a collection agency only as a last resort.** Collection agencies are expensive, charging up to 50 percent of the receivable for their services. Also, collection agencies are not known for their consideration and politeness. Be sure that you are willing to kiss your customer goodbye forever should you elect to hand your slow-paying accounts over to an agency.

And finally, remember that your accounts receivables represent cash, and cash is the ultimate measure of your business's liquidity. Liquidity is always the first place lenders and investors will look when appraising the health of your business. You want to make sure that your receivables are current before showing your financial statements to people who have a reason for reading them.

The Three Ways to Improve Profitability

Every small-business owner spends a significant amount of time trying to increase the business's profitability — the difference between revenue (the money you take in) and expenses (the money you pay out). No one succeeds in increasing profitability all of the time, no matter how hard he or she tries. Some succeed often enough to grow a small business into a big one. Some succeed just often enough to survive; and, unfortunately, some don't succeed at all.

Only three ways are available for you to increase your business's profitability:

✔ Decrease expenses.

✔ Increase margins. (Margin is the difference between sales price and the cost of the goods or services that were sold. Margins can be increased by raising prices, lowering the costs of the goods or services sold, or both.)

✔ Increase sales.

Or you can do all three at the same time — that is, if luck and the small-business gods are with you.

Instead of proceeding by trial-and-error, today's successful entrepreneur can use a thorough understanding of how these options work to know exactly where to look when a business's profits aren't what they should be. In the sections that follow, we explain what you need to know about each of these three options.

Decreasing (or controlling) expenses

The biggest advantage that comes from controlling your expenses is that the right expense cuts have a direct short-term impact on the bottom line. For every dollar you save by eliminating an expense, you earn an extra dollar of profit. (Sure, increasing sales is another way of increasing profits, but an extra dollar in sales may only bring in 25 cents of profit. We explain more about that shortly.)

Of course, you see a world of difference between reducing the expense of your phone bill by switching to a company with a lower cost but comparable quality long-distance service and reducing the cost of your product by switching to a supplier that offers lower cost *and* lower quality. Higher returns from disgruntled customers — or worse, lawsuits from harmful products or services — can do more harm than good to your business's long-run profitability.

So, although we're strong advocates of operating a lean business, you must be thoughtful about where and how to reduce your expenses. You must consider *all* the effects of cost cutting, not just the short-term bottom-line effects.

Controlling expenses is a cultural issue, which means that controlling expenses is a lead-by-example issue that begins with you, the business owner, and carries over to your employees (presuming that you've hired the right ones). From the day you open your business's doors, you must pay close attention to its expenses, being careful not to spend money carelessly and being tactfully critical of those who do. If the boss sets the right example, the rest of the company is certain to follow. That is how a company culture flourishes.

The following sections give you guidelines for successfully controlling expenses.

Zero-based budgeting

After you determine what kind of expense controlling culture you want (and make the commitment to act accordingly), the next step is to introduce a zero-based budgeting program. Zero-based budgeting requires that you begin each year's annual budget process by setting each expense category to zero. In other words, you do not assume that the dollar amounts in the preceding year's expense account were legitimate; you question every dollar that went into that expense account. Hence the term "zero-based." For the purpose of budgeting expenses, you begin the budgeting process with a "zero-base" in every expense account.

This zero-based budgeting approach contrasts with the manner in which many businesses budget expenses. Most businesses add a "percentage increase" to the preceding year's expenses, with the prior year's inflation increase being the most frequently used common denominator. If last year's inflation rate was 3 percent, just plug 3 percent into this year's budget and move on to something more exciting.

The primary advantage of budgeting by the percentage-increase method is that it is quick and easy. The primary disadvantage is that it means that last year's fat is destined to be carried forward into this year's diet. And ditto with next year's, and forever — unless that particular expense category is eventually purged through the zero-based budgeting technique.

Here's an example of how zero-based budgeting works: Suppose it's time to budget your telephone expense for the year. The quick and easy solution is to take the preceding year's telephone expense figure, add 3 percent (or whatever inflation is) and move on to the next line item on the Profit & Loss Statement. The zero-based budgeter, however, assumes that last year's telephone expenses were zero, and begins the laborious process of pricing competing telephone services. He calls alternative carriers, collects quotes on their services, and oftentimes awards his business to a less-expensive carrier. More often than not, the additional time spent budgeting will be rewarded with a decrease in expenses.

Tips for controlling the fat

In addition to zero-based budgeting, effective control of expenses requires understanding the 80-20 rule as it applies to your various expense categories. The 80-20 rule maintains that 80 percent of your wasted expense dollars can usually be found in 20 percent of your expense categories.

Challenge expenses in all categories, large and small. You can usually find quick-and-easy dollars to save by rooting around in such overlooked expense categories as utilities, travel and entertainment, insurance, and the compost heap of them all, the miscellaneous category.

These important tips provide a framework in which you can effectively control your expenses:

- ✔ **Avoid overstaffing.** Finding and hiring a good employee is costly, and after you've hired one, it's difficult and expensive to unhire him or her. Use outside contractors, temporary services, and part-timers if you're on the fence about the need to hire a full-time employee.

- ✔ **Automate where possible.** Technology is usually cheaper than people (and it can be depreciated). When possible and where it won't compromise the quality of your products or services, purchase software in lieu of hiring additional employees. Functions such as accounting, inventory control, accounts receivable, and payroll lend themselves to automation. Let technology do your detail work.

- ✔ **Don't wait until a crisis arrives to do something about your expenses.** Institute an expense-control program when things are going well; you don't have to wait until the roof caves in. Be motivated by efficiency, not by fear.

- ✔ **Put the responsibility for controlling expenses where it belongs — in the hands of the employees who spend the money.** Also, make them accountable for their actions. Reward them when they meet their goals, and provide corrective feedback when they don't.

After you've made the *commitment* to maximize your profitability, the "controlling your expenses" option should always be the first place to turn. Everything you do in the process of controlling expenses will have a direct — and immediate — impact on your earnings.

The preceding tips are intended to provide you with an overview of how to control your expenses. Following are several specific cost-controlling measures, intended not only to give you specific ideas but also to put you in the frame of mind for getting specific on all your expenses:

- ✔ **Don't pay unnecessary bank charges.** Shop around if your bank is charging for services that you think you shouldn't have to pay for. Some banks today are aggressively pursuing small businesses. Just about everything is negotiable.

✔ **Shop your telephone service every year or so.** Everyone is discounting telephone services as technology and deregulation make prices more competitive.

✔ **Ask for price quotes before you obligate yourself to services.** This is true for everything from lawyers, accountants, and financial advisers to computer repair people, plumbers, and consultants. (Often the quotes won't hold up but they will give you a basis on which to negotiate subsequent charges.) Also, always ask for itemized invoices.

✔ **If you have employees, review your experience ratio with your insurance agent.** Your experience ratio is the factor that determines your worker's compensation payment. (See Chapter 8.)

✔ **Speaking of insurance agents, how long has it been since you've shopped for insurance?** So, what are you waiting for?

Incidentally, we're not suggesting here that price should be your only consideration or that after you've found a lower price, you should automatically wave goodbye to your current supplier. Rather, we're suggesting that you be aware of the going rate in the marketplace and, where appropriate, either change suppliers or press your current supplier to reassess the prices he's charging you. Squeaking wheels get the grease, and the effective control of expenses is no exception to this rule.

The preceding tips are a few of the many possible ways for you to control your business's expenses. Remember that effective expense control is not a one-time event; it is an ongoing occurrence whose success or failure lies entirely in your hands.

Increasing margins

Gross margin represents the difference between the selling price and the cost of the product or service in question. If your product sells for $15 and the cost of that product (including shipping charges) is $10, then your gross margin is 33 percent (the $5 in margin or markup divided by the $15 gross sales price) and your gross margin dollars are $5 (the difference between the $10 cost and the $15 sales price). For more on gross margin, see the discussion on pricing in Chapter 9.

The magic of increasing margins is that, similar to decreasing expenses, every dollar of income derived from the margin increase, assuming no reduction in sales, ends up as profit on the bottom line. In the preceding example, if the price of the product is raised to $16, the margin jumps from 33 percent to 37.5 percent, and the gross margin dollars increase from $5 to $6. Because it generally costs little to increase prices, the entire $1 of the price increase will be realized as profit, again assuming no reduction in purchasing from customers.

Consider the case of the small business doing $500,000 in sales in a year. If the owner, at the beginning of the year, decides to increase the prices of his products by an average of 1 percent, that would mean an additional $5,000 in profits at the end of the year. An average of 2 percent would add another $10,000, 5 percent a solid $25,000 (again, all this assumes that the price increases would not reduce sales).

It should be added that the tolerance of your customers to accept price increases will depend on such issues as competition, alternative products, and most of all, the customer relationships you maintain. (See Chapter 10 for tips on keeping your customers happy.)

We strongly recommend that every small-business owner review the margins on every product or service at least once a year. Determine a time of the year when it makes the most sense to raise prices (usually at the beginning of the business's fiscal year), mark that date on your calendar in indelible ink, and start with your lowest-priced item and work up. Be sure to analyze the percentage of price increase on each individual item. Don't simply increase prices using an across-the-board percentage increase; look at each individual item. Also, be sure to aim for higher margins on the lower priced items and on those products that do not need to be as competitively priced.

You don't have to wait until the end (or the beginning) of the year to consider increasing your prices. You may want to consider a price increase when the demand on your product suddenly increases. Perhaps a competitor has raised his prices, or perhaps the law of supply and demand is hard at work — in other words, maybe more demand than supply for the product in question can provide a perfect scenario for raising prices. (You needn't feel guilty for taking advantage of such situations — you will encounter plenty of occasions when the law of supply and demand works in reverse, and you will be forced to *cut* your prices.)

Increasing sales

After your expenses have been zero-based and after your margins have been increased, it is time to do what every entrepreneur worth his weight in loan guarantees loves to do. Increase sales.

After all, increasing sales is what most of us are born to do, and besides, offense (increasing sales) is always more enjoyable than defense (cutting expenses). We love to roll out a new product, hire a new salesperson (it's always more fun to hire a salesperson than it is a bookkeeper), or develop a new sales promotion. What's more, the results of a plan to increase sales can be easily measured.

Chapter 12

Escaping the #1 Cause of Failure on the Road to Success

In This Chapter

▶ The number one cause of small-business failure

▶ The options to learning by trial-and-error

*A*ll right, here's an important question:

> *What's the number one cause of small-business failure?*

Hands shoot up.

> *What's that? No, it isn't a lack of money. Sorry, not lousy location. No, not poor distribution either. Give up?*

All heads nod.

> *The answer is isolation. The small-business owner's isolation.*

All right now, dear reader, admit it. You were wrong, too.

A lack of money and lousy location and poor distribution aren't causes of failure, they're only symptoms . . . symptoms of that dreaded sickness, Owner's Isolation Syndrome. These symptoms affect every small-business owner at one time or another in the course of his or her career — generic symptoms that won't occur if the small-business owner commits to preventing the disease. In the end, the owner's isolation does not itself cause the demise of his or her small business; the mistakes caused by the trial-and-error system of management that follows are what does it in. How unfortunate and unnecessary this situation is, when so many options exist for overcoming it.

Overcoming Isolation

In light of our status as charter members of the never-bring-up-a-problem-without-an-accompanying-solution club, we present a collection of options that will help you do away with the trial-and-error method of small-business management. We recommend that you make room for them all in your repertoire.

Soak up information like a sponge

Magazines and books (and associated videos, audiotapes, and CDs) abound. Where small business is concerned, you name it, and a book has been written about it —including this one!

In addition, read your industry trade publications (which you can often find through the industry's trade association(s) discussed later in this section). Also, check out the *Small Business Sourcebook* (Gale), which you can find in most public libraries.

Find a mentor

We know two things for sure:

- If we had our small-business careers to live over again, the first thing we would do is find ourselves a mentor.
- Somewhere out there is a veteran small-business owner who would agree to be *your* mentor if you approach him or her correctly.

Mentors are in the experience business, and that experience is the best teacher of them all (that's why it's so expensive!). But what everyone doesn't know is how to find the veteran who would agree to become a mentor and provide that experience. Us to the rescue. Here's our three-step Mentor Search Plan:

1. **Compile a list of prospective mentors.**

   Ask your banker, your accountant, your lawyer, and those folks around town (Chamber of Commerce, Service Corps of Retired Executives, Small Business Development Centers) who are wired into the small-business community for the names of veteran small business owners who might be interested in helping you succeed.

2. Pick up the telephone and call the person that your research and intuition indicate may be the best mentor for you.

Use the following suggestions to aid both your research and your intuition:

> Remember, this is a "relationship" you are seeking here; where possible, you want to make sure that you and your mentor will be compatible.

> The best way to approach your prospective mentor would be to write him or her a letter introducing you and your business and the reason for your interest. Then follow up the letter with a phone call (see below).

> Of course, the best mentor would be someone who (currently or previously) has experience within your industry, but this is not a prerequisite. (General business knowledge is a prerequisite.)

3. Persuade your prospective mentor to take the job.

Proceed as follows:

> "Mr. (or Ms.) Veteran, my name is Wanda Wannabe. Mr. Legal Beagle, a mutual friend of ours, suggested I call you.

> "Mr. Veteran, I'm not looking for your money, but I am looking for your advice. Would you agree to spare a small amount of your time to meet with me if I promise not to waste one nanosecond of it, if I organize that hour and provide you with a complete agenda in advance of every meeting, if I follow up on your suggestions, and if you can name the place and time of that meeting, along with your price?

> "Mr. Veteran," you conclude, with just a touch of a plea in your voice, "as you have probably surmised, I am looking for a mentor. Would you consider being that person?"

Hey, this pitch works. We should know; it's been successfully used on both of us, and on other business owners we know.

Here are several tips on how to keep your mentor and make the most of the relationship:

✔ Don't ask a mentor for money.

✔ Understand that mentoring is a personal experience, not a business one. If the chemistry is right, the relationship works well. If the chemistry doesn't work, the relationship won't work either.

✔ Follow up, follow up, follow up. Drop your mentor a note, or the next time the two of you talk, let your mentor know how implementing the advice turned out and how much you appreciate the help.

- Be honest and straightforward with your mentor about the problems and issues you face. No sugarcoating allowed. Your mentor will see through that anyway, and think less of you.

- Leave your thin skin at home. Good mentors speak their minds and aren't shy about shooting down poor ideas.

- Don't blindly follow all your mentor's advice. Your mentor may have different priorities, ethics, and needs than you do. So in the end, follow your heart as well as your head in making decisions based on your mentor's input. Just make sure to show respect and consideration in your disagreements.

- Most mentors prefer to deal with strategic issues (long term, fundamental and always critical) as opposed to operational issues (short term, day-to-day, and often temporary).

- A mentoring experience may endure for one day, one month, one year, or the lifetime of your business. The only determinant is how well the relationship works for both parties involved.

Network with peers

Although nobody knows the business of small business better than a veteran of the fight, finishing a close second in the antidote-to-lonely-decision-making competition is a current small-business owner. A peer. A peer who is facing the same day-to-day issues that you face.

Imagine the power of putting a dozen or so current small-business owners in the same room. Imagine the wealth of solutions that appear when one of the members presents a nagging problem or a thorny issue. You say you have a problem with an employee who can't seem to get to work on time? Someone else has had the same problem before . . . discover what has worked for him. You say you don't have a personnel manual yet? Someone else has already gone to the trouble of assembling one and could lend hers to you.

This kind of peer networking works because, as we say throughout this book, many of a small-business's problems are generic — that is, they're not unique to the industry or niche a particular small business finds itself in. Thus, most solutions to these common problems are generic, too.

Second only to what a good mentor can offer, peer networking is the best of the small-business owner's learning devices, *if* you can locate the right networking resource. (Sorry, we're not talking Rotary Clubs or Chambers of Commerce here, although they are a step in the right direction.) Some cities already have peer networking programs up and running, ask at your local Chamber of Commerce or your city's or state's small-business magazine or newspaper to find out what and where these programs are.

Several for-profit and/or non-profit peer networking organizations have surfaced across the country in the past several years, as the value of this concept has spread. These organizations include

- ✔ The Executive Committee (TEC), San Diego, California
- ✔ Entrepreneurs Edge, San Diego, California (associated with TEC)
- ✔ American Women's Economic Development Corp. (AWED), Washington, D.C.
- ✔ The Alternative Board (TAB), St. Louis, Missouri
- ✔ President Resource Organization (PRO), Chicago, Illinois
- ✔ Opportunity Knocks (OK), Bend, Oregon (Jim founded this organization)

One or more of these organizations (or another with a similar agenda) may surface in your city if one isn't there already. Keep your eyes peeled.

Form a Board of Advisors

Boards of Advisors are like breath mints; almost everybody could benefit from one, but too few of us partake.

Similar to mentors, boards provide the isolated small-business owner with an affordable, outside perspective. Boards replace trial-and-error with experience and knowledge. They act as sounding boards, and rebound boards, and boards of inquiry. They open needed doors and close unnecessary ones, while giving the small-business owner an inside look at the outside world.

Incidentally, we're not talking about a Board of Directors here, we're talking about a Board of Advisors. Directors are responsible for directing the company; advisors are responsible only for advising the president or CEO (Chief Executive Officer). Because directors, by virtue of accepting their positions, assume the "fiduciary responsibility" (meaning they are responsible to the shareholders for the financial state of the business) of directing the company, they are legally liable for its direction. Since directors can be sued, smart companies that use a Board of Directors must also carry an expensive Directors and Officers Insurance package on their positions. For the above reasons, most public companies utilize Boards of Directors while most privately held small businesses use Boards of Advisors.

There are few valid reasons not to have a Board of Advisors. Yes, they do take time to organize and coordinate, but that time will be repaid many times over if your board is a good one. They are also inexpensive — most board members will gladly donate an hour or two of their time every three months for the price of a good lunch (if, that is, your board meetings are well organized, and if the board members feel that their time isn't being wasted, and if they feel their advice is being heeded).

Most small-business boards consist of five or so members, including the owner. (If you're a home office business, perhaps you might want only three board members.) Here are some tips on how to assemble and utilize your own Board of Advisors:

- **Select advisors from outside your company, not inside.** No board of employees here, all nodding their heads in unison in case dissent becomes grounds for dismissal. Besides, you're looking for knowledge that doesn't already exist in the company.

- **Balance your own skills with the skills of the board members.** If your strengths are sales and marketing, make sure that the finance and operational bases are covered through advisory board members. Could you use a banker on the board? A lawyer? An accountant?

- **Include a customer as a board member.** No viewpoint can equal the viewpoint of a customer. Never go to a board meeting without one.

- **Schedule meetings regularly and well in advance.** Give at least one month's notice, maybe more. Quarterly meetings are usually the best.

- **Avoid surprises.** Send out an agenda in advance of the meeting and then stick with it, unless an emergency prompts some last-minute changes.

- **Focus on strategic and overview issues.** Do not discuss operations; limit the meetings to two hours, keep them meaty and keep the advisors interested. (The difference between operations and strategy? Strategic issues are issues of business direction and positioning; they include such subjects as distribution systems, marketing plans, and sales initiatives. Operational issues include specific problems such as administrative snafus, shipping and receiving roadblocks, and invoicing issues. And what about the biggest issue of them all, cash flow? Although a shortage of cash is really an operational problem, it is always caused by a strategic problem — not enough sales, inadequate margins, or out-of-control expenses.)

- **Be truthful.** Lose your credibility, and you lose your advisors. Be candid — no sugarcoating or truthbending allowed.

- **Follow up on suggestions.** Follow up on your board's recommendations, not just those you consider to be valid. You don't have to *act* upon every recommendation; you should, however, have the courtesy to *respond* to all seriously considered recommendations and ideas.

- **Pay the board.** If you can afford it, you should pay them anywhere from $50 per meeting on up. If you're a start-up and money is tight, at least buy them lunch until you can afford to compensate them.

After your advisors are comfortable with you and your business, you can ask to use their credibility and contacts to help you gain new customers, new vendors, and new sources of financing. If you've developed a good working relationship with your board, most board members are willing to let you use their names and their contacts.

Get a partner

For sure, you may have plenty of reasons not to want to take a partner (or multiple partners) into your business. Everyone knows juicy horror stories about business partnerships that turned sour and even ended up in court, destroying the business in the process (assuming anything was left to destroy by the time the opposing partners made it that far). Warring partners seldom go down alone.

Well, partnerships are just another example of how the risk-reward equation works. Sure, partnerships present a distinct risk that doesn't exit when you go it alone. After all, partnerships are really nothing more than organized relationships, and we all know what can happen to relationships, organized or not. Even the good ones are difficult to maintain.

But here's a fact that not everyone knows. According to studies, partnerships outperform sole proprietorships by a wide margin. Although the studies don't differentiate, we're sure the success ratio is highest when the two partners have complementary skills. You're a salesnik? Find an operations type for a partner. Your skills are in product development? Find someone who has experience in getting the product to the marketplace and subsequently sold. You're a mover and shaker? Find someone who can count the beans that you have been moving and shaking.

How does one find a partner (or partners)? The same way you'd find a key employee, or find a consultant or find a mentor. You'd identify what it is you'd need (in this case the skills you'd be looking for) and then network your available resources. (For much more on partnerships, see Chapter 5.)

The number one rule of a partnership? **Don't enter into a partnership without first consulting a lawyer.** The lawyer will advise you and your prospective partner about the many obstacles that lie in the path of a successful partnership. Then the lawyer will assist you in drawing up an ironclad, airtight, cast-in-stone, buy-sell partnership agreement to overcome those obstacles — an ironclad, airtight, cast-in-stone, buy-sell partnership agreement, by the way, that will be tested many times over the life of the business, if not by you then by your next-of-kin. Or by your partner's. (For much, much more on partnerships and partnership agreements, see Chapter 5.)

Testing the partnership waters

So, how can you test a partnership before you get in so far you can't get out? First, ask your attorney or accountant for the names of partners who currently own a business together. Meet with them (without your prospective partner), ask questions, find out the pros and cons of partnering. And, yes, ask your attorney or accountant for the names of the people who have been involved in failed partnerships, too. You can learn just as much from people's failures as you can from their successes.

We also suggest you give your partnership a trial run before you open your business. For starters, write your business plan together; doing this will give you an immediate insight into whether or not you're capable of working side by side. Next, investigate your financing options together; meet with your probable vendors, interview potential customers, do everything just short of hanging out your shingle for business and guaranteeing the bank loan. Sure, the time involved in testing a partnership this way may cost a month or two of doing business, and it may make the business formation process a tad messier than it would have been if you'd started from ground zero. But we can guarantee you this: No matter how messy the formation process may be, it will never be as messy as the dissolution of a failed partnership.

As someone once said, business is life. And so it is with partnerships. Shotgun weddings don't usually work; shotgun partnerships don't usually work either.

So why might a partnership make sense? Let us count the reasons:

1. **Complementary skills**

   We discuss this earlier in this section as the most important benefit of partnerships. Although most of us are aware of our own individual strengths, our human nature lets us more easily overlook our weaknesses. Ask those who know you well — family, friends, and current or previous co-workers — what complementary skills you should seek in a business partner. And, try doing some honest introspection.

2. **Additional capital**

   Two savings accounts are better than one.

3. **Additional problem solving capacity**

   Two heads are usually better than one.

4. **More flexibility**

   One partner goes on vacation or gets sick, the other one minds the store.

5. **Ease of formation**

   Partnerships are easier, and less expensive, to form than corporations (but not as easy, or inexpensive, as sole proprietorships).

6. **Less risk**

   Profits aren't the only thing partnerships share.

The most important thing to remember when forming a partnership is that you are beginning what you hope is a long-term relationship — a long-term relationship that sometimes rivals a marriage in terms of complexity. If you're smart, you'll determine a way to test the chemistry of the partnership before you get so far involved that you can't get out. Otherwise, you may learn the same lesson that too many marriages teach — a lifetime can be a long time.

Join a trade association

Thousands of trade associations exist in the United States. No matter who you are or what industry you're in, a trade association is probably available for you. The best trade associations offer a wide range of potential benefits, everything from business contacts to skill-building workshops to industry-specific information. In addition, most trade associations host an industry-wide trade show at least once a year during which you can mingle with suppliers and peers.

Two kinds of trade associations exist: industry-specific trade associations and small-business-specific trade associations.

- **Industry-specific trade associations:**

  Consult your local library for the trade association or organization that caters to your industry. The *Encyclopedia of Associations* (published by Columbia Books, Washington, D.C.) lists more than 30,000 trade associations in the U.S. today. Your local library should have a copy. Or, search your Web browser by keying in the name of the specific industry that you're in, followed by the word "association," as in **sporting goods association**.

- **Small-business-specific trade associations:**

  Small-business-specific trade associations include:

    - **National Small Business United (NSBU):** This association watches congressional action and reports on issues affecting small business. See its Web site (`bizserve.com/nsb`) for details.

- **National Association for the Self-Employed (NASE):** NASE offers resource materials and a monthly magazine. Call 800-232-NASE for details.

- **National Association of Women Business Owners (NAWBO):** This association brings together women entrepreneurs for support and assistance. Call 800-55-NAWBO for details.

- **National Business Association (NBA):** The NBA assists the small-business person in achieving his or her personal and professional goals. Call 800-465-0440 for details.

- **National Federation of Independent Business Owners (NFIB):** The NFIB is the largest lobbying organization for small business in the country. Call 615-872-5800 for details.

- **American Home Business Association (AHBA):** This association is aimed at the small business owner who works out of the home. Call 800-664-2422 for details.

Trade associations are not without their warts. First, don't assume that products and services marketed to the association's members are necessarily the best of what's out there. Many associations, for example, offer insurance programs to their members that could be purchased at a lower cost elsewhere. Remember that the programs a trade association offers are only as good as the people who determine what that association will offer its members and what it won't.

Also, don't limit yourself to providing a product or service just the way people in the trade association say to provide it. For example, when Eric began offering personal financial counseling services, he chose to do so exclusively on an hourly basis even though most other financial advisors either worked on commission or managed money for fees. Eric knew their way was not the only way, and the path he chose reflected his belief that a financial counselor should have no personal financial stake dependent on any of the products or services that he or she recommends. This policy has worked well for him.

Stay informed

Magazines and books (and associated videos, tapes, and CDs) abound. Where small business is concerned, you have a wide variety of topics and programs to choose from.

As the Internet continues to grow, the small-business resources available continue to grow as well. Familiarize yourself with this medium and keep up to speed on the new offerings under the small-business category. See Chapter 19 for our top resource recommendations, and Chapter 3 for helpful government resources, such as the Small Business Administration.

Part IV
Keeping Your Business in Business

The 5th Wave   By Rich Tennant

Disney Corp. vs. Diznee's Magic Kingpin Bowling Alleys

Okay, we'll change the name of the bowling alleys, but about our bowling ball caps, do these really look like mouse ears, your honor? I mean really now...

In this part . . .

Once you start your business, the real fun begins — staying in business, and growing your business. This part puts you through your paces, covering employee issues, government regulations, taxes, and everything else we could think of that didn't fit elsewhere in this volume.

Chapter 13

Finding and Keeping Superstar Employees

● ●

In This Chapter

▶ Hiring superstar employees

▶ Training and motivating your employees

▶ Rewarding a job well done and offering corrective feedback

▶ Terminating an employee — when all else fails

▶ Assembling an employee manual

▶ Determining whether or not to lease employees

● ●

*H*ow times have changed! Unlike a generation ago, today's good employees generally have a large number of employment options available to them at any given time.

As a result, today's employer must learn to savor employees — at least the good ones — or they'll exercise those options and move on. "Savoring employees" is another way of saying "solving their problems." After you solve their problems, they can reciprocate by solving yours.

The management procedures in this chapter are designed to help you keep your employees happy, and in the process, keep them exactly where they belong: working for you, not for your competition or someone else.

Why You Need Superstars

If you're like most small-business owners we know, you may work without any employees at all for a period of time and then, after you decide to hire employees, you may find that you only need or want to hire one or two. However, if you have ambitions to really grow your business, you'll probably end up hiring many employees. After all, employees mean leverage (increased means of accomplishing your mission) in the world of business, and leverage opens up the opportunities for growth.

No matter what size company you aspire to own, you still want to hire the best employees possible. For those of you who make the decision to grow, you should know that one of the entrepreneur's most important duties is to assemble a team of superstars in gamebreaker positions (the key roles that will make or break your company).

Every business has a number of gamebreaker positions. When you're just starting out, that position may be yours alone, as you may be the only employee. In larger, established small businesses those gamebreaker positions may include the president/CEO/grand poobah (that's you), the financial person, the sales manager, the marketing manager, the production manager, maybe the office manager, maybe the purchasing agent, maybe the art director. . . . well, you get the point. The number of gamebreaker positions depends upon the type of business, the size of the business, and the number of tasks that the owner assigns to herself.

Every successful, growing business must have superstars filling its gamebreaker positions.

A superstar is an employee who

- Is capable of taking on increasing responsibilities and contributing to the company's continued growth
- Is loyal to the entrepreneur's vision
- Shares the entrepreneur's ethics and principles
- Is creative within his or her area of expertise
- Adds to the synergy of the team — superstars aren't superstars unless they can work effectively with other team members
- Welcomes positive change

You should have no trouble recognizing a superstar when you see one. The trick, of course, is finding and keeping them.

Assembling your team of superstars is a three-part process — hiring, training, and motivating. Unfortunately, in the process of hiring people who you hope are superstars, you will sometimes stumble and hire someone who doesn't work out. Sadly, that calls for a related process: Firing.

Assembling a Team of Superstar Employees

The best employees go to the entrepreneur who is willing to go to the most trouble to find them.

Hiring is mostly science, not art, it's science, and a darn sight less exciting a science than, say, oceanography or archeology. It's methodical, it can be repetitive, and it's a drawn-out, brain-dulling process.

You must first collect a roster of worthwhile applicants for the position, by running an ad, by putting out a sign or a Web site posting, or by encouraging referrals from employees, vendors, and customers. Referrals are usually the best of the options; referrals are more likely to be skilled applicants (those doing the referring don't want the embarrassment of referring a weak applicant) and it is always the least expensive. Referrals cost next to nothing — just get the word out and let your employees, vendors, or customers do the talking.

You may, on occasion, when hiring for a part-time position or a minimum-wage job, receive applicants who don't have resumes. Be sure you have an application form ready for them to fill out (ask your accountant or any active business for a copy of the form they use). Never accept an applicant for a responsible position (responsible for managing employees, for handling money, for dealing with customers and so on) without a resume. If the applicant hasn't taken the time to complete a resume, that alone will tell you all you need to know about her potential for the job.

After you've collected the resumes comes the tough part — you must interview, then reinterview, and then reinterview again. You must check those often-camouflaged references, whose primary function, you soon learn, is to tell you as little as possible about a candidate's faults in between glowing adjectives.

Hints for hiring

Following is a list of hiring hints to help you locate and hire that elusive superstar:

- ✔ When running an ad, remember, you are selling an opportunity, not offering a job — write the ad with this in mind. You want (we're assuming) to attract a career-minded employee who wants to grow with your company, thus you must paint your company, and the position, in a similarly attractive light. Review a large number of existing ads carefully, and then use bits and pieces of the best ones.

- ✔ Establish a reward system to encourage your employees to introduce qualified candidates. The best candidates often come from inside-the-company referrals. Rewards can include anything from cash to vacation days.

- ✔ Always prepare a job description (see "Writing performance expectations" later on in this chapter) in advance. Good applicants want to know exactly what the job entails and what is expected of them. Include the job definition, performance expectations, salary, expected bonus, perks, and the chain-of-command, as it relates to the position being interviewed.

✔ Try to open the door to more candid conversations when you're talking to the applicant's references. Look for areas of commonality in order to put the person at ease. Tune in for the little things as you listen. Ask about the applicant's weaknesses, and then multiply — most references are prone to sugarcoating. And remember, the reference's reluctance to provide information on the applicant should not necessarily be construed as negative to the applicant; the reference may simply be protecting himself.

✔ Review the applicant's resume, looking for businesses or people you may know who are not listed as one of the candidate's "official references." The most informative references may be those the applicant doesn't list. Such "third-party references" are usually more candid with their comments than the official references are.

✔ Look for the applicant's ability to listen. If he doesn't listen well during an interview, he's unlikely to listen well after you hire him and he's on the job.

✔ Find out what research the applicant has done on you and your company. If she comes to the interview unprepared and devoid of knowledge about your company and industry, you are learning something about either her work habits or the depth of her desire for the job.

✔ Remember that the hiring process usually requires you to wear two hats:

- The detective's hat, as you interview and separate potential superstars from the rest of the pack

- The salesperson's hat, to be donned after the superstar is found

Don't forget to prepare for the second role, and don't incorrectly assume your company is the only, or the best, opportunity in town. Show your prospective superstar how working for you will also benefit her.

Hiring right brings you an endless list of benefits. The biggest is that the better the employee you hire, the less time you have to spend managing him. Instead, you can spend your time on other product (or service) development, business-building activities, such as marketing and sales, hiring more employees, supervising the production floor, or doing those things you enjoy most.

The interview process

The following process should be used when hiring any employee who is not either part time or in line for a minimum wage position. Yes, the process is time-consuming and will take you away from other projects that may appear to be more meaningful and are certainly more enjoyable. But remember, the price you'll pay for doing a second-rate job of hiring is that you'll have to do the process costly and time-consuming over again.

The process of hiring superstar employees should proceed along these lines:

✔ **Interview #1:** Takes place in your office with you asking probing questions and the interviewee doing about 90 percent of the talking. (If he isn't doing that much of the talking, then *you* are talking too much.) Immediately following the interview, assuming it went well, begin the reference-checking process, while the details are still fresh in your mind.

✔ **Interview #2:** Meet on neutral turf this time, maybe for breakfast or lunch. Relax the interviewee, loosen him up, get a look at his social and personal side (though be careful, here; simply observe the behavior; personal questions may get you into areas that you legally can't enter; we discuss those later). Ask any puzzling questions that may have emerged as a result of the reference checks.

✔ **Interview #3:** If all has gone well, have the applicant go through the interviewing process with other key employees who have a stake in the hire. Ask their opinions. Compare. If the applicant isn't going to mesh with your key employees, better to find out now than later.

✔ **Interview #4:** Review, negotiate, and close — if the applicant still passes muster. Then cross your fingers — employees don't come with guarantees, no matter how thorough a job you do. (Your odds do improve with experience, however.)

Don't forget to ask open-ended questions in the interview. Open-ended questions are those that can't be answered well with a simple yes or no; the questions are designed primarily to get the interviewee talking. Following are a few of our favorite open-ended questions to help discover those superstar job applicants:

✔ **What is the number one trait that differentiates you from other applicants?** Look for something measurable here — specific accomplishments, specific skills, specific prior jobs. Get inside the general statements such as, "I'm a people person" or "I meet my deadlines" or "I'm a hard worker" by asking specific questions: "What makes you a people person — give me an example." Watch out for egotistical and egocentric responses; large egos usually get in the way of becoming a team player.

- ✔ **What is your most significant business achievement?** Again, look for specifics. If this is the person's first job, ask for her most significant achievement in whatever else she has done — schooling, homemaking, and so on.

- ✔ **What was your biggest failure and what did you learn from it?** Look for honesty here. Everyone has had failures. Promising applicants have no trouble admitting theirs and are quick to tell you what they learned from them. Insecure applicants have trouble admitting failure and thus may have a difficult time learning from it.

- ✔ **What are your weaknesses?** Everyone has weaknesses. The honest and mature applicant readily admits his or hers. Where the applicant can't come up with any, soften the question to "What kind of work do you dislike?" or "What aspects of this job will you enjoy the most and what will you least enjoy?"

- ✔ **What are your strengths?** Specifics again. Ask for examples. Does the candidate's strengths match the needs of the position?

- ✔ **What do you want to be doing five years from now?** The "right" answer to this question is determined by the position you are hiring for and your own personal goals for the company. For gamebreaker positions in a growing company, for instance, you may look for an answer signifying that the candidate wants increasing responsibility over the next five years. On the other hand, if you are hiring someone into, say, a truck-driver position from which you don't anticipate promotion possibilities, you may hope that the candidate's response is that he wants to be doing the same thing five years from now that he would be doing today — driving a truck.

Be aware that some questions could land you in court if you ask them. You shouldn't ask the applicant's age, race, religion, nationality, or political persuasion. And you shouldn't inquire about his or her marital status, parental status, or wealth.

Training Your Team: It's an Investment

Training is the most-efficient and least-expensive answer to employee improvement. Unfortunately, however, training remains close to the bottom of too many small-business owners' priority lists.

A young friend of ours who took his initial job out of college with Xerox relates that in his first year of employment he spent five full months in formal training. Tack on another full month of reading and study, and several more months of on-the-job training, and our friend had more training in one year than many small-business employees get in 20.

We're not sure that the Xerox approach is the best one (because such a well-trained employee can easily be lost to another employer), but we do know this: Too often, small-business owners view training as an expense and not as the investment it really is.

Think about it, the money you spend on leasing an automobile, buying a mahogany desk, represents money gone forever. Meanwhile, the money you invest in training good employees is money that comes back to you later in the form of increased productivity.

We've heard small-business owners complain about the cost of training, especially when that training results in the employee moving on to greener pastures — and taking her knowledge with her. Although such occurrences definitely do take place, part of the reason that employees move on is because they don't get the training they need. Besides, as the saying goes, "if you think training employees and watching them leave is expensive, try not training them and watching them stay!"

Training comes in many forms and from various sources. Unlike Xerox Corp., which generates much of its training from in-house sources, small-business training usually comes from the outside. The most obvious options are shown in the following list:

- ✔ **Consultants** have perhaps the most potential as trainers, but are also the most expensive and risky (see Chapter 8).

- ✔ **Vendors** can also be an excellent resource for training, and less costly than consultants. Some vendors provide free training on their products or services (see Chapter 8).

- ✔ **Seminars** can be expensive in both dollars and time, and their potential value is difficult to predict. Good seminars are great bargains; bad ones are outlandish scams. Potentially the best seminars, and usually the least expensive, are those put on by your trade association.

- ✔ **Schooling** (universities, colleges, night schools, and vocational training), although probably more dependable than seminars, is also difficult to predict. The benefit of the course depends entirely on the quality of the instructor.

   Consider offering a tuition-reimbursement program whereby employee's expenses for related-to-the-business outside studies are reimbursed. The benefits to the company from such a program include goodwill, the development of a self-improvement culture, and the infusion of new ideas in its employees. Require a B grade (or better) for reimbursement, to be paid after the course is completed.

- ✔ **Books** are a great value. In fact, a good book is the ultimate training bargain. Read it (or have your employees read it) between projects, put it down when you please, and refer to it always. Keep it forever or pass it on to a friend or another employee. Extract and implement one good idea, no matter how small, and the $20 you've shelled out is quickly repaid, many times over. Every good idea after the first one is a bonus. (Audiotapes, audiocourses, and videotapes fall into this same category.)

✔ **The Internet** is becoming an increasingly valuable training tool for both small-business owners and employees. More and more training classes are found on the Net — some are "for pay" and some are "for free." Be sure to investigate the agenda of the "course" sponsor.

Motivating Your Team: Issues of Pay and Performance

If you've read John Gray's book *Men are from Mars, Women are from Venus* about how the differences between men and women affect their relationships with one another, you definitely have a head start when it comes to dealing with employees. That's because similar principles often apply: Employees are from Mars, employers are from Venus. Yes, the two oftentimes don't reside on the same planet. No, make that the same solar system!

People who study such things tell us that the typical employee is motivated by the following (in this particular order):

✔ Recognition/appreciation

✔ Being part of a team

✔ Having problems solved

✔ Security

✔ Money

Meanwhile, the typical entrepreneur is motivated by one or more of the following (in no particular order):

✔ Creativity/growth

✔ Money

✔ Power

✔ Freedom

✔ Survival

Although the two lists have some overlap, what motivates you, the employer, is probably quite different from what motivates your employees. So, if you expect your employees to perform as you want them to, you must learn to motivate them differently than you motivate yourself.

What employees really want

Employees are like spouses. Just when you think you have them figured out, they do or say something that leaves you scratching your head. Here's what we mean.

An acquaintance of ours is the local manager of a small (20 employees) wholesale business. One day, the home office sent a consultant to his branch to conduct an employee survey. It seems that the home office wanted to delve deeper into its employees' wants and needs, to learn what they liked and didn't like about the company, and to determine ways to improve the workplace environment. "A waste of time and money," our friend groused, as some managers (and owners) are prone to do when consultants come bearing suggestions. "I already know what my employees want: more money, more benefits, more vacation, and longer coffee breaks."

Well, the results from the survey came in and guess what? The employees asked for more of only one thing.

Training.

That's a pleasant commentary on human nature, if you ask us — a commentary that says most people want to learn more about their jobs, improve their skills, and be better off tomorrow than they are today. Most thinking employees (especially your potential "superstars") recognize that ongoing training is what gives them the opportunity to realize their goals.

Our friend went on to increase training, whereupon his company's 15 percent growth in profits suddenly spurted to 30 percent. And then, because the company paid its employees monthly bonuses (that's right, monthly!) based on profits, each employee received a healthy bonus.

Training — it's a win-win situation, if ever there was one.

To be a successful employer, you must adjust the way in which you envision the motivational process. The biblical Golden Rule needs its own special twist for employees; you should amend it to state: *Do unto your employees as they would have done unto themselves.*

The following sections discuss the tools that play a primary role in the motivational process: compensation, goal-setting, performance expectations, and performance reviews. Look for the Mars/Venus-type differences between you and your employees as you read.

Designing a compensation plan

Compensation is #5 on the typical employee's list of key motivators. Although this news may be encouraging to the U.S. economic future as well as to that of your own business, it becomes irrelevant when salary review time comes around — Pee Wee Herman suddenly turns into Mike Tyson when his wages are on the line.

The next time the annual salary-setting time comes around in your company, try saying no to a few expected (and deserved) raises among your employees. Or try cutting the salary for a few of your good employees. Number five on his list suddenly becomes number one!

Nothing is more important than compensation on *that* particular day — the day you tell your employee if he's getting a raise and how much. Compensation is a black-and-white issue — your employees can look at it, compare it, and show it off to their loved ones. Compensation states what that particular employee is worth — in the eyes of that particular employer anyway. Oh yes, and compensation can also be the first foot in the door when competitors come snooping around to hire away your best employees. (A healthy salary increase is usually used as the opener for negotiations between an employee and a prospective new employer.)

Types of compensation

You can compensate employees in a number of proven ways:

- ✔ **Hourly:** The original tool of the "paying for time" compensation method. It works for Starbucks, General Motors, and Wal-Mart, and it will also work for you, especially for your part-time and entry-level employees.

- ✔ **Salaried:** The long-term version of "paying for time." Salaries usually come with annual cost-of-living raises and bonuses typically ranging anywhere from 3 percent to 25 percent of base salary. (These bonuses are based on performance-to-plan and/or achievement of goals.) Salaries, as a rule, represent security to their recipients, and most employees value security.

- ✔ **Commission:** Always the best compensation method for the hungry, hard-charging, sales types. Security isn't important to these folks; open ends and opportunity are.

- ✔ **Pay-for-performance:** Also called *gain-sharing* or *success-sharing*, this method is an increasingly popular alternative to the traditional "paying for time" compensation plans. Pay-for-performance usually involves a relatively small base salary — often without annual cost-of-living adjustments — with all other compensation based on either individual or team performance (or a combination of both). Specific pay-for-performance plans are as varied and creative as the small business itself, and they always require an efficient measuring system to back them up.

- ✔ **Hybrids:** A mix of annual salary, pay-for-performance, annual bonuses, stock option plans (see Chapter 13), and whatever else the creative small-business owner can devise.

Ways to create a plan that works

Here's our advice for devising a compensation plan that will work for *your* business:

- Be sure to design your compensation plan before you hire your first employee. This will assure that you will have a defined plan in place and won't set precedents for your first employee that will later have to reset.

- Make sure that your employees thoroughly understand whatever method you use to compensate them. Paying-for-performance may make all kinds of motivational sense, but only if the employee understands the concept behind the performance formula being used and how he or she can impact the results.

- Make sure that you can measure whatever it is that needs measuring before you agree to pay for it. Measurement is always easier said than done.

- Be consistent within employee groups. For example, with your sales people, have one compensation method and be consistent within that group.

- Remember that benefits are an important part of the compensation package — important to your employees' security and to your bottom line. Consider them carefully and be sure you (and your employee) knows exactly how much they are worth. (See Chapter 14.)

- Keep the time between bonus payments as short as possible. Rewards, financial and otherwise, lose their impact when stretched out too long.

- Contact your industry trade association for information on what similar-sized businesses are paying employees in comparable positions if you're unsure of how much to pay your employees.

- Make any period-ending bonus meaningful in size (at least 3 percent of the employee's annual salary) and give it personally — mano a mano or womano a womano.

This subject of compensation is one of those eyes-of-the-beholder kind of issues. If you view compensation as an expense when you establish a plan for your business, then that's exactly what it will turn out to be — an out-of-pocket, painful expense, with all the downsides that term implies.

On the other hand, if you view your compensation plan as a motivational tool, you won't be creating an expense account, you'll be developing an instrument to increase your employee's performance.

Think about it. The best employees are those who believe they are valued and being treated fairly. The best measurable (key word here!) method of that valuation is their salary. If they believe it is consistent with the value they deliver to your business, you won't have to motivate them — they will motivate themselves. Poof! The salary expense account suddenly becomes a salary investment account. A huge difference!

The bottom line? You can willingly spend a fortune compensating your employees, but if the dollars you pay don't help motivate the people you pay them to, your compensation plan may be less than effective. The possibility exists too, that you hired the wrong employee for the position. If that's the case, see the earlier section on hiring for upgrading your hiring skills as well as the following section on firing.

Solve your employees' problems to solve your own

Joe, the owner of a small machine parts business, tells the following story:

"Fred, my shipping and receiving supervisor, had been unusually quiet — bordering on morose — for the past several weeks. The rest of my employees started doing whatever they could to avoid communicating with him. Fred was also making an unusual number of mistakes, and whenever I corrected him, Fred shrugged his shoulders and made the same mistake again. Finally I called Fred into my office.

"Fred," I began, "you've worked for me for four years now, and I know the quality work you can do. What you've been doing lately isn't up to your usual standards. This can't continue."

Fred's shoulders slumped, but he didn't argue. "I know," he whispered, his eyes gazing at the floor. "I'm sorry Joe, but I can't keep my mind on my work anymore."

"Okay, Fred, 'fess up. What's the trouble?"

"It's the IRS. I owe them $1,200, and I don't have the money. I don't know what they're going to do if I can't pay them by Friday."

I briefly excused myself, walked into the adjoining office, and returned with a check for $1,200 made out to Fred.

"Fred, here's an interest-free loan," I said, handing him the check. "I'll deduct $25 a pay period until the loan has been repaid.

"That was six months ago. Fred went back to being a great employee and enjoying his job again. Best darn investment I ever made."

"Hey, it was a no-brainer," Joe laughed, explaining why he decided so quickly to write Fred the check. "$1,200 is a small price to keep a good employee. Aside from the fact that I owe Fred something for his past performance, think how much I would spend hiring and training a new supervisor to replace him."

Get SMART! Goal-setting that works for everyone

Everyone can use goals as a motivational tool, and not just when relating to the workplace. You can also use goals in raising kids, pursuing financial security, and improving your golf game. And we're not talking lighthearted New Year's resolutions here — we're talking goals, as in commitments to objectives.

Although the purpose of this section is to assist you in working with your employees to set goals that will motivate them, these suggestions can also help you with your own personal goals.

LIFO, FIFO, DOS, TQM: Acronyms are everywhere these days. Even goal-setting comes with its own acronym. That acronym is SMART, and here's how it works:

- ✔ **S** = *Specific.* Goals must be clear, direct, and definable.

- ✔ **M** = *Measurable and meaningful.* Goals must be measurable, in the sense that employer and employee can assess whether or not the goal is achieved. And, of course, goals must be meaningful to both parties.

- ✔ **A** = *Appropriate:* Goals should be appropriate to the employee's experience, training, potential, and responsibilities.

- ✔ **R** = *Realistic.* Goals should challenge but be achievable. Eighty percent of the goal should be relatively easy to meet, 20 percent a stretch.

- ✔ **T** = *Time limit.* The goals should be achievable within a specified time frame.

The two biggest mistakes business owners make when setting goals for themselves, their business, or their employees are creating goals that are not measurable and giving a time frame that is not specific. Consider the following examples:

- ✔ **Non-SMART goal:** "Increase sales and increase profitability by working smarter and harder." Nothing measurable here and no time frame to measure it in.

- ✔ **SMART goal:** "Increase sales by 15 percent and increase profitability by 20 percent by the end of this fiscal year." Are these goals measurable? Yes. Is a workable time frame given? Yes. Are they achievable? You make the call.

Here's how you and your employees can set and achieve SMART goals:

✔ Never set goals without first planning how to reach them. (For instance, wanting to increase sales by 15 percent is not enough; you must have a marketing game plan for how to do so.)

✔ Don't wait until the end of the goal-setting period to measure. Check progress informally as the mood strikes and, formally, at defined time intervals between now and the end of the goal-setting period.

✔ Allow for the unexpected. Changing goals midstream is acceptable if the reasons are right.

✔ Make a public announcement within the business (occasionally outside of the business when the goals reached are extraordinary) as soon as your business or your employees have achieved their goals. Let the celebration begin, let it be spontaneous, and let it be loud.

✔ Understand that an employee may come up short on his goals occasionally. What's not okay is for an employee to consistently come up short. In that event, something is wrong with either the employee or with the goal-setting process.

Effective goal-setting should be a communal, bottoms-up process. The more involved the employee is in establishing her goals, the more committed she'll be to achieving them. Ask her to prepare her goals first, and then review them together, hone them together, and be sure to *write them down,* giving one copy to the employee and adding a second to her personnel files. Documenting goals makes the goal-setting process official, and minimizes potential misunderstandings when the employee's performance-review time comes around.

Writing performance expectations

Many years ago, this section would have been entitled, "Writing job descriptions." No longer. In these days of empowered and enlightened employees, the term "job description" is to small business what good sportsmanship is to professional basketball. A remembrance of the past.

Today the correct term is *performance expectations.*

Although some companies may get by without using performance expectations (or the old-fashioned job descriptions) in running their business, we think that most small-business owners would agree that employees need some degree of structure in their jobs. Performance expectations provide just that — used correctly, they provide a loose but reliable framework to help the employee focus on the *results* of his activities, not on the activity itself. And that's the key difference between job descriptions and performance expectations: Job descriptions focus on the activity of the position; performance expectations focus on the anticipated results.

An example? A typical "job description" would state that a salesperson would be responsible to sell the company's products at the published prices, to write sales orders correctly, and to make sure that the sales orders were submitted within a specified time. On the other hand, a "performance expectation" for the same position would require that the salesperson would represent her company professionally (and then define the word "professional"), to build ongoing relationships with customers and buyers, and to assist the entire business team in realizing the specified departmental goals.

Writing a performance expectation is not as hard as you may think. You write the performance expectation, the employee reviews it, and the two of you either sign off on it or suggest revisions. Here's how the writing process works:

- ✔ Include a brief explanation at the beginning of the performance expectation of the position's objective (mission) and how it relates to the business's overall mission.

- ✔ Describe the position's location on the organization chart (discussed later in this chapter) — include the immediate supervisor's title and the positions (if any) of those being supervised.

- ✔ Define the performance evaluation process — who will perform the evaluation, when will it be done, and on what basis the employee's performance will be appraised.

- ✔ Concentrate on output, not on activity, and be careful not to limit the ways in which the job can be accomplished. Define the responsibilities and allow the employee the freedom to make the job work.

- ✔ Be flexible. The world changes. So do expectations. (See later in this chapter for more on flexibility.)

Employees are not robots; the biggest mistake you can make is to develop performance expectations that restrict the employee's options. You should write the performance expectation before you advertise for the position, and then once you've hired the new employee you and she should review the performance expectation together and agree on the expected results. Then, you should give the employee the leeway to achieve those results.

Reviewing your employees' performance

How important is the performance review? How important is anything that assigns a value to someone's existence in a place where he likely spends more than 50 percent of his waking hours during the work week? If performance reviews aren't important, then breathing isn't either!

The biggest problem with performance reviews is that the typical entrepreneur perceives the review to be an opportunity to criticize the employee's performance rather than to improve it. Sure, negative criticism of past performance may be involved in the review process, but so is the positive critique of performance — both are necessary elements of the process. Also, it must be remembered that the intent of that criticism should be to improve future performance, not to punish nor complain about past performance. Everything you do in the performance review (including increases in compensation) is a means to improving performance.

Good performance reviews don't just happen. They evolve, as a result of a well-defined review process. Take a look at the basic components of a successful review process:

- **Goal-setting:** Working with the employee, you must establish — and agree upon — applicable SMART goals. These goals should be developed as soon as the employee is comfortably settled in her new job. (See section on goal-setting earlier in this chapter.)

- **Writing performance expectations:** You must also have written, meaningful standards by which to measure performance. (See the previous section for more information.)

- **Creating critical-event memos:** Critical events in an employee's day-to-day performance should be written and filed in the employee's personnel file at the time they occur. Extract them at review time to add objective support to your otherwise subjective observations.

  These critical-event memos should include occurrences of positive as well as negative behavior. Because reviews are intended to *improve performance,* you can earn more motivational mileage by pointing out the employee's successes than you can by itemizing his or her failures.

  In between performance reviews, you should informally and regularly give employees feedback. Thus, by the time the next performance review comes around, the employee shouldn't have any surprises. If you are consistent in providing feedback to your employees, they will have plenty of time in between reviews to work on their behavior.

- **Conducting the annual performance and salary review:** At last, the main event — the time when you compare actual performance with expectations and goals. The time when you review critical-event memos, assign new wages, and agree on bonuses and perks, all the while discussing goals and expectations for the upcoming year. All of which, lest you forget, are intended to motivate the employee to improve his or her performance in the upcoming period.

- **Scheduling the follow-up review:** The follow-up review should be held quarterly or semiannually; if the situation is dire enough, however, you should hold it monthly until the performance has improved to your expectations. These follow-up reviews should be informal but well-prepared, intended to provide feedback on progress since the annual review.

As discussed, the employee evaluation process is a natural progression that begins with performance expectations and setting goals and ends with the performance and salary review and necessary follow-up review. The performance review itself is but one piece of the process: Without the other pieces the evaluation is incomplete. Don't expect earth-shattering results from performance reviews if you don't adhere to the entire process.

Following are guidelines for providing effective performance reviews:

- ✔ Hold the review once a year, either on the employee's anniversary date or sometime around the beginning of your business's upcoming fiscal year.

- ✔ Schedule the review in advance, giving both parties plenty of time to prepare. No phones, no interruptions. Go off-site if you expect the review to be stressful.

- ✔ Prepare for the review with the same thoroughness as you would for any important business meeting. Remember, reviews are benchmarks in the employee's career.

- ✔ Begin each review with a generous helping of compliments, citing specific accomplishments and good work. Get things off to a positive start. Reinforce the intent of the review early — to improve the employee's performance.

- ✔ Evaluate the employee based on the past year's performance, not just the past month's. We're talking careers here, not trends.

- ✔ Back up subjective comments with objective facts and stories, extracted from the critical-event memos you've filed in the employee's personnel file.

- ✔ Don't forget that this is a performance review, not a character review. Keep personalities out of it.

- ✔ Discuss changes in compensation after your critque of the employee's performance but before soliciting feedback from the employee about the company. Ask how she feels about the way the company is being run and what things might be better managed. (***Note:*** The order here is important. You won't get frank feedback from most employees until they have the assurance — in the form of a pay change commitment from you — that negative comments won't get in the way of their pay increase. If you discuss pay changes first, the employee may not listen well to the review.)

When there is no pay increase, make sure during the course of the review that the employee knows exactly why an increase will not be forthcoming, and then conclude the review by asking the employee if he thoroughly understands why the cupboard is bare. Also, be sure he knows when the next opportunity for pay increases will come and if he understands what he must do to get his performance up to the level where he can expect an increase.

If the review is a failure — if you perceive that the employee does not go away motivated — one of two things may have happened:

1. **You didn't conduct the review correctly.**

   If this is the case, we recommend you try it again a week or so later — after upgrading your presentation and explaining to the employee that you made some mistakes you'd like to correct. Yes, bosses and owners are human — they make mistakes, too!

2. **You performed the review correctly, but the employee falls into the category of people who simply can't take criticism, constructive or otherwise.**

   If this is the case, the employee may not be the right person for the job. Observe the employee's performance over the next few weeks to watch for signs of improvement. If there are none, you may need to start considering termination.

The best way to judge the immediate results of a performance review is by observing and asking how the employee feels about the review and change in compensation. If the employee is visibly upset and goes away angry, the review is a failure. If he or she goes away motivated, the review is a success.

Parting company — firing an employee

Firing an employee, as much as you'd like to avoid it, has its place in the growth of a successful business. Not often, hopefully, if you hire right, train right, and motivate right. But the need to fire will happen. As a matter of fact, if you never fire an employee, you're bound to have a handful of nonperforming employees on your payroll, a financial burden few small businesses can afford and a condition that won't be acceptable to those who are performing.

We doubt that even George Steinbrenner (owner of the New York Yankees, a team whose managers are as dispensable as tissue paper) enjoys the firing process, but the timely performance of it plays an integral role in your drive to surround yourself with a team of superstars.

Unfortunately, the fear of the dismissal process is usually worse than the event itself. After all, most employees know when they're not performing, and they're usually as unhappy in their jobs as you are in having them there. Yet they're too afraid or insecure (or motivated to be fired rather than quit by unemployment compensation laws) to make the first move, leaving the difficult work up to you.

Having to sometimes let an employee go is a fact of business life, and in the end can be justified by your obligation to your business's existence and to those employees of yours who *are* performing. You have an obligation to them to build a team that is good as it can be, and you can't meet that obligation when nonperforming employees are included on your team.

You're not passing judgment on the person being dismissed; you're passing judgment on the performance of the employee in that particular job. His or her talents, which may be many, may simply lie elsewhere.

Here's our advice to help you get through the unpleasant task of firing an employee:

- **Explore all the alternatives before settling on dismissal.** Alternatives include demotion, grace periods, personalized retraining, and consultant contracts (hiring the employee as an consultant only to do specific one-time jobs) outside of the business. When the alternatives won't work, record the reasons why. The employee may ask.

- **Do the firing as soon as possible after the decision to terminate is made.** In business, as in life, postponed problems usually don't get better, they often get worse. And, the longer you wait, the more likely it is that word will leak out to the soon-to-be-fired employee.

- **Arrange for outplacement services.** Small business can learn this lesson from watching its Fortune 500 cousins perfect the ritual of downsizing. Being fired can be softened by helping the employee to get back on his feet again.

- **Check with your attorney before firing a longtime employee or a member of a minority if the reasons for the termination may appear vague to the person being terminated.** Attorneys should also be involved when the firing is for an offense (sexual harassment, fighting, and other such incidents) that might wind up as a lawsuit.

- **Prepare the firing package in the same organized and documented manner you would the hiring package.** Include, where applicable, severance pay, continuance of health insurance, duration of benefits and perks (memberships, subscriptions, and so on), and returning company assets (computers, and so on).

- **Plan the firing meeting as you would any other important business meeting.** Organize in advance, outline your presentation, and have handouts prepared if necessary. Make the dismissal as businesslike as possible, and above all, avoid sentimentality and reminiscing. Keep emotions subdued; they only make matters worse.

✔ **Don't argue.** State the reasons and the facts surrounding the termination. Show the supporting documents. Arguing will only serve to further incense the person being fired. Let the employee rant and rave if he chooses — he may feel better when he's done, and you may learn something about how to be a better manager for the future.

✔ **Perform the termination first thing in the morning.** Doing so allows the employee to leave the company and have the rest of the day to gather his composure. At a minimum, pay the employee through the end of that day and perhaps even the rest of the week or month to help him stay on his feet financially.

Firing an employee plays a role in the process of building a company, but it will never be an enjoyable part, no matter how much practice you may have at it. When you're feeling especially sorry for yourself because you have to fire an employee, keep in mind that the situation is a heck of a lot tougher on the person on the other side of the desk.

Use exit interviews for fresh perspective

Your company will inevitably have people who quit their jobs for one reason or another. These employees can be a valuable resource that you need to tap into before they leave. During an exit interview, as the name implies, you interview the departing employee to gain insights into the company that a current employee may be reluctant to provide. Exit interviews can be an excellent tool for seeing your business through the eyes of others, especially because you — the person at the top — have a unique perspective that may too often become narrow or skewed.

Be sure to include at least the following questions in an exit interview:

✔ What was the main factor in your decision to quit?

✔ What did you like the most about our company?

✔ What did you like least?

✔ How do you rate such issues as working conditions, cooperation and teamwork, on-the-job training, supervision, opportunity for promotion, and communication?

✔ If you could change one thing about this company, what would it be?

Always interview employees who quit on their own volition. Where possible, also give employees you fire an exit interview, remembering that the terminated employee may exaggerate your and your business's shortcomings. Never exit-interview an employee at the same time you are firing him — wait until later, when he returns to pick up a severance paycheck or personal belongings.

Working Relationships: Designing a Flexible Organization Chart

Some say that organization charts — a graphic depiction of your company's chain of command — are out of style. All you have to do, these people tell us, is empower your employees and then step aside while the job gets done. No layers, no politics, no people caught in the middle — or so the story goes. Today's empowered employees don't require management, they conclude; they simply need a flexible and lenient environment.

We disagree. We believe in organization charts and in the chain of command, but only when the person at the top of the chain is worthy of the position. We further believe that someone must manage employees, someone must motivate them, and someone must help improve their performance. Someone must also promote them, demote them, and on occasion, fire them. Employees, we believe, have to work for somebody, like it or not.

Organization charts, however, don't have to be carved in stone. You should feel free to use them flexibly, circumventing their layers and tiers in order to accomplish specific projects. You can even assemble creative and temporary secondary charts from time to time to accomplish those complicated projects and one-time jobs.

Here's how to construct your organization chart and use it effectively:

- ✔ **Construct the organization chart for the employees, not for the "organization."** For instance, if one person is particularly knowledgeable about the project-du-jour, give her the senior responsibility for that job. (This structure means that your sales manager may be working on a project headed by a computer clerk, if the computer clerk knows more about the project than the sales manager.)

- ✔ **Pay by the quality of the employee's performance and the contribution to the team, not the position on the organization chart.** (So, although the sales manager and the operations manager might be on the same tier of the chart, they could be compensated quite differently based on the relative importance of sales and operations to the overall success of the company.)

- ✔ **Determine how many employees one person can supervise.** The answer depends on the quality of the team you've assembled. One is plenty if that one is like some people we've seen over the years. On the other hand, eight employees would be a snap to manage if those eight were good ones.

- ✔ **Remember that flatter organization charts (fewer tiers) are better, when you have the right employees.**

You don't want to live or die by the constrictions of your organization chart. It should serve as a structural guideline for making decisions and assigning responsibility — nothing more — so use it administratively, but bend it and mold it to fit the skills of your employees and the needs of your company.

And remember, the organization chart is no better, and no worse, than you — the person at the top of the chart. Where you lead, your employees are sure to follow. Don't expect to turn weak leadership into a strong team through the use of an organization chart, no matter how uniquely you shape it. The team can only be as good as the person at the top.

Why You Need an Employee Manual

In terms of excitement, the employee manual ranks right up there with ordering toner cartridges for your copying machine. Most entrepreneurs don't rank it in the top ten list of Things We Can Hardly Wait to Do.

However, once employees are on the payroll, employee manuals should be a must in every small-business owner's preventive medicine kit. Like Novocain, a well-prepared manual can save a lot of pain later on. The employee manual is important because of the varied and important functions it fulfills. Behold what a well-prepared employee manual will do for you:

- ✔ The employee manual provides the first opportunity to publicly define your corporate missions and goals to your employees.

- ✔ The employee manual sets the tone for what's to come. Imagine the message that a well-prepared employee manual sends to the recently hired employee when his or her questions are quickly and succinctly answered in an organized manner.

- ✔ The employee manual saves time — time spent on resolving problems that established policies would have resolved in the first place. And, the employee manual saves time spent explaining the basics of the job — such basics as hours of work, vacation and sick days, and termination policies.

- ✔ The employee manual saves time and effort and money spent on lawyers by establishing company policies for all to see. By stating company policies publicly and in writing, potential problem employees are quickly and succinctly alerted that they must either find a way to work within those policies or seek employment elsewhere.

The best way to assemble your employee manual is to use someone else's (a neighboring small business or a vendor or small business that you have frequented over the years) good manual as a guide for constructing yours.

Good employee manuals tend to make the rounds from small business to small business, and with good reason, too. The ones that have survived have already been tried and tested.

When compiling your employee manual (whether you prepare it yourself or use someone else's), be sure to do the following:

- ✔ Include a statement of your company's mission and goals. Make it brief, make it specific, and put it at the beginning of the manual where you know it will be read.

- ✔ Include an "employment at will" statement if you reside in a state where it is applicable; an attorney experienced in small-business management can advise you of the laws of your state. (*Employment at will* means that you aren't restricted to firing only for cause.)

- ✔ Declare early on that the employee manual is not a contract and that it can, and undoubtedly will, change.

- ✔ Include an equal opportunity statement.

- ✔ Spell out the benefits you offer — health insurance, maternity leave, pensions, profit sharing, company-reimbursed education policies, etc. Where applicable, include the details of the health insurance plan as an attachment.

- ✔ Define policies concerning the workday. Also include policies regarding overtime pay, time off, and breaks, as well as those concerning performance reviews, promotions, and wage increases.

- ✔ Include paid holiday and vacation policies.

- ✔ Develop and define a drug and alcohol policy, including pre-employment screening, and post-accident testing (if any).

- ✔ Define standards of conduct such as dress, timeliness, and consideration of others. Include causes for disciplinary actions and termination, along with severance pay policies.

- ✔ Keep the employee manual current as you go, assuring that your employees are kept abreast of the changes. Post any changes on the bulletin board at the same time you hand out revision attachments for your employees' manuals.

Before you distribute the completed manual to employees, have an attorney experienced in working with small businesses and employee handbooks review it. That review could save you a great deal of grief and money down the road.

What Makes a Successful Employer?

No two small businesses are alike. The reasons behind one small business's success are often entirely different than the reasons behind a second one's success. One succeeds because of its marketing, another because of its product or service quality. One focuses on customers, another on employees. One has an awesome in-house sales force, another utilizes an eye-catching catalog to sell its products.

However, every successful small business (those that include employees anyway) have three identifiable characteristics, no matter what its niche, product, or service. Those three characteristics are flexibility, accountability, and follow-up.

Flexibility: Some rules are meant to be bent

Consider the following small-business participants and issues, all of which need to be managed flexibly:

- **Employees:** The sidebar "Solve your employees' problems to solve your own" tells a story about Joe, who lent his employee $1,200 — interest free — to keep the IRS at bay. Joe's employee manual said nothing about employees in debt or noninterest bearing loans, but Joe flexibly managed around the situation by creating a loan, thus solving his employee's problem. You say you have a good employee who needs additional time off to resolve a family situation? Nuts to the rules, give him the time off, help him solve his problem. You say you have a good employee who needs a flexible work schedule in order to honor her responsibilities at home? So what are you waiting for, create a flexible work schedule, help her solve her problem.

- **Loyal, paying customers:** Rules are always meant to be bent when it comes to loyal, paying customers. You say you have a good customer who needs an additional 30 days to pay an especially large invoice? Then 30 days it is. You say you have a good customer who needs his products individually shrink-wrapped instead of bulk-wrapped? Then shrink-wrapped it is.

- **Visions, missions, goals, strategies, and plans:** Darn right visions, missions, goals, strategies, and plans must be managed flexibly. After all, they are based on the activities of people and, well, you know the rest.

- **Organization charts:** As we said earlier, organization charts are to be used for administrative and structural purposes only.

If you look at your business as providing solutions rather than as merely following rules, you'll be better able to meet the demands of today's ever-changing business life.

Don't get us wrong, we're not saying that everything in your business should be managed flexibly. To the contrary, a small business does need a number of inflexible rules and regulations included among its management tools. For instance, it needs inflexible rules and regulations to manage these things:

- ✓ **Ethics and principles:** If ethics and principles aren't inflexible and inviolate, they aren't ethics and principles.

- ✓ **Expense controls:** The best small businesses are those that are as aware of their expenses as they are of their sales. Expenses need to be controlled inflexibly.

- ✓ **Quality:** Quality cannot be flexible. The product or service is either fit for your most-demanding customer at that price or it's unfit for any of your customers. There is no middle ground.

But where people enter into the picture, flexibility is the order of the day because people are different and unique. One employee's reward may be another employee's punishment. Just as no two people are alike, no two responses to management are the same.

Accountability: Performers and non-performers are accordingly noted

Your employees really have two options when you ask them to perform a task. Either they do it. Or they don't. When they don't perform the designated task, the next question you must ask is, "What was the reason they didn't do it?"

The answers to that question can include the following:

- ✓ **The employee is incapable of performing the task.** Your options are to reassign the task, reassign the employee, or replace the employee.

- ✓ **The employee is not properly trained.** You must train the employee.

- ✓ **The task and its priority was not clearly communicated.** It's your job to communicate the task more clearly.

- ✓ **The employee saw no good reason to accomplish the task and thus elected not to do it.** In which case, either your company does not include accountability as part of its culture, or you made a serious hiring mistake.

Accountability — being responsible for one's actions — is a cultural issue. It begins with you holding those employees working for you accountable, which results in the same behavior trickling down through your organization. In the process of creating an accountable culture, you must provide a system of rewards when employees perform and punishments when they don't. Just as employees need a reason to do something, they also need a reason not to.

In order to determine whether your small business has an accountable culture, ask yourself the following four questions:

- ✔ Do your employees have the motivation to achieve what you want them to achieve?
- ✔ Does achievement make a difference in the success of the team and do you and your employees know how to recognize that difference?
- ✔ Can the other members of the team tell when an employee has achieved or not achieved?
- ✔ Do your employees know that they have to achieve, or is achievement only one of their options?

In the process of asking yourself these questions, you'll quickly recognize the four elements required to differentiate an accountable culture from a nonaccountable one.

- ✔ Employees have to have a reason to achieve.
- ✔ Achievement has to be recognized throughout the company.
- ✔ Employees should receive rewards when they do achieve.
- ✔ Consequences have to be in place when employees do not achieve the goals the two of you have agreed upon.

Put these elements together and you can quickly create a culture that promotes accountability. Although the manner in which you install these elements may vary, they all have one thing in common: They begin at the top.

Follow-up: The more you do it, the less you need it

Why should you follow up? After all, you've already gotten whatever-it-was off your desk the first time. Why must you do it all over again? What the heck, if *you* were an employee you sure wouldn't have to be followed up.

But (and this is the last time you'll hear this) you aren't an employee, you are an entrepreneur, and if you don't remember the difference you may not be in business for long. If you don't follow up your employees, missions and goals won't be missions and goals anymore, they'll be hopes and wishes, and hopes and wishes don't build businesses, they only create dreams.

The good news is that once your employees know that follow-up is coming, the need for it decreases. Translation: Once an accountable culture is firmly in place you won't have to follow up as much anymore.

In the beginning, however, when your culture is being established, every commitment made, large or small, must be followed up. A simple notation on the calendar followed by a transfer to the to-do list on the appropriate day should complete the process. You should never stop trying to collect that team of superstars we mention earlier in the chapter. After all, superstars don't need to be rigorously followed up (if they do, they're not superstars!), which means that they allow you to spend more time growing your business.

The Option of Leasing Employees

More than 2,000 employee-leasing companies — also known as professional employer organizations (PEOs) — exist in the United States today, which means that at least one is probably in or near your hometown. The employee-leasing company's primary customer is you — the small-business owner — because most large businesses develop the wide variety of human resource services in-house.

Employee leasing means that the leasing company assumes the paperwork and administrative responsibilities of dealing with employees, allowing you to concentrate on their operational activities. Thus, in effect, you are simply outsourcing your human resource needs. In this way, you and your employee leasing company become "co-employers" of the employees.

Employee-leasing companies are not to be confused with temporary employment agencies. They both have similar objectives — to simplify the complexities of hiring employees for your business and handling the related administrative details. But where temporary services provide instant, disposable workers, employee-leasing companies offer a more permanent, yet hassle-free workforce.

In return for the services the employee-leasing company provides, it charges its customers an "administrative fee" (in effect its markup over their costs) of anywhere from 2 percent to 8 percent, depending upon the dollar amount of the transaction.

We are not advocating employee leasing for every small business — the decision to lease or not to lease is a gray area. Leasing employees makes sense for a number of reasons:

- ✔ Employee-leasing companies do what they do best (hire and handle the administration of employees) and you do what you do best (run your business).

- ✔ You write one check and they do all the rest.

- ✔ Employee-leasing companies can serve as unofficial employment agencies. You hire the best, send back the rest.

- ✔ By pooling employees, employee-leasing companies can cut costs in such areas as insurance rates.

At the same time, leasing has the following disadvantages:

- ✔ When an employee-leasing company goes under, it can take your payroll cash and prepaid insurance along with it, leaving you, the employee, or both, holding the bag.

- ✔ If you can provide comparable employee services at the same cost, you are, in effect, cutting your expenses by hiring your own employees. (Remember, every dollar saved by not paying a leasing company fee results in an extra dollar of profit.)

After you decide to lease your employees, be extremely careful in selecting the company you use as your "co-employer." Ask for referrals and check it thoroughly, network with other small-business owners, and remember that everything is negotiable when signing a leasing contract. You may even want to customize the leasing agreement to meet your specific needs. Also, you may want to check with the Institute for the Accreditation of Professional Employer Organizations in Bethesda, Maryland (301-656-1476), to verify that you are dealing with an accredited PEO. This self-regulating industry group has accredited PEOs representing workers in 50 states. When in doubt as to where to look for a PEO, this is a helpful resource.

In the final analysis, most small-business owners make the decision to lease employees based on whether or not they think they can save all or part of that 2 to 8 percent "administrative fee" by hiring themselves and how much of their time and energy they wish to spend dealing with human resource issues. The fact that the employee-leasing industry is growing at a rapid rate indicates that increasing numbers of small-business owners have made the decision that the 2 to 8 percent charged in fees is worth the expense.

Chapter 14

Providing Employee Benefits

- -

In This Chapter

▶ What is the most valuable employee benefit?

▶ Selecting a retirement plan for you and your company

▶ Deciding whether to share equity with your employees

▶ Designing and securing a good health insurance plan

▶ Disability, life, and other insurance plans

▶ Flexible benefit plans, vacations, and other odds and ends

- -

*Q*uiz question: What do you think is the most valuable benefit you receive from your employer?

If you answered health insurance, you have lots of company. According to the Employee Benefit Research Institute (EBRI), about six in ten American workers view their health insurance as their *numero uno* employee benefit.

If you answered retirement benefits, your answer agreed with only 17 percent of employees — but you would have answered correctly.

If you examine the monetary value of all benefits that employers offer, retirement plan benefits are by far the most financially valuable. Employer contributions into all types of employee retirement plans account for about 45 percent of employer benefits received by individuals, according to the U.S. Department of Commerce. Health benefits account for just 28 percent of benefit payments. The disparity between the value of retirement and health care benefits becomes even larger when you factor in the long-term value of the tax-deferred compounding of retirement account money (discussed later in this chapter). For example, for every $1,000 that a 35-year-old employee (or his or her employer) in the 35 percent tax bracket (combined federal and state) contributes into a retirement plan that is able to generate a 9 percent annual return, he or she will have about $3,100 *more* by age 65 by being able to invest that money inside, rather than outside, a tax-sheltered retirement account.

Among larger employers, however, employer contributory plans, such as pension plans and profit-sharing plans, are declining in importance. Among small employers, most don't offer retirement plans at all — even plans such as 401(k) plans, which are funded largely or completely from employee paycheck contributions. Among firms with fewer than 25 employees, just 19 percent offer some sort of retirement plan, according to EBRI. We explain in the next section why so few small-business employers offer retirement plans and why more should do so.

Small-Business Retirement Plans: The Underappreciated Benefit

One of Eric's financial counseling clients, Alice, operates a 14-employee architecture firm. Alice is unusual in offering extensive retirement plan benefits to her employees. The architecture firm offers both a 401(k), which matches 25 percent of employee contributions, and a profit-sharing plan, which is totally funded by her firm's contributions that in recent years, have averaged around 6 percent. "It's important to have a good benefits package to attract and keep employees," says Alice.

For sure, other benefits such as life and disability insurance may be important to many employees. These benefits, however, are far less valuable/costly than retirement plan benefits, and employees can relatively easily purchase them on their own as long as they don't have a preexisting medical condition. Although health insurance is usually more costly to replace than disability or life insurance, employees can purchase it, too, as long as they don't have a preexisting condition.

So, if retirement benefits are so much more valuable than other benefits, why do so few workers think so? Several reasons may explain why people value their health benefits more than their retirement benefits:

- ✔ **The absence of health benefits can be financially catastrophic should a major illness arise.** If you do have a preexisting health condition, being able to jump into an employer's group plan without a health evaluation can mean the difference between getting health care coverage and going without.

- ✔ **Younger employees view retirement as something far in the future and not tangible.** "I personally believe in the importance of retirement savings and wish I had started sooner. While some younger employees also may not value these benefits, eventually they probably will and will be grateful," says Alice.

✔ **Employees often don't know what retirement benefits are worth because many companies do a poor job educating and promoting such benefits' value.** For example, with a pension plan, an employer is setting aside money separate from an employee's salary to fund the monthly pension payment to be paid during the employee's retirement years. Unlike with a retirement savings plan, such as a 401(k), where you can see your current account value, employers generally don't prepare individual pension statements showing the total amount contributed for each employee and the investment returns on that money.

So, if you're still dreaming about starting your own business, don't view your employer's benefits package as a ball and chain tying you to your current job. As a small-business owner, you can replace the benefits provided by your former employer on your own, and you can establish a SEP-IRA or Keogh retirement plan to tax shelter your self-employment earnings. SEPs and Keoghs, which are discussed later in this chapter, allow you to shelter far more money than most corporate retirement plans do.

Getting the Most Value from Your Small-Business Retirement Plan

Retirement plans are a terrific way for small-business owners and their employees to tax shelter a healthy portion of their earnings. If you don't have employees, regularly contributing to one of these plans is usually a no-brainer. With employees, the decision is a bit more complicated, but contributing is still often a great idea because of the benefit's value in attracting and retaining good employees. Self-employed people may contribute to Keoghs or Simplified Employee Pension Individual Retirement Accounts (SEP-IRAs). Small businesses with a number of employees should also consider 401(k) and SIMPLE plans.

With SEP-IRA and Keogh plans, if you have employees, you are required to make contributions on their behalf that are comparable to the company owners' contributions (as a percentage of salary) under these plans. Some part-time (fewer than 500 or 1,000 hours per year) and newer employees (less than a few years of service) may be excluded. Small-business owners often set up plans for themselves but fail to cover their employees because either they don't know about this requirement or they choose to ignore it. Be forewarned — the IRS and state tax authorities may discover that you have neglected to make contributions for eligible employees, sock you with big penalties, and disqualify your prior contributions. Because self-employed people and small businesses get their taxes audited at a relatively high rate, don't mess up in this area.

Don't avoid setting up a retirement savings plan for your business just because you have employees and you don't want to make contributions on their behalf. In the long run, you build the contributions that you make for your employees into their total compensation package, which includes salary and other benefits like health insurance. Making retirement contributions need not increase your personnel costs.

SEP-IRAs

Simplified Employee Pension Individual Retirement Account (SEP-IRA) plans require little paperwork to set up. They allow you to sock away about 13 percent (13.04 percent, to be exact) of your self-employment income (business revenue minus expenses) up to a maximum of $24,000 (for 1998) per year. Each year, you decide the amount that you want to contribute — the plan has no minimum requirement. Your contributions to a SEP-IRA are deducted from your taxable income, saving you on federal and state taxes. As with other retirement plans, your money compounds without taxation until withdrawal.

Keoghs

Keogh plans require a bit more paperwork to set up and administer than SEP-IRAs. The appeal of certain types of Keoghs is that they allow you to put away a greater percentage (20 percent) of your self-employment income (revenue less your expenses), up to a maximum of $30,000 per year.

Another appeal of Keogh plans is that they allow you, the small-business owner, to maximize contributions relative to employees in two ways that you can't with SEP-IRAs:

- ✔ **Vesting schedules:** Keogh plans allow *vesting schedules,* which require employees to remain with the company a specified number of years before they earn the right to their full retirement account balances. Vesting refers to the portion of the money in a retirement account that is owned by the employee. After a certain number of years, employees become fully vested and, therefore, own 100 percent of the funds in their retirement accounts. If they leave prior to being fully vested, they lose the unvested balance, which reverts to the remaining plan participants. Thus, you've given employees a good reason to stay rather than leave.

- ✔ **Social Security integration:** Keogh plans allow for *integration,* which allows high-income earners at your company (usually you and the other owners/executives) to receive larger percentage contributions for their accounts than the less-highly compensated employees. The logic behind this idea is that Social Security taxes top out after you earn more than $68,400 (for 1998). Social Security integration allows you to make up for this ceiling. If Keoghs sound attractive to you, you should know that you can choose from four major types of Keoghs:

✔ **Profit-sharing plans:** These plans have the same contribution limits as SEP-IRAs. Profit-sharing plans appeal to owners of small companies who want to use vesting schedules and Social Security integration, both of which cannot be done with SEP-IRA plans.

✔ **Money-purchase pension plans:** You can contribute more to a money-purchase pension plan than you can to a profit-sharing plan or SEP-IRA. The maximum tax-deductible contribution here is the lesser of 20 percent of your self-employment income or $30,000 per year. Although these plans allow you to make a larger contribution, they offer no flexibility on the percentage contribution that you make each year — it's fixed. Thus, these plans make the most sense for high-income earners who are comfortable enough financially to know that they can continue making large contributions.

If the simplicity of the money-purchase pension plan appeals to you, don't be overly concerned about the consequences of some unforeseen circumstance that may render you unable to make the required contribution. You can amend your plan and change the contribution percentage starting the next year. As long as you have a reason, the IRS generally allows you to discontinue the plan altogether. Prior contributions can remain in the Keogh account — you can even transfer them to other investment companies if you like. Discontinuing the plan simply means that you won't be making further contributions. You don't lose the money. However, if you have employees, you need to notify them and vest them 100 percent.

✔ **Paired plans:** These plans combine the preceding profit-sharing and money-purchase plans. Although they require a little more paperwork to set up and administer, paired plans take the best features of both individual plans. You can attain the maximum contribution possible (20 percent) that you get with the money-purchase pension plan but have some of the flexibility that comes with a profit-sharing plan. For example, you can fix your money-purchase pension plan contribution at 8 percent and contribute anywhere from 0 to 12 percent of your net income to your profit-sharing plan. Thus, in any given plan year, you may contribute as little as 8 percent of your net income and as much as 20 percent.

✔ **Defined-benefit plans:** These plans are for people who are able and willing to put away more than $30,000 per year. As you can imagine, only a very small percentage of people can afford to do this. Consistently high-income earners older than age 45 or so who want to save more than $30,000 per year in a retirement account should consider these plans. If you are interested in defined-benefit plans, you need to hire an actuary to crunch the numbers to calculate how much you can contribute to such a plan.

401(k) plans

Larger for-profit companies generally offer 401(k) plans. The silly name comes from the section of the tax code that establishes and regulates these plans. The 401(k) plan generally allows you to save up to $10,000 per year (for 1998). An individual plan's contribution limits may be lower, however, if not enough employees save enough in the company's 401(k) plan. Your contributions to a 401(k) are generally excluded from your reported income and thus are free from federal and, in most cases, state income taxes, but not Social Security and Medicare taxes. An employer may make contributions to an employee's accounts as well. Similar to the employee's contribution, these contributions are tax-deferred until retirement.

Because of the significant costs of establishing and maintaining a 401(k) plan, such plans generally make the most sense for larger small companies — those with 20 or more employees. You may want to make employees wait a year before contributing to a 401(k) plan to ensure that you have adequate time to educate them about the virtues of your plan and so that they'll view it as a valued benefit. To encourage participation, you may also consider matching a portion of employees' contributions.

The best investment companies through which to consider establishing a 401(k) plan are the bigger and better mutual fund companies, such as T. Rowe Price (800-492-7670), Vanguard (800-662-2003), and Fidelity (800-343-0860), as well as the premier discount brokerage firms, including Charles Schwab and Jack White. In some cases, your company may need to work with a separate plan administrator, in addition to one of these investment firms. These excellent investment companies can also recommend an administrator to help you with all the tedious aspects of 401(k) plan paperwork and accounting.

403(b) plans

If you happen to be running a nonprofit organization, you can offer a 403(b) plan to your employees. As with a 401(k), contributions to these plans are federal and state tax-deductible. Unlike a 401(k) plan, a 403(b) plan includes virtually no out-of-pocket set-up expenses or ongoing accounting fees. The only requirement is that the organization must deduct the appropriate contributions from employees' paychecks and send the money to the investment company handling the 403(b) plan.

Nonprofit employees generally are allowed to contribute up to 20 percent or $10,000 of their salaries, whichever is less. Employees who have 15 or more years of service may be allowed to contribute a few thousand dollars beyond the $10,000 limit.

The best place to establish a 403(b) plan is through the leading mutual fund companies that are mentioned in the previous section — Vanguard (800-662-2003), Fidelity (800-343-0860), or T. Rowe Price (800-492-7670) — all of which offer terrific mutual funds and 403(b) plans to invest in. Don't invest through tax-sheltered annuities, the name for insurance-company investments that satisfy the requirements for 403(b) plans. Such plans have much higher fees and worse investment performance than the better mutual fund company 403(b) plans.

SIMPLE plans

If you think that the people in Congress have nothing better to do with their time than to keep tinkering with our tax laws and cooking up even more retirement plan options, you're right! In the tax bill passed in 1997, yet another retirement plan, the SIMPLE plan, was allowed. *SIMPLE* stands for Savings Incentive Match Plans for Employees.

SIMPLE-IRAs have a contribution limit of $6,000 per year. Relative to 401(k) plans, SIMPLE plans are expected to help employers more easily reduce their costs, thanks to easier reporting requirements and fewer administrative hassles.

Employers *must* make small contributions on behalf of employees, however. Employers can either match, dollar-for-dollar, the employee's first 3 percent contributed or contribute 2 percent of pay for everyone whose wages exceed $5,000. Interestingly, if the employer chooses the first option, the employer has an incentive not to educate employees about the value of contributing to the plan because the more employees contribute, the more it costs the employer. And, unlike a 401(k) plan, greater employee contributions do not enable higher-paid employees to contribute more.

Convincing employees that retirement plans matter

The single biggest mistake that people at all income levels make with regard to retirement planning is not taking advantage of retirement accounts. In your 20s and 30s (and for some even their 40s and 50s), living for today seems a whole lot more fun than saving for the future.

But, assuming that you don't want to work your entire life, the sooner you start to save, the less painful saving for retirement will be each year, because your contributions have more years to compound. Each decade that you delay approximately doubles the percentage of your earnings that you need to save in order to meet your goals. For example, if saving 10 percent per year in your early 30s would get you to your retirement goal, waiting until your 40s may mean putting away about 20 percent of your pretax (gross) earnings.

Naming beneficiaries on retirement accounts

With any type of retirement account, you're supposed to name beneficiaries who will receive the assets in your account when you die. You usually name primary beneficiaries (your first choices for receiving the money) and secondary beneficiaries, who receive the money in the event that the primary beneficiaries are also deceased when you pass away.

The designations are not cast in stone; you can change them whenever and as often as you desire by sending written notice to the investment company or employer holding your retirement account. Note that many plans require spousal consent if you want to name a beneficiary other than your spouse. You can designate charities as beneficiaries.

If you want to reduce the amount of money that is required to be distributed from your retirement accounts annually, name beneficiaries who are all at least ten years younger than yourself. The IRS allows you to calculate the required minimum distribution based on the joint life expectancy of you and your oldest-named beneficiary. However, you can't use a difference of greater than ten years for a nonspouse. If a nonspouse is named as the beneficiary and is more than ten years younger, for tax purposes of calculating required withdrawals, the nonspouse is considered to be just ten years younger than you.

The longer you wait, the more of your income you'll need to save and, therefore, the less you'll have left over to spend during your earning years. As a result of not starting soon enough, you may not meet your retirement-savings goal, and your golden years may be more tarnished than golden.

We use the preceding brief economics lesson to emphasize the importance of considering *now* the benefits that you achieve by saving and investing in some type of retirement account. These benefits include the following:

- ✔ **Contributions offer immediate tax savings.** Retirement accounts should really be called tax-reduction accounts. If you're a moderate income earner, you probably pay at least 35 percent in federal and state income taxes (see Chapter 2 to determine your tax bracket). Thus, with most of the retirement accounts described in this section, for every $1,000 you contribute into them, you save yourself about $350 in taxes in the year that you make the contribution.

- ✔ **Investment earnings accumulate tax-deferred.** Once inside a retirement account, contributions accumulate interest, dividends, and appreciation without being taxed. You get to defer taxes on all the accumulating gains and profits until you withdraw the money, presumably in retirement. Thus, more money is working for you over a longer period of time. Even if your retirement tax rate is the same as your tax rate during your employed years, you still come out ahead by contributing money into retirement accounts. In fact, because you defer paying tax and have more money compounding over more years, you can end up with more money in retirement even if your retirement tax rate is higher than it is now.

As we mention earlier in the chapter, most people don't value retirement plan benefits for the simple reason that they don't understand them. So, as an employer, to get the most mileage from your retirement plan, do the following:

- ✔ **Educate your employees.** Educate your employees about the value of retirement savings plans. For example, people on average need about 75 percent of their preretirement income throughout retirement to maintain their standard of living. Personal finance primers such as *Personal Finance For Dummies* (IDG Books Worldwide, Inc.), which Eric wrote, offer lots of helpful background about why we all should be planning ahead financially for our golden years. Get your employees to understand and appreciate your investment in their financial futures.

- ✔ **Use the plan as an incentive to retain employees.** Many small businesses have trouble with employee turnover. With particular types of Keogh plans, for example, employees must stay a certain number of years to become vested in their contributions. (For more on vesting, see "Keoghs," earlier in this chapter.)

- ✔ **Select the plan that best meets your business needs.** If you have more than 20 or so employees, consider offering a 401(k) or a SIMPLE plan, which allows employees to contribute money from their paychecks.

To Share or Not Share the Equity

As we discuss in Chapter 5, one decision that all small-business owners must confront in the early days of their small business is whether to go it alone or take on partners. Should you decide to take on partners, you probably will be sharing ownership with some or all of those partners. And even if you're going solo, over time, you may benefit from sharing equity with key employees or even all of your employees.

The reason to consider sharing equity with key employees or even all of your employees is that it aligns their incentives with yours. After all, one of the reasons that you may have started your small business was to share in the economic rewards of doing good work. If your employees are simply drawing a paycheck, they have less incentive to work toward boosting the short- and long-run profitability of your business.

Not surprisingly, sharing equity also has some downsides. One is that some small-business owners end up giving away too much, too quickly, and too easily. And, if you give away too much ownership to employees or outside investors, you may find yourself a minority shareholder (owning less than 50 percent of your business) and no longer in control of the destiny of your enterprise nor having your own job security.

Additionally, minority shareholders have, as a result of their ownership, rights that may not always align with yours. This disparity in interest is especially true when a minority shareholder leaves the company either from his own volition or from yours. Be sure to use a lawyer whenever creating an ownership position (no matter how small) within your business, and be sure to inquire of the downsides of sharing ownership.

Stock and stock options

In Chapter 13, we discuss the importance of hiring the best people that you can into key positions in your company. In order for you to attract and retain star employees for the critical positions in your company, you may need or want to offer some equity to those employees.

Shares of ownership in a company are known as *stock.* The number of shares of stock in a company is an arbitrary item. Suppose for example that your company is worth $500,000. You could have 1,000 shares of stock, 10,000 shares of stock, 100,000 shares of stock, or any number of shares of stock your heart desires. If you have 1,000 shares of stock, then the price or value per share will be $500; whereas if you have 100,000 shares of stock, the price per share will be $5.

When hiring a key employee, you can simply grant that person a certain number of shares of stock that they will receive after they've stayed with you for certain periods of time. Alternatively, you can grant them *stock options,* which allow the key employee to buy your company's stock at a predetermined price.

Continuing with the previous example, suppose you have 100,000 shares of stock in your company and the share price is $5 per share for a total value of $500,000. You've been interviewing a person who you think will be your star marketing manager, and you'd like to offer her some financial upside if she is able to help you expand your company. After some conversations with her, you decide that you'll offer her stock options to purchase up to 5,000 shares of your company's stock (5 percent of the total company stock) within the next five years at a price per share of $5. Five years from now, if your marketing manager and other key players have done their jobs, your company should be worth a whole lot more than it is now and your stock should be worth much more than $5 per share, thus enriching the stock option holder's compensation.

Here are some tips for offering stock and stock options to key employees:

- **Make sure that the employee is a keeper.** Just as you should want to date a person before marrying, make sure that you've had ample opportunity to observe firsthand an employee's abilities and shortcomings before you offer him equity. Just because someone has an impressive resume and comes across well in a job interview doesn't mean that she will work well in your company and is worthy of offering equity to from day one.

- **Make 'em earn it.** In most cases, you should vest your key employee(s) in a certain portion of the stock. Vesting them at the rate of 15 to 20 percent per year so that they are fully vested after five to seven years makes good sense.

- **Get expert help.** Issuing stock and granting stock options can get complicated fairly quickly. You'll want to have good tax and legal advisors on your team (see Chapter 8).

Employee stock ownership plans (ESOPs)

The Washington, D.C.-based ESOP Association defines an ESOP as "an employee benefit plan which makes the employees of a company owners of stock in a company." ESOPs are most often used when the owner of a privately held small business readies for retirement, has no family successor, and wants to pass the company on to the employees. The federal government encourages small-business owners to consider ESOPs by way of granting tax breaks. The only big expense is the eventual cost to the company of buying out retiring employees.

You can obtain more information on this unique and growing-in-popularity equity-sharing tool by writing or calling: The ESOP Association, 1726 M Street N.W., Suite 501, Washington, D.C. 20036; phone 202-293-2971. Or you can visit the company's Web site at `www.the-esop-emplowner.org`.

Buy-sell agreements

In the event that you and a minority shareholder have a dispute (and you can bet that eventually you'll have one, especially if you have more than one minority shareholder), a buy-sell agreement is a necessary legal document for your business. *Buy-sell agreements* specify that owners/shareholders must sell their stock upon separation from the company, and at the same time establish a method to set the price of the buy-back. Buy-sell agreements also make provisions for the death of a shareholder.

As we say earlier in this chapter, you need to involve a lawyer several times in the life of a business — and making equity decisions is certainly one of them. Never create a minority shareholder without one!

Insurance and Other Benefits

A variety of insurance and related benefits are tax-deductible to corporations for all employees. If the business is *not* incorporated, with the exception of health insurance plans (see the next section), business owners can't deduct the cost of the insurance plans discussed in this section for themselves, but they can deduct these costs for their employees.

Health insurance

As we discuss in the introduction to this chapter, employees usually value their health insurance coverage over other traditional employee benefits. Of course, not all of your current and prospective employees will equally value health insurance coverage. For example, some married employees may already be covered through their spouse's plan and may not need nor want health coverage through your small business.

Unfortunately, if you're self-employed, only a portion of your health insurance premiums are deductible (45 percent of your health insurance costs for yourself and your covered family members is deductible for tax years 1998 and 1999, and this percentage will be increasing to 100 percent by the year 2007).

Issues to consider when establishing health insurance

Shopping for a quality health insurance plan requires patience and time to understand the myriad attributes of plans as well as to address your needs and those of your employees. Here are some issues to consider when establishing a health insurance plan:

✔ **Commitment of the insurer to its health insurance business:** Some insurance companies have their fingers in lots of pots — they may dabble in many lines of insurance including a bit in health insurance. One problem with choosing such insurers for your company's health plan is that the insurer may pull the plug on your coverage. In the worst case, your employees with preexisting medical conditions may be unable to secure new coverage. So, while you receive no guarantees that any particular insurer is going to stay in the health insurance business for the long haul, we suggest that you choose among the biggest plans in your area. Besides increased likelihood of staying in the business, larger players can negotiate better rates from providers. In most areas, Kaiser Permanente, and Blue Cross and Blue Shield Plus are among the larger health insurers.

✔ **Comprehensive, catastrophic coverage:** So-called major medical coverage pays for the potentially large expenses such as hospitalization, physician, and ancillary charges (such as lab work). Health insurance plans specify the maximum total benefits ("lifetime maximum benefits") that they'll pay over the course of the time that you're insured by their plan. With the high cost of health care today, $1 million is a minimally acceptable level of total benefits, and a plan that has no maximum or that has a maximum of at least several million dollars is preferable.

✔ **Choice of health care providers:** Increasing numbers of health insurance plans contract with specific health care providers, which restricts your choices but helps to keep costs down. Health maintenance organizations (HMOs) and preferred provider organizations (PPOs) are the main plans that restrict your choices. The major difference between HMOs and PPOs is that PPOs pay the majority of your expenses if you use a provider outside their approved list. If you do this with an HMO, you typically won't be covered at all.

If you and your employees want to be able to use particular physicians or hospitals, check which health insurance plans they accept as payment. If you can't use their services in the restricted-choice plans, ask yourself if the extra cost of the open-choice plan is worth being able to use their services.

✔ **Guaranteed renewability:** Only consider health insurance plans that will keep renewing your coverage without you and your employees needing to take more physical examinations to prove your continued good health.

Select higher deductibles and co-payments

As with other insurance policies, the more you are willing to share in the payment of your claims, the less you will have to pay in premiums. To reduce your health insurance premiums, choose a plan with the highest deductible and co-payment that you and your employees can comfortably afford. Most policies have annual deductible options, such as $250, $500, or $1,000, as well as co-payment options, typically 20 percent or so.

Know that a 20 percent co-payment does not mean that you would have to come up with $10,000 for a $50,000 claim. Insurers typically set a maximum out-of-pocket limit on your annual co-payments of $1,000 to $2,000 and then cover 100 percent of medical expenses over that cap. With HMO plans, most insurers offer options such as $5, $10, or $20 for a physician's office visit. Again, the higher the per visit charge you're willing to accept, the lower your health insurance premiums will be.

Sharing costs with your employees is a good way to provide better policies at a fair price for all. We suggest that you as the employer pay half the cost of the health insurance premiums and have your employees pick up the other half.

Be sure to shop around

Most health insurance plans are sold through insurance agents, but some are sold directly from the insurer. If the plan is sold both ways, going through an agent shouldn't cost you any more. Start by getting plan proposals from Blue Cross and Blue Shield, Kaiser, or other large health insurers in your area. Also check with professional or other associations that you may belong to. A competent independent insurance agent who specializes in health insurance can help find insurers willing to offer you and your employees coverage.

Health insurance agents have a conflict of interest common to all financial salespeople working on commission: The higher the premium plan they sell you, the bigger the commission they earn. So an agent may try to steer you into higher-cost plans and not suggest some of the strategies discussed in the previous section to reduce your cost of your company's coverage.

When you try to enroll with a particular health insurance plan, you may have trouble securing coverage if any employees have health problems, also known as a preexisting conditions. Try health insurance plans that don't discriminate — some plans such as Blue Cross and Blue Shield, and some HMO plans such as Kaiser will sometimes take you regardless of your condition. Also, some states provide plans for people with preexisting conditions who are unable to find coverage elsewhere. Contact your state's insurance department.

Disability insurance

Most small businesses do not offer disability insurance to their employees. The purpose of *disability insurance* is to protect your income and that of your employees from being lost in the event of a disability. Anyone who is dependent upon their own income should have disability insurance. If you suffer a total disability, you probably won't be able to earn an income or as much income but you'll have the same or higher living expenses.

As an employer, you may be required by your state to pay into a state disability or worker's compensation program (the latter only covers injuries and disabilities suffered on the job). Additionally, through the Social Security system, you and your employees have minimal disability benefits. While coverage through government disability programs is often not sufficient, it's better than nothing; so you as the employer shouldn't beat yourself up for not offering disability coverage to your employees.

Good reasons to offer disability coverage to your employees would be that your competitors offer their employees coverage and/or you can afford to pay for such coverage. As with health insurance, we strongly encourage you to have your employees share in the cost of disability coverage — perhaps you could pay 50 percent.

If you're in the market for disability protection for you and your employees, here's how to get the best coverage at a competitive price:

- ✔ **Replace about 60 percent of income.** A person generally needs enough disability coverage to provide him or her with sufficient income to live on until other financial resources are available. If you pay for a portion of your employees' disability coverage, that portion of the benefits then becomes taxable. You may also get a policy with a so-called "residual benefits" feature, which pays a partial benefit to a person with a disability that prevents him or her from working full time. Lastly, consider getting a cost-of-living adjustment rider, which increases a benefit payment by a set percentage or in accordance with changes in inflation and helps retain the purchasing power of a policy's benefits.

- ✔ **Get benefits through age 65.** A good disability policy should pay benefits through an age at which the employee becomes financially independent, which for most people occurs around age 65, the approximate age at which Social Security retirement benefits begin. If you'd like to offer your employees coverage but find that policies until age 65 are too costly, you can get five-year benefit policies instead.

- ✔ **Use an adequate definition of disability.** An adequate definition of disability in a policy is that the policy pays benefits if you cannot perform work for which you are "reasonably trained." "Own-occupation" policies, which pay benefits if you are unable to perform the duties of your current occupation, are the most expensive because there's a greater chance the insurer will have to pay out benefits.

- ✔ **Buy policies that are noncancelable and guaranteed renewable.** These features ensure that the disability policy cannot be canceled because an employee falls into bad health.

- ✔ **Accept a lengthier waiting period.** The waiting period, which can also be thought of as the deductible on the policy, is the time between the onset of your disability and the time you begin collecting benefits. Accepting a longer waiting period — at least three months and preferably six months — greatly reduces the cost of the disability insurance.

- ✔ **Shop around.** In addition to soliciting proposals from insurance agents who specialize in disability coverage, also check through professional associations to which you already belong or can join. USAA (800-531-8000) is also worth soliciting proposals from because it offers competitively priced policies.

Life insurance

We recommend that you not waste your precious compensation and benefits dollars on life insurance. Why? First, few small employers (your competitors) offer life insurance coverage. Second, it's not a wise benefit to offer for the simple reason that many of your employees won't need it. Life insurance is needed by those who have financial dependents. The vast majority of your single employees and childless employees won't have the need for life insurance.

Should you decide that you really want to offer the Cadillac of benefits packages and include some life insurance coverage, buy term life insurance not cash value life insurance. With term life insurance, you pay an annual premium for a set amount of life insurance coverage. During the term of the policy, if you stay alive, your beneficiaries collect no death benefit and you're out the premium, but of course you're eternally grateful you're not deceased. With cash value life insurance (also known as whole life, universal life, or variable life), you pay a much higher premium for a combination of life insurance coverage and a savings type account. For the same amount of coverage, cash value policies cost a whopping eight times more than comparable term policies.

Dependent care plans

A *dependent care plan* enables you and your employees to put away money from your paycheck on a pretax basis, which you can then use to pay for child care expenses or to care for an ill or aging parent. Doing so saves you federal, state, and even Social Security taxes. These plans allow you to put away up to $5,000 per year ($2,500 for those of you who are married filing separately).

Dependent care spending accounts are a "use it or lose it" benefit. If you or your employees aren't able to spend the money for child care expenses in the current tax year, at the end of the year the IRS forces you to forfeit all the money that you haven't used.

Flexible benefit plans

Flexible benefit or "cafeteria" plans allow employees to pick and choose the benefits on which to spend their benefit dollars. These plans are also known as Section 125 for the section of the IRS tax laws that sanctions such plans.

Under a *flexible benefit plan,* employees have a choice for a portion of their compensation to receive it as pay or to put those dollars toward purchasing benefits of their choosing from a menu offered by their employer. The virtue of such a flexible plan is that it allows employees to customize their own benefits package to suit their own needs and wants. For example, a married employee with young children may prefer to spend his benefit dollars on dependent care expenses, whereas a single employee may prefer simply to receive more cash compensation or take more vacation days.

Unless and until you offer a number of insurance benefits to your employees, offering a flexible plan won't be necessary and worthwhile. However, if you are offering a generous number of benefits and would like to offer your employees maximum flexibility in using their benefits, a flex plan may make sense.

Among the types of benefits that employers may offer to their employees to choose from in a flexible benefit plan are:

Worth Considering

Health insurance and health care spending accounts (which allow employees to pay for out-of-pocket medical expenses with pretax dollars)

Group life insurance

Disability insurance

Vacation days

Employee contributions to a 401(k)

Dependent care plans and spending accounts (which allow employees to pay for dependent care with pretax dollars)

Don't Bother

Dental and vision insurance

Group legal insurance plans

You'll notice in the previous list that we've differentiated between benefits that we think are worth including in a flexible benefit plan and those we think aren't worth including. In the latter category are insurance programs that ultimately cover small-potato items. You should spend your insurance dollars on coverages that protect you and your employees against potentially financially catastrophic losses, such as those that could be incurred from a long-term disability or major medical problem.

Because flexible benefit plans are time-consuming and fairly costly for small businesses to establish (around $1,000) and administer (about $1,000 per year), your small business likely won't have one, especially if you have fewer than ten employees. You will need and want to hire competent tax and benefit advisers to help you design your flexible benefit plan and to help you comply with the myriad tax issues that must be dealt with on an ongoing basis with such plans.

If you're going to go to the trouble and expense of putting a flexible benefit plan in place at your company, also invest the necessary time and cost to explain the specific benefits in the plan and how employees can choose among them. For many employers, small and large, too many employees' lack of understanding hampers them from making good use of these plans and appreciating the employer's providing them.

Vacation

We all need down time, and weekends don't just cut it. A full week or two off can do wonders for you and your employees.

Two weeks of paid vacation is the norm for new hires. For key employees and employees who have been with you for several or more years, three weeks is the norm. Many small businesses offer a graduated vacation schedule that may, for instance, offer 4 weeks after 10 years and 5 weeks after 20.

Some employees may value flexibility and more time off, so if your business allows, try to accommodate such wants to keep good employees happy. For example, if an employee would rather have an extra week's vacation each year rather than 2 percent of a pay raise, financially you should be indifferent, unless of course, that employee is difficult or impossible to replace during that extra vacation period.

Chapter 15

The Long Arm of the Law: Regulatory and Legal Issues

. . . .

In This Chapter

▶ Complying with governmental licensing, registrations, and permits

▶ Protecting your ideas and plans

▶ Managing legal issues related to employees

. . . .

*O*ne of the least-pleasant aspects of starting and running a small business is attempting to comprehend the myriad of government regulations that affect how and where you do business, as well as the plethora of legal issues that can blow up in your face and culminate in a lawsuit. So we can understand what's probably a strong desire on your part to skip this chapter. Please don't; doing so could ensnare you in government fines and legal fees that could prove fatal to your business.

And, if the thought of these penalties isn't enough, we have what we hope is an incentive for you to familiarize yourself with the issues raised in this chapter. *We can save you time and headaches.* How? By showing you how to get important legal and regulatory tasks completed correctly while minimizing time spent.

A Whole Lotta Laws for Small Business

You may think that if you're starting or operating a truly small, small business, you don't need to know much on the legal and regulatory fronts. We wish that were true, but it's not. Consider the following types of issues that most small-business owners must grapple with both in the early years of their businesses and on an ongoing basis:

✔ **Selecting a name for your business:** You can't simply choose a name and start using it for your business. Why not? Because you may select a name that's already being used by another business, the owner of which surely won't be pleased by your apparent plagiarism and who could take legal action against you. Besides, you'll probably be spending a lot of marketing money over the years to distinguish *your* business, and you don't want it confused with someone else's.

✔ **Complying with government licensing and permit requirements:** Federal, state, and sometimes even local governments regulate and license certain types of businesses, such as restaurants or taxi cabs or beauty shops.

If you're operating a business that requires you to register with particular government entities and/or pass certain exams or satisfy particular licensing requirements, you will be breaking the law and may be out of business if you don't comply. The possible penalties for running afoul of such laws can be steep, including monetary fines and even outright prohibition against practicing your line of work for months or even years. And, if that weren't bad enough, your transgressions may be public knowledge, which can hamper your ability to get your business up and running again after you're legally able to do so.

✔ **Protecting your ideas and work:** If you prepare a business plan and distribute it for comment or to raise money, you don't want those ideas stolen, do you? Or, if you invent or create something new and unique — you don't want someone to copy your creation and profit from it would you? Well, if you don't properly protect your ideas, work, and other creative developments through trademarks, copyrights, and patents, someone could very well rip you off, and you would have little, if any, legal recourse.

✔ **Establishing a retirement plan:** Perhaps you've heard of retirement plans such as profit sharing, money purchase pension plans, SEP-IRAs, and so on. Over the years, these plans can slash tens and maybe even hundreds of thousands of dollars off your tax bill. However, if you have employees, those employees are entitled to certain benefits in retirement plans subject to federal regulations. Your reward for violating retirement plan rules can be the disallowance of your contributions into the plan, thereby owing the IRS lots of taxes and penalties — ouch! Retirement plans are covered in Chapter 14.

✔ **Tax filings:** As a business owner and self-employed person, you are responsible for the proper filing of all federal, state, and local taxes for yourself and your business. And when you employ others, you must withhold appropriate taxes from your employees' wages and submit the withheld taxes in a timely fashion to the various tax regulatory authorities. More than a few small businesses have failed because the owners have fallen behind and subsequently been buried by past-due tax payments. Chapter 16 will help you stay on the good side of the IRS.

✔ **Hiring and managing employees:** Employment law is a vast and growing area of the legal profession. When you hire and employ workers, you must be thoughtful and careful about what you say to them and how you manage and behave around them. If you're not careful, you can face big legal bills and possible lawsuit damages, while your own and your hard-earned business reputations are dragged through the mud during legal proceedings.

✔ **Contracts:** In many ways, contracts make the business world go 'round. When properly prepared, contracts function as legally binding and enforceable agreements that your business makes with suppliers, employees, and others relating to the operation of your business. If you offer a contract to another person or business or seek to change the terms and conditions of a contract, you must understand, up front, the legal ramifications. If you don't understand these ramifications, at a minimum you'll have upset parties on the other end of the contract; in the worst cases, you could end up in court with soaring legal bills and potential lawsuits.

Regulatory Concerns of the Start-Up

Before you begin working with your first customer, you should be investing time and money into getting your legal and regulatory ducks in a row. In the start-up phase of a small business, however, few business owners have the luxury of spending much time or money on these issues. Thus, in this section, we attempt to save you some of both while helping you protect your business.

Licensing, registrations, and permits

Years ago, when Eric started his financial counseling practice, the first thing that he did was to investigate what government regulatory organizations he needed to register with. To his surprise, he had to register both with the federal Securities and Exchange Commission and his state's Department of Corporations. He was surprised because he figured that a profession as full of deception, conflicts of interest, and outright cases of corruption as the financial planning profession would have had little government oversight. (Then again, government "oversight" of a profession can literally result in oversights!)

To discover the various ways in which various government bodies regulate your line of business, we suggest you check with the following:

- ✔ **Trade associations for your business or profession:** Zillions of trade associations exist, and the better ones can provide a wealth of information on government regulations and other such subjects. The *Small Business Sourcebook* discussed in Chapter 6 can help you locate the associations in your industry.

- ✔ **Others in your profession:** The simplest way to network with others in your line of work is to attend conferences or conventions for your industry or profession. Again, trade associations should be able to help you locate such events. Alternatively, you can network in your local area. A problem with this strategy is that people in the same line of work in your town may view you as competition and be less than forthcoming with assistance.

- ✔ **Contact the state agency that oversees corporations:** Check the government section in your local white pages phone directory for the phone number. Be persistent because if the person who answers the phone is poorly trained or having a bureaucratic bad day, you may not get the information that you're looking for, or you may be transferred to the wrong department.

- ✔ **Trade publications:** You may be surprised at how many specialized occupational publications exist. (See Chapter 6 for how to identify and locate them.) You can then research past articles on industry regulations in such publications. (You may need to contact the publication for a listing of topics covered in prior issues.)

- ✔ **Chamber of Commerce:** Most communities have a local Chamber of Commerce that may be able to suggest the applicable government organizations for you to check in with and other people to speak to.

The realities of compliance

Imagine a world where your business has to deal with only one government agency for all required licenses, registrations, and permits. Further imagine that when you're ready to open a particular type of business, that one government agency has a neatly organized, concise, and easy-to-understand packet of information that details exactly what registrations and paperwork you need to file in order to comply with government regulations. All you have to do is pay one fee, spend a few minutes completing a few pieces of paperwork, and turn it over to a friendly, service-minded government employee who, on the spot, issues you all the licenses and permits you need and sends you on your merry way.

Now snap out of it and get yourself back to reality!

In the real world, numerous governmental agencies — at the local, regional, state, and federal levels — impose all sorts of licensing, registration, and permit requirements on small-business owners. If you've ever arrived in a new city without a map and tried to get around by yourself in a car, then you can begin to understand what it may be like as you try to discover all the agencies and paperwork required for the particular type of business you want to operate.

Miss applying for one important permit or license, and the government can slap you with hefty fines, and you could be sued by disgruntled customers who use your lack of compliance with government regulations as an indicator of slipshod business practices. And, even if you are a good enough detective to ferret out and understand each and every government regulation with which you must comply, you can go mad when you realize that, just as in finding your way out of a maze, the order in which you obtain your permits and licenses is critical and that the only correct order is non-apparent.

Consider the experience of our friend, Jason. He played in a local band that was getting lots of gigs and starting to generate a bit of income. The band members agreed that this was no longer just a hobby and that they should register as an official business. Jason, to his later chagrin, agreed to take care of this.

One afternoon, he hopped on his bike (being in his mid-20s and cost conscious, Jason commuted by bicycle) and headed to City Hall. On the second floor, he found the business tax registration office, where he was told that he needed a federal Employer Identification Number (EIN) before he could register with the city. The federal building was two blocks up the street, so off he went to fill out the necessary federal form.

Back at City Hall, Jason was now informed that he couldn't register his business until he made sure that his business name wasn't taken by anyone else in the county. Also, because he would be filing his business under a fictitious name (the name of the band rather than the real name of a person), he needed to fill out a "doing business as (dba)" form. "Can I do that here?" he asked. "No," he was told, "You need to go the County Clerk's office."

The County Clerk's office was three blocks down the street. He was directed to an old computer in the corner where he could do a search for his business name. The name wasn't taken. "So can I go ahead and register our fictitious name?" Jason asked. "No," he was told, "We need to have proof that you've paid your business tax registration fees."

So back to City Hall, where he was finally allowed to fill out the business tax paperwork and pay his registration fee. When the clerk who was handling his paperwork heard that the band planned to sell recordings at its gigs, Jason was told to get a seller's permit for collecting state sales tax. "How many blocks away is that?" Jason asked. "The state office is on the other side of town," he was told.

But first, back to the County Clerk's office three blocks down the street. By showing proof that he had filled out the business tax registration forms and paid the filing fee, he was now allowed to fill out the dba registration forms and pay that filing fee.

As it was getting late in the day, Jason raced to the other side of town to get his seller's permit . . . but the office was closed. Time flies when you have to tour every regulatory office in town. "I'm nervous about going back down there tomorrow," Jason admitted to his bandmates that night. "I'm afraid of where they'll send me next."

Don't despair. Life could be a lot worse — you could live in Russia! Just remember to keep your eyes and ears open. Talk to as many people as you can and remember that the burden for compliance falls on your shoulders. Don't toss your hands in the air and say that compliance with government regulations is too hard to figure out so you're just going to wing it. And remember that the success or failure of a business often lies in the details — or more specifically, the owner's willingness to pay attention to them. This is an early test!

Local regulations: Taxes, zoning, and health

The town, city, and county in which you operate your business more than likely impose some requirements on businesses like yours. Even if you operate a home-based business (see Chapter 18), you can't assume that you can do what you want, when you want, and where you want — home-based businesses are often more restricted than their office park counterparts.

Here are the more common local regulations affecting small-business owners:

- ✔ **Taxes:** In most areas, if you're selling products through a retail store, you'll more than likely have to collect sales tax. Even if you don't operate a retail store but sell products, you may also have to collect sales tax. And some (primarily larger) cities tax all revenue from small businesses. Last but not least, you may be surprised to learn that some communities levy an annual property tax on certain business assets such as inventory, equipment, and furniture.

- ✔ **Fictitious name:** As with our friend Jason and his band mentioned previously, if the name of your business is different from your own, you need to file what is known as a fictitious name or "doing business as (dba)" certificate. Filing is usually done through the county. You are often also required to publish your dba filing in a local newspaper.

- ✔ **Real estate:** All real estate is affected by zoning, which restricts the usage of a given property. If you don't like the idea of local government telling you what you can and can't do on your property, consider how you would feel if your next-door neighbor opened a chicken and pig farm on his property! Whether you're leasing or buying a property, your business will be affected by zoning ordinances. You need to investigate whether you can operate your desired business out of a given location as well as plan on dealing with the good folks in City Hall if you want to do any renovations to your place of business. And if those renovations raise any environmental concerns, such as disturbing or removing potentially hazardous substances like asbestos, your local health department may get involved as well.

✔ **Health and safety:** Small-business owners whose enterprise involves food are subject to all sorts of regulations from their local health department. You may need to have your water occasionally tested if you're lucky enough to live in a less-densely populated area where well water is used. And, don't overlook the myriad safety regulations such as local fire codes and elevator inspections.

So, you may or should be wondering, how the heck do you discover what local regulations affect your type of business? Here's a short list of the best ways that we know of to learn more:

✔ **Call relevant local government agencies.** Let your fingers do the walking through the government pages section of your local phone directory. For tax issues, look under "Tax Collector." For real estate issues, look under terms like "Planning Department" or "Building Inspection Department." For health-related issues, the heading in the phone book is almost always "Health Department." Should you get stuck and not be able to reach the correct department, most cities and towns have a city clerk or town clerk who can transfer you to the right department.

✔ **Contact the local Chamber of Commerce.** Most communities have a Chamber of Commerce; the better ones have helpful information for prospective and current small-business owners.

✔ **Speak with other small-business owners in your field.** Those who have "been there" and "done that" can tell you of their experiences and what they've learned. Although you can learn a tremendous amount speaking with fellow small-business owners, please keep in mind that others may or may not have done a thorough job of researching regulatory requirements and may have chosen to not comply with certain regulations.

✔ **Tap the collective experience of trade associations.** Most lines of business have active trade associations (see Chapter 12 for how to locate a trade association) whose management and members can share war stories and information about regulations. Obviously, association members in your local area will have far more relevant experiences to share.

✔ **Chat with real estate agents and building contractors.** If your business is going to be in a commercial or retail space, you can acquire much knowledge conversing with agents who sell or lease space and/or contractors who develop and renovate space similar to what your business will occupy.

✔ **Work with experienced small-business advisors.** Tax and legal advisors, as well as consultants experienced with businesses like yours, can help point you in the right direction. Although such advisors charge a hefty hourly fee, they may be willing to offer gratis tips on general regulatory issues in order to cultivate your future business.

State regulations: More taxes, licensing, insurance, and the environment

In addition to regulations at the local level, states all impose requirements on businesses that you'll need to be aware of and comply with. Fortunately, most states have established agencies to assist business owners with doing business in the state. States do have some vested interest in trying to attract and retain businesses within their state because business tax revenues fill their coffers.

Here are the primary issues that may affect your small business due to state regulations:

✔ **Licenses:** If all people in a given occupation were competent and ethical, we would have little need for government regulation. However, as we all know from personal experiences, each and every profession has its share of bad apples. State licensing is primarily intended to reduce the consumer's likelihood of being fleeced or victimized. Although some occupations (such as doctors and lawyers) are universally required to be licensed, each state has a unique list of occupations it regulates. The only way you can know for sure if your occupation requires a license in your state is to ask.

State licensing requirements vary by occupation and by state. In some states, you can get certain licenses if you're able to complete a few forms and write the state a check to pay your fees. In most cases, however, you have to take a test or complete some certification in order to get a license. However, as we all know again from personal experience, just because a person can pass a test or gain some credential does not mean that he or she will be a competent or ethical practitioner in his or her chosen field. But it's at least a start, indicating your willingness to strut your stuff.

✔ **Taxes:** As we discussed in the local regulations section, some businesses, such as retailers, will need to collect sales tax on products sold. And in most states, all businesses, regardless of type, must pay income taxes at the state level (see Chapter 16).

✔ **Insurance:** To you, the small-business owner, having to pay for employee-related insurance will feel like another tax. Common state-required coverages include worker's compensation, which compensates workers for lost wages due to job-related injuries, and unemployment insurance, which pays laid off employees for a certain amount or until they are able to secure another job.

✔ **Environment:** If you are a manufacturer and your plant emits things into the air or water, you can be pretty certain that your state and possibly other government agencies will regulate your activities. And for good reason — left to their own devices, some business owners would pollute away because installing control devices would add to the cost of doing business, effectively reducing profits.

Federal regulations: Still more taxes, licenses, and requirements

In addition to local and state regulations, small-business owners also must comply with U.S. federal government regulations. Myriad governmental regulations cover taxes, licenses, as well as the health, safety, and welfare of your employees. In this section, we cover the critical ones that you should know about. Note that not all federal labor laws affect all small businesses, because some issues only apply to employers with a certain number of employees. So, the good news may be that your small business is small enough that you don't have to concern yourself with the following topics.

Here are the key federal regulations you need to think about:

✔ **Licenses:** Most businesses that require a license or permit to operate generally obtain such licenses and permits at the state level. Some businesses (mostly ones you won't be attracted to), however, are permitted and licensed at the federal level. They include alcohol manufacturers, drug companies, firearm manufacturers and dealers, investment advisers, meat packing and preparation companies, radio stations, tobacco manufacturers, television stations, and trucking and other transportation companies.

✔ **Taxes:** All businesses that are incorporated, or their owners if the business is not incorporated, must file a federal income tax return. Additionally, most small-business owners, especially those who hire employees, will apply for and utilize a federal Employer Identification Number (EIN). See Chapter 16 for the lowdown on small-business tax issues.

✔ **Americans with Disabilities Act:** In 1991, Congress passed the Americans with Disabilities Act (ADA), which was sweeping legislation to prohibit employers with 15 or more employees from discriminating against prospective and current employees or customers with disabilities. Such discrimination is barred in the hiring, management, and dismissal of any employee.

For example, in the process of interviewing job applicants, you can get yourself into a lot of legal hot water if you exclude from consideration qualified candidates who are in some way disabled.

✔ **Family Medical Leave Act:** Employers with 50 or more employees
(within 75 miles) are required by this 1993 legislation to provide up to
12 weeks of unpaid leave to employees who desire or need the leave for
personal health reasons due to a serious medical condition that affects
the employee's ability to perform the regular duties of his or her job; to
spend time with a newborn or adopted child; or to care for a family
member who has a serious medical condition. During the term of an
employee's leave, the employer must continue to cover the employee
under the company's group health insurance plan under the same
conditions as when the employee was working.

Eligible employees (who have been with the employer for at least one
year and who have worked at least 125 hours over the previous year)
who take a leave under the Family Medical Leave Act can generally do
so with the understanding that they can return to their same position
with the same pay and benefits. So-called highly compensated employees are not guaranteed the same position and compensation package if
their return would lead to significant economic harm to the employer.

Selection of a business entity

In the start-up phase of your business, you should think about what type of
organization or business entity (for example, sole proprietorship, partnership, corporation, limited liability company) makes the best sense for your
enterprise. Although the different corporate entities that you may form for
your business can provide some legal protection for you and your personal
assets, establishing such entities involves significant time and expense and
does not completely insulate you and your company from lawsuits.

Given the excitement and stresses inherent in the early days of a small
business, we can understand why you may not care to spend your precious
time and money on researching and consulting with legal and tax experts
about what type of organization you should establish for your business
entity. As we discuss in Chapter 5, however, because of tax and other issues,
you should choose sooner rather than later which entity will best serve
your needs.

Protecting ideas and plans: Trademarks, patents, NDAs, and copyrights

Odds are good that the business idea you have or the business plans you
have aren't unique. After all, the U.S. alone has tens of millions of businesses. Some business owners, however, do take a different twist on something or a have a truly unique product or service to offer. And even if you
don't have something unique or different to offer, who wants to have his
plans and ideas literally ripped off? In circulating copies of your business
plan, you may be giving away much of your hard work and ideas to someone
or some company that can end up being a competitor.

Here are some tips for how to protect your business plan, your ideas, and yourself:

- ✔ **Be careful about who sees the plan.** A friend or advisor who happens to know a lot about your type of small business or small businesses in general is unlikely to have unsavory motives in looking at your plan. On the other hand, a potential competitor who peruses your plans may not have your best interests at heart.

- ✔ **Keep proprietary information out of your plan.** Product designs, manufacturing specifications, unique resources, and other information unique to your company, should not be included in copies of your business plan that you distribute to others. Share such information with serious investors only if needed to gain their investment.

- ✔ **Place a nondisclosure statement in the front of your business plan.** In the event that your plan does fall into the hands of someone who may be inclined to steal your ideas, a nondisclosure statement (discussed in the next section) should scare them off.

- ✔ **Get legal assistance where necessary.** If your work and ideas are proprietary and protectable, speak with an attorney concerning copyrights, trademarks, and patents. We explain these important legal protections in the upcoming section "Patents, trademarks, and copyrights."

If you haven't yet developed your business plan and need help doing so, see Chapter 4.

Nondisclosure agreements (NDAs)

A nondisclosure agreement should always be attached to the beginning of a business plan before you circulate it for review. Its purpose is to warn the reader that the enclosed contents are your property and not to be spread around without your consent. Following is a sample nondisclosure:

> This confidential Business Plan has been prepared in order to raise financing for Wowza Widgets, Inc. This material is being delivered to a select number of potential investors, each of whom agrees to the following terms and conditions:

> Each recipient of this Business Plan agrees that, by accepting this material, he or she will not copy, reproduce, distribute, or discuss with others any part of this plan without prior written consent of Wowza Widgets, Inc.

> The recipient agrees to keep confidential all information contained herein and not use it for any purpose whatsoever other than to evaluate and determine interest in providing financing described herein.

This material contains proprietary and confidential information regarding Wowza Widgets, Inc., and is based upon information provided to Wowza Widgets by sources deemed to be reliable. Although the information contained herein is believed to be accurate, Wowza Widgets, Inc., expressly disclaims all liability for any information, projections, or representations (expressed or implied) contained herein from omissions from this material or for any written or oral communication transmitted to any part in the course of its evaluation for this financing. The recipient acknowledges that this material shall remain the property of Wowza Widgets, Inc., and Wowza Widgets, Inc., reserves the right to request the return of the material at any time and in any respect, to amend or terminate solicitation procedures, to terminate discussions with any and all prospective financing sources, to reject any and all proposals, or to negotiate with any party with respect to the financing of Wowza Widgets, Inc.

The projections contained in the pro-forma Financial Section are based upon numerous assumptions. Although Wowza Widgets, Inc., believes that these assumptions are reasonable, no assurance can be given as to the accuracy of these projections because they are dependent in large part upon unfore-seeable factors and events. As a result, the actual results achieved may vary from the projections, and such variation can be material and adverse.

Patents, trademarks, and copyrights

You may have created something unique that you would like to protect others from copying. Or, you may simply wish to restrain others from using and profiting from the name of your business or literary, musical, or artistic creations.

Welcome to the wonderful and often confusing world of patent, copyright, and trademark law. You'll be happy to hear that this is not a legal book, in part because your two humble authors are, happily (for us at least), not lawyers. And most small-business owners need not spend much time or legal expense on these issues.

Here then are some brief definitions of some important terms:

- ✔ **Patent:** If you've invented something (such as a new type of toy or computer disk), you may explore patenting your invention. The reason: By filing a patent with the federal government, you then have exclusive rights to manufacture, sell, and use the patented invention. You can, if you so choose, license usage of the patent to others.

- ✔ **Trademark:** Companies invest significant time, effort, and money into creating brand names (for example, *Coca-Cola, ...For Dummies*), marketing, advertising slogans (The Real Thing, A Reference for the Rest of Us!), and logos (see the *...For Dummies* guy on this book's cover), and so on. The point of the trademark is to protect your brands and prevent other enterprises from using and profiting from the recognition and reputation you've developed through your business's brand names, marketing/advertising images, and the words associated with your product. Trademarked items can also include things such as the packaging, shape, character names, color, and smell associated with a product. If you think your business has identifying characteristics you don't want copied by competitors, think about applying for trademark protection.

Most small-business owners need not be as concerned with protecting their own trademarks as they are with infringing on someone else's. For example, when you're starting your business, make sure that the business name you have in mind is not currently in use by another small business. An attorney can help you with this.

✔ **Copyright:** Copyright laws cover such works as musical and sound recordings, literary works, software, graphics, and audiovisuals. The owner of the copyright in a work is solely allowed to sell the work, make copies of it, create derivations from it, and perform and display the work. The creator of the work is not always the person or part of the organization that holds the copyright. For example, writers will sometimes do freelance writing for publications that hold the copyright to the work that their writers create for them.

In addition to hiring an attorney (which we discuss in Chapter 8), you can also check out books and other resources explaining small-business law. We strongly encourage you to understand as much as you can *before* sitting down with a lawyer.

Contracts with customers and suppliers

All small businesses have customers as well as suppliers. In both of these relationships, the small-business owner will find himself or herself engaging in contracts, whether formally written or verbal. Certain expectations are created as well in these relationships due in part to advertising. Here are our tips for dealing with contracts with your customers and suppliers:

✔ **Get it in writing.** Otherwise, you have no or little recourse if someone doesn't deliver (such as a supplier) as promised.

✔ **Don't make promises verbally that you wouldn't be willing to put into writing.** Yes, this may sound like it contradicts our first tip but especially when it comes to your customers and advertising, what you say can get you into trouble.

✔ **Get a legal perspective.** As we discuss in Chapter 8, there will be various times when you should get legal assistance. When you are drafting contracts is one of those times.

Hiring and Labor Laws

When your business begins to hire employees, the good news is that your business has probably gotten off the ground sufficiently well enough to afford the cost of hiring an employee. The bad news is that, besides the salary you pay your employees, myriad "hidden" costs to hiring and retaining employees arise, such as the following:

- ✔ **Taxes:** On top of your employees' salaries, you'll also be responsible for paying Social Security taxes on their earnings, as well as other taxes, such as unemployment insurance. When hiring, you also must be careful about whether you hire people as employees or independent contractors. Many small-business employers prefer to hire people as independent contractors because it lowers their tax bill, but the IRS has strict rules for who qualifies as an independent contractor. If you're treating someone as a contractor who should be treated as an employee, you could end up with stiff penalties. Small-business tax issues are covered in detail in Chapter 16.

- ✔ **Employee benefits:** Various insurance programs, paid vacation, and retirement plans, if you provide them to attract and retain employees, are possible company benefits that can add to your personnel costs. Most truly small, small businesses won't be able to afford offering many employee benefits, but you should know your options and what your competition is offering. (We cover employee benefit programs in Chapter 14.)

- ✔ **Complying with government regulations:** Are you surprised that a host of local, state, and federal government regulations dictate, mandate, and cajole your hiring, management, and dismissal of employees? You shouldn't be if you've made it this far in this chapter!

- ✔ **Employee lawsuits:** Don't think that just because you're not running a billion-dollar enterprise you can't and won't be sued. Although some employee suits are frivolous, others are caused by employers not exercising proper care when dealing with their employees. (In addition to working with a small-business-experienced attorney, see Chapter 19 for legal resources.)

Chapter 16

Taming Your Small Business's Taxes

. . . .

In This Chapter

▶ Managing your business taxes

▶ Finding good tax advice

▶ Understanding employee tax issues

▶ Using sensible tax write-offs

▶ Selecting a tax-friendly corporate entity

. . . .

*O*ne of the more painful aspects of owning your own business is the far-too-many hours you'll spend on bookkeeping chores for tax reporting and on completing and filing a myriad of tax forms. In addition to federal income tax requirements, most states assess income taxes and, as we discuss in Chapter 15, some local governments levy taxes on small businesses, too.

When you were an employee, you may very well have taken for granted how much simpler your tax life was. As a wage-slave, you have the appropriate taxes withheld by your employer from each of your paychecks, and your employer submits the money to the required government entities. When time comes for you to file your annual tax return, your employer provides you with Form W-2, which neatly summarizes on postcard-size documents your total pay for the year just passed as well as the dollar amount of taxes paid at the federal, state, and local levels. Being a wage-slave, from a paper-work standpoint anyway, isn't really so bad!

By contrast, as a small-business owner, you are now the employer, and you have many new tax responsibilities. Throughout the year, you are personally responsible for paying estimated taxes as you earn money, and you must also withold and submit payroll taxes for all of your employees. And, then, when time comes to file your annual tax return, the real fun begins. Therefore, many small-business owners seek help from tax professionals when completing their annual income tax returns and when filing their payroll tax payments throughout the year. As we discuss in Chapter 8, as your company grows, you may choose to hire an in-house bookkeeper. Even then, however, you're unlikely to be able to go it alone on your income and payroll taxes and be assured of doing things correctly and taking advantage of lawful ways to minimize your tax bills.

Whether you hire professional tax help or not, we don't want you to pay more taxes than you are legally required to pay. Although you may have heard tales of small-business owners who cheat on their taxes, surprisingly, we know some small-business owners who pay more taxes than they should. Why? Because they haven't taken the time to understand the tax laws or because they or their tax preparers are being too conservative in preparing their income tax returns. Also, small-business owners (and sometimes their tax preparers) believe that it's better to not claim legal deductions if doing so will trigger an audit. Frankly, we find that philosophy to be generally foolish. There's no reason to fear an audit, except for the hassle of time and possible out-of-pocket expense for representation if you so choose, if you're staying within the boundaries of the tax laws.

In this chapter, we highlight strategies for reducing your small-business taxes.

Get Smarter About Taxes

Whether you hire tax advisors or deal with taxes completely on your own, your best strategy for reducing your taxes and complying with tax laws is to educate yourself. For those who can afford to and who enjoy doing so, you can hire outside bookkeeping and tax preparers/advisors. However, we believe that you'd be making a mistake if you hire such assistance without investing a small amount of your own time to better understand the tax laws and how they fit into your small-business and personal financial situation. Thus, the last thing we cover in this section is how to go about hiring tax preparers and advisors.

Reading income tax guides

Free for your asking (call 800-TAX-FORM) — actually, you've already paid for them through your tax dollars — are the following sometimes helpful booklets from the Internal Revenue Service (IRS):

- ✔ Publication 17, *Your Federal Income Tax,* is designed for individual tax-return preparation.
- ✔ Publication 334, *Tax Guide for Small Businesses,* is for small-business owners to use in their tax-return preparation.

It should go without saying that in its publications, the IRS doesn't go out of its way to suggest ways for you to cut your tax bill. It should also go without saying that the IRS doesn't have a knack for clearly and concisely stating things in plain English. If it did, we wouldn't all get frustrated and annoyed when it comes time to complete our tax forms.

Fortunately, you don't have to rely solely on IRS booklets to understand taxes and file your tax returns. You can obtain tax preparation, planning, and advice books that highlight wise and legal tax-reduction moves. We're partial to *Taxes For Dummies,* which Eric co-authored with David J. Silverman. Another good book to check out is *J.K. Lasser's Your Income Tax.* Don't be put off by the girth of these books — the portions relevant to small-business owners aren't lengthy and are well worth your time to read. Those who understand our tax system can legally reduce their tax bills by tens of thousands of dollars during their working years.

Using income tax-preparation software

Good income tax-preparation computer programs explain how to complete your tax return, highlight what could cause an audit, and suggest some tax-reduction strategies. Tax-preparation software also enables you to quickly recalculate all your tax numbers if something changes.

Among the major programs, our favorites are Kiplinger TaxCut and TurboTax. If you use bookkeeping software, check if the income tax package you're interested in allows you to transfer data from your financial program into the tax-preparation program.

Hiring help

Hiring a tax preparer/advisor — particularly when you're confronted for the first time with completing a tax return as the owner of your own business — can save you time and reduce your tax bill. If you are a person who has a static tax situation year after year or if you take sufficient interest in under-standing the income tax system, we don't believe you need to hire a tax person, unless you feel you have something better to do with your time.

If and when (as do most small-business owners) you end up seeking the services of a tax practitioner, do your homework to find a good one. As in any field, the quality and competence of tax preparers and advisors vary widely.

What's in a title?

In the income tax field, you'll find practitioners who go by all sorts of names and titles. There are folks who simply go by the title of preparer, there are enrolled agents, certified public accountants, tax attorneys, and so on. Here are the common ones you'll encounter along with our take on when each might be appropriate for a small-business owner to hire:

✔ **Preparers.** Tax preparers, such as those who work for large chains such as H&R Block and Jackson Hewitt, as well as a myriad of sole practitioners and small partnerships, tend to focus on tax preparation and sometimes don't work in the tax field year-round. Although they are among the least costly of tax people, most preparers don't have adequate expertise to handle the typical small-business owners' tax returns and other tax questions. As is the case with so-called financial planners, no regulations nor licensing applies to preparers. A good preparer, who should have completed an adequate training program, makes sense for small-business owners with simple situations and businesses.

✔ **Enrolled agents.** Enrolled agents, also known as "EAs," tend to focus their practices upon income tax-return preparation. EAs, whose prices tend to be higher than those of preparers, complete significant training as well as continuing education. Unlike a preparer, should you ever get audited, an EA can represent you before the IRS or state tax authorities.

✔ **Certified public accountants.** Like enrolled agents, certified public accountants, also known as "CPAs," go through significant training and examination to receive their credential and then must complete continuing education. CPA fees tend to be a bit higher than EAs.

✔ **Tax attorneys.** Most tax attorneys don't prepare tax returns and instead typically get involved in court cases dealing with tax problems. Attorneys with sufficient small business experience also can help with your buying or selling of a business.

A tax person with a credential isn't necessarily competent, ethical, or cost-effective. What credential a given tax advisor has should have little impact in your decision about whether or not to retain his or her services.

When searching for tax help, as with seeking out any other competent professional, you need to take the time to get the names of several leads and interview your prospects. Then check their references carefully. Word-of-mouth referrals are good places to start finding people to interview. (Lawyers, bankers, and other small-business owners are the traditional sources for referrals.) Networking with other small-business owners is the best way to find an experienced and capable professional. What should you be looking for and asking about? We're glad you asked! Here are our suggestions:

✔ **Small business focus.** As a small-business owner, you have unique income tax requirements, quite different from those of a retired person or one who draws an employer's paycheck. As a result, one of the first questions you need to ask a tax person you're interviewing is to describe the makeup of his or her practice in terms of income, assets, and client occupation. Don't say that you're a small-business owner as that may bias their answers. Another way to verify the tax advisor's experience with businesses like yours is to ask for such references.

✔ **Tax focus.** The United States income tax system can get complicated. Good tax advisors will tell you that keeping up with it is a full-time job. Thus, you should seek the services of a tax person who focuses full-time on tax preparation and advice. Be careful — some tax preparers struggling to build their businesses or seeking fat commissions try to sell financial products under the guise of performing financial planning for their clients. You don't want or need a sales pitch for investments and insurance products. Hire professional tax advisors who are selling their time and tax expertise, and nothing else.

✔ **Solid training and experience.** As we discuss in the sidebar "What's in a title?," tax advisors come with varied credentials. Far more important than a credential is the relevant training and experience the tax advisor brings to the table.

✔ **Tax advisors, not number crunchers.** Some tax practitioners only complete tax returns and don't offer advice or much other assistance throughout the year. We'd rather you seek out the services of a tax advisor — someone who has a broader view of the job than simply plugging numbers into your annual tax return and then forgetting about you until the next spring.

A good tax advisor should help you plan ahead to reduce your taxes and should help you file other important tax documents throughout the year. He or she should also make sure that you're not overlooking deductions or making costly mistakes that may lead to an audit, penalties, and interest.

✔ **Cost-effective.** As you interview them, ask prospective tax advisors what their hourly billing rate is and what total fees they expect to charge you for specific services (such as completing your annual income tax returns, helping with employee payroll tax issues, preparing financial reports, and so on). You should hold them to their quotes unless you dumped more work on them than you originally told them.

More-experienced advisors charge a higher hourly rate, but they should be able to complete your work in less time than someone less experienced.

✔ **Insured.** When interviewing prospective tax advisors, be sure to ask if they carry liability or what is sometimes known as *errors and omissions insurance.* Should your tax advisor make a gaffe, especially a major one, the insurance increases your chances of being compensated for your damages.

✔ **Glowing references.** Ask tax advisor candidates to provide you with three clients in similar work to yours who have used the advisor's services the past couple of years. As you check references with these clients, ask them such questions as what they like or don't like about working with that tax advisor and how aggressive and proactive the advisor is with regard to tax-reducing tactics.

✔ **Speaks your language.** Advisors who use lots of confusing jargon and don't give straight answers are a waste of your time and money. Sure, taxes can get complicated. But a good advisor should be able to explain things in plain English. If he or she can't, then you'll be going on blind faith that the advisor is taking the best path for you.

You can be your own best tax advisor. Understanding how the income tax system works and how to make it work best for you can save you tens of thousands of dollars in taxes, as well as tax advisor fees. Use advisors to increase your knowledge and save you money, not as replacements for your own responsibility.

Keep Good Financial Records

Small-business owners such as ourselves, who've survived more than a few years running our own shops, know from experience the value of tracking and documenting our business financials. Consider the following tax benefits from keeping good records and staying on top of your business bookkeeping:

✔ **Reduced taxes.** The better the financial records you keep for your business, the better able you will be to come up with lawful, tax-reducing deductions when the time comes to fill out that dreaded annual tax return. Also, good records enable you to stay on top of your income tax payments for yourself, and your business, and payroll tax payments for your employees throughout the year — saving you late interest and penalty charges.

✔ **Easier and less-costly income tax return preparation.** If you don't keep a proper accounting of your income and expenses during the tax year, you won't be able to complete the necessary tax forms accurately when the time comes to file them for your business. Your tax preparer may actually be happy at your slipshod practices, however — the more time he or she needs to spend assembling and organizing your documentation, the fatter the tax-preparation fee you'll need to pay.

✔ **Documentation for audits.** Getting audited isn't a picnic for anyone — especially not for small-business owners, who get audited at a much higher rate (about 3 percent per year) than employees who draw a paycheck (because the IRS uncovers more mistakes and fraud on small business returns than on ordinary employee returns). The better records you keep, the better able you will be to effectively substantiate your tax return if you do get audited.

In Chapter 8, we discuss how to establish a bookkeeping system for your small business.

Know Your Income Tax Bracket

Over the course of time as you own and operate your small business, your income will, hopefully, be increasing; most likely, your income will also be fluctuating. Because of the way that income is taxed by the IRS and most states, your changing income from year to year will probably place you in different income tax brackets from year to year.

So, you may be thinking, who cares? Well, you should care! And we tell you why it matters.

You may be able to legally shift some of your business's income and expenses from one tax year to another, saving yourself some tax dollars — perhaps even thousands of dollars. If you operate your business on a "cash basis" — meaning, you recognize or report income in the tax year in which that income was received and expenses in the tax year that they were paid — you can control the amount of profit that your business reports in a given tax year.

If your income fluctuates from year to year, you may be able to lower your income tax burden by doing a little shifting of income and expenses. Sole proprietorships, partnerships, S Corporations, LLCs (Limited Liability Corporations) and personal service corporations typically can shift revenue and expense. On the other hand, C Corporations (and partnerships that have C Corporations as partners) may not use the cash accounting method.

Suppose that, like most business owners, you expect your next year's income to be higher than this year's and that you expect to be in a higher tax bracket next year (see Table 16-1 to approximate your federal income tax bracket). Therefore, you can likely reduce your total tax bill for both this year and next by paying more of your expenses in the next year, thus reducing your next year's taxable income, which you expect to be taxed at a higher rate. Although you can't expect your employees to wait until January for their November paychecks, maybe you can delay buying a new photocopying or fax machine or delay paying a December invoice for expenses (so long as no penalties are involved) until the beginning of the next tax year.

Table 16-1	Estimating Your Federal Income Tax Bracket	
Singles Taxable Income	*Married-Filing-Jointly Taxable Income*	*Federal Tax Rate (Bracket)*
Less than $24,650	Less than $41,200	15%
$24,650 to $59,750	$41,200 to $99,600	28%
$59,750 to $124,650	$99,600 to $151,750	31%
$124,650 to $271,050	$151,750 to $271,050	36%
Over $271,050	Over $271,050	39.6%

* for 1998 tax year

Your *marginal tax rate* is the rate of tax that you pay on your *last* or so-called *highest* dollars of income. In the example of a single person with taxable income of $30,000, that person's federal marginal tax rate is 28 percent. In other words, she effectively pays 28 percent federal tax on her last dollars of income — those dollars in excess of $24,650.

Stay on Top of Employment Tax Issues

As we discuss in Chapter 13, hiring and keeping good employees is no small challenge. Unfortunately, one of the administrative unpleasantries that comes with hiring employees is needing to withhold proper taxes for a myriad of government entities. Here's our advice for dealing with the sometimes sticky issues of employee taxes.

Know your benefits options

As a small-business owner, you can deduct the cost of various benefits — including retirement savings plans and insurance — which are for yourself as well as employees in your company. As a self-employed person, you may find it funny to think of yourself as an employee, but you are an employee in addition to being the owner. You've got to look after your own as well as your employees' benefit needs.

Please be sure to thoroughly read Chapter 14, which covers the ins and outs of benefits, including which benefits are tax-deductible as an expense related to your business.

Keep current on those taxes

When you're self-employed, you're responsible for the accurate and timely filing of all taxes owed on your income. Without an employer and a payroll department to handle the paperwork for withholding taxes on a regular schedule, you need to make estimated tax payments on a quarterly basis.

As we note in Chapter 8, all businesses except certain sole proprietors are required to obtain an Employer Identification Number (EIN) from the Internal Revenue Service. The application form, known as an SS-4, is available at your local IRS or Social Security office or by calling 800-TAX-FORM.

If you have employees, you also need to withhold payroll taxes on their income from each and every paycheck you cut them. And you then must make timely payments to the IRS and to the appropriate state authorities. To discover all the amazing rules and regulations of withholding and submitting taxes from employees' paychecks, ask the IRS and your state agencies for informational brochures.

In addition to witholding federal and state income tax, you also need to withhold and send in Social Security and any other state- or locally-mandated payroll taxes from your employee's paychecks.

If you aren't going to keep current on taxes for yourself and your employees, hire a tax advisor and/or payroll service (good tax advisors can recommend a payroll service) who will force you to jump through the necessary tax hoops. Too many small businesses have been sunk by falling behind in taxes.

Be careful with "independent contractor" hirings

Many small businesses start off hiring people as part-time independent contractors rather than full-time employees. Why? For the simple reason that hiring a contractor is less of a financial commitment.

- ✔ Committing to pay someone for part-time work without any benefits is much less of a big deal than hiring a full-time employee.

- ✔ If you hire an employee, your business must withhold federal (including your share of the employee's Social Security taxes) and state taxes and any other mandated taxes and then send those tax payments to the appropriate tax authorities.

- ✔ Finally, you don't have to offer an independent contractor any benefits, such as health insurance or retirement plan coverage.

Although you as the small-business owner may be attracted to hiring people as contractors rather than employees, the people you hire also may often prefer to be classified as independent contractors, too. Why?

- ✔ Contractors have greater ability to write off business expenses on their personal income tax return.

- ✔ Being themselves self-employed, contractors can establish and fund retirement savings plan such as a SEP-IRA or Keogh, which allow for tax sheltering as much as 20 percent of employment income.

The IRS dislikes independent contractor arrangements because it believes such workers tend to underreport their income and inflate their business expenses.

Not surprisingly, the IRS has rules for determining whether someone you hire should be classified as a contractor or as an employee. The general rule is that, unless the person doing the work is clearly another business, you have an employee. Neither the length of employment nor how much you pay matters. Even if you and the other person both agree that you are using an independent contractor, the only thing that matters is whether the business (person) meets both state and federal guidelines. Here are some of the many guidelines for making the determination:

- ✔ **Amount of employer's direction.** Employees are directed in their work by their employers. Independent contractors largely figure out for themselves, without much direction or instruction from the employer, how to accomplish the work that they're hired to do. Employees also usually have set hours of work, whereas independent contractors have more latitude in setting the hours that they will work for a given employer.

- ✔ **Number of employers.** Independent contractors tend to perform work for many employers at the same time; they may even have their own employees. Employees typically work for just one employer.

- ✔ **Where the work is performed.** Employees typically do their work at the employer's place of business; independent contractors usually do their work elsewhere.

IRS Publication 15, *Circular E, Employer's Tax Guide,* spells out all the parameters to consider in classifying someone who works with your firm as an employee or independent contractor. If that still confuses you — and it very well may — seek out a tax advisor experienced in working with small-business owners. You can also allow the IRS to make the determination by completing Form SS-8, *Determination of Employee Work Status,* and mailing it to the IRS.

If a business hires legitimate independent contractors to perform work, the contractors are responsible for paying all their taxes. However, this doesn't absolve you as the small-business owner from reporting on independent contractors that your firm works with. In fact, you are required to file **Form 1099** with the IRS (and some state tax agencies), which details the amount of money paid to companies (who are not corporations) who receive $600 or more from your business for services (not the product they provide).

Hire your kids!

If your kids can perform a useful job in your business, consider hiring them.

✔ First, you'll be showing them firsthand the value of their efforts.

✔ Second, this could be an important bonding opportunity for you and your kids. (Just be sure they wash their greasy popcorn hands before coming to work!)

✔ Last but not least, if you are a sole proprieter, you could be saving your family taxes.

Your kids are surely in a lower income tax bracket than you so by paying them some of your income, you're effectively lowering your income tax bill. Also, if your kids are under the age of 18, they won't have to pay Social Security on their earnings as you must do for your own earnings.

To make the most of hiring your kids, follow these guidelines to keep the IRS off your back and you and your kids happy:

✔ Make it real work.

✔ Pay fair market wages.

✔ Highlight the value of working for work's sake and for the accomplishment of broader goals such as saving for college or for major purchases.

Don't make the work part of their household chores, and don't treat your child differently than you treat your other employees. Keep your business relationship businesslike.

Spend Your Money Tax-Wisely

As a small-business owner, you'll have many opportunities for how and where to spend your money. In this section we explain how part of your spending decisions should hinge on tax factors.

Take equipment write-offs sensibly

When you buy equipment such as computers, office furniture, bookshelves, and so on, each of these items can be depreciated — meaning that each year you claim a tax deduction for a portion of the original purchase price of the equipment. Alternatively, through a so-called Section 179 deduction, you can deduct the entire amount spent on the equipment as long as the deduction does not contribute to showing a tax loss. You must also be within IRS limits for the amount of equipment purchases expensed for your business (see Table 16-2).

Table 16-2	Maximum IRS-Allowed Equipment Write-offs via Section 179
Tax Year	*Amount*
1998	$18,500
1999	$19,000
2000	$20,000
2001-2	$24,000
2003 and after	$25,000

Although you may think it attractive to expense the full amount of an equipment purchase in the tax year that the purchase is made, doing so isn't always the best thing. Looking ahead, if you expect your business profits to increase, pushing yourself into higher tax brackets, you may be able to reduce your taxes by depreciating rather than deducting — thus pushing more tax write-offs into future years when you expect to be in a higher tax bracket. (See the section "Know Your Income Tax Bracket" earlier in this chapter.)

Don't waste extra money on a business car

If you use your car for business, you can claim a deduction. Some small-business owners mistakenly buy a costly car for business use, reasoning that a splashy car will impress clients and customers and, because auto expenses for business are tax-deductible, the IRS is helping to foot the bill.

We think you should buy a car within your means — just as you should buy any other piece of business equipment within your means. Money not spent on an expensive business car can be much better spent on marketing, customer service, a new computer system, and so on. You should also know that the IRS limits the depreciation write-off you can take for a car, thus negating some of the potential tax write-offs on more expensive cars. Without boring you with the details, suffice it to say that, for tax purposes, you shouldn't spend more than about $20,000 on a car for use in your business.

Minimize entertainment and travel expenditures

With meal and entertainment expenses, only 50 percent of your business expenses are deductible. You should also know that the IRS does not allow deductions for club dues such as health, business, airport, social clubs, or entertainment facilities like executive boxes at sports stadiums, apartments, and so on.

The IRS has clamped down on writing off travel, meal, and entertainment expenses because of abuse by business owners and employees who try to write off nonbusiness expenses.

Taxes and Selecting the Right Corporate Entity

Corporations, as we note in Chapter 5, are taxed as entities separate from their individual owners. This situation can be both good and bad. Suppose that your business is doing really well and making lots of money. If your business is not incorporated as a C Corporation, all the profits from your business are taxed on your personal tax return in the year that those profits are earned.

If you intend to use these profits to reinvest in your business and expand, incorporating can potentially save you some tax dollars. If your business is incorporated (as a regular or so-called *C Corporation*), the first $75,000 of profits in the business should be taxed at a lower rate in the corporation than on your personal tax return (see Table 16-3). One exception to this rule is personal service corporations, such as accounting, legal, and medical firms (which pay a flat tax rate of 35 percent on their taxable income).

Table 16-3	Corporate Tax Rates for C Corporations
Income	*Tax Rate*
$0–$50,000	15%
$50,001–$75,000	25%
$75,001–$100,000	34%
$100,001–$335,000	39%
$335,001–$10,000,000	34%

One possible tax advantage for a corporation is that corporations can pay — on a tax-deductible basis — for employee benefits such as health insurance, disability, and up to $50,000 of term life insurance (see Chapter 14 for the details). Sole proprietorships and other unincorporated businesses can only take tax deductions for these benefit expenses for employees. Benefit expenses for owners who work in the business are not deductible.

Resist the temptation to incorporate just so you can have your money left in the corporation, which may be taxed at a lower rate than you would pay on your personal income (refer to Table 16-1 for the personal income tax rates). Don't be motivated by this seemingly short-term gain. If you want to pay yourself the profits in the future, you could end up paying *more* taxes. Why? Because you pay taxes first at the corporate tax rate in the year your company earns the money. Then you pay taxes *again* on these profits (this time on your personal income tax return) when you pay yourself from the corporate till in the form of a dividend.

Another tax reason not to incorporate (especially in the early days of a business) is that you can't immediately claim the losses for an incorporated business on your personal tax return. You have to wait until you can offset your losses against profits. Because most businesses produce little revenue in their early years and have all sorts of start-up expenditures, losses are common.

With all entities except C Corporations, the business profit or loss passes through to the owner's personal tax returns. So if the business shows a loss in some years, the owner may claim those losses in the current year of the loss on the tax returns. If you plan to take all the profits out of the company, an S Corporation may make sense for you.

The only significant advantage for most businesses to incorporation is that the corporate "shield" protects you from some liabilities (suits against the company) — if the corporation is properly organized. Because incorporation has legal and tax consequences, we recommend that you consult a tax preparer and an attorney before making a decision.

See Chapter 5 for a full discussion of the pros and cons of incorporation.

Chapter 17

Issues for Growing Businesses

· ·

In This Chapter

▶ Deciding to grow your business

▶ Understanding the evolution of a growing business

▶ Making the transition from entrepreneur to manager

▶ Addressing human resources issues

▶ Managing time in a growing business

▶ Troubleshooting business problems

· ·

*G*iven the choice, most small-business owners would prefer that their companies grow, rather than not grow, stagnate, or even fail. After all, growth is the American way — not to mention that it's also one of the typical entrepreneur's primary motivators.

This chapter then is for those of you whose businesses are either presently on a growth track or soon will be. We provide you with insights into what awaits you on your journey, along with tips on how to survive the trip and prosper as you go.

We warn you, however, that growth, especially that of the consistent and relentless variety, can feel like a climb up an uncharted mountain, especially for the small-business owner who sets out on the journey unprepared to make the transition from entrepreneur to manager.

If you choose to remain in the driver's seat throughout your company's growth, you can depend on the fact that five years from now, your business will not resemble your business as it is today. Furthermore, 10 years down the line, you can count on another entirely new look — ditto 15 years, 20 years, and any other marker on your business's timeline.

The changes to your growth-fueled business will be apparent everywhere. Five years from now, your customers will be different, their demands and needs will be different, and many of the products and services you offer them will be different, too. You'll also have a number of brand-spanking-new superstar employees (sadly, some of your earlier hires won't have the necessary skills to keep up with your growth), and employee-related matters will take up more and more of your time.

Finally, you, Mr. or Ms. Grand Poobah yourself, will be constantly in the midst of change, engrossed in the not-always-enjoyable-but-always-necessary process of making the transition from entrepreneur to manager, perhaps adopting along the way skills such as delegation, focus, and holding people accountable — skills that every successful manager must eventually learn in order to effectively lead a growing team of employees. Your financial, communication, and leadership skills also will be tested and, we hope, improved. In other words, you will not be the same Grand Poobah as you are today!

The only characteristics of your business that won't change (hopefully) as your company grows are its mission, ethics, and principles. However, if your top management (which is probably just you at this point) changes during the business's growth years, as happens in so many growing entrepreneurial companies, then even your company's mission, ethics, and principles may be subject to change. Growth holds nothing sacred.

Recognizing the Three Stages of a Business

A small business does not just happen. Some fairly predictable but not-very-orderly stages characterize its evolution. Those entrepreneurs caught up in the day-to-day goings on in a business don't recognize these stages until they have passed.

The following sections describe the three stages of that evolution:

The start-up years

These are the years when survival motivates the thoughts, actions, and reactions of the small-business owner. Everything that happens within the business is dominated by its owner; words such as "delegation," "team," and "consensus" are generally not yet part of the business's vocabulary. These are the hands-on years. For some owners, they're the most enjoyable years of the business; for all owners, they're an integral part of the learning process.

The work is hard — often the physically draining kind of hard. The hours are long and sometimes tedious, but by the end of the day, you can see, touch, and feel the progress you have made. The gratification is instantaneous.

The duration of this first stage can vary greatly. Some businesses may fly through the start-up stage in less than a year, but most spend anywhere from one to three years growing out of the stage. Others spend as many as five or more years in the start-up stage.

You'll know you've graduated from the start-up stage when profitability and orderliness become a dependable part of your business. The hectic days of worrying about survival will be replaced by the logical, orderly days of planning for success.

The growth years

These are the years when the small business achieves some sense of order, stability, and profitability. The evolving organization has survived the mistakes, confusion, and chaos of the start-up years, and now optimism, camaraderie, and cooperation should play an important role in the organization. Key employees surface, efficient administrative systems and controls become part of the business's daily operating procedures, and the need to depend on the owner for everything disappears.

The business of doing business remains fun for most small-business owners in this stage, as increasing sales translate into increasing profits — every small-business owner's dream. The balance sheet puts some flesh on its scraggly bones, the owner learns to delegate many of those unpleasant tasks that he or she performed in the past, and survival is no longer the entrepreneur's primary motivator. At last, the daily choices that the owner makes can be dictated by lifestyle goals instead of by survival.

There's further good news: This stage can last a long time if growth is gradual and remains under control, and if the business and its expanding population of employees is managed properly. More than likely, however, this stage lasts anywhere from a few years to decades, before the next stage raises its ugly head.

The transition period

The third stage, the transition period, could also be called the Restructuring Stage or the Diversification Stage. This is the stage when something basic to the success of the growth years has changed or gone wrong. As a result, in order for the business to survive, a strategic change in direction is required.

The transition period can be brought about by many factors. Often, relentless growth initiates it. This is because relentless sales growth requires relentless improvement in the business's employees, systems, procedures, and infrastructure; and many businesses simply cannot keep up with such pressures. The transition period can also be brought on by the opposite of growth — the shrinkage of sales and the disappearance of profits — or even by prolonged periods of stagnation. The causes for this shrinkage or stagnation can come from anywhere and everywhere, and often include such uncontrollable factors as new competitors, a changing economy, and changes in consumer demand.

The solution to transition period problems involves the business and its owner making a strategic change — a transition — in the fundamentals of the company. This transition often involves a change in top management, and it is not unusual for a rapidly growing company to outgrow its founding entrepreneur. Additionally, the transition may involve the introduction of new products or services, the establishment of new distribution systems, or the paring of unperforming parts of the business.

The good news to the displaced founding entrepreneur? If yours was a profitable (and thus salable) company, you can then afford to go back to what you do well, and what you enjoy. You can go back to entrepreneuring again. Or, if you are financially able, you can move on to other pursuits.

Feeling the Impact of Human Resources Issues

As we discuss in Chapter 13, the day that you hire your first employee is the same day that the bottomless pit of human resources issues appears on your path. After all, that newly hired employee has needs, privileges, and rights, the last of which, lest you forget, is protected by a host of government agencies.

Human resources concerns

Consider, if you will, a partial list of those human resources issues, the mere mention of which make a government inspector's mouth water:

- ✔ Sexual harassment
- ✔ Discrimination
- ✔ Wrongful discharge

> ✔ Hiring violations
>
> ✔ Workplace safety violations
>
> ✔ Working conditions violations
>
> ✔ Wage and hour violations

Unfortunately, much of this concern for the employee's welfare is well founded and necessary, as too many greedy and uncaring business owners over the years have created the need for such government scrutiny. This means that law-abiding and people-caring small-business owners like yourself must pay the price in the form of red tape and regulations. And the more your company grows, the larger that price becomes.

It makes no difference, incidentally, whether you break the law or violate a regulation by intent or by accident. What *does* make a difference is whether the person who perceives that he or she has been violated decides to do something about it. Furthermore, at the time of this writing, the depth and complexity of this dilemma shows no signs of letting up. (We deal with legal and regulatory issues in Chapter 15.)

The three stages of human resources development

So how do you deal with such a wide spectrum of human resources issues? The answer depends on which of the three stages of human resources development your company happens to be in.

Stage 1: Dealing with human resources issues yourself

This is the start-up stage when your business has, for example, fewer than ten employees. This is the stage when there's no one on the payroll to whom you can delegate human resources issues. In this stage, you must interrupt the activities that you probably prefer performing — sales, product development, and customer service — and deal with those that you don't — working conditions, drug and alcohol policies, and employee conduct. Stage 1 is the hands-on stage when the owner is up to his neck in the day-to-day details of running a business. The good news is that the human resources lessons you learn at this stage of your business will remain with you forever. The bad news is that dealing with some human resources issues may consume a large part of your time.

For those of you struggling through Stage 1, we recommend you read Chapter 13. Also, when dealing with those sticky issues that have the potential to become even stickier (harassment, wrongful termination, employee theft, and the like) we recommend you consult a professional (human resource consultant or lawyer) before you act.

Stage 2: Delegating human resources responsibilities to others

As the number of employees in your company grows, you should look for the opportunity to offload some of those human resource details onto either someone else in the business (most likely a full-time bookkeeper or the person who manages your office) or, as we explain in Chapter 13, a professional employer organization. Whatever option you choose, those functions will remain until your business enters Stage 3.

Stage 3: Hiring a human resources director

You may think you're in heaven when your business grows to the point where you are finally able to afford the small-business owner's greatest luxury: your very own human resources director. (Our experience is that this will happen when you get somewhere in the neighborhood of 50 to 100 employees.) We know that it's hard to believe that people actually make a 9-to-5 living dealing with human resources' seemingly endless details, but some people enjoy making a living of it, and imagine, you could have one on your very own payroll!

Strangely, people capable of becoming human resource directors are like consultants; there seems to be one on every street corner. Run an ad for a Human Resources Director in the paper and measure your responses in the dozens. You can expect a number of quality applicants; see Chapter 13 for tips on how to hire the best one for you.

Addressing Time-Management Issues

The faster a company grows and the bigger it becomes, the more time-management issues become important. The increased size of an organization requires increased communications between its members — which in turn increases the demands on your time and that of your employees.

Time, and the efficient use of it, is one of those cultural issues that starts at the entrepreneur's desk. By your actions, you, the owner and grand poobah, determine how your business uses its time. If you ensure that meetings start on time, that the workday begins at 8 o'clock sharp, and that prolonged gatherings around the coffeemaker are not acceptable behavior, your company will have a culture of efficient time management. On the other hand, if you don't pay attention to such issues, human nature takes its natural course, which will not bode well for your business's efficient management of time.

Time wasters

Let us present a number of ways that a small business's team member's time can be wasted:

- ✔ By missed deadlines and appointments
- ✔ By meetings that last an hour but should have lasted only ten minutes
- ✔ By people who arrive late to meetings
- ✔ By meetings that shouldn't be held in the first place
- ✔ By the telephone, in so many ways: long voice mail messages, phone calls not returned, ringing phones not picked up, and unnecessary calls
- ✔ By unnecessary or long-winded e-mail
- ✔ By employees conducting personal matters on the job (making calls to friends, surfing the Internet looking for their next vacation, and so on)
- ✔ By people taking 15 minutes to say what could be said in 5
- ✔ By waiting — in waiting rooms or outside offices, or for someone to get off the phone or fax machine or away from the copier
- ✔ By equipment that malfunctions, by systems that don't work, and by supplies that run out

Time savers

A small-business culture that allows such time-abusive behavior does not *have* to happen. You, and you alone, can insist on employee attitudes that value time rather than abuse it and respect the fact that because your employees are paid to do the work of your business, they should focus upon that end while at work.

For example, you can insist on a culture within your business that

- ✔ Requires people to be on time for the start of the day, for meetings, for conferences, for whatever
- ✔ Never holds a meeting when a conversation around a desk would suffice
- ✔ Requires every employee to use some kind of a time-management system, whether it be a simple to-do list or an intricate store-bought system
- ✔ Has definitive rules governing such issues as surfing the Internet and playing computer games on company time

✔ Deals with its in-house nonstop talkers and time abusers (every office has at least one)

✔ Requires that telephones be picked up after the first or second ring, voice mail messages be shortened, and telephone calls returned promptly

✔ Respects visitors' time (How do you like it when you visit another business and are made to wait in the lobby for a half an hour?)

✔ Encourages delegation (Don't waste your time doing a task that some-one else could do faster. Or better.)

✔ Understands that shorter and quicker is better when it comes to meetings, memos, letters, manuals, and rules

✔ Insists on employee accountability (Accountability to perform such tasks as keeping the supply inventory at adequate levels, maintaining equipment to minimize downtime and designing and implementing workable internal systems and controls.)

✔ Uses time-proven technology

Imagine what your company would be like if effective time management were practiced by everyone in your company. How much additional work would each employee get done? How much time would he or she save? Five hours a week? Ten?

What could every employee do with another 5 hours a week — 250 hours a year? And what could your company do with those 250 hours a year, multi-plied by the number of employees?

Time management itself is impossible to measure. What can be measured is results — results when compared to plans, results when compared to budgets, and results when compared to goals. You can usually figure, whenever you see improving results in the areas you *can* measure, your management of time is improving too.

You alone can make effective time management a part of your company's culture. After hiring the best people that you can, set the right example. Your employees will take it from there.

Choosing the Best Management System for Your Small Business

Little is new in the world of small business. Other organizations have needed restructuring, other employees have needed motivating, and other cultures have needed change.

So what are you, the small-business owner who is looking for ways to continue growing your company, supposed to do when you think it's time for a dose of something new? What system should you use to assure continued growth, whose advice should you take, and how can you possibly know which of the latest fads to glom onto?

You can't. The truth of the matter is that there isn't just one thing that will turn your company around. And there isn't just one thing that will change your culture, correct your infrastructure, or unite your employees, just as there isn't one thing that wins football games, loses customers, or makes roses grow.

We suggest that when you're considering adopting the latest fad, wait instead and let someone else be the pioneer. (Someone once said, "You can always tell the pioneers — they're the ones with the arrows in their backs.") Be aware of the fads making the rounds of the small-business arena, but don't bet the farm on the latest one. Cherry-pick the fad's key components that make the most sense to you.

The following tips will help you determine whether a new management system will work for you:

- ✔ Don't be the first kid on the block. See if you can determine which similarly sized businesses have already pioneered the system, and then solicit their suggestions and advice. (This is particularly true of new software applications. Make sure the program you are considering has been time-tested and has many satisfied users.)

- ✔ Make sure your key employees agree with the need and the basics of the new system before you introduce it.

- ✔ Consider the downsides of the new system as well as its upsides. Make sure you know what it will cost you to pull the plug in midstream.

- ✔ Understand the time frame needed to implement the system and measure its success, and be sure you can live within that time frame.

- ✔ And, finally, make sure that you, the owner and chief culture-setter of your business, have the time and the energy to devote to the implementation of the new system. New management systems require total commitment from the grand poobah; if you aren't willing — or able — to make that commitment, don't even think about initiating a new system.

If your business is working well (as measured primarily by profitability), don't break it. (It's okay, however, to bend it.) If it isn't working, consider a change. Your job is to be the matchmaker. Keep current of the latest and greatest management systems, and then match the need for the change with the applicable system.

Consider the following list of management fads. Each of the fads has at least one key component that makes sense, ranging from setting goals to redefining processes, from paring expenses to sharing financial information. Every fad offers some management wisdom, but that doesn't mean that you should adopt the entire system.

Management by objective (MBO)

An old-timer for sure, the basic components of MBO — setting and reaching goals — have endured and are used, to one degree or another, by many successful businesses. The process of goal setting is discussed at length in Chapter 13; most businesses — small and large — use goal setting in one form or another. Yours should be no exception.

Participatory management

Great in theory (*all* employees take part in determining the direction and policies of the company), participatory management can work wonders when organized carefully and phased in over long periods of time. But don't give away the keys to the car too soon. It takes years of training and preparation to learn how to drive a small business. Besides, not all employees *want* the responsibility that goes with being behind the wheel.

Participatory management works for two reasons. First, given a voice in the decision-making process, employees are much more likely to make a personal commitment to the decisions reached. Secondly, given the fact that employees see the business through eyes that the owners don't, their input enhances the quality of the decisions.

Employee ownership

Although we're certainly proponents of offering employees the opportunity to own a piece of the company, sharing the pie isn't always as easy as it sounds. Sometimes there isn't enough pie to go around, sometimes the pie isn't divided the way everyone would like it to be, and sometimes your employees would rather bet their future on T-bills. Besides, minority shareholders can be a pain in the keister.

But, for many people, there is no better motivator than ownership. That is why, despite the problems of sharing the pie, there is more and more pie-sharing going on than ever before. Even the federal government recognizes this fact, which is why it offers a number of incentives to companies to establish Employee Stock Ownership Plans (ESOPs). For more on offering employees equity in your company, see Chapter 14.

Quality circles

Quality circles are ad hoc groups or temporary teams of employees assembled to solve specific problems. Forms of this team approach to problem-solving are used every day in most successful businesses, as specially formed teams are assembled to solve a problem, and then disbanded once the issue has been resolved.

The appeal of quality circles is the age-old theory that two heads are better than one. Especially when those two (or more) heads are focused on solving a specific problem, and especially when those two heads bring differing perspectives to the problem-solving table.

Total Quality Management (TQM)

TQM is an all-encompassing phrase that means *"the involving and empowering of employees to increase profits by increasing quality, increasing focus on the customer, and decreasing costs."* Whew. Sounds like a synonym for *"sound business practices"* to us.

After all, the management of quality, the focus on customers, and the ongoing control of expenses is nothing more than plain old common sense. Which, come to think of it, is what TQM is all about.

What makes it a fad is beyond us.

Reengineering

Called *process analysis* by some, and Business Process Reengineering (BPR) by other, reengineering refers to putting each of a business's functions under the microscope and refining them. Given the choice, we'd call reengineering either *expense management par excellence* or *fat cutting extraordinaire.*

Again, similar to TQM, reengineering is just another fancy word for managing your business efficiently and logically. Which makes the fad itself another excuse for consultants to write books on the subject.

The faster the growth, the harder it is to keep up

Joan owned what had been (for its first five years) a very successful sign company. Her sales had grown at an annual rate in excess of 25 percent and had reached $15 million per year in less than eight years. As a result of Joan's previous job in sales, she had developed an effective sales staff within her company, a staff that kept the orders coming. And coming.

Unfortunately, the business's systems and controls had not kept up with the 25 percent annual increase in sales. Neither had the skills of its managerial, administrative, and production employees. As a result, despite the consistent increase in sales, Joan's inefficient business lost money in its sixth, seventh, and eighth years and eventually forced her to file for bankruptcy.

"The more rapid the sales growth," Joan told us later, "the more difficult it is to keep up. A 5 percent sales growth rate provides ample time for the employees to learn and react. A 25 percent sales growth rate and the accompanying crush of new problems does not."

Here are some lessons to learn from businesses like Joan's that are consumed by sales growth:

✔ Unless your business has large fixed costs that you can lower, you can't grow yourself out of profitability difficulties. Consequently, never try to throw more sales at profitability problems. More sales will only magnify existing deficiencies. Forget focusing on sales growth. Focus instead on improving profitability (see Chapter 11).

✔ A strategic change (that is, a transition) is needed at this stage in your business. Missions, goals, and strategies must be evaluated and changed. Systems and controls must be repaired or, more often, replaced. The organizational structure must be reviewed and upgraded. Most important, key employees must be trained, and where necessary, replaced — including, when the shoe fits, you, the founder.

✔ Do not give yourself, your managers, and your key employees aspirin (cheerleading speeches) when they require penicillin (training). A fight for life is going on here, and the fight will be won or lost by the employees.

✔ Be willing to go outside of the organization for management help. A promote-from-within strategy in the face of exploding sales may mean a team of secure and unthreatened employees, but the strategy could also mean that their secure and unthreatened days will be numbered if your staff doesn't have the objectivity to honestly evaluate the business's weaknesses.

Open-book management

The latest of all management fads, open-book management teaches that "informed employees" are capable of making key decisions that are usually reserved for management — within, that is, their areas of expertise. An "informed employee" is one who is privy to nearly everything that goes on within the company, including a variety of tools usually reserved for management, including financial statements.

Similar to any other management system, there are upsides and downsides to the open-book management system. The upside is that informed employees tend to make better day-to-day decisions than uninformed ones. Informed employees are also more likely to be committed to the cause — in this case to increasing the profitability of their company.

Troubleshooting Your Business

From time to time, small-business consultants are called in to assist businesses. Although troubleshooting can be an effective tool any time, it's usually done when a growing business suddenly slows down. When this situation occurs, most consultants bring along checklists to help them determine the seriousness of the problems.

Here's a checklist that one consultant we know uses:

Troubleshooting checklist

(Rank each category from one to ten; 1 = poor, 10 = excellent)

1. **Quality of cash-management procedures (cash-flow reporting and forecasting)**

   1   2   3   4   5   6   7   8   9   10

2. **Quality of financial reporting (profits and losses and balance sheet)**

   1   2   3   4   5   6   7   8   9   10

3. **Quality of financial forecasting (budgets)**

   1   2   3   4   5   6   7   8   9   10

4. **Dependence upon borrowed funds (1 = heavy, 10 = none)**

   1   2   3   4   5   6   7   8   9   10

5. **Late with payroll tax deposits (1 = never, 10 = often)**

   1   2   3   4   5   6   7   8   9   10

6. **Lag between sales growth and profit growth (1 = substantial, 10 = none)**

   1   2   3   4   5   6   7   8   9   10

7. **Employee turnover (1 = heavy, 10 = nonexistent)**

   1   2   3   4   5   6   7   8   9   10

8. **Quality and frequency of strategic planning**

   1   2   3   4   5   6   7   8   9   10

9. **Owner has more work to do than time to do it (1 = too much work, 10 = balances time efficiently)**

   1   2   3   4   5   6   7   8   9   10

10. **Owner's feelings about the business (1 = hates it, 10 = loves it)**

   1   2   3   4   5   6   7   8   9   10

Using this checklist, how does your business check out? On how many items would you give yourself a ten? How many only receive a one?

Although there is no overall key to grading the answers, we would suggest that where any of the above questions were answered with a 5 or below, immediate attention be given to upgrading the number. Sixes or sevens? Put the issue on your long range to-do list. Eights and above? Pat yourself on the back and make sure that the employees responsible for the rating are publicly recognized and, where possible, rewarded.

If you were your own business consultant, how would you rate your business overall?

What areas would you target for improvement?

Taking the five-minute appearance test

Appearance *is* important. With this in mind, we devised a simple "appearance test" for your business — or, for that matter, any business. Five minutes is all it takes.

Start with a business other than your own. Offer to give a friend's business the following five-minute appearance test. Simply drive into the parking lot, walk into the general office area, peek into a few offices here and there, step into the restroom for a quick look around, and then check out the area around the coffee-maker and fax and copying machines on your way out the door.

Note the following as you go, ranking your observations from one (poor) to five (excellent):

THE EXTERIOR:

Parking lot: Indicates care and upkeep

> 1   2   3   4   5

Grounds and exterior: Well-maintained, trimmed, and inviting

> 1   2   3   4   5

Windows: Clean, unsmeared, and uncluttered from the inside

> 1   2   3   4   5

Signage: Well maintained, readable, understandable

> 1   2   3   4   5

INSIDE:

General neatness: Desks and working areas neat and uncluttered

> 1   2   3   4   5

Restrooms: Neat and clean

> 1   2   3   4   5

Expense awareness: Unnecessary lights turned off, unused equipment turned off, no gurgling waterfalls in the lobby

> 1   2   3   4   5

Time management: Employees appear focused and busy, no gossipy gatherings around the coffee or copying machines

1   2   3   4   5

Employee attitudes: Polite, alert, attentive, focused

1   2   3   4   5

Employee appearance: Neat, clean, dressed appropriately

1   2   3   4   5

Sense of urgency: Employees "going about their business" at a pace that indicates they don't have time to waste

1   2   3   4   5

THE BEST AND THE WORST:

The one thing I saw that impressed me the most:

The one thing I saw that bothered me the most:

Then give the questionnaire to the owner. Ask your friend to repay you the favor. Your business could use the five-minute appearance test, too.

Finding Your Role in an Evolving Business

Owning a business is like raising a teenager: As it grows, the business is sure to get into trouble, yet you can never be sure what the trouble will be, how severe it will be, and how the company will weather the experience. Whether the business and the teenager will survive and thrive or fail depends on the quality of leadership that someone provides.

That leadership, in the case of your business anyway, must come from you.

You *can* judge a business by its looks

Most people who work with small-business owners have learned that the health of a business can often (but not always) be prejudged accurately by its physical appearance. Here's a telltale example of how a few simple details can provide a surefire indication of what a growing business's culture is really like and how it can be translated into the health of that business.

Jim was asked to visit an automobile recycling business (a.k.a a "junkyard") and help the owner devise a commission plan for its sales employees. Driving into the parking lot, Jim noticed the well-kept wooden fence, the neat landscaping lining the front office, and the freshly asphalted and well-marked parking facilities. Upon entering the office, he was immediately struck by how neat and clean the facilities appeared, the professional counter and wall displays of the company's "recycled" products, and the staff of employees with matching, embroidered shirts. The busy atmosphere and the prevailing sense of urgency reminded Jim of a McDonald's restaurant at lunchtime.

Well, Jim could tell you one thing about this man's business within 30 seconds of walking into the place, without so much as talking to its owner or glancing at its financial statements. The business looked, felt, and yes, even smelled like a profitable business.

And so it was. The financial statements revealed rapidly growing sales and robust profitability in excess of a 10 percent return on those sales. Additionally, the company boasted a low employee turnover, excellent employee benefits, and an inventory system that was second to none Jim had seen in any small business.

In short, this business's performance lived up to its appearance, a relationship that usually goes hand in hand.

Dealing with growing pains

So why is growth, especially that of the rapid variety, so hard on the typical small-business owner?

The reasons are twofold. First, most small-business owners aren't prepared for the managerial demands of a growing business. In most cases, the owner's expertise is in a specialized area, such as sales or accounting, or is related to the product or service that the company offers. As a result, owners are often untrained and unskilled in the management aspects of running a business. To make matters worse, many of the management skills required to run a growing business usually are counter to the way the owner is accustomed to doing things.

Second, the bigger your company becomes, the further you fade from the center of the action. Visions get blurred as a result of that distance, missions fade, and communications falter. Also, the more the business grows, the more layers there are to separate you from your customers, vendors, and employees. It's an entrepreneurial axiom that with distance comes misdirection — unless the management skills of the owner can keep pace with the growth.

A number of traits are required of a proficient manager. Most of these traits aren't required for a successful start-up but only come into play as a company grows. The ability, or inability, of the entrepreneur to adopt these skills determines the ultimate success of the business.

Making the transition to manager

Here's another entrepreneurial axiom: "The day you hire your first employee is the same day you begin making the transition to manager." This is not an easy transition to make because many of the typical small-business owner's personal traits run counter to those of a successful manager. Consider the following required traits of the successful manager — traits that aren't always near the top of the entrepreneur's skills list:

- ✔ **Focus:** The successful manager focuses on the project at hand, no matter what else is going on around him. The typical entrepreneur stops in the middle of the task to respond to the latest crisis.

- ✔ **Attention to detail:** The successful manager dots his *i's* and crosses his *t's* religiously. The typical entrepreneur is often too busy or simply not the type that enjoys dealing with the details.

- ✔ **Follow-up:** The successful manager knows that employees need to know their work will be evaluated. The typical entrepreneur thinks that employees' work shouldn't have to be followed up; she believes that the employees should do it right the first time.

- ✔ **Conflict resolution:** The successful manager views resolving conflict as an important part of his job description. The typical entrepreneur sees it as an intrusion on his time.

- ✔ **Training:** The successful manager views training as an investment. The typical entrepreneur sees it as an expense.

This is not to say all small-business owners fit this entrepreneur's profile, nor is it to say that they can't make changes in some, if not all, of those managerial traits that they lack. However, the transition to manager is not an easy one and involves some basic — and often wrenching — changes in the person who originally founded the business.

Making big changes

The Peter Principle (that is, sooner or later, everyone peaks and ends up in a job beyond his or her capabilities) is constantly creeping up on all of us as our companies grow. For one entrepreneur, it may arrive when his company has only one employee; for others, it may creep up when their companies reach 1,000 employees. But we all have our limitations — managerial and otherwise. Having limitations doesn't make us bad people; it only means that where the management of a business is concerned, there may come a time when we should either move over or move on.

When you notice that the Peter Principle is hanging over your management skills and you are having a difficult time making the transition from entrepreneur to manager, it may be time to consider the four alternatives available:

Downsizing your business

This alternative involves shrinking your business back to the point where you are able to spend your time doing those things you enjoy. For example, you may decide to limit your customer base to only those within your own market area, thereby cutting your sales and allowing you to shrink the number of employees you must manage.

Before making this choice, ask yourself:

- ✔ What are the downsides of shrinking the business (loss of income, reduction in the market value of the business, letting go of customers, and possibly laying off of employees)?
- ✔ Will you be able to emotionally and financially cope with these losses?

If the answer is no to either of these questions, then consider the following alternative:

Taking a personal inventory

This alternative includes assembling your own "managerial defect list" a list of personal traits that make managing your business difficult, such as inattention to detail or fear of conflict. Consider which entries on the list you could, and would, change in order to make the managerial transition. (Ask your spouse, friends, and key employees to help you make the list.)

Questions that you should ask yourself include

- ✔ How many of the traits on your managerial defect list can you hire around?
- ✔ How many of the traits can you train around?

> ✔ How many of the traits can you delegate around?
>
> ✔ Of those traits that you cannot hire, train, or delegate around, how many can you reasonably expect to change?

This exercise will tell you what you need to do to improve your managerial skills and how to go about it. Assuming, as a result of the answers given, you decide you can make the transition, then get busy. Start hiring, training, delegating, and where applicable, making changes.

Assuming you decide you can't — or won't — make that transition, it's time to consider the following alternative:

Hiring a replacement

This alternative includes hiring a president or COO (Chief Operating Officer) to run your company while you become CEO (Chief Executive Officer). The president or COO takes control of the day-to-day management of the business, while you concentrate on long-range, strategic matters.

Before hiring a replacement, ask yourself

> ✔ Is your company big enough and profitable enough to afford a COO or CEO?
>
> ✔ Can you let go, keeping your nose out of the day-to-day operating functions of your business?

If the answer to either of these questions is no, you'll have to either go back to the preceding alternatives (downsizing your business or making personal changes) and decide how you can adapt one (or both) to your situation or consider the fourth alternative:

Selling the business

Before you decide to take such a big step as selling your business, ask yourself:

> ✔ Will you emotionally be able to sell and walk away from the company you have built?
>
> ✔ Is your company salable at a price that works for you?

Ultimately, you may decide to sell your business and move on to something you're better suited to do.

Part V
The Part of Tens

The 5th Wave   By Rich Tennant

So—what the heck are you selling?

In this part . . .

This part provides tens of things you need to know in order to build your business and keep it growing. These chapters share a collection of suggestions, advice, and tips on subjects designed to make the difference between maintaining a mediocre business and growing a healthy one. We provide tips on such topics as operating a home-based business, effectively using computer software and the Internet, and improving your personal management skills. Consider this section as a mentor-in-print. Mentors guide and teach, and that is what these chapters are intended to do.

Chapter 18

Ten Tips for Home-Based Businesses

● ●

Make no mistake about it: Opening a home-based business is in vogue these days. A recent study by the National Federation of Independent Businesses (NFIB) indicates that more than twice as many businesses are now being started at home as in storefronts and offices.

Your humble authors account for two of those 20 to 25 million home-based businesses, and we can tell you from experience that starting a home-based business definitely has its advantages. The four most typically cited advantages include the following:

- ✔ Lower start-up costs
- ✔ Lower overhead
- ✔ Tax benefits
- ✔ Lifestyle advantages gained by being "close to home"

Furthermore, for us anyway, having our own home-based businesses sure beats the heck out of being someone else's employee — punching a clock, packing a cold lunch, or sharing a cubicle with someone who forgot to take a shower this morning. Furthermore, when compared to owning our own office-based retail, manufacturing, or service business (again, for us anyway), running our home-based businesses sure beats the heck out of managing a warehouse filled with inventory, motivating a team of march-to-their-own-drummer employees, or attempting to comply with ever more government regulations.

Not everyone, however, is home-based business material. You need more than a computer and a modem to create a successful home-based business. You also need large doses of dedication, discipline, and self-accountability.

In this chapter, we share a collection of tips we've learned from our home-based business experience and those of other home-based business owners we've known to help you start and grow one of your own.

Run your business like a business

After you've made the decision to set up shop in the den or the extra bedroom of your home, remember that this is a business you're running, not a hobby — unless it is just that, a hobby. The two are very different. Businesses are intended primarily to be profitable; hobbies are intended primarily to be fun. (The key word here is *primarily*. Businesses can obviously be fun, and hobbies can also be profitable.)

If your business *is* a hobby, then feel free to let the daily events of the home come first. Do the dishes between phone calls, let the kids doodle on your business stationery, chat with a neighbor in your office over a cup of coffee. Be cool. Stay relaxed. Have fun.

If, however, you have started what you intend to be an honest-to-goodness business, then treat it like an honest-to-goodness business. Make the door to your office an imaginary line in the sand; cross it and you enter into the world of debits and credits and deals. Set rules for whoever is on the other side of that line, and then make sure that you enforce those rules.

We're not saying that you can't take time out to answer the doorbell, have lunch with the family, or dial 911 if your garage catches on fire. But we *are* saying that, during the course of your stated business hours — whatever those hours may be — business should come first, just as business would come first if you had an office on the corner of Wall Street and Broad Street.

Keep things legal

Perhaps in part because working out of the home is not like working in a downtown, high-rise office building, some home-based business owners feel that they can cut corners legally. Of course, people who run their businesses out of glitzy high-rises break the law, too.

Just because you work out of your home, don't assume that you won't get caught or you won't draw attention to yourself if you do break the rules. If you cheat on your taxes or don't get the proper licenses and permits to run your business, you should expect to get caught and to pay a dear price.

Do things right the first time around!

Chapter 15 explains how to comply with the myriad legal and regulatory issues that small-business owners face, and Chapter 16 details how to stay on the right side of the various tax authorities. While you're keeping legal, we would also suggest you protect yourself in the insurance department. Consulting? You'll probably need some business liability protection. Customers or vendors visiting your home office regularly? You may need an add-on to your homeowner's insurance to cover personal liability. Your business up, running, and successful? You may want to consider business interruption insurance. (For more about insurance, see Chapter 8.)

Put on a professional face

Someone once said that "you don't get a second chance to make a first impression," a statement that is especially true where a home-based business is concerned. With this thought in mind, your first impression had better be a good one!

Part of making a good first impression is making a professional one. Today's customers, at least the ones who will be willing (and able) to pay top dollar for your products or services, are looking for professionalism from their vendors. Use these tips to help you make that first impression a professional one:

- ✔ **Office:** Physically separate your office from the rest of the house. If that's not possible, find a way to close the doors and shut out the sounds (and smells) of the house. Try to keep background noise (the television playing, children crying, carpenter hammering, washing machine churning) to a minimum.

- ✔ **Telephone:** The telephone is the front door of your business and is oftentimes the first impression a potential customer has of you. If your customer must dial your number six times before getting through, or if your answering machine sounds scratchy and unprofessional, or if you don't return your customer's call within a reasonable amount of time, then your relationship is off to a rocky start.

  Many local phone companies offer voice mail service, providing you the benefit of having your calls answered while you're on the phone. Another option is to get two telephone lines, one for incoming calls and/or one for outgoing calls and (where necessary) the modem and fax. You could have three lines — one for incoming calls, one for your modem and outgoing calls, and the third dedicated to your fax. Obviously, the more phone lines, the more expense.

✔ **Answering service and/or voice mail:** Unless you can afford a full-time secretary, this is your best alternative. (It is our experience that most people would rather leave their message on voice mail than with a secretary — voice mail doesn't lose words or garble messages in the translation.)

✔ **Consider a toll-free number:** Toll-free 800 or 888 numbers are relatively inexpensive ($20 per month), yet present a professional image to your potential customers. At the same time, they send a loud message that yours is a sales-minded, customer-responsive business.

✔ **Fax:** Over an extended period of time, you can pay for a fax with the money you save not using the mail or the various overnight services. Besides, faxes don't waste telephone time by chatting or being put on everlasting hold or having to convince a secretary to let your call through. (Be sure to develop a professional-appearing cover sheet; it can serve as an advertising piece as well as an introduction to your communication.)

✔ **E-mail:** E-mail is usually the quickest and least-expensive method of communication. Pay the $20 or so monthly fee (some Internet providers offer free e-mail) and type away to your heart's content, regardless of where the message is headed. (Sending a message to Rome costs the same as sending a message to Chicago.)

✔ **Letter-writing ability:** Despite all the new technology, sooner or later you will have to write letters. Your business will be judged by the professionalism of those letters. You should learn to word-process your own letters, as most word-processing programs come with a spell-check and grammar-check feature, assisting you in giving your written communications a professional appearance. If you are unable for some reason to word-process your letters, be sure and have a secretarial service lined up to handle your important written communications.

✔ **Business cards:** Don't scrimp on business cards; they will probably turn out to be one of your primary marketing vehicles. (Don't believe it? The next time someone slips you his business card, make a mental note of how you judge that person's business by the appearance of the card.)

So, you ask, why all this fuss about your business's appearance? After all, are you in the image business or are you selling widgets?

The answer is: You are in both the image business and the selling business. The selling of your widgets is made easier by the establishment of your image. Like it or not, people (potential customers) *do* judge businesses by their appearance and image. If yours doesn't stack up on first impression, chances are those people won't even try to do business with you.

Choose the right technology

We can't imagine a home-based business today that wouldn't benefit from a computer and some of its related technologies. No matter what service you provide or product you sell, you must perform one or more of the following duties in the conduct of your business:

✔ **Write a business plan.** (See Chapter 4.)

✔ **Write a business letter.**

✔ **Communicate efficiently with other businesses in the same town or halfway across the world.** Nothing compares in price or quickness to a fax or e-mail. Of course, where a personal touch is needed, don't use such impersonal communication methods.

✔ **Invoice a customer, pay your bills, and track your business financials.** A host of financial software packages is available, and even the most inexpensive has advantages over a manual system.

✔ **Maintain a customer database.** You can have customers' names, addresses, and whatever else you need to know, ranging from the name of the purchasing agent's spouse to the date of his or her birthday. A computerized database package has far-reaching advantages over a manually maintained system.

✔ **Maintain a to-do list and an appointment calendar.** Manual versus computerized to-do list? One man's meat is another man's potatoes.

Here is a quick overview of the technology that you should consider when starting your own home-based business. Some basic needs include

✔ **The Hardware:** The computer itself. The choices you'll have to make will include

> PC or MAC
>
> Laptop or desktop
>
> New or used
>
> A wide range of horsepower options

Your choices will be dictated by the kind of business you're in, your budget, and your personal preferences.

✔ **The Software:** The software that you'll need to tell your computer what to do and how to do it will depend on what applications you intend to use: word processing for letter-writing and reports, spreadsheets for accounting and other number-crunching functions, a drawing for charts and graphs, scheduling and e-mail programs, presentation graphics for slides, or database packages for customer information.

If your budget allows, you might consider purchasing one of the many office-manager suites available. (Microsoft Office is the best-selling package.) The applications in a typical office suite include all of the above, and because they're from the same manufacturer, they are designed to work more easily together.

✔ **Printer:** Laser printers or inkjet printers are generally favored over the older dot matrix printers as the copies they produce are more professional in appearance and the colors are clearer. (If you plan on preparing your own marketing materials, a color printer will be necessary. Also, if you plan on downloading and printing from the Internet, color is preferable.) Color is available with laser printers but is more expensive — more than double the cost of black-and-white printers and about five times the cost of ink-jet. Laser printers are better suited for high-volume work.

✔ **The Modem:** The modem is the mechanism that connects your computer with the telephone line, thereby allowing you to send e-mail and connect with the Internet. Modems come in both internal (as part of the computer) and external models and can vary in price, depending on the speed of the modem. The faster the modem, the less time you wait. *Warning:* When you buy a mail-order computer, it may come with a slower modem. You may need to upgrade that modem if you intend to spend a lot of time on the Internet.

✔ **Fax Machine:** The fax machine (short for facsimile) is behind only the telephone, computer, and printer in importance to the typical home-based business. Fax machines send their images via telephone lines and allow you to transmit documents in a matter of seconds.

You can also get fax machine services at most copy centers. So you don't have to purchase the machine yourself to send or receive faxes. (You can use the copy center's fax number and have incoming faxes held there for you.)

Sending your documents via a fax machine is, in most cases, less expensive than alternative methods, including the U.S. mail and the various overnight services.

✔ **Answering machine:** Answering machines record incoming messages on a tape recorder and come in two different models, digital and tape. Although both are effective, the digital is faster because you don't have to wait for the tape to rewind before you can hear your messages. Some people prefer voice mail because it sounds more professional and can answer a number of calls at once.

You can buy both fax machines and answering machines as add-on features to your printer and computer. Our experience is that, although stand-alone faxes and answering machines may be a bit more expensive than the add-on units, the added expense is worth it. Stand-alones generally perform better.

Develop a marketing strategy

If you are like most people who operate home-based businesses, your number one critical issue from day one will be your need to sell and market your services or products. This is almost always the most difficult task, and not surprisingly either, because it is also one of the issues at or near the top of the office-based business's list as well.

One of the primary differences between home-based and office-based marketing is that, in the home-based business, you must make all the decisions and do all of the work yourself. No one is available to provide feedback on your latest and greatest idea, to be the devil's advocate, or to suggest that what you are doing may not work. You *are* the marketing department — lock, stock, and barrel.

The most frequently used marketing tool for the home-based business is word of mouth. Word-of-mouth referrals from satisfied customers lead to more satisfied customers and more referrals. This is the major reason that the typical home-based business takes so long to become successful — a solid base of satisfied customers takes time to build.

The best home-based marketers are those who are able to take that base of satisfied customers and do something with them. Although they may be satisfied, these customers may also need to be encouraged to broadcast their satisfaction, which is where the aggressive home-based business owner comes in. The meek may well inherit the earth, but they shouldn't own home-based businesses.

Word-of-mouth referral techniques vary. Use these techniques and others that you may come up with to "advertise" your business:

- ✔ Call your satisfied customers and ask them to call one potential customer for you.
- ✔ Ask for the names of potential customers and the right to use the satisfied customer's name in a conversation with a potential customer.
- ✔ Use your satisfied customer's name and quote of praise in such advertising materials as flyers, brochures and media ads.

Second only to word-of-mouth advertising is networking. Networking comes in many forms, from joining the Chamber of Commerce, to volunteering to flip burgers at the Rotary picnic, to introducing yourself to the person sitting next to you on the airplane.

The best way to find out about the marketing techniques that work (or don't work) in your industry is to join your industry trade association, become a member of one of the home-based business associations, or subscribe to a home-based business magazine. Any of these resources worth their salt will include a number of self-training vehicles and suggestions on how to market your products or services.

Finally, for those of you who are contemplating starting your own home-based business, remember the primary lesson from Chapter 8. No matter how good you are at performing your service or how wonderful your product is, your business will sink or swim based on your ability to promote and sell your product or service, get paid for it, and account for the proceeds. In other words, the key to your success will be your ability to manage your business.

Manage your time effectively

Effective time management is especially difficult for the typical home-based business owner. This is primarily due to the fact that within most home-based businesses there is typically no one to delegate all those mundane details to, so you must do them all yourself.

Out of stamps? *You* buy them. UPS driver knocking at the door? *You* answer it. Dog needs to go outside? *You* open the door and let him out. *You* must also clean up the office at the end of the day, answer the telephone, and monitor your accounts receivable — all this between solving your customer's problems. Everything that happens in your home-based business either goes *through* or goes *to* you.

We suggest that you review the section on time management in Chapter 17. Most of the same parameters that apply to office-based businesses also apply to home-based businesses.

Similar to the office-based small-business owner, you too must use a time-management system of one sort or another. Whether it's a simple to-do list (we suggest two to-do lists — one for short-term issues and one for long-term projects) or one of the many commercially developed systems (manual or computerized) that manage your time down to the nanosecond, you must initiate a time-management plan and then stick to it religiously.

Always end your workday by preparing the following day's to-do list. This allows you to get off to a good start in the morning, cuts down on the likelihood of your omitting an important item from the list, and reduces the stress of feeling that you have a zillion things hanging over your head without a plan for how to tackle them.

Keep your to-do list alongside your appointment calendar. (If you use one of the commercially prepared or computerized time-management systems, the appointment calendar will likely be a part of the system itself.) Get in the habit of consulting both the to-do list and your appointment calendar first thing when you enter your office in the morning. Doing this will cut down on missed appointments, something that is a problem for most home-based business owners.

Also, get in the habit of using e-mail instead of the telephone, especially when your phone call is a reminder call or a call that doesn't require a give-and-take conversation. You won't get dragged into a one-hour conversation on e-mail, you won't be hung up on, and you won't get involved in playing telephone tag. E-mail can't put you on hold either. And you'll also have a record of your action, complete with time and date.

Finally, don't try to do every menial chore yourself, in the interest of saving a few bucks. Allocate your time, making sure to spend it where the leverage is. Plenty of outsourcing companies are available to perform many of the menial tasks. If you have a direct-mail piece to get out and it's going to take four hours to do the addressing and stamping, outsourcing the project to a mailing house may be a better choice, allowing you to spend those four hours on a project that is more worthy of your time.

Motivate yourself (if you don't, who will?)

Goal-setting exercises are important when it comes to motivating you in your personal life, as well as in your home-based business. See Chapter 13 on setting "SMART" goals for your business and employees, if you have them.

You should remember, however, that setting the goals isn't what will make you achieve them. Writing goals down, and then publishing them, will help motivate you to achieve them.

By publishing your goals, we don't mean sending them to *The Wall Street Journal* and hoping that they get included in the next press run. We mean showing them to your spouse, mounting them on the refrigerator, and including them in your business plan right below your mission statement.

Include your spouse or significant other

If your office is in your home, that makes your spouse or significant other — whether he or she is around the house during the day — at least a silent partner in your venture. After all, your spouse, in addition to being your dinner date, is also your landlord, investment partner, and eternal soulmate, and as such, has a vested interest in the stresses and successes of your business.

Use these tips to help you work with your spouse or live-in significant other in regard to your home-based business:

- ✔ Before opening the door of your business, you should both agree to ground rules for the input each of you will have as to the direction of the business. Minimize down-the-road surprises by defining each partner's input and the parameters from the beginning. The silent partner will be able to contribute some things, but not all.

- ✔ If your spouse is involved in your business, he or she deserves to know what's going on. This is especially true when, from time to time, your spouse is involved in the business — talking to your customers, greeting the UPS driver, and picking up your fax paper when you run out. Keep your spouse in the loop.

- ✔ In the event that you and your spouse are considering working together in the business, recognize that if you haven't been able to solve your personal problems amicably in the past, being in business together will probably just make things worse. Don't burden your marriage with the heightened difficulties of being in business together if the marriage isn't strong. Address your relationship issues first before going into business together.

  The best partnerships are those where the partners bring different skills to the table. If you and your spouse don't have complementary skills, don't consider going into business together.

- ✔ Always make sure that the marriage and the family come first.

- ✔ Remember to compete with your competitors and not with each other.

Stay in the loop

One of the common misconceptions about the home-based business is that it is a safe place for people who are hermits or loners or Howard Hughes types. Old stereotypes abound: Many home-based business owners are perceived as people who don't need or like people.

Although it may be true that some of us have had less-than-desirable experiences with our fellow *homo sapiens,* either as part of a team of employees or as the leader of a team, this doesn't mean that we got into the home-based business because we wished to lose contact with the world. In the end, the success or failure of our businesses will be because we've discovered a way to interest people (a.k.a. customers) in our products or services. We've discovered a way to provide a service or deliver a product that people are willing to pay for, solving their particular problem in the process. We've found that all of us must depend on someone, whether we want to or not.

What this dependence on people means is that, when you're out of the social or local business loop due to working out of your home office, you must find a way to stay in it or risk losing touch with the people whose needs can influence your product or service. Here are several of our suggestions for staying in the loop:

✔ Join at least one local business organization, such as the Chamber of Commerce, the Rotary, or one of the community's business networking organizations.

✔ Join at least one national organization, such as a home-based business association or an industry trade association. Not only will this help you remain in the loop, many associations offer its members a number of other advantages, such as health plans, travel discounts, and educational programs. (Ask for the *Encyclopedia of Associations* at your local library for a list of applicable associations.)

✔ Subscribe to at least one business magazine.

✔ Make an educational goal for yourself each year, and then stick to it. Goals should include such activities as schooling, reading books, and attending educational seminars (especially those put on by your trade association), conferences, and industry trade shows.

✔ Familiarize yourself with the Internet (without getting hooked on it). Learn where the Web sites are that have good information related to your industry. See Chapter 19 for how to best use the Internet in your small business.

Every business, home-based and otherwise, is a living, breathing organism, and thus is always in one stage or another of growing or dying. In order to keep your business growing, you need to have a constant pulse on how the world is changing. The best way to keep your finger on the world's pulse is by staying in touch.

Recognize that working from home isn't a free lunch

Some small-business owners believe that they are getting something for nothing by working from home rather than from a business office. The truth is, however, that the space your business occupies in your home and the costs of that space are real, not imaginary.

Sure, assuming that you qualify, you get tax deductions for the costs of operating your business out of your home (see Chapter 16 for tax information). But that's no different than if you operated a business outside your home and paid for office space, the expense for which will be tax-deductible too.

If you have the choice of running your business from your home versus securing outside office space, base the decision as much as possible on what makes the best overall business sense for your enterprise. Ask yourself: What are your business's and customers' needs?

✔ If you don't need fancy office space to present an image of success or in which to meet with clients, then it may well make sense to work at home. Likewise, if you're in a creative enterprise, such as copywriting or graphic design, that can be done at any time of the day or night, working at home can be ideal.

✔ If you operate a retail business that requires a constant flow of customers, obtaining outside office space is probably the best (and legally correct) choice. Likewise, if you're in warehousing or manufacturing, you may have problems in a home environment.

✔ Professionals such as doctors, lawyers, or accountants and tax consultants may have more versatility in their choice of work setting, depending on their specialties and the customers they want to attract.

Be sure to check with the governing authorities of your town or city to learn what regulations exist for home-based businesses. You may find that government regulations prohibit you from conducting certain kinds of business from your home.

Also ask yourself what it will cost you personally to work from home. At home, you must have the discipline to work the number of hours you need. Will you be tempted to make half a dozen snack trips to the kitchen and turn on the television for late-breaking news? Will you get caught up in the details of running your house rather than running your business?

The hardest time to discipline yourself is usually in the early days of your business when you don't have enough work to fully occupy your time. The sometimes-amorphous challenge of figuring out how to grow the business may cause you to focus your energies elsewhere.

Above all, ask what it will cost to conduct business within your house in terms of your home life. If you're single and living alone, home life may be less of an issue because you need consider only your own needs and schedule.

If you're a parent, working at home may be an advantage because you can be a more involved parent. If nothing else, the one to two hours per day that many people spend commuting can be spent with your kids! Just be sure to set specific work hours, during which time you're off limits for the child-care or other family stuff.

Talk to other family members to find out how they feel about your working at home. Get specific about what you plan to do, and where, when, and how you intend to do it. Will you have clients come to your home? What time of day and where in the home will you meet with them? How will you assure that your home-based business won't override the needs of your family?

Chapter 19

Ten Ways Computers Can Help Your Small Business

• •

Most of the time computers enable small-business owners to run their businesses more efficiently and profitably. However, like any tool, computers and accompanying technology can be misused and become more costly than necessary.

We encourage you to keep a finger on the pulse of technology and its role in your type of business. In fact, if you fail to track and take advantage of useful technology, your business could end up getting swallowed by your competition.

We need to warn you against embracing new technology blindly, however. At the entrance to every software program or Web site, we would post a sign that says: "Small-business owners, proceed at your own risk." Why? Because whether you're a current small-business owner or a wannabe entrepreneur, time is probably your most precious commodity, and time is where computers can sometimes make you or break you.

Software programs and Web sites should do two things for your business:

✔ Save you time instead of wasting time.

✔ Stimulate ideas that can help make your business grow larger and more profitable instead of leading to dead ends and pipe dreams that burn through your cash reserves.

As a group, small-business owners are particularly susceptible to buying software programs that they don't need.

A common tactic Web sites employ is to offer seemingly altruistic "small-business services" — business news, business plan advice, and so on — to keep you clicking through the site. Don't get sucked in to these time- and money-burners.

Never buy expensive new business software until you've talked with several other small-business owners who've used the software for at least a year. Be sure to exercise self-discipline when you're surfing the Web for small-business services or to identify software you may want to purchase. Computers are incessantly sold as time- and money-savers, but anyone who has dealt with them knows that computers can also make things more difficult and can end up costing more than they save if used inefficiently.

This chapter contains our suggestions for the best ways to use computers in your business, including software programs and Web sites.

Brainstorming and researching business ideas

The Internet can be a useful place to jog your imagination and brainstorm your business ideas. And, no, we're not referring to the business pitches that junk up your e-mail box every day. Even if you're more interested in starting a business than buying one, check out a few Web sites that list businesses for sale, such as BizBuySell (www.bizbuysell.com). Such an exercise will often expand your horizons and could perhaps steer you into your true life's calling — running a surf shop in Hawaii, for example. Also check out the "Start Up Ideas" on the Web site for the Home Office Association of America (www.hoaa.com).

More and more trade associations are establishing a presence on the Web, and these sites can be a great resource for getting information on a specific line of work. The popular search engine, Yahoo! (www.yahoo.com) has a good list of these types of sites under "Trade Associations." (A search engine is a program that lets you use keywords to search through the Web and identify sites that may meet your needs.) Also try adding .org to a type of business that you're interested in and plugging that into the URL (Uniform Resource Locator, which is another name for Web address) box in your Web browser; you'll be amazed how often this works. If you're skeptical that a site is available for a particular kind of business, remind yourself that www.coinlaundry.org exists!

For those interested in starting a home-based or freelance business, the Web sites for the Home Office Association of America (www.hoaa.com) and Working Solo (www.workingsolo.com) include comprehensive directories to various resources — trade associations, seminars, Web sites, and so on. If you don't yet have a computer or internet access, try public libraries in your area, many of which can perform computer searches (sometimes for a nominal fee) for small-business owners and help you get on the Internet.

Finding a mentor

Another way to get perspective on starting a particular type of small business is to talk to someone who has "been there" and "done that." The Service Corps of Retired Executives (SCORE) discussed in Chapter 3 has thousands of volunteer business counselors who offer their services free of charge. SCORE's Web site (www.score.org) helps you track down these potential mentors. Choose from the vast list of business categories — everything from furniture finishing to management consulting — and the site will give you the e-mail addresses of SCORE volunteers with experience in that area. You can also enter your zip code to find the location of your local chapter, where you can attend a seminar or meet with a SCORE counselor face to face.

Buying a business or franchise

The Internet has a long way to go before it becomes a major meeting place for business buyers and sellers, but you may find promising leads with these sites.

BizBuySell (www.bizbuysell.com) has all the ingredients for a good business-for-sale online database: a pleasing design, a smooth search engine, and a decent description of each listed business that includes the asking price, gross income, cash flow, year established, number of employees, details on the competition, and growth possibilities. The only problem, albeit a big one, is the lack of critical mass: Some states only have a handful of businesses listed for sale. Still, with such entries as a surf shop in Hawaii and a swinging door saloon in Oregon, this site helps jog your entrepreneurial imagination!

If you're interested in owning a franchise business, check out Be the Boss (www.betheboss.com), a site that matches up its client franchise companies with your selection criteria and profile as a potential franchise owner. The site gives good specs on each franchise — companies such as 7-Eleven, Subway, and Baskin-Robbins — including the company history, number of stores, description of company support, franchise fee, and necessary capital to get started.

Searching for financing

Nobody helps finance more small businesses than the Small Business Administration (SBA), a federal government agency created to foster American small businesses. Its Web site (www.sba.gov) is a good source of information on SBA loans, as well as a host of other things, including helpful tips for start-ups.

Approach with caution the many online "directories" of financing resources that exist on the Web. Hardly objective, many of these sites typically list sources of financing that have paid the site to be represented there and don't necessarily offer competitive rates.

A fun site to check out is MoneyHunter (`www.moneyhunter.com`), a media company that helps small businesses get off the ground. On the Web site, you'll find the "Golden Rolodex" — a mix-and-match bulletin board where investors and entrepreneurs can find each other. The site also helps the company dig up good stories for its PBS television show. If you think your business idea is good enough, fill out the online application for the show!

Marketing your business

As we discuss in Chapter 9, marketing is among the biggest and most important challenges that you face in getting your business off the ground and ensuring that it's on a dependable growth trajectory. The Internet and e-mail can certainly assist you in marketing your business, but e-mail is no substitute for personal contact and your customers' ability to see and touch your products and services. For a nominal fee, you can develop a Web site for your company to communicate your vision and promote your wares.

Beware of all the hype about how the Internet can be the sole focus for your business. Few companies have successfully used the Internet to market their businesses. For every company such as `Amazon.com`, the large online bookseller, hundreds if not thousands of companies have expended significant sums on the Web to no avail. And even `Amazon.com` has yet to make a profit as of this writing.

Maintaining and analyzing your financials

One area in which computers have made a real contribution to small business is bookkeeping. Programs such as Intuit's Quickbooks and Peachtree Accounting (see Chapter 8) can take a lot of the grunt work out of small-business bookkeeping. These programs can pay for themselves if you use them to track and categorize your income and expenses and then use that information to generate financial reports and project cash flow (see Chapter 11).

On the Web, *Entrepreneur* magazine has established a site with several interactive worksheets for generating financial statements (`www.edgeonline.com`).

Filing your taxes

Another benefit of using an accounting software package is that it helps organize your records for filing taxes. You can easily print out a report that breaks down your revenue and expenses. But an accounting software package won't help you transfer these numbers onto those bewildering IRS forms that you have to file. For that, you need a tax-filing software package such as *TurboTax for Business*. This program asks you a series of easily understandable, non-IRS-phrased questions and then converts your answers to the lines on the IRS forms. Going through this process will help you not only understand how taxes work but also better plan your finances for next year's tax return.

Believe it or not, the normally inscrutable IRS has a good Web site (www.irs.ustreas.gov). All IRS forms are available for downloading here, and the site includes how-to articles that are uncharacteristically easy to understand.

Avoiding attorneys

Paying an attorney $100 to $300 per hour for what you know is rather simple legal help is one of the toughest bills for a small-business owner to stomach. That's why self-help legal software is such a growing business.

Our favorite package is put out by Nolo Press and is called *Small Business Legal Pro*. At less than $100, this package is a great value; included on the CD-ROM is the text for a number of well-done self-help legal books for small-business owners from Nolo Press, as well as more than 100 ready-made legal forms for you to fill in and edit. All kinds of basic contracts and simple legal issues can be handled by this package. Even if you're up against something that demands the services of your lawyer, your background knowledge of the subject should reduce the hours that your lawyer has to bill you. Also be sure to check out the various self-help legal books from Nolo.

For those of you who want to build your business around a new invention, check out the Web site at www.gibbsgroup.com. Andy Gibbs, author of books on the invention business and owner of an inventor's services company, has established this site for what he calls "Inventrepreneurs." This site has quite a bit to share: "yellow pages" for inventor networking and inventor services, a bulletin board for inventors to post patents and inventions for sale or license, downloadable "inventor assessment forms" written by Gibbs for helping you gauge whether your invention can really sustain a business, and a comprehensive Web directory to patent forms and offices all over the world.

Saving time and money

Computers, when properly used, can save time and money in countless ways. Consider these:

- ✔ **Letters and memos:** Write it, sign it, and mail it — instead of dictating it, someone else writing it, sending it back to you to edit and sign, and *then* mailing it. Computers make this task quicker, less expensive, and more private (no administrative assistants nosing around in your hallowed company secrets).

- ✔ **Communications:** E-mail, when you don't need an immediate response, is the quickest, easiest, and least-expensive way to communicate.

- ✔ **Filing:** Electronic filing of letters, worksheets, financial statements, and so on is quicker, neater, less expensive, and less space-consuming than manual filing. Just make sure that you back up your files in case your computer crashes!

- ✔ **Worksheets:** After you know how to work with the software, electronic spreadsheets can be developed and filled out in half the time (or less) than manual spreadsheets. Also, they're generally more professional-looking, easier to file, and easier to update and change.

- ✔ **Mailing:** Computer-generated mailing labels are much faster than hand-addressed envelopes. And you can also customize a promotional letter — generating your very own "junk mail"! For all its bad press, mass mailings when done right can result in increased sales.

Of course, computers and the accompanying technology can also waste your time if you happen to get hooked on surfing the Internet, fiddling with the latest presentation software, or reading endless computer manuals. Be aware that, as with any other item that is part-tool-part-toy, computers can become an obsession.

Keeping track of technology

Two good resources that keep tabs on changes that relate to small-business owners are the Web sites for *Inc.* (www.inc.com) and *Entrepreneur* magazines (www.edgeonline.com). Both sites maintain a well-culled and annotated list of links to practical business-related sites on the Internet. For each listed link, you'll find a brief summary of what the site purports to do, saving you from clicking on a misleading title. In addition to their link lists, both sites feature lots of articles that report on big picture changes and trends in the industry.

Chapter 20

Ten Tips for Managing Your Growing Business

. . . .

*L*ike it or not, the larger your company grows, the more you must learn to take off your entrepreneur's hat and put on your manager's hat. This is not an easy transition for most small-business owners to make, and it involves adopting a number of new management skills, skills that do not come naturally to many of us.

This chapter provides a collection of time-tested tips that will help you to work through this transition and to better manage your growing company.

Keep focus on what you can do and what you do best

How many small businesses do you know that try to offer too many services than they can successfully provide ? Or too many products? How many do you know that try to provide the best quality along with the fastest delivery as well as the lowest prices — all at the same time?

The successful small business is one that is operated with the recognition that its resources are finite, that the business can only do so much and do it well. Hence, the business is focused on what it does best; then, it goes ahead and does it *better* than anyone else.

You, as the owner of a growing business, must recognize your need to focus, too. Your personal resources are finite, and you can only do so much before you start doing *too* much and losing *your* focus. Learn to keep your focus on what you can reasonably accomplish, leaving that which you can't do well to someone else — an employee, an outside vendor (lawyers or accountants, for example), or perhaps to a consultant or mentor.

Use these tips to help you focus appropriately and, therefore, better manage your finite time and talents:

- ✔ An overflowing plate is the enemy of focus. You don't have to be all things to all people. Determine what you can delegate, and how.

- ✔ When one project must give way to another, make sure that the first project is temporarily concluded at a convenient spot. Then adopt a steadfast plan for its resumption.

- ✔ *Interest* and *focus* are directly related. Don't expect to focus for long periods of time on subjects that don't interest you. Delegate them to someone else who is interested in such projects.

- ✔ Focus, and the lack thereof, is an issue of company culture. If you, the owner/boss, don't finish the projects you begin or follow up on your initiatives, your employees will most likely adopt the same behavior over time. Your lack of focus can lead to their lack of focus; nothing will get done well or on time; and you'll be left with plenty of time to focus on the failure of your business.

The best small-business managers know that the ability to focus pays dividends. They have learned that solving one problem forever is far better than having three problems in various stages of irresolution.

Bend the rules when necessary

A small business is a place where Katharine Hepburn undoubtedly would have enjoyed herself. You may recall that Hepburn was once quoted as saying: "If you obey all the rules, you miss all the fun."

And, with one slight change, Katharine's quote works for today's successful small business too: "If you obey all the rules, you miss many of the opportunities."

We are certainly not suggesting that you bend the rules you hold flexible *all* the time. The act of rule-bending is not to be considered lightly. Those for whom the rules are bent need to understand why the rules are being bent, and that the bending is an exception, not a rule. The same holds true for when the rules need to be bent because of circumstances, rather than individuals.

When people and institutions become perfect and problems become predictable, then rigid and inflexible rules may work. Until then, however, flexibility is the key to making the best of any imperfections.

Hold your employees accountable

Remember the best teacher you ever had? Chances are, that teacher made you accountable as she went about the teaching process — accountable to do your homework, to participate in class, and to pay attention to whatever it was she was teaching. When she told you to do something, by golly, you did it.

In the process of making you accountable, this teacher no doubt communicated to you in advance what would happen if you didn't do what was asked of you. Conversely, she also told what would happen if you accomplished what she asked. So you knew exactly what to do and exactly what to expect in terms of reward or punishment. Most importantly, you knew that she would follow up her words with actions. So if you didn't do your homework, you could expect to stay after school, or receive a lower grade. You could control the outcome by your choice to follow or not follow her instructions. Somewhere along the line, your best teacher had learned the necessary role of accountability in attaining desired results.

Two elements make up this process of establishing accountability: communication of expectations and follow-up. Without the two working in unison, accountability will not be present. And the lack of accountability will result in spotty performance, at best, and at worst, no performance at all.

Right or wrong, people need a rationale — a sense of the purpose and consequences of the task — before they can do whatever it is you want them to do. Providing this rationale is the role of accountability — yours for setting expectations and follow-up; theirs in accomplishing the expected result — in managing your employees.

The same tools that worked for your best teacher can also work for you. If your employees aren't held accountable for their actions, then they usually won't succeed. And, in the long term, if your employees don't succeed, your company won't either. The time-tested "win-win" formula won't kick in unless both sides are involved.

Consider the 80-20 rule

The 80-20 rule is alive and well in everything the small-business owner does. Consider the following examples of the 80-20 rule.

✔ **The 80-20 rule for your customers:** *"Eighty percent of your profits come from 20 percent of your customers."*

What this means to you: Focus your time and energy on those customers who have the potential to be profitable. Stop wasting your time on those who don't.

✔ **The 80-20 rule for your employees' output:** *"Eighty percent of your company's output will come from 20 percent of your employees."*

What this means to you: Work harder to improve, or cull, the 80 percent that isn't contributing and take good care of the 20 percent that is doing so much of the work.

✔ **The 80-20 rule for your employee problems:** *"Eighty percent of your employee problems come from 20 percent of your employees."*

What this means to you: Do something about that 20 percent. Either solve *their* problem (by training or motivating them) or solve *your* problem (by replacing them).

✔ **The 80-20 rule for your expenses:** *"Eighty percent of your waste come from 20 percent of your expense categories."*

What this means to you: Focus on the 20 percent — that's where your leverage lies.

✔ **The 80-20 rule for your accounts receivable:** *"Eighty percent of your slow pay dollars come from 20 percent of your customers."*

What this means to you: Determine the source of that 20 percent; you usually find a common denominator. One salesperson, maybe? One product? One market?

✔ **The 80-20 rule for your success:** *"Eighty percent of your successes will come from 20 percent of your efforts."*

What this means to you: Learn how to leverage your talents as well as your time. Find a way to spend more time on the things you do well, while delegating those things that you don't do well.

Think ahead: What happens today was yesterday's fault

Have you ever noticed that the hottest month of the year is July, even though the sun is at its peak in June? Ditto with any given day: The hottest time of the day is midafternoon even though the sun is at its highest around noon.

The point? Lags in time are a reality of life, and we must learn how to live with them. Such lags in time have a place in the small-business world as well. Use these examples to help you deal with your business's hot spots:

✔ When your sales hit the skids in June, it isn't because your salespeople have suddenly become ineffective. They may have become ineffective months earlier. The results have just caught up.

✔ When your days-in-receivables (how long it takes your customers to pay you) suddenly doubles, it isn't because your credit manager went on vacation this week. It's because he went on vacation three months ago.

✔ When your inventory soars out of sight, it isn't because of what you ordered last week. It's your prior month's purchases that killed you.

And so it is with any small-business bad news. What happens today is yesterday's fault.

So how do you compensate for this lag in small-business time? Using the examples above, you do the following:

✔ Use an early warning system, such as a Salesperson's Call Report. This report will tell you how many calls your salespeople are making, giving you an indication of how hard they are working in those months before the actual sales will increase.

✔ Hire a temporary employee during the credit manager's absence or find the credit department a capable employee from another department.

✔ Put a purchasing system in place that sounds bells and whistles when purchases exceed a certain level. Today's bells and whistles will negate any chance of tomorrow's soaring inventory.

This business of doing small business is a 12-month proposition, but people and business cycles have their ups and downs, and so does their performance. Your job is to manage your small business around those ups and downs, making sure that this lag in time does not cause a lag in results.

Sleep on it

Following are the guidelines the President of the United States is supposed to observe when he has an important decision to make. These guidelines also apply to the President of General Motors and the President of Acme Plumbing. You should apply them to your business as well:

✔ **Be steady.** That's what Americans most want from their president and what adversaries most respect.

✔ **Don't get captured by the event.** History is full of presidents who have been obsessed with a crisis or an impending decision.

✔ **Don't act until you must.** Rash decisions based on emotion and insufficient information are the biggest dangers in a crisis.

✔ **Talk, talk, talk. Think, think, think. Negotiate, negotiate, negotiate.** Take your time and consider all the options and don't rush into something that you'll later regret.

The underlying strategy here for all presidents of organizations large and small is to keep cool, stay in control, and allow plenty of time to reach a decision. Wait until your emotions are subdued before making big decisions.

Whether you like it or not, the biggest decisions in life and in business usually come only once. Rarely will you be allowed a second chance.

"I'll get back to you tomorrow," are the words for those make-it-or-break-it times. Then go home. Take a drink of something tall and cool. Go for a bike ride with the kids.

And sleep on it.

Resolve conflicts (the meek may inherit the Earth, but their employees may revolt)

Employees and conflict are directly related. The more employees you have, the more conflict you will have in your company. Also, the stakes involved in that conflict become more important and the antagonists become more skilled at that conflict as your company grows.

Effective managers must also be professional conflict resolvers. Conflict and the quick and easy resolution of it does not come naturally to many of us. Resolving conflict almost always calls for compromise and understanding in the heat of emotion, something many of us are unable or unwilling to do.

Walk your talk: The message you send is vital

Imagine the following scenario:

Annual performance review time has come. One of your employees fidgets nervously on the far side of your desk. You begin the review with a complimentary remark, and then dive into the guts of the presentation.

Your intent? To improve the employee's performance.

Ten minutes later, your employee storms out of your office, slamming the door behind him. He perceived that you were attacking him personally.

And that's how perception works. Facts and intent don't mean diddly-squat. It's only perception that counts — that perception is reality until the perception is changed.

So what, you ask?

✔ So remember when leading people (as small-business owners are supposed to do), what you think or believe doesn't matter. What matters is what your employees *perceive* that you think or believe. If they perceive that you don't give a hoot about their problems, they won't give a hoot about your problems. If they perceive that quality is not important to you, then quality won't be important to them. If they perceive that you think the customer is a pain in the posterior, then so the customer shall be to them.

✔ Presentation is everything. Employee review? Shareholder meeting? Customer presentation? What you intend to communicate isn't the issue here; the way your presentation is perceived is what counts.

Try this. Ask a collection of your employees (allow anonymity, of course) how you and your company are perceived. Ask them for a 1-to-10 rating on whatever you deem important to the success of your business. Ask about cultural issues, management issues, leadership traits, ethics, respect for the individual, customer responsiveness, trust, follow-up, accountability, and focus — whatever perception you want to measure.

Then compare your employees' rating to yours. Does their perception agree with yours?

Our guess? On some issues, it isn't even close. Like it or not, when it comes to dealing with people, or being dealt with by people, facts hardly matter at all. Perception is what counts.

Remember and review your mission

In a growing business, you can easily get caught up in the heat of the battle and the excitement of the day-to-day challenges that growth presents. But some businesses and their owners lose sight of why they started the business in the first place. As a result, they lose sight of the other, more important, priorities in their lives.

Growth for the sake of growth or growth to fatten your wallet isn't worth the struggle for most of us. Learn to live within your means, and don't lose sight of the value of family, friends, and your personal health. No business success is worth sacrificing those higher priorities.

And finally, never compromise your ethics and values for the sake of growth. Although building a solid reputation can take years, that reputation can be destroyed overnight if you compromise your ethics and values. And as with a good first impression, a reputation for honesty and integrity, once lost, is never really regained.

Follow the Rule of Many Reasons

When Joe Montana used to quarterback the San Francisco 49ers, people would say that the team won consistently because of him. So what happened? The 49ers traded Montana and continued winning anyway.

Once more, the old adage was proved: There isn't only one reason why a football (or any other) team wins or loses — there are many reasons.

And similarly, if your business is successful, a myriad of reasons is behind that success. You've hired right, and fired right, and focused, and made a great product or provided a great service, and put the right distribution system in place, and planned and strategized. The list goes on forever of the things you've done right.

And if your business is in trouble, you'll find an equal number of reasons why. You've hired poorly, or you haven't fired when you should, or your product quality is poor, or your sales force needs training, or your culture lacks accountability. You get the idea.

That's how the Rule of Many Reasons works, and it applies to everything you do, whether it's running your company, or raising your kids, or shuffling along the backroads of life.

So what does this Rule of Many Reasons mean when your company hits one of the many speed bumps that lurk along the road to success?

It means that no easy fixes are available. Sure, you have priorities, but your company won't do an about-face tomorrow simply because you've put a quality program in place. Or started a program to hire better. Or decided to install accountability in your culture. Or whatever it is you've started to do that you weren't doing before.

And it means that the winner in the small-business game is the owner who has learned that everything makes the difference — the big things and the little things and all the in-between things. Success is a combination of everything.

Index

• *Numbers* •

3M, 30, 66
80-20 rule, 385–386
401(k) plans, 302, 305
403(b) plans, 302–303
504 Loan Program, 96

• *A* •

accountability, of employees, 293–294, 295, 350, 385
accountants. *See also* tax advisors
 certified public (CPAs), 332
accounting. *See also* financial statements
 accrual-basis, 171
 cash-basis, 171, 335
 defined, 165
 double-entry, 170, 171
 outsourcing, 165
 responsibility for, 78
 terminology, 171
accounting systems
 manual, 168–170
 need for, 167–168
 selecting, 168, 173–174
 software, 170–173, 380, 381
accounts payable
 aging, 172
 on balance sheet, 143
 examples, 13
 of existing businesses, 143
 managing, 178
 tracking, 172
accounts receivable
 aging, 172, 251
 collecting, 249–251
 defined, 142
 80-20 rule, 386
 examples, 14
 of existing businesses, 142
 interest rates on overdue balances, 251
 as loan collateral, 93
 number of days in, 247, 387
 tracking, 172
accrual-basis accounting, 171
ACE-Net (Angel Capital Electronic Network), 97
ADA. *See* Americans with Disabilities Act
advertising
 call to action in, 191
 defined, 193
 developing, 194
 Internet, 198
 jobs, 271
 magazine, 197–198
 newspaper, 195
 options, 198–199
 plans, 75
 radio, 196
 strategies, 193–194
 television, 196–197
 Yellow Pages, 195
advertising agencies, 194
advisors. *See also* attorneys; tax advisors
 boards of, 261–263
 consultants, 149, 184
 on regulatory issues, 322
 when buying small businesses, 126, 148–149, 151–152, 155
The Advisory Board (TAB), 72
agents, 202
AHBA. *See* American Home Business Association
The Alternative Board (TAB), 261
Amazon.com, 380
AMC, 221
American Home Business Association (AHBA), 266
American Stock Exchange (AMEX), 104
American Women's Economic Development Corp. (AWED), 261
Americans with Disabilities Act (ADA), 323
AMEX. *See* American Stock Exchange
Angel Capital Electronic Network (ACE-Net), 97

angels. *See also* investors
  defined, 96–97
  finding, 97, 100
  investment criteria, 98
answering machines, 370
appearance. *See* physical appearance
appraisers, business, 151
aptitude test, small-business owner's,
    20–25
asset-based financing, 93, 94
assets. *See also* accounts receivable;
    balance sheets
  on balance sheet, 142
  depreciation, 142, 339
  examples, 14
  of existing businesses, 142–143, 144, 154
  fixed, 142
  goodwill, 144
  other, 143
  personal, 39
  property and equipment, 142–143,
    339–340
attorneys, consulting
  buying businesses, 149, 152, 154, 156
  contracts, 327
  employee manuals, 291
  employee stock ownership plans, 308
  fees, 183
  finding, 183
  firing employees, 287
  incorporating, 103, 109
  itemized invoices, 183
  limited liability corporations, 111
  negotiating leases, 164
  relationships, 181–183
  self-help software as alternative to, 381
  setting up partnerships, 103, 263
  startups, 105
  taxes, 332
  when to consult, 182–183
audit trails, 170–171, 172
automation. *See* computers; software
automobiles
  business use, 340
  manufacturers, 221
average sales days, 247
AWED. *See* American Women's Economic
    Development Corp.

• *B* •

Bailey, Keith, 232
balance sheets
  in business plans, 81
  defined, 240
  of existing businesses, 142–144, 150
  four-column format, 240
  using, 240–242
bankruptcies
  personal, 36
  risk of, 28–29
banks
  asset-based financing, 93, 94
  fees, 254
  floor planning, 94
  letters of credit, 94
  lines of credit, 93
  loan committees, 182
  loans from, 92–93, 180–181
  minority-owned, 99
  relationships with, 179–181
  SBA loans, 95–96, 379
  use of technology in loan application
    process, 94
bartering, 13
Be the Boss Web site, 379
Bean, L. L., 51
Ben & Jerry's, 52
BizBuySell, 378, 379
Bizcomps, 152
Blue Cross and Blue Shield, 308, 310
boards of advisors, 261–263
boards of directors, 261
Boeing, 66
Bogle, John, 51
book value. *See* net worth
book value valuation method, 150–151
bookkeeping
  defined, 165
  double-entry, 171
  function, 233
  manual systems, 168–170
  outsourcing, 165
  responsibility for, 78
  single-entry, 171
bootstrapping. *See also* partners
  common use of, 88–89
  defined, 85

estimating cash needs, 86
examples, 89–90
golden rule of, 91
life insurance cash value, 91
loans from family members and friends, 90, 91
locating funds, 90–92
BPR. *See* Business Process Reengineering
break-even point, 209, 212
Brodsky, Norm, 98
brokerage firms, 223
brokers. *See* business brokers
budgets
  personal, 42–43
  zero-based, 176–177, 253
business appraisers, 151
Business Assistance Service-Office of Business Liaison (Commerce Department), 63
business brokers
  commissions, 127, 153
  comparable market analysis, 153
  finding, 125, 128
  licensing and regulation, 128
  pitfalls of using, 127–128
  roles, 127, 149
  selecting, 128, 153
business cards, for home-based businesses, 368
business incubators, 100
business interruption insurance, 162
business plans
  adjusting over time, 83
  competitors described in, 72–73
  Description of Business section, 71–73
  Financial Management section, 80–82
  as financing tool, 69, 73, 78
  importance of, 68, 69–70
  lengths, 70
  Management Plan (Operations), 77–78
  Management section, 73
  marketing plan, 73–76
  mission statements, 65–67, 71
  for newly-purchased businesses, 157
  nondisclosure agreements, 324–326
  purposes, 68–69
  Risks section, 68, 78
  software, 82
  writing, 70

Business Process Reengineering (BPR), 353
business triangle, 218
Business Valuations by Industry, 152
buying small businesses. *See also* franchises
  advisors, 126, 148–149, 151–152, 155
  allocation of purchase price, 154–155
  as alternative to startup, 31–33, 116–119
  background needed, 121–122
  capital needed, 120, 122–123, 125
  company culture, 138–139, 158
  customer base, 118, 136, 144, 157
  determining value, 149–153
  disadvantages, 119–121
  down payments, 122–123
  due diligence, 153, 155–156
  employees, 119, 135, 136, 139, 144, 158
  evaluating, 134–135, 140–144
  financial statements, 140–144, 156
  finding candidates, 124–128, 379
  first steps after purchase, 139, 157–158
  identifying growth potential, 117, 125, 150
  inspections, 119, 153
  motivated sellers, 138
  non-disclosure agreements (NDAs), 140
  owner's reasons for selling, 136–137
  prices, 117, 125
  purchase offers, 134–135, 148–155
  risks, 32, 133–134
  seller financing, 123, 154
  transfer of ownership notice, 157
  vendor relationships, 144
  wrong reasons, 120
buy-sell agreements, 103, 109, 263, 307

• C •

C corporations, 109–110, 341
capital. *See also* bootstrapping; outsourcing startup financing
  estimating startup needs, 86–87
  needed for buying small businesses, 120, 122–123, 125
  requirements for startups, 81
  reserve, 87
  working, 86, 87

Carlson, Curt, 214
cash flow
   compared to profitability, 81, 234–235
   defined, 81
   effects of efficient inventory manage-
      ment, 249
   of established businesses, 117–118
   importance of, 234–235
   projections, 81, 235–236
cash reserves
   estimating, 87
   personal, 44
cash-basis accounting, 171, 335
catalogs, mail order, 203–204
Certified Development Companies
      (CDCs), 96
certified public accountants (CPAs), 332
Chamber of Commerce, 318, 321
Charles Schwab, 223, 302
checks, signing, 165
children
   hiring, 338–339
   working at home with, 376
Chrysler, 221
COBRA health insurance, 46
Cognetics, 15
Cohen, Ben, 52
collection agencies, 251
collections, accounts receivable, 249–251
Collins, James C., 66
Commerce Department
   Business Assistance Service — Office of
      Business Liaison, 63
   Minority Business Development
      Agency, 99
company policies
   employee manuals, 290–291
   flexibility, 222, 224, 292–293, 384
compensation plans. *See also* employee
      benefits
   bonuses, 279
   for employees, 77–78, 277–280, 289
   as motivation, 277–278, 279–280
   salary reviews, 284, 285
   types, 278
competitive advantage, 62
competitors
   description in business plans, 72–73

evaluating, 61, 74
   prices, 210–211, 212
complaints, customer, 229, 230–232
computers. *See also* Internet; software
   benefits, 377, 382
   games, 349
   printers, 370
   uses in home-based businesses, 369–370
conflict resolution, 388
consultants, 149, 184
contracts
   with customers and vendors, 317, 327
   franchise, 147–148
copyrights, 316, 324–325, 326, 327
corporations
   benefits of incorporating, 108
   buy-sell agreements, 109
   C, 109–110, 341
   disadvantages, 109
   Fortune 500, 15
   number in United States, 105
   personal service, 341
   subchapter S, 110–111, 342
   taxes, 109, 111, 341–342
cost of goods, 13
cost-based pricing, 208, 212–213
CPAs. *See* certified public accountants
credit. *See* banks; outsourcing
credit applications, for customers, 250
credit cards
   charges to retailers, 202
   financing startups with, 92
   interest rates, 40
   problems with, 40
credit histories
   business, 94
   of customers, 250
   of franchisers, 147
   personal, 94
credit policies, 76, 250–251
critical-event memos, 284
culture
   accountability, 294, 295, 350, 385
   of existing businesses, 138–139, 158
   expense control as part of, 175, 253
   focus in, 384
   physical appearance as clue to, 359
   time management, 348, 349–350

current ratio, 83
customer receivable ledgers, 172
customer retention
 flexibility in company policies,
   222, 224, 292
 importance of, 219, 220, 224–225
 increasing value, 222
 learning from defections, 224–226
 quality and customer service, 221, 223
customer satisfaction, 219
customer service
 after sale, 229
 before sale, 228
 complaints, 229, 230–232
 departments, 227
 during sale, 228–229
 examples, 226–227
 flexibility, 222, 224, 292
 importance of, 219–220, 221
 as responsibility of all employees, 227
customers
 on advisory boards, 262
 building relationships with, 205,
   217–218, 220
 in business triangle, 218
 collecting accounts receivable, 249–251
 contracts, 317, 327
 database, 369
 demand for product or service, 210, 256
 80-20 rule, 385
 of existing businesses, 118, 136, 144, 157
 extending credit to, 250–251
 good, 220
 listening to, 230–231
 loyalty, 224–225
 new product ideas, 190
 potential, 75
 referrals from, 192–193, 371
 training, 178

• *D* •

dba. *See* doing business as (dba)
   certificates
debit cards, 41
debt
 on balance sheets, 143
 comfort level with, 26
 credit card, 40

of existing businesses, 143
 good and bad, 40
 personal, 40–41
 problems with consumer, 35–36, 40
debt to equity ratio, 83, 246
decision-making, 387–388
defined-benefit plans, 301
dental insurance, 48–49
dependent care plans, 312
depreciation, of assets, 142, 339
direct cost allocation, 209
direct mail, 202–203
direct selling companies. *See* multilevel
   marketing (MLM) companies
directors, boards of, 261
Directors and Officers insurance, 261
disability insurance
 as employee benefit, 310–311
 for owner, 41, 46–47
discount brokers, 223
discount retailers, 205–206
Disney, 66
distribution
 channels, 201
 defined, 188, 201
 direct, 201, 202–204
 direct mail, 202–203
 indirect, 201, 202, 204–206
 Internet sales, 204
 mail-order catalogs, 203–204
 plans, 75
 product versus service, 201–203
 repackaging, 206
 retail, 202
 selecting channels, 206
 wholesalers and distributors, 205–206
doing business as (dba) certificates,
   106, 320
double-entry accounting, 170, 171
Drucker, Peter, 17
due diligence, before buying small
   businesses, 153, 155–156

• *E* •

E.F. Hutton, 223
EAs. *See* enrolled agents
EBRI. *See* Employee Benefit Research
   Institute

80-20 rule, 385–386
EINs. *See* Employer Identification Numbers
electronic commerce, 173
e-mail, 368, 373, 380
Employee Benefit Research Institute
    (EBRI), 297, 298
employee benefits
  dependent care plans, 312
  descriptions in employee manuals, 291
  disability insurance, 310–311
  flexible benefit plans, 312–313
  health insurance, 297, 298–299, 308–310
  life insurance, 311–312
  replacing when starting business, 45–49
  retirement plans, 297–298, 299–305
  stock and stock options, 305–307
  tax deductions for, 336, 341
  vacation, 314
employee manuals, 290–291
employee stock ownership plans (ESOPs),
    307, 353
employees. *See also* human resources
  accountability, 293–294, 295, 350, 385
  business plan section on, 77
  in business triangle, 218
  children as, 338–339
  compensation plans, 77–78, 277–280, 289
  conflict resolution, 388
  customer service responsibility, 227
  customers lost by, 226
  dishonest, 162
  distinction from independent contrac-
    tors, 328, 337–338
  education and training, 30, 166, 178,
    274–276, 277
  80-20 rule, 386
  exit interviews, 288
  expense control responsibility, 254
  firing, 286–288
  gamebreaker positions, 270
  helping, 280
  hiring, 270–274, 317, 328
  improving skills as alternative to starting
    business, 29–30
  incentives to cut expenses, 176
  interviews, 272, 273–274
  job descriptions, 271–272, 282
  leasing, 295–296
  legal issues, 317, 328, 346–347

  motivating, 276–277
  moving from large to small com-
    panies, 31
  organization charts, 289–290
  part-time, 337
  perceptions, 388–389
  performance and salary reviews, 283–286
  performance expectations, 282–283
  of purchased small businesses, 119, 135,
    136, 139, 144, 158
  records, 164
  salespeople, 214, 215, 216, 217, 278
  security of, 36–37
  as shareholders, 103, 305–306, 352–353
  successful management of, 292–295
  superstars, 269–270
  as team members, 270, 289
  withholding tax payments, 336–337
  workers' compensation insurance, 163,
    255, 322
Employer Identification Numbers (EINs),
    323, 336
"employment at will" statements, 291
Encyclopedia of Associations, 265
enrolled agents (EAs), 332
entertainment and travel expenses,
    340–341
Entrepreneur magazine, Web site, 380, 382
entrepreneurs. *See also* owners
  compared to managers, 360
  definition of, 17
  inside large companies, 30–31
Entrepreneurs Edge, 261
environmental regulations, 323
equipment
  depreciation, 339
  of existing businesses, 142–143
  Section 179 deduction, 339–340
equity, sharing with employees, 103,
    305–307, 352–353
ESOP Association, 307
ethics, 293, 389
The Executive Committee (TEC), 261
exit interviews, 288
exit strategy, 109
expenses
  controlling, 175–176, 252–255
  defined, 140

80-20 rule, 386
estimates in business plan, 80
examples, 13
of existing businesses, 141, 142
fixed, 175
operating, 238
personal, 42–43
startup costs, 32, 86, 87
travel and entertainment, 340–341
variable, 175
zero-based budgeting, 176–177, 253
experience modification factors, 163, 255
exports, by small businesses, 15

• *F* •

family
   hiring children, 338–339
   impact of starting small businesses,
      37–38
   loans from, 90, 91
   roles in home-based businesses,
      373–374, 376
Family Medical Leave Act, 324
fax machines, 367, 368, 370
federal government. *See* U.S. government
Federal Reserve System, 186
Federal Trade Commission (FTC), 145, 147
Fidelity Investments, 42, 43, 302, 303
financial management. *See also* expenses;
      personal finances
   basics, 13–14
   business plan section on, 80–82
   key business functions, 233
   newly-purchased businesses, 157
   signing checks, 165
   time lags and problems, 386–387
Financial Research Associates (FRA), 152
financial statements. *See also* accounting
      systems
   audited, 140
   balance sheets, 81, 142–144, 150, 240–242
   in business plans, 80–82
   cash-flow projections, 81
   cost to produce, 242
   evaluating before buying businesses,
      140–144, 156
   frequency of, 237

as management tool, 233–234, 242–243
   open-book management, 355
   preparing, 80, 82
   pro forma profit and loss, 80
   profit-and-loss (income) statements,
      140–142, 237–240
   ratios and percentages, 244–247
   separate set for tax purposes, 143
   unaudited, 140
Financial Studies of the Small Business, 152
financing. *See* bootstrapping; outsourcing
      startup financing
firing employees, 286–288
fiscal years, 171
504 Loan Program, 96
five-minute appearance test, 357–358
fixed assets, 142
fixed expenses, 175
flexible benefit plans, 312–313
floor planning, 94
Ford Motor Co., 221
forecasting. *See* budgets
Form 1099, 338
Fortune 500 companies, 15
401(k) plans, 302, 305
403(b) plans, 302–303
FRA. *See* Financial Research Associates
franchises
   advantages, 129–130
   centralized purchasing, 130
   customers, 129–130
   defined, 129
   disadvantages, 130–131
   evaluating, 145–148
   fees, 146–147
   fraudulent, 131
   Hallmark stores, 54
   motives of franchisers, 146
   negotiating contracts, 147–148
   regulation of, 145, 147
   royalties, 146
   Web sites on, 379
fraud. *See* pyramid schemes
freelancers. *See also* independent
      contractors
   Web sites, 378
friends, loans from, 90, 91
FTC. *See* Federal Trade Commission

• *G* •

gain-sharing. *See* pay-for-performance
Gateway 2000, 89
General Electric (GE), 16
General Motors (GM), 221, 278
General Sports Corp., 182
Gentes, Jim, 51
Gerber, Michael, 7
Gibbs, Andy, 381
GM. *See* General Motors
goals, setting, 281–282, 373
Golden Rule of Bootstrapping, 91
goodwill, 144
governments. *See also* state governments;
    U.S. government
  local, 163, 320–322, 337, 376
  policies, 186
  regulations, 315–316, 317–320
  relationships with employees of, 185
  resources for small businesses, 62–64, 99
Gray, John, 276
Greenfield, Jerry, 52
gross margin, 238, 245–246, 255

• *H* •

Hallmark stores, 54
health insurance
  deductibles and co-payments, 309
  as employee benefit, 297, 298–299,
    308–310
  for owner, 41, 46
  sharing cost with employees, 309
  shopping for, 308–309, 310
Health Insurance Portability and
    Accountability Act, 46
health maintenance organizations
    (HMOs), 309
health and safety regulations, 321
Hepburn, Katherine, 384
hiring employees, 270–274, 317, 328
HMOs. *See* health maintenance
    organizations
home equity loans, 92
Home Office Association of America, 378
home-based businesses
  advantages, 365
  business cards, 368

  computers, 369–370, 372–373
  costs, 375–376
  discipline required, 376
  growing numbers of, 365
  insurance, 367
  legal issues, 366
  marketing strategies, 371–372
  motivation, 373
  offices, 367
  opportunities advertised, 19–20
  professionalism, 366, 367–368
  roles of family members, 373–374, 376
  staying in touch with outside world,
    374–375
  telephone service, 367, 368
  time management, 372–373
  trade associations, 266, 375, 378
  Web sites, 378
  zoning regulations, 320–321, 376
hooks, for publicity, 200
human resources. *See also* employees
  development stages, 347–348
  directors, 348
  leasing employees, 295–296
  legal issues, 317, 328, 346–347
  outsourcing, 166

• *I* •

icons, defined, 6–7
IDG Books, Worldwide, Inc., 190
Inc. magazine, 61, 66, 88, 98, 382
income, net, 238, 239
income statements. *See* profit and loss
    statements
income taxes
  brackets, 335
  corporate, 109, 111, 341–342
  deductions for employee benefits, 336
  estimated payments, 336
  as factor in spending decisions, 339–341
  federal, 323
  guides, 330–331
  on limited liability corporations, 111
  manual preparation of returns, 169
  marginal rates, 336
  on partnerships, 107

reducing, 335
savings from retirement accounts,
    299, 304
Section 179 deduction, 339–340
software, 331, 381
on sole proprietorships, 106
state, 322
withholding for employees, 336–337
independent contractors, 328, 337–338
industries. *See also* trade associations
fastest growing companies, 61
publications, 125, 152, 197, 318
saturation points, 61
inspections, when buying small
    businesses, 119, 153
Institute for the Accreditation of Profes-
    sional Employer Organizations, 296
Institute of Business Appraisers, 151
insurance
business interruption, 162
costs, 162
dental and vision, 48–49
Directors and Officers, 261
disability, 41, 46–47, 310–311
health, 41, 46, 297, 298–299, 308–310
for home-based businesses, 367
liability, 162
life, 47–48, 91, 311–312
property damage, 162
quotation services, 48
for sole proprietorships, 106
theft, 162
unemployment, 322, 328
workers' compensation, 163, 255, 322
insurance agents, 47
intellectual property protection, 316,
    324–325, 326–327
interest rates
credit card, 40
Federal Reserve policies, 186
on overdue receivables, 251
Internal Revenue Service (IRS)
business tax deductions, 143
count of small businesses, 15
Form 1099, 338
independent contractor rules, 337–338
limited liability corporations
    allowed by, 111

publications, 330–331
retirement account regulations, 299
self-employment tax deduction, 49
travel and entertainment expenses rules,
    340–341
Web site, 381
Internet. *See also* Web sites
advertising on, 198
brainstorming business ideas on, 378
doing business on, 173, 204, 380
e-mail, 368, 373, 380
search engines, 378
surfing, 349
as training tool, 276
interviews, prospective employees, 272,
    273–274
inventions. *See* patents
inventory
of existing businesses, 143
insuring, 162
as loan collateral, 93, 94
managing, 247–249
obsolescence, 247
physical counts, 248
software, 172, 248
thefts, 247, 248
inventory turn, 246–247
investments, personal
mutual funds, 43
in other small businesses, 33–34
retirement accounts, 42, 43
investors. *See also* angels; partners;
    shareholders
importance of business plan, 69, 73, 78
venture capital firms, 92, 97
IRAs (individual retirement accounts), 48.
    See also SEP-IRAs
IRS. *See* Internal Revenue Service
isolation
overcoming, 258–266
of small-business owners, 257–266

Jack White, 302
Jack White Insurance Services, 48
job descriptions, 271–272, 282

• K •

Kaiser Permanente, 308, 310
Keogh plans, 45, 299, 300–301, 305
Kilcullen, John, 190
Kmart, 215

• L •

labor. *See* employees
lawsuits
  by customers, 220
  by employees, 328
lawyers. *See* attorneys
leases
  of existing businesses, 144–145, 156
  financing startups with, 95
  long-term, 164
  negotiating, 164
leasing companies, 95
leasing employees, 295–296
legal entities
  choosing form, 105, 324
  corporations, 105, 108–111
  limited liability corporations, 105, 111
  sole proprietorships, 105, 106
  tax considerations, 341–342
  unincorporated, 105–108
legal issues. *See also* attorneys
  home-based businesses, 366
  labor law, 317, 328, 346–347
  lawsuits, 220, 328
  self-help software, 381
Leland, Karen, 232
lenders. *See* loans
letters, writing, 368
letters of credit, 94
liabilities. *See also* balance sheets; debt
  accounts payable, 143
  on balance sheet, 142
  examples, 14
  of existing businesses, 142, 154
  personal, 39
liability, personal
  in limited liability corporations, 111
  in partnerships, 107
  in sole proprietorships, 106
liability insurance, 162

licenses, 316, 317–320, 322, 323
liens, on existing businesses, 156
life insurance
  as employee benefit, 311–312
  for owner, 47–48, 91
  using cash value to finance startups, 91
Limited Liability Corporations (LLCs),
    105, 111
limited partnerships (LPs), 223
lines of credit, 93
liquidity, 246
LLCs. *See* Limited Liability Corporations
loans
  bank, 92–93, 180–181
  from family members and friends, 90, 91
  home equity, 92
  importance of business plan, 69, 73, 78
  negotiating terms, 181
  personal guarantees, 181
  SBA, 62, 92, 95–96, 379
  from seller of business, 123, 154
local governments
  regulations, 320–322, 376
  taxes, 163, 320, 337
loss leaders, 212
LPs. *See* limited partnerships

• M •

magazine advertising, 197–198
mail order catalogs, 203–204
mailing lists, 203
management by objective (MBO), 352
management systems, 350–353, 355
managers
  business plan section on, 73
  compared to entrepreneurs, 360
  conflict resolution, 388
  employees and, 292–295
  hiring, 362
  owners as, 347, 359, 360, 361–362
  traits of successful, 360
manual bookkeeping systems, 168–170
Manufacturers' Agents National
    Association, 217
manufacturers' representatives, 166, 214,
    215–217

manufacturing businesses
  buying, 116
  defined, 55
  distribution channels, 205
  fixed assets, 142
  inventories, 143
  personality traits needed, 60
  risks, 60
manufacturing function, outsourcing, 166
margin
  defined, 207
  gross, 238, 245–246, 255
  increasing, 252, 255–256
  of individual products, 213
marginal tax rates, 336
market research, 12, 189
market share, increasing, 211
marketing. *See also* advertising; promotion
  defined, 188
  home-based businesses, 371–372
  importance of, 187
  on Internet, 198, 380
  plan, 73–76
  pricing strategies, 207–214
  product and service development,
      188–190
Marriott, 66
Mary Kay, 19, 66, 132
MasterCard, 41
MBO. *See* management by objective
media. *See also* advertising
  public relations, 75–76
  publicity, 199
  trade publications, 125, 152, 197, 318
Medicare taxes, 49
mentors
  finding, 258–259, 379
  relationship with, 259–260
Merrill Lynch, 223
Midas Muffler, 129–130
Minority Business Development Agency
      (Commerce Department), 99
minority shareholders, 103, 306–307
minority-owned businesses, 99
mission statements
  in business plan, 71
  defined, 65
  displaying, 67

examples, 66
for newly-purchased businesses, 157
reviewing, 389
writing, 67
MLM. *See* multilevel marketing (MLM)
      companies
model companies, researching, 74
modems, 370
MoneyHunter Web site, 380
money-purchase pension plans, 301
Montana, Joe, 390
motivation
  of employees, 276–277
  goals, 281–282
  in home-based businesses, 373
  of small-business owners, 276
multilevel marketing (MLM) companies,
      18–19, 131–132
multiple of earnings valuation method,
      150, 151
mutual fund companies, 302
mutual funds, 43

• *N* •

Naisbitt, John, 15
names
  business, 106
  registering, 316, 319, 320, 327
NASDAQ. *See* National Association of
      Securities Dealers Automated
      Quotation system
NASE. *See* National Association for the
      Self-Employed
National Association of Securities Dealers
      Automated Quotation system
      (NASDAQ), 104
National Association for the Self-Employed
      (NASE), 266
National Association of Women Business
      Owners (NAWBO), 266
National Bankers Association (NBA), 99
National Business Association (NBA), 266
National Business Incubation Asso-
      ciation, 100
National Federation of Independent
      Business Owners (NFIB), 266, 365
National Small Business United
      (NSBU), 265

NAWBO. *See* National Association of
  Women Business Owners
NBA (National Bankers Association), 99
NBA (National Business Association), 266
NDAs. *See* non-disclosure agreements
net income, 238, 239
net worth
  on balance sheet, 240
  definition, 14
  of existing businesses, 150
  personal, 39
network marketing. *See* multilevel
  marketing (MLM) companies
networking
  with peers, 260–261, 318
  promoting business through, 191–192
New York Stock Exchange (NYSE), 104
news releases, 199
newspapers
  advertising, 195
  public relations, 75–76
NFIB. *See* National Federation of
  Independent Business Owners
Nolo Press, 381
non-disclosure agreements (NDAs)
  for business plans, 324–326
  when buying business, 140
nonprofit organizations, retirement plans,
  302–303
NSBU. *See* National Small Business United
number of days in receivables, 247, 387
NYSE. *See* New York Stock Exchange

• *O* •

OK. *See* Opportunity Knocks
open-book management, 355
operations
  business plan, 77–78
  distinction from strategy, 262
  managers, 362
Opportunity Knocks (OK), 261
options, stock, 306–307
organization charts, 289–290
outsourcing, of tasks
  accounting and bookkeeping, 165
  decision factors, 166–167
  defined, 165

of home-based businesses, 373
  human resources, 166
  manufacturing, 166
  sales, 166, 214, 215–217
outsourcing startup financing. *See also*
  investors; loans
  angels, 92, 96–97, 98, 100
  banks, 92–94
  business incubators, 100
  defined, 85
  estimating cash needs, 86–87
  minority funding resources, 99
  sources, 92, 95–98, 379–380
  venture capital firms, 92, 97
owners. *See also* personal finances
  aptitude test, 20–25
  background needed to buy businesses,
    121–122
  consulting with former, 154, 158
  daily tasks, 52–53
  dealing with business growth, 344,
    358–362, 383
  deciding to become, 26–29
  decision-making, 387–388
  definitions, 17–18
  finding niches, 51–53
  focus needed by, 383–384
  hiring replacements, 362
  isolation, 257–266
  leadership, 358, 388–389
  management responsibilities, 347, 359,
    360, 361–362
  matching skills to business type, 56–59
  mentors, 258–260, 379
  motivations, 276
  reasons for selling, 136–137, 362
  replacing employee benefits, 45
  salaries and bonuses, 142, 156, 245
  skills needed, 20–26
  teams, 72
  traits needed, 26, 59–62
  value of business experience, 122
ownership forms. *See also* shareholders
  choosing, 99–100, 101–102
  partnerships, 101, 102–103, 107
  public corporations, 103–104
  sole ownership, 101–102

• P •

paired plans (Keoghs), 301
participatory management, 352
partners
    advantages, 263, 264–265
    buy-sell agreements, 103, 263
    as financing source, 90
    general, 107
    limited, 107
    need for, 101, 102–103
    personal liability of, 107
    trial runs with, 264
partnership agreements, 107–108, 263
part-time small businesses, starting as, 32, 44
patents, 316, 324–325, 326, 381
payables. *See* accounts payable
pay-for-performance compensation, 278, 279
payroll software, 172
payroll taxes, 336–337
peer networking, 260–261, 318
PEOs. *See* Professional Employer
        Organizations
performance expectations, 282–283
performance reviews, 283–286
permits, 316, 317–320
personal finances. *See also* insurance;
        retirement accounts
    assessment of position and goals, 39–42
    bankruptcies, 36
    cash reserves, 44
    credit histories, 94
    cutting spending, 42–43
    debt, 40–41
    investments, 42, 43
    managing after starting small business,
        49–50
    net worth, 39
    preparing to start business, 36–38
    retirement planning, 42
    savings, 39, 41–42
personal service corporations, 341
Peter Principle, 361
physical appearance of business
    five-minute test, 357–358
    as indication of company culture, 359
point-of-sale systems, 248
preferred provider organizations
        (PPOs), 309

President Resource Organization
        (PRO), 261
price-earnings ratio, 150, 151
prices, of small businesses, 117, 125
pricing strategies
    business plan section on, 76
    of competitors, 210–211, 212
    cost-based, 208, 212–213
    developing, 207–211
    discounting, 208
    follow-up services, 229
    increasing market share, 211
    for new products or services, 211–212
    objectives, 208
    premium, 211
    relationship to marketing, 207
    special services, 224
    specials and loss leaders, 212
    trial and error, 213
    updating prices, 212–214, 255–256
printers, computer, 370
PRO. *See* President Resource Organization
pro forma profit and loss statements, 80
Pro Source Fitness, 31
process analysis, 353
products and services. *See also* distribu-
        tion; marketing; pricing strategies
    break-even point, 209, 212
    comparative value to customer, 210
    costs, 209
    customer demand, 210, 256
    development, 188–190
    new ideas, 190
professional associations, disability
        insurance plans, 47
Professional Employer Organizations
        (PEOs), 295–296
profit. *See also* margin
    defined, 140
    example, 13
    of existing businesses, 141
profit and loss statements (P&L)
    defined, 237
    of existing businesses, 140–142, 156
    four-column format, 237
    preparing, 238–239
    pro forma, 80
    using, 239–240

profitability
   analyzing causes of changes, 239
   compared to cash flow, 81, 234–235
   effects of efficient inventory
      management, 249
   improving, 174–175, 251–252
profit-sharing plans (Keoghs), 301
promotion. *See also* advertising
   networking, 191–192
   publicity, 199–200
   purpose, 190–191
   word-of-mouth, 192–193, 371
property and equipment
   autos, 340
   of existing businesses, 142–143
   tax write-offs, 339–340
property damage insurance, 162
property taxes, 320
Prudential, 223
public relations, 75–76
publicity, 199–200
purchase offers
   contingencies, 134–135, 153–154
   making, 148–155
   negotiating, 153–154, 155
   noncompete clauses, 154
   valuing business, 149–153
purchasing function, 130, 248, 387
pyramid schemes, 18, 131–132

• *Q* •

quality, 221, 293
quality circles, 353
Quick & Reilly, 223
quick ratio, 246

• *R* •

radio advertising, 196
ratios
   comparing, 244
   current, 83
   debt to equity, 83, 246
   gross margin, 245–246
   industry norms, 244
   inventory turn, 246–247
   number of days in receivables, 247, 387
   quick, 246

return on equity (R.O.E.), 245
return on sales (R.O.S.), 245
variations in, 83
real estate
   business incubators, 100
   leases, 144–145, 156, 164
   property taxes, 320
   zoning, 320–321, 376
receivables. *See* accounts receivable
reengineering, 353
referrals
   from customers, 192–193, 371
   of new employees, 271
registration, of new businesses, 317–320
regulations
   environmental, 323
   federal, 323–324
   home-based businesses, 320–321, 376
   importance of compliance, 318–320
   labor laws, 317, 328, 346–347
   local, 320–322, 376
   new businesses, 315–316, 317–318
   state, 322–323
Reichheld, Frederick, 224–225
relationship investing, 90, 91
relationship lending, 90, 91
relationship selling process, 205, 217–218
repackaging, 206
restaurants, buying, 133–134
retail businesses
   buyers, 205
   buying existing, 141
   defined, 54–55
   discount chains, 205–206
   as distribution channel, 202, 204–205
   insurance needed, 162
   inventories, 143
   leases, 144
   personality traits needed, 59
   point-of-sale systems, 248
retirement accounts
   asset allocation, 43
   beneficiaries, 304
   contributions for employees, 299–300
   as employee benefit, 297–298, 299–305
   401(k) plans, 302, 305
   403(b) plans, 302–303
   government regulations, 316
   importance of, 42, 303–305

IRAs, 48
Keogh plans, 45, 299, 300–301, 305
for self-employed, 45–46, 299, 300–301
SEP-IRAs, 45, 299, 300
SIMPLE plans, 303, 305
tax savings, 299, 304
retirement planning, workbooks and
software, 42
return on equity (R.O.E.), 245
return on sales (R.O.S.), 245
revenues
by product line or store, 141
defined, 140
estimates in business plan, 80
growth rates, 141
in profit and loss statements, 238
risk
ability to deal with, 26
business failure, 28–29
business plan section on, 68, 78
in buying small businesses, 32, 117
of manufacturing businesses, 60
recognizing, 79
of startups, 32
R.O.E. *See* return on equity
R.O.S. *See* return on sales
Rule of Many Reasons, 390

• *S* •

safety regulations, 321
sales
defined, 188
examples, 13
gross, 238
growth, 346, 354
importance of, 118–119, 214
increasing, 256
outsourcing, 166, 214, 215–217
relationship selling process, 205, 217–218
sales taxes, 320, 322
sales terms, 76, 250
sales-driven companies, 217–218
salespeople. *See also* manufacturers'
representatives
compensating, 278
in-house, 214, 215, 216
perceived by other employees, 217
San Francisco 49ers, 390

savings
financing startup from, 91
personal, 39, 41–42
Savings Incentive Match Plans for
Employees. *See* SIMPLE plans
SBA. *See* Small Business Administration
SBDCs. *See* Small Business Development
Centers
SBICs. *See* Small Business Investment
Companies
SCORE. *See* Service Corps of Retired
Executives
search engines, 378
SEC. *See* Securities and Exchange
Commission
Section 125 (flexible benefit) plans, 312–313
Section 179 deduction, 339–340
securities brokerage firms, 223
Securities and Exchange Commission
(SEC), 104, 223, 317
SelectQuote, 48
self-employment
estimated tax payments, 336
freelancers, 378
health insurance premiums, 308
independent contractor rules, 328,
337–338
retirement accounts, 45–46, 299, 300–301
taxes, 49
trade associations, 266
Web sites, 378
SEP-IRAs (Simplified Employee Pension
Individual Retirement Accounts), 45,
299, 300
service businesses
defined, 55
distribution channels, 201–202
insurance needed, 162
personal service corporations, 341
personality traits needed, 60
Service Corps of Retired Executives
(SCORE), 63, 69, 379
services. *See* products and services
shareholders
buy-sell agreements, 109, 307
employees, 103, 305–306, 352–353
majority, 103
minority, 103, 306–307
public, 103–104

shares
  exchange listing requirements, 104
  issuing to employees, 103, 305–306,
    352–353
  issuing to public, 103–104
shipping and receiving, 248
Silverman, David J., 331
SIMPLE (Savings Incentive Match Plans for
    Employees) plans, 303, 305
Simplified Employee Pension Individual
    Retirement Accounts. *See* SEP-IRAs
single-entry record-keeping, 171
skills
  of employees, 29–30
  inventory of, 56–59
  needed by small-business owners, 25–26
  Small-Business Owner's Aptitude test,
    20–25
Small Business Administration (SBA)
  ACE-Net, 97
  assistance available from, 62, 99
  Certified Development Companies
    (CDCs), 96
  definition of small business, 15
  504 Loan Program, 96
  loans guaranteed by, 62, 92, 95–96, 379
  LowDoc program, 96
  minority funding information, 99
  Web site, 96, 379
Small Business Answer Desk, 62
Small Business Development Centers
    (SBDCs), 63
Small Business Investment Companies
    (SBICs), 92, 96
Small Business Sourcebook, 126, 244, 318
small businesses. *See also* buying small
    businesses; startups
  advantages of ownership, 27
  alternatives to starting, 29–34
  basics, 12–14
  categories, 54–55
  definitions, 11, 15
  disadvantages of ownership, 28–29
  export markets, 15
  failures, 28–29, 257
  growth, 343–344, 345, 361–362
  as model for big business, 16

  names, 106, 316, 319, 320, 327
  number of employees, 15
  selling, 136–137, 362
  similarities among, 17
  specialists, 62
  stages, 344–346
  transition stage, 345–346
  types of products or services, 16
small-business consultants, 149
small-business owners. *See* owners
SMART goal-setting, 281–282
Smith Barney, 223
Social Security taxes
  integration in Keogh plans, 300–301
  paying, 328, 337
  on self-employed, 49
software
  accounting, 170–173, 380, 381
  benefits, 377, 382
  business plan preparation, 82
  cutting labor costs with, 254
  for home-based businesses, 369–370
  inventory management, 172, 248
  new products, 351, 378
  office suites, 370
  point-of-sale systems, 248
  retirement planning, 42
  self-help legal, 381
  spreadsheets, 80
  tax-preparation, 331, 381
  time-management, 372–373
sole ownership, 101–102
sole proprietorships, 105, 106
spreadsheets, 80
Starbucks, 278
startups. *See also* bootstrapping; business
    plans; outsourcing startup financing
  accidental opportunities, 56
  choosing form of ownership, 99–100
  choosing type of business, 51–53, 56–63
  costs, 32, 86, 87
  details, 161
  duration of stage, 344–345
  impact on family members, 37–38
  names, 106, 316, 319, 320, 327
  other income sources, 44–45
  part-time, 32, 44

preparing personal finances, 36–38
regulatory issues, 317–324
state governments
disability insurance programs, 310
franchise regulation, 147
licenses, 322
regulations, 322–323
regulatory agencies, 318
resources for small business, 63, 99
taxes, 163, 322, 337
Steinbrenner, George, 286
stock. *See* shareholders; shares
stock exchanges, 104
stock options, 306–307
strategy
changing, 346
distinction from operations, 262
subchapter S corporations, 110–111, 342
success-sharing. *See* pay-for-performance
suppliers. *See* vendors
sweat equity, 32

• T •

T. Rowe Price, 42, 43, 302, 303
TAB (The Advisory Board), 72
TAB (The Alternative Board), 261
tax advisors
accountants, 332
attorneys, 332
enrolled agents, 332
evaluating purchase of businesses, 149, 155
functions, 158
hiring, 152, 331–334
preparers, 332
relationships with, 183
taxes. *See also* income taxes
deferred, 143
filing, 316, 329–330
financial records for, 143, 233, 334
information on, 330–331
local, 163, 320, 337
Medicare, 49
paying, 163
payroll, 336–337
property, 320

sales, 320, 322
self-employment, 49
Social Security, 49, 300–301, 328, 337
state, 163, 322, 337
TEC. *See* The Executive Committee
technology. *See* computers; Internet; software
telephone service
answering machines, 370
costs, 255
in home-based businesses, 367, 368
toll-free numbers, 368
voice mail, 367, 368
television advertising, 196–197
temporary employment agencies, 295
term life insurance, 47–48, 312
The Advisory Board (TAB), 72
The Alternative Board (TAB), 261
The Executive Committee (TEC), 261
theft insurance, 162
3M, 30, 66
time management, 348–350, 372–373
Total Quality Management (TQM), 353
TQM. *See* Total Quality Management
trade associations, 244, 265–266, 375, 378
trade publications, 125, 152, 197, 318
trademarks, 316, 324–325, 326–327
training, of employees, 30, 166, 178, 274–276, 277
transfer of ownership notice, 157
travel and entertainment expenses, 340–341
troubleshooting
checklist, 355–356
five-minute appearance test, 357–358
Rule of Many Reasons, 390
time lags, 386–387
Tupperware, 19

• U •

UFOC. *See* Uniform Franchise Offering Circular
unemployment insurance, 322, 328
Uniform Franchise Offering Circular (UFOC), 145, 147
unincorporated businesses, 105–108

U.S. government. *See also* Internal
    Revenue Service; Small Business
    Administration
  Commerce Department, 63, 99
  Federal Trade Commission (FTC),
    145, 147
  regulation of businesses, 323–324
  resources for small business, 62–63, 99
USAA, 47, 48, 311

• V •

vacations, as employee benefits, 49, 314
valuation of businesses
  appraisers, 151
  book value method, 150–151
  comparable companies, 149,
    151–152, 152
  multiple of earnings method, 150, 151
Vanguard Group, 42, 43, 51, 302, 303
variable expenses, 175
vendors
  business plan section on, 78
  contracts, 317, 327
  evaluating new, 179
  relationships with, 144, 177–179
  selecting, 248
  training provided by, 178, 275
venture capital firms, 92, 97
vesting schedule, in Keogh plans, 300
VISA, 41
vision insurance, 48–49
voice mail, 367, 368
Volcker, Paul, 186

• W •

Waitt, Ted, 89
Wall Street firms, 223
Wal-Mart, 64, 215, 249, 278
Walton, Sam, 64, 249
Web sites. *See also* Internet
  businesses for sale listings, 378, 379
  company, 198, 380
  financial statement preparation, 380

financing sources, 379–380
  finding, 378
  franchise listings, 379
  as resources, 378, 379–380, 382
  retirement planning, 42
  time wasters, 377
  trade associations, 265, 378
Welch, Jack, 16
Wholesale Insurance Network, 48
wholesaling businesses
  defined, 55
  distributing products through, 205–206
  insurance needed, 162
  personality traits needed, 60
women-owned businesses
  financing resources, 99
  trade associations, 266
word-of-mouth advertising
  negative, 219
  positive, 192–193, 371
workers' compensation insurance, 163,
    255, 322
working capital, 86, 87
Working Solo Web site, 378

• X •

Xerox Corp., 274

• Y •

Yahoo!, 378
Yellow Pages advertising, 195
Yellow Pages Publishers Association, 97

• Z •

zero-based budgeting, 176–177, 253
zoning regulations, 320–321, 376

IDG BOOKS WORLDWIDE
BOOK REGISTRATION

Register This Book and Win!

We want to hear from you!

Visit **http://my2cents.dummies.com** to register this book and tell us how you liked it!

✔ Get entered in our monthly prize giveaway.

✔ Give us feedback about this book — tell us what you like best, what you like least, or maybe what you'd like to ask the author and us to change!

✔ Let us know any other *...For Dummies*® topics that interest you.

Your feedback helps us determine what books to publish, tells us what coverage to add as we revise our books, and lets us know whether we're meeting your needs as a *...For Dummies* reader. You're our most valuable resource, and what you have to say is important to us!

Not on the Web yet? It's easy to get started with *Dummies 101*®: *The Internet For Windows*® *95* or *The Internet For Dummies*,® 5th Edition, at local retailers everywhere.

Or let us know what you think by sending us a letter at the following address:

...For Dummies Book Registration
Dummies Press
7260 Shadeland Station, Suite 100
Indianapolis, IN 46256-3945
Fax 317-596-5498

BUSINESS AND
GENERAL
REFERENCE
BOOK SERIES
FROM IDG

COMPUTER
BOOK SERIES
FROM IDG